TH

MW00811241

Twenty-Seven "Divine Revelations"

CONTAINING

A DESCRIPTION OF TWENTY-SEVEN BIBLES, AND AN
EXPOSITION OF TWO THOUSAND BIBLICAL ERRORS IN
SCIENCE, HISTORY, MORALS, RELIGION, AND
GENERAL EVENTS

BY

Kersey Graves,
AUTHOR OF "THE WORLD'S SIXTEEN CRUCIFIED SAVIORS" AND
"THE BIOGRAPHY OF SATAN"

FOURTH EDITION

Published by
**Research Associates School Times Publications/
Frontline Distribution Int'l Inc.**

Distributed by
Frontline Distribution Int'l Inc.
751 East 75th Street
Chicago, IL 60619 USA
773-651-9888

CHICAGO•JAMAICA•LONDON
REPUBLIC of TRINIDAD and TOBAGO, CARIBBEAN

Research Associates School Times Publications
and
Frontline Distribution Int'l Inc.
751 East 75th Street
Chicago, IL 60619
Tel: (773) 651-9888
Fax: (773) 651-9850
E-mail: info@frontlinebooks.net
www.frontlinebooks.net

Second Reissue
Published 2004 by
Research Associates School Times Publications/
Frontline Distribution Int'l Inc.

In Association with
Miguel Lorne Publishers, Jamaica
P.O. Box 2967
Kingston 8, Jamaica
Tel/Fax: (876) 922-3915
E-mail: Headstartp@hotmail.com

© 2002

All Rights Reserved

No part of this publication may be reproduced, stored in a
retrieval system, or transmitted in any form or by any means,
electronic, mechanical, photocopying, or otherwise, without the
prior permission of Frontline Distribution Int'l Inc.

Edited and Typeset by
Dorothy M. Johnson

ISBN 0-94839-067-0

Library of Congress Control Number: 00132273

CONTENTS

The Bible of Bibles

Contents

The Bible of Bibles

Contents

Contents

The Bible of Bibles

PREFACE TO THE 2002 FRONTLINE EDITION

"Today man sees all his hopes and aspirations crumble before him. He is perplexed and knows not whither he is drifting. But he must realize that the solution of his present difficulties and guidance for his future action is the Bible. Unless he accepts with clear conscience the Bible and its great message, he cannot hope for salvation. For myself, I glory in the Bible."

Emperor Haile Sellassie I

The Bible of Bibles or Twenty-seven "Divine Revelations" is a well documented book that analyses the Holy Bible and other Holy Books such as the Vedas, the Quran, and other scriptures, with an abundance of concrete evidence and facts being put forward by the author.

In *The Bible of Bibles* (p. 129), Kersey Graves states:

The Old Testament is principally a history of the Jews and their God Jehovah—a narrative of their trials, troubles, treachery, quarrels, and faithless dealings toward each other. No other God ever had so much trouble with his people; and no other nation ever showed so little respect for their God, or so little disposition to obey him, or live up to his commands.

Kersey Graves, the author of *The Sixteen Crucified Saviors* and *The Biography of Satan*, writes very objectively and candidly about the contradictions and errors within the Bible, i.e., both the Old and New Testaments. He reviews and shows the many flaws found within the pages of the Holy Scriptures.

Graves, a former member of the Quaker Church who later adopts the position of a free thinker, first published *The Bible of Bibles* sometime in the 1870's. In *The Bible of Bibles*, the fallacy of the scriptures is brought out after immense research by the author and his group of religious researchers.

The Bible of Bibles is very thorough. It spells out, lists references, and also makes pertinent cross-references to other religious Holy Books and other religions. It refers to the Egyptian text, i.e., the *Book of Coming Forth By Day* or the *Egyptian Book of Life*, sometimes called the *Egyptian Book of the Dead*.

He discerns the misgivings and misconceptions within the Holy Bible in a very dignified manner, by making the appropriate cross-references, checks and balances by way of demonstrating the actual scriptures where the mistakes are blatantly erroneous.

In republishing this book in 2002, we hope it will contribute to the ongoing debate and discourse as it relates to the revelations of these so-called Holy Texts. The ongoing questions are: Were the scriptures revealed by a Supreme Being called God or the Creator to his prophets or apostles? Or are these scriptures, e.g., the Old Testament in the Bible, a history of the Jews and their search to create a God in the form of Jehovah? Did God create man or did man create God? These are some of the burning questions that wise minds continue to discuss in the midst of new scientific research and development which shows that our planet earth belongs in antiquity, long before the Christian Bible or any other form of religious texts were written or supposedly revealed; or long before the first man and woman in the Christian Bible came forward into existence. A fossil of a man found in Chad, said to be over seven (7) million years old, was revealed on the ABC six o'clock news on July 10, 2002.

And there is scarcely a book, or even a chapter, in the whole Bible that does not evince a spirit of religious devotion, and an effort for the right, though often misdirected. Taken as a whole, the Bible may be regarded as an exposition of the condition of science, morals, religion, government, and domestic policy of the era in which it was written, and suited to the temporal and spiritual wants of the people of that age, for whom it was written, but not for this age. When regarded in this light, and as simply a human production of the best minds of the age and times in which it was written, many portions of it can be read with interest and instruction. But when read, as it has been for centuries, as a perfect, divine composition, designed for all time and as a finality in faith and practice and moral progress, it becomes a stumbling block in the path of progress, an embargo upon free thought, a fetter upon the soul, a fog of bewilderment to the mind, and a drag-chain to the moral and intellectual reformation of the world. (Emphasis in original)

The Bible of Bibles, p. 44

The Bible of Bibles is a must read for all students of religious doctrines, especially the Holy Bible. In reading this book, one will look at the Bible from a historical or fable perspective, or a combination of both. However, as the reader, please be the judge. Read the book.

Peace and Blessings
SEKOU S. TAFARI

July 2002

NOTES AND EXPLANATIONS
FOR THE THIRD EDITION

1. On page 73, it is stated that no geologist or philosopher believes in either a creation or a creator. It is admitted that some men, called geologists, may believe so; but we hold that no man thoroughly versed in geology and philosophy can thus believe.

2. On page 141, contradiction 146, it should be stated in the first part that Ahaziah's reign began in his thirty-second year, instead of the eleventh year of Joram. The second part should state that he began in his forty-second year, instead of the twelfth year of Joram.

3. On page 143, contradiction 181, the anointment of Christ is spoken of. But the text refers to the feast of the passover.

4. On page 315, it is stated that the Unitarians believe in a hell. It should be understood, however, that they believe in a hell merely as a state or condition, and not as a place.

5. On page 364, it is staled that the weight of the tables of the law was fifty times as much as Hilkiah could carry. This, of course, would depend upon the quality and condition of the stone used and the manner of engraving this law, if not, what is assumed to constitute the law. It is stated that some considered the Pentateuch the law. This, however, was only in a general sense. They, of course, knew that the law as described in Deuteronomy was the law proper, or special law.

6. The charge of falsehood against Christ, on page 403, is not intended to imply that it is certain he designed telling a falsehood. But, as he stated he would not go up to the feast at Jerusalem, and yet did go, it shows that he either intended to deceive, or was ignorant of what he would do in the future; and either defect would prove he was not an omniscient God.

7. On page 414, it is stated that a Jew could not be a full Roman citizen in the time of Paul, and that Tarsus was not at that time a Roman city. But it may be stated also that authors differ on these points, and we leave the matter for them or their critical readers to settle. Let it be noted that it is not claimed that Paul, while professing to be first a Roman citizen, and then a Pharisee, and then a disciple of Jesus Christ, could not be all three at once, but it indicates his policy of changing.

THE PERSONALITY OF GOD

As the denial of the personality of God, as set forth in Chapter 44, has been warmly assailed by Orthodox professors since the work was issued, and as that dogma constitutes one of the principal pillars of the Orthodox faith, I propose to examine it a little further in the light of reason and science. I will present other absurdities of the doctrine in the form of questions.

1.   If God is an organized personality, what should we assume to be his form, size, shape, and color?

2.   How large is his body?

3.   Does it occupy more than one planet?

4.   If not, how can he be present in other worlds?

5.   What is his physical type—Malay, Mongolian, Anglo-Saxon, or African?

6.   What is his complexion—white, black or tawny?

7.   What is the color of his eyes and hair?

8.   What are the dimensions of his body and the length of his arms and legs?

9.   What is his position—lying, sitting, or standing?

10. How is his time occupied?

11. And as personality implies sex, and one sex not only implies the other sex, but also creates a necessity for the other sex, we are driven to ask, who is God's wife, and where is she?

12. Are they both on the same planet?

13. And have they ever been divorced? Or is he still a bachelor?

14. And as sex also implies offspring, we desire to ask, how many children have they had?

15. And whether they are all boys?

10. And as personality also implies parentage, this brings up the question, who was God's father, grandfather, etc.?

17. And as personality implies the susceptibility to anger, and the Bible-God is often represented as getting angry, and anger has been shown to be a species of insanity, would not this imply and prove that heaven is ruled by an insane God—an omnipotent lunatic?

18. And would not this virtually make heaven a lunatic asylum, and consequently a very unsuitable and disagreeable place to live in?

As all these and many other absurdities are involved in the assumption of a personal God, it is difficult to see how any reasonable being can swallow the doctrine.

MORE BIBLES

As the notices of several bibles prepared for the first edition were left out from fear of making the book too large, I have concluded to insert a brief notice of some of them here.

1.   *Dhammapada,* or "Path of Virtue."   This sacred book has constituted the moral and religious guide of several hundred millions of Hindus for many centuries.   It is probably the oldest record of the Buddhistic faith.   It is assumed to be a collection from the *pitakas,* which

are principally compilations from the discourse of the incarnate god Gautama, written out by his disciples. It was pronounced genuine and canonical by a famous council which met in 246 B.C., under the reign of King Asoka. Max Müller says, "Its moral code, taken by itself, is one of the most perfect the world has ever known." Spence Hardy and Johnson both speak highly of the work. It contains many wise, beautiful, and lofty moral precepts, of which we will give a few specimens: "Haste to do good." "Give to those who ask." "Master thyself, and then thou canst control and teach others." "Select for friends the best of men." "Be just, speak truly, act nobly," etc.

2. *Tripitaka.* This book is divided into three parts, hence its name, which means "the three *pitakas*" or "Three Baskets." Like the Dhammapada, it is a history of some of the gods, and sets forth their lives and precepts. It forbids the commission of sin, and enjoins the practice of the highest virtues. "In no system," says Amberly, "is benevolence and charity more emphatically inculcated." Chastity is recommended, and a life of spotless virtue in every respect enjoined. The former work appears to be made up principally by selections from this.

3. Other sacred books might be mentioned, such as "The Paradise of Fo," "Confucius and his Disciple," "Catena of the Chinese Buddhistic Scriptures," "The Bhagavad Gita," "The Samhita," "Sutras" (appendages to the Sunhita), "Divine Opherisms of Kanada," "The Upanishads" (a commentary on the Vedas), "Saddharma Pundosika" (another commentary), "Worship and Psalmody of the Maharadas," etc. Some of these works are either other titles for those previously described, or are additions, appendages, or commentaries. And thus, it will be observed, the world is full of bibles and scriptures.

THE LEADING POSITIONS OF THIS WORK

We maintain, first, that man's mental faculties are susceptible of a threefold division and classification, as follows: First, the intellectual department; second, the moral and religious department; third, the animal department (which includes also the social).

Second, that all Bibles and religions are an outgrowth from some or all of these faculties, and hence of natural origin.

Third, that all Bibles and religions which originated prior to the dawn of civilization in the country which gave them birth (i.e., prior to the reign of moral and physical science) are an emanation from the combined action and cooperation of man's moral, religious, and *animal* feelings and propensities.

Fourth, that the Christian Bible contains (as shown in this work) several thousand errors—moral, religious, historical, and scientific.

Fifth, that this fact is easily accounted for by observing that it originated at a period when the moral and religious feelings of the nation which produced it cooperated with the *animal propensities* instead of an *enlightened intellect*.

Sixth, that, although such a Bible and religion may have been adapted to the minds which originated them, the *higher* class of minds of the present age demands a religion which shall call into exercise the *intellect*, instead of the *animal* propensities.

Seventh, that, as all the Bibles and religions of the past are more of an emanation from the *animal propensities* than the *intellect*, they are consequently not suited to this age, and are for this reason being rapidly abandoned.

Eight, that true religion consists in the *true exercise* of the moral and religious faculties.

Ninth, as the Christian Bible is shown in this work to inculcate bad morals and to sanction, apparently, every species of crime prevalent in society in the age in which it was written, the language of remonstrance is frequently employed against placing such a book in the hands of the heathen, or the children of Christian countries; and more especially against making "the Bible the fountain of our laws and the supreme rule of our conduct," and acknowledging allegiance to its God in the Constitution of the United States, as recommended by the American Christian Alliance. Such measures, this work shows by a thousand facts, would be a deplorable check to the moral and intellectual progress of the world.

Tenth, if any clergyman or Christian professor shall take any exceptions to any position laid down in this work, the author will discuss the matter with him in a friendly manner in the papers, or through the post-office, or before a public audience.

KERSEY GRAVES

Richmond, Indiana

CHAPTER 1

THE SIGNS OF THE TIMES

We live in the most important age in the history of the world. No age preceding it was marked with such signal events. No other era in the history of civilization has been characterized by such agitation of human thought; such a universal tendency to investigation; such a general awakening upon all important subjects of human inquiry; such a determination to grow in knowledge, and cultivate the immortal intellect, and mount to higher planes of development. The world of mind is in commotion. All civilized nations are agitated from center to circumference with the great questions of the age. And what does all this prove? Why, that man is a progressive being; that the tendency of the human mind is onward and upward; and that it will not always consent to be bound down in ignorance and superstition. And, thanks to the genius of the age, it is the prophecy of the glorious reformation and regeneration of society—an index of a happier era in the history of the human race. Old institutions are crumbling and tumbling to the ground. The iron bands of creeds and dogmas, with which the people have been so long bound down, are bursting asunder and permitting them to walk upright and do their own thinking. In every department of science, in every arena of human thought and every theater of human action, we see a progressive spirit, we behold a disposition to lay aside the traditions and superstitions of the past, and grasp the living facts of the age. We everywhere see a disposition to abandon the defective institutions, political and religious, which were gotten up in the childhood of human experience, and supplant them with those better adapted to the wants of the age. In a word, there is everywhere manifested a disposition and determination to unshackle the human body and set free the human mind, and place it with its living aspirations on the road to the temple of Truth. An evidence of the truth of these statements, the reader can gather by casting his eyes abroad, or by reading the periodicals of the day.

At this very time, nearly all the orthodox churches are in a state of commotion. The growing light and intelligence of the age, penetrating their dark creeds and dogmas, are producing a sort of moral effervescence. The question of "hell" is now the agitating theme of the churches. Posterity will ridicule us, and class us with the unenlightened heathen, for discussing a question so far behind the times, and one so childish and so absurd in this intelligent and enlightened age. To condescend to *discuss* such a question *now* must be *hell enough* for scientific and intelligent minds. And other important religious events mark the age. When the Roman-Catholic Church, through its Ecumenical Council, dragged the Pope from his lofty throne of usurped power, and robbed him of his attribute of infallibility, it proclaimed the *downfall* of the Pope and the *death-knell* of the Church. Already thousands of his subjects refuse longer to bow down and kiss the big toe of his sacred majesty. His scepter has departed, his spiritual power is gone, his temporal power is waning. And the same spirit of agitation is operating as a leaven in the Protestant churches also. All the orthodox churches are declining and growing weaker by their members falling off. The Methodist Church has recently lost more than two hundred of its preachers; and the Baptist Church, according to the statement of a recent number of "The Christian Era," has lost twenty-two thousand of its members within a period of five years. The agitation in the churches is driving thousands from their ranks, while many who remain are becoming more liberal-minded.

The orthodox Quaker Church has, in many localities, "run clear off the track." It has abandoned its old time-honored peculiarities in dress and language, once deemed by them sacred and essential to true godliness. The use of "thee" and "thou" is laid aside by many of its members; and even leading members have given up the "shad-bellied coat," and the round-crowned hat with a brim broad enough to "cover a multitude of sins." They no longer wait for "the Holy Ghost" to move them to preach; but, as a member once remarked, "they go it on their own hook, like the Methodists, hit or miss." Music, once regarded by many of them as an emanation from "an emissary of the Devil," is now admitted into many of their churches. Thus, it will be seen, they are making some progress. The *light without* is benefiting them *more* than "the light *within*."

All the orthodox systems committed a fatal error at the outset in assuming that their religions were derived directly from God, and consequently must be *perfect* and *unalterable,* and a *finality* in moral and religious progress. Such an assumption will cause the downfall, sooner or later, of any religious body which persists in propagating the error. Religious institutions, like all other institutions, are subject to the laws of growth and decay. Hence, if their doctrines and creeds are not improved occasionally to make them conform to the growing light and intelligence of the age and the principles of science, they will fall behind the times, cease to answer the moral and religious wants of the age, and become a stumbling-block in the path of progress. Common sense would teach us that the doctrines preached by the churches two hundred years ago must be as much out of place now as the wooden shoes and bearskin coats worn by the early disciples would be *for us. Their spiritual food* is by no means adapted to *our moral and religious wants.* We are under no more moral and religious obligation whatever to preach the doctrines of original sin, the fall of man, endless punishment, infant damnation, etc., because our religious forefathers believed in these doctrines, than we are morally bound to eat beetles, locusts, and grasshoppers, because our Jewish ancestors feasted on these nasty vermin, as we learn by reading Lev. xi.

Why is it that in modern times there has arisen great complaint in all the orthodox churches about the rapid inroads of infidelity into their ranks? It is simply because, while the people are beginning to assume the liberty to do their own thinking, the churches refuse to recognize the great principle of universal progress as applicable to their religion, which *would* and *should* keep their doctrines and precepts improved up to the times. Instead of adopting this wise policy, they try to compel their members to be content with the old stale *salt* junk of bygone ages, in the shape of dilapidated, outgrown creeds and dogmas; but it will not do. It is as difficult to keep great minds tied down to unprogressive creeds as it would be to keep grown-up boys and girls in baby-jumpers. Enlightened nations are as capable of making their own religion as their own laws; that is, of making its tenets conform to the natural outgrowth of their religious feelings as they become more expanded and enlightened. And it is a significant historical fact that great minds in *all* religious nations have wholly or partially outgrown and abandoned the current and popular religions of the country. It is only moral cowards, or the ignorant and uninformed, who throw themselves into the lap of the Church, and depend upon the priest to pilot them to heaven.

Moses, Jesus Christ, Muhammad, Martin Luther, John Wesley, Emanuel Swedenborg, George Fox, Elias Hicks, and many other superior minds, strove hard unconsciously to rise above the religion in which they were educated; and all succeeded in making some improvement in its stereotyped doctrines or practices. The implied assumption of the churches that their doctrines and precepts are too perfect to be improved and too sacred to be investigated, and their Bible too holy to be criticised, is contradicted both by history and science; and this false assumption has already driven many of the best minds of the age from their ranks. Theodore Parker declared that all the men of great intellects had left the Church in his time, because, instead of improving their religion to keep it up to the times, they bolt their doors and hang curtains over their windows to keep out the light of the age. There could not be one inch of progress made in anything in a thousand years with the principle of non-progression in religion adopted by the churches; for, if it will apply to religion, it will apply with still greater force to everything else: and hence it would long ago have put a dead lock upon all improvement, had it not been counteracted by outside counter-influences. It is because a large portion, and the *most enlightened portion,* of the community have assumed the liberty and moral independence to *think* and *act for themselves,* that society has made *any* progress either in science, morals, or religion. A religion which sedulously opposes its *own improvement* can do nothing essential toward improving *anything else,* unless *forced* into it by outside influences; and it cannot feel a *proper degree* of *interest* in those improvements essential to the progress of society. On the contrary, it must check the growth of everything it touches with its palsied hands. Here we can see the reason that no church in any age of the world has inaugurated any great system of reform for the improvement of society, but has *made war* on nearly every reform set on foot by that class of people which it has chosen to stigmatize as "infidels." Such a religion will *decline* and *die* in the exact ratio of the enlightenment and progress of society.

The Coming Revolution

That there is a general state of *unrest* in the public mind, at the present time, on the subject of religion, must be apparent to every observing person. Theological questions, long since regarded as settled forever, are being overhauled and discussed with a freedom and general interest far transcending that known or practically realized at any previous period. This is premonitive of a *speedy* religious revolution. That it will come sooner or later is as *certain* as that seed-sowing is succeeded by harvest. Reforms no longer move with the snail's pace they did a century ago. This is an age of steam and electricity, and everything has to move with velocity. We cherish no unkindly feelings toward any church or people; but we must rejoice that the strongholds of orthodoxy are being shaken, and error exposed, and that creeds are loosening their iron grasp upon the immortal mind. Old, long-cherished dogmas, myths, and blinding superstitions are passing away, to make room for something better.

Yes, the signs of the times indicate the *dawning* of a brighter day upon the world—a day which shall be illuminated by the rays of reason and science. And, if this work shall contribute anything toward *speeding* the dawning of that glorious era, we shall feel amply rewarded for the labor and personal sacrifice required in its production.

Reason Will Soon Triumph

The march of science and the rapid growth of the reasoning faculties peculiar to this progressive age are daily revealing the errors of our popular theology, and exposing their demoralizing effects in repressing the growth and healthy action of the intellect, and perverting the exercise of the moral faculties. And this progressive change and improvement must be a source of great rejoicing to every true-hearted philanthropist, and furnishes a strong incentive to labor with zeal in this field of reform. It should be borne in mind that all the dogmas and doctrines of our current religious faith originated at a period before the sun of science had risen above the moral horizon, and anterior to the birth of moral science, and hence, like other productions of that age, are heavily laden with error. But rejoice, O ye *lovers of* and *laborers for* truth and science! The dark clouds of our gloomy theology are *rapidly* receding before the sunlight of our modern civilization, and will soon leave a clear and cloudless sky! And all will rejoice in having learned and practically experienced the glorious truth, that true religion is not incorporated in Bibles, or inscribed on the pages of any book, and cannot be found therein, but is a natural and spontaneous outgrowth of man's moral and religious nature, and is "the *most beautiful flower* of the *soul*."

CHAPTER 2

APOLOGY AND EXPLANATION

Although books are constantly issuing from the press, and the country kept literally flooded with new publications, yet few of them meet the real wants of the age, and many of them are of no permanent practical benefit to the world. Such a work as is comprised in "The Bible of Bibles" is a *desideratum.* It has been long and loudly called for. It is a moral necessity, and partially supplies one of the great moral wants of the times. It is true, hundreds of works have been published embracing criticisms on the Bible, and attempting to expose some of its numerous errors, and portray some of its evil influences upon those who accept it as a moral guide. Yet it is believed that the present work embraces the first attempt to arrange together, or make out anything like a full list of, the numerous errors of "the Holy Book." And yet it falls far short of accomplishing this end; for, although more than two thousand errors are brought to notice, a critical research would bring to light several thousand more. It will be observed by the reader that there has been a constant effort on the part of the author to abridge, contract, and compress the contents of the volume into the smallest compass possible to be attained compatible with perspicuity. Every chapter, and almost every line, discloses this policy. In no other way than by the adoption of such an expedient could two thousand biblical errors have been brought to notice in a single volume. The adoption of the most rigid rules of abbreviation and compression alone could have accomplished it; and this policy has been carried out even in making citations from the Bible. Such superfluous words and phrases have been dropped as could be spared without impairing the sense or real meaning of the text. And yet, with this unceasing effort to compress and abridge the work, it falls so far short of portraying fully all the errors and evils which a critical investigation shows to be the legitimate outgrowth of our Bible religion, that the author contemplates following it with another work, which may complete an exposition of nine thousand errors now known to be comprised in "the Holy Book." The title will probably be "The Bible in the Light of History, Reason, and Science." He intends also to rewrite and republish soon, and probably enlarge, his "Biography of Satan," so as to make it entirely a new work.

JEHOVAH NOT OUR GOD

The author desires the reader to bear it specially in mind that his criticisms on the erroneous conceptions and representations of God, as found in the Christian Bible, appertains in all cases to that mere imaginary being known as the Jewish Jehovah, and has no reference whatsoever to the God of the universe, who must be assumed to be a very different being.

Apology and Explanation

The God of Moses, who is represented as coming down from heaven, and walking and talking, eating and sleeping, traveling on foot (and barefoot, so as to make it necessary for Abraham to wash his feet); and who is also represented as eating barley-cakes and veal with Abraham (Gen. xviii.); wrestling all night with Jacob, and putting his thigh out of place; trying to kill Moses in a hotel, but failing in the attempt; and as getting vanquished in a battle with the Canaanites; and also as frequently getting mad, cursing and swearing, etc.—such was the character of Jehovah, the God of the Jews—a mere figment of the imagination. Hence, he is a just subject of criticism.

THE RELATIONSHIP OF THE OLD AND NEW TESTAMENTS

Some of the representatives of the Christian faith, when the shocking immoralities of the Old Testament are pointed out, attempt to evade the responsibility by alleging that they do not live under the *old* dispensation, but the *new*, thereby intimating that they are not responsible for the errors of the former. But the following considerations will show that such a defense is fallacious and entirely untenable:

1. It takes both the Old and the New Testaments to constitute "the Holy Bible," which they accept as a whole.
2. Both are bound together, and circulated by the million, as possessing equal credibility and equal authority.
3. Both are quoted alike by clergymen and Christian writers.
4. The New Testament is inseparably connected with the Old.
5. The prophecies of the Old form the basis of the New.
6. Both are canonized together under the word "holy."
7. Nearly all the New Testament writers, including Paul, endorse the Old Testament, and take no exception to any of its errors or any of its teachings. For these reasons, to accept one is to accept the other. Both stand or fall together.

Note: Christ modified some of Moses's errors, but endorsed most of the Old Testament errors.

CHAPTER 3

WHY THIS WORK WAS WRITTEN

There are in this and other Christian countries more than one hundred thousand clergymen who spend a portion of each recurring sabbath in presenting the claims, and dilating upon the beauties and benefits (some real and some imaginary), of the religion of the Christian Bible. They claim that it is the religion for this age, and a religion that should be adopted by the whole human race, but they present but one side of the picture, and but one phase of the argument. A witness before a jury is required to "tell the truth, and *the whole* truth," but the priesthood dare not do this with respect to the errors and defects of their religion. They would lose their congregations and their *salaries* also. But few clergymen possess the moral courage to turn state's evidence against their pockets or their "bread and butter." It is a sad reflection that they are hired, and required to *conceal* whatever errors may loom up before their moral vision in the investigation of the principles of their religion, or the Bible on which it is founded. They are placed in the position of an attorney who is sworn to be true to his client at any sacrifice of truth and moral manhood. Whatever may be their moral convictions with respect to the sinfulness or evil consequences or demoralizing effects of continuing to breach the *intellectually dwarfing* and *morally poisoning* doctrines originated in, and adapted only to, the dark and undeveloped ages of the past, when the race was under the dominion of the animal and blind propensities, yet *they must do it*. They must continue to preach these errors, to sustain these evils, and maintain their false positions, or lose their salaries and their popular standing in society. It is a very unfortunate position to be placed in, but self-interest being the ruling principle of the age, we cannot reasonably expect the clergy will do anything toward enlightening the people on the errors and immoral influences of their religious doctrines, or the substitution of a better system, until human nature has advanced to a higher moral plane. On the contrary, we must expect they will continue to blind the people, pervert the truth, and magnify every imaginable good quality of their religious system; while, on the other hand, they will as sedulously attempt to hide every defect which either they or others may discover in their Bible. This state of things in the religious world imposes upon the moral reformer the solemn necessity of employing the most effectual lever, and of adopting every available moral means to counteract this morally deleterious influence of the clergy, and arrest the tide of evil which follows in their wake as the legitimate fruits of a course of conduct dictated by *policy* instead of *principle.*

Why This Work Was Written

THE MORAL TRUTHS OF THE BIBLE

Some of our readers will doubtless be disposed to ask why we have not occupied a larger portion of this work in exhibiting the beauties and benefits of the religion and system of morals set forth in the Bible. The answer to the question is fully anticipated in the preceding remarks. It is simply because fifty thousand tongues and pens are almost constantly employed in this work. They do it and overdo it. This renders it a work of supererogation on our part; while, on the other hand, we find the errors and evils of the Bible and its religion, which they overlook or neglect to expose, so very numerous, that we cannot exhibit them in a single volume, unless we allow but a limited space to a repetition of what is done by them every week. This is our reason for *appearing* to pursue a one-sided policy.

WHY RESORT TO RIDICULE?

We hope we shall not be misunderstood or condemned by any reader for appearing to indulge frequently in a spirit of levity in attempting to expose the logical and moral absurdities of the Bible. We have assumed this license more from an apprehended moral necessity than from a natural disposition. Ridicule is now generally acknowledged by moralists to be a most potent weapon for the demolition of error. Moral and religious absurdities, according to Cicero, can be arrested and put down much sooner by "holding them up to the light of ridicule, than by any other means that can be employed." Let no one, then, oppose the use of such means simply because it may disturb a sensitive feeling in his own mind, derived from a false education. A critical investigation of religious history discloses the important fact that the conviction established in the popular mind that it is wrong to indulge in a feeling of levity when writing or discoursing on religious subjects is the work of the clergy. Having discovered that many of the narrations of their Bible, and likewise many of the tenets of their creeds, are really ridiculous when examined in the light of science, reason, and sound sense, in order to prevent these ridiculous features of their systems from being exposed, they taught the people that ridicule is entirely out of place in matters of religion, and that such feelings, or language *expressive* of such feelings, should be entirely suppressed. And it is principally by the invention of this expedient, and the establishment of this conviction in the public mind, that the clergy have succeeded in keeping the ridiculous errors of their creeds concealed from age to age. And to continue this policy longer is only to yield to their interests, and prolong those evils still longer, which have been perpetuated for centuries by the adoption of this expedient.

9

The Bible of Bibles

No other argument or apology is necessary than this as a justification of the limited extent to which the language of ridicule has been employed in this work. It is an egregious error, which is the offspring of an erroneous education and habit, to suppose that ridicule is more out of place on religious subjects than on other subjects. O. S. Fowler has fully established this as a scientific fact on phrenological grounds. We should be quite sorry to wound the feelings of any sensitive mind by any language made use of in this work, and hope this explanation will prevent such results.

THE PRINCIPAL DESIGN OF THIS WORK

As a critical examination of the Christian Bible discloses the fact that it contains several thousand moral and scientific errors, and as experience proves the tendency of such errors is to corrupt the moral feelings and check the intellectual growth of all who read and believe "the Holy Book," we have, since arriving at this conviction, considered it to be our duty not only to expose these errors, but also to discourage the habitual reading of the Bible with any other view than to learn its real character. And more especially do we earnestly advise parents not to place the Bible in the hands of their children until they arrive at an age when a more mature judgment can enable them to discriminate between its truths and its errors. We likewise entreat all moralists and philanthropists, and all lovers of truth and virtue, as they desire the moral growth and moral reformation of the world, to exert their influence to stop the shipment of the Christian Bible to foreign lands to be circulated among the uncultured and credulous heathen. Here is disclosed one of our principal reasons for writing this work. We wish to make it a voice of remonstrance against placing any of those morally defective books called Bibles in the hands of the ignorant and impressible heathen, or the children of Christian countries, until their minds become sufficiently fortified by age and experience to resist or withstand the demoralizing influence of their bad precepts and bad examples as exposed in this work.

DON'T READ PERNICIOUS BOOKS

The Quaker Church (of which the author was once a member) has a clause in its discipline forbidding its members to read pernicious books, which are defined by one of the founders of the Church (William Penn) to be "such books and publications as contain language which appears to sanction crime or wrong practices, or teach bad morals." And hundreds of cases cited in this work prove that the Christian Bible may be ranked with works of this character. If the advice of the Hindu editor had been complied with many years ago—to "revise all Bibles, and leave out their bad precepts and examples," and change their obscene language—the Christian Bible might now be a very useful and instructive book. But we are willing to leave it to the conscience of every honest reader, who places truth and morality above Bibles and creeds, to decide, after reading this work, whether the Bible, with all its ennobling precepts, does not contain too strong an admixture of bad morality to make it a safe or suitable book to be relied on as a guide in morals and religion.

According to Archbishop Tillotson, Bibles shape the morals and religion of the people in all religious countries—they are derived from the examples and precepts of these "Holy Books." If this be true, we most solemnly and seriously put the question to every Bible reader, What must be the effect upon the morals and religion of Christian countries of such moral examples as Abraham, Moses, Noah, Isaac, Jacob, David, Solomon, and nearly all the prophets, with their long string of crimes, as shown in this work? Let us not be guilty of the folly of suffering our inherited, stereotyped predilections, and exalted veneration for "the Holy Book," to rule our moral sense, and control our judgment in this matter, but muster the moral courage to look at the thing in its true light. Let us be independent moralists and philanthropists, rather than slaves to Bibles and creeds. "Every book," says a writer, "has a spirit which it breathes into the minds of its readers"; and, if it contains bad morals or bad language, the habitual reading of it will gradually reconcile the mind to those immoral lessons, and finally cause them to be looked upon as God-given truths. Such is the omnipotent force of habit. And we appeal to all Bible readers to testify if this has not been their experience. All Christian professors, when they first commenced reading the Bible, doubtless found many things in it which shocked their moral sense, did violence to their reasoning faculties, and mortified their love of decorum. But a perseverance in reading it, through the force of habit and education, has finally reconciled their minds to those immoral lessons, and blinded the judgment, so that they are not now conscious of their real character and deleterious influence upon the mind.

TWO THOUSAND BIBLE ERRORS EXPOSED

One of the strongest and most solemn lessons of human experience, and proofs of the blinding effect of a false religious education, may be found in the fact that the two thousand Bible errors brought to notice in this work have been overlooked from age to age by the great mass of Bible readers. So absolutely and deplorably blinded have they been in some cases as to lead them to conclude, like Dr. Cheever of New York, that "the Bible does not contain the *shadow* of a *shade* of *error* from Genesis to Revelation." Such a perversion and stultification of the reasoning faculties was never excelled in any age or country. St. Augustine furnishes another striking illustration of the total wreck of mind and moral principle which an obstinate determination to accept the Bible with all its errors is capable of effecting. Having found a great many absurdities in the Bible, which he could not reconcile with reason and sense, and hence discovering he must either give up his Bible or his reason, he chose the latter alternative, and declared in his "Book of Sermons" (p. 33), "I believe things in the Bible because they are absurd. I believe them because they are impossible" (as glaring an absurdity as ever issued from human lips). Such a desperate expedient to save his Bible and creed from going overboard shows that they had demoralized his mind, and made a complete wreck of his reason. This is the writer who declared he found and preached to a nation of people who had but one eye, and that situated in their foreheads, and another nation who had no heads, but eyes in their breasts. It seems a pity that this single-eyed nation became extinct; for Christ declared, "If thine eye be single, thy whole body shall be full of light." Such an embodiment of light might have done much to enlighten the world. And this St. Augustine is the writer whom Eusebius pronounces "the great moral light of the Christian Church." And St. Irenaeus furnishes another deplorable example of the prostration or perversion of the moral faculties by accepting the Bible as a standard for morals when he *justified* the *crime* of *incest* by pointing to the example of "righteous Lot" and his daughters.

The celebrated Albert Barnes was made a victim of great mental suffering for many years by his laborious but ineffectual attempts to reconcile the Bible with the dictates of reason. Hear what he says about the matter. We will present the case in his own language: "These difficulties (of reconciling the teachings of the Bible to reason) are probably felt by every mind that ever reflects on the subject; and they are unexplained, unmitigated, and unremoved. I confess, for one, that I feel them, and feel them more sensibly and powerfully the more I look at them, and the longer I live. I do not understand them, and I make no advance toward understanding them. I do not know that I have a ray of light upon this subject which I had not when the subject first flashed across my soul. I have read what wise end good men have written upon the subject; I have looked at their theories and explanations; I have endeavored to weigh their arguments—for my whole soul pants for light and relief on these questions, but I get neither; and, in the anguish and distress of my soul, I confess I get no light whatever. I see not one ray to disclose to me the reason why sin came into the world, why the earth is strewn with the dying and the dead, and why man must suffer to all eternity. I have never seen a particle of light thrown on these subjects that has given a moment's ease to my tortured mind.... I trust that other men ... have not the anguish of spirit which I have. But I confess, when I look on a world of sinners and sufferers, upon death-beds and graveyards, and upon a world of woe filled with hosts to suffer forever; and when I see my friends, my parents, my family, my people, my fellow citizens—when I look upon a whole race—all involved in this sin and danger; and when I see the great mass of them wholly unconcerned; and when I feel that God only can save them, and yet he does not do it, I am struck dumb. It is all dark—dark—dark to my soul; and I cannot disguise it" (Practical Sermons, p. 124).

There, reader, you have the candid confession of an honest-minded, orthodox, and one of the ablest and most talented writers that ever wielded the pen in defense of the Christian faith. And if such a talented and logical mind could find no reason, consistency, or moral principle in the dogmas of orthodoxy, we may readily ask, Who can? Thousands of other orthodox clergymen have doubtless been perplexed with the same difficulties, but have not had the honesty to confess it. Those who do not now perceive them can find the reason by putting their hands on their own heads. They will find their intellects or logical brains defective. Moral philosophers now find no difficulty in solving any of those problems which so much perplexed the mind of Mr. Barnes. They are all false and unfounded dogmas except the prevalence of death and disease in the world. And these casualties are now known to be amongst the wisest and most useful dispensations of nature. (See chapter headed "Natural and Moral Evil.") And had Mr. Barnes ascended to the plane of mental and moral science, instead of remaining down in the dark, orthodox, theological cellar, trying to squeeze truth out of old, dead, dried-up, dusty, theological dogmas, he would have readily found the solution to all his problems, and would have rejoiced in thus emerging into the glorious sunlight of truth.

BIBLES USEFUL IN THEIR PLACE

We do not question that Bibles served a useful purpose for those nations and tribes by whom and for whom they were written; but as they only represent the imperfect moral and religious conceptions of that age, and have always been sacredly guarded from improvement, to make them the rule of action for any subsequent age would be to stop all moral and religious improvement. It is strikingly evident that society can make no improvement while it follows a Bible which is interdicted from improvement. It must remain stationary, with respect to religion and morals, so far as it is tied to an unchangeable book. Bibles in this way become masters of human thought, and shackles for the soul, and thus inflict serious evils upon society by their tendency to stop all moral and religious progress. Three thousand or ten thousand years may elapse, and no improvement can be made in the religion or morals of the people while the Bible from which they emanate is prohibited from improvement. Thus, Bibles inflict a death-like torpor and stagnation upon the moral and intellectual progress of society so far as their precepts are lived up to; that is, so far as the assumption that there can be no improvement in the teachings of the Bible is practically observed. It is the source of a pleasing reflection, however, to know that most Bible believers habitually violate their own principles by trampling this assumption under foot. Otherwise, we would have remained eternally in a state of barbarism.

CHAPTER 4

THE BEAUTIES AND BENEFITS OF BIBLES

There is displayed in all Bibles a devout recognition of moral principles and a strong manifestation of moral feeling. The disciples of all Bibles manifest an ardent aspiration for something higher, something nobler—a mental struggle to reach a higher plane. This moral aspiration is displayed in almost every chapter, and there are in all Bibles veins of beautiful thought coursing through their pages. All of them contain moral precepts which are in their nature elevating and ennobling, and which, if practically recognized, would have done much to improve the morals and enhance the happiness of their disciples; and all Bibles are valuable as fragments of religious history, and as indicating the state of religion and morals of the people who originated them. Their numerous outbursts of religious feeling indicate the depth of their devotion, while their many noble moral aphorisms indicate an appreciation of, and a desire for, a higher moral life than they were able to practice because of the strength of their animal feelings. This is especially true of the Jews, and also of the early Christians. They had a partial perception of a true moral life, and a desire at times to practice it, but that desire was counteracted and held in check by their still stronger animal natures and animal propensities.

A HIGHER PLANE OF DEVELOPMENT HAS BEEN ATTAINED

There can be no question, from the light derived from the twofold avenues of science and history, but that the great principle of universal progress, which is carrying everything forward to a higher plane and state of perfection, has elevated the most advanced nations of the present age *beyond* and *above* the religion and morals prevalent in the world when the Jewish and Christian Bible was written, which makes it very unsuitable for the *present* advanced state of society. An investigation of the science of anthropology discloses the very significant and important fact that the religious feelings of the founders and early representatives of the Jewish and Christian religions were under the control of their animal natures, which accounts for their frequent use of obscene language, and their frequent indulgence in the practice of every species of crime with the full sanction of the principles of their religion. And they cherished the conviction that those things had the divine sanction.

The moral and religious feelings of the early Jews and Christians *cooperated* with their *animal propensities*, and the *latter held supreme sway* over the former; while the moral and religious feelings of the finest advanced minds of the present day cooperate, not with the *animal,* but with the *intellectual.* This makes a very important and very marked difference, and makes the semi-animal religion of the past very unsuitable for the present age. Please note this point, friendly reader.

BIBLE WRITERS HONEST

It may readily be conceded that the writers and compilers of all Bibles were honest, and that all the errors which those Bibles embrace, and the crimes which they sanction, were honestly believed to be right, and in accordance with the will of God. For all sacred history teaches us, as an important lesson of human nature, that no errors are too gross, no crimes too enormous, no statements too false or absurd, no contradictions too glaring, and no stories too preposterous or too ridiculous, to receive the fullest endorsement of the most honest and pious minds, and to be even cherished by them as *God-given* or divinely revealed *truths,* when such has been their teaching every day of their lives, in connection with the habitual *suppression* of the voice of reason, and the inherited conviction of their truth deeply implanted in the mind, derived from a thousand preceding generations. A strong and unyielding cord of religious conviction thus grows in the human mind, which no reason, no philosophy, and no science can ever sever or even shake. It becomes a moral canker, which no remedy can reach, or arrest in its progress. It seems to grow into the very heartstrings. Such is the strength of religious prejudice, such the weak side of human nature. Three hundred millions of people believe in the Hindu religion, one hundred millions in the Chinese religion, two hundred millions in the Muhammadan religion, and one hundred and fifty millions in the Christian religion, all for the same reasons—because their parents so believed, and taught them, and their neighbors still believe it—and surrounding influences have caused them to continue in their erroneous belief.

After the illuminating rays of the sun of science had to some extent dispelled the religious errors of our early education, the case was so plain that we entered upon the work of trying to convince others, with sanguine hopes of success. But experience has established the conviction in our mind that if every text of the Christian Bible were a falsehood, and every line of their creeds an absurdity, there are many devout admirers of the book who could never be made to see it, because they are ruled by their *religious feelings,* and not by their *reasoning faculties*; and hence, they will live and die in their moral and religious errors. But we rejoice in the omnipotent power of truth, which will finally dispel all error from progressive minds.

The Beauties and Benefits of Bibles

More than twenty sacred books have been found in various countries, which, if not in all cases denominated Bibles, have at least been venerated and used as such, and, properly speaking, are Bibles. Hence, we shall call them Bibles. The list in this chapter comprises nearly all which recent research has brought to light. A brief synopsis of the character and contents of each will be presented, so far as a comparative view with the Christian Bible seems to make it requisite.

All of these Bibles possess some common characteristics:

1. All of them were claimed to be inspired.

2. All were claimed to be an embodiment of wisdom and knowledge far transcending the ordinary attainments of man.

3. All were penned by inspired men, who were shielded from the possibility of erring while writing them.

4. Each Bible is a finality in religious knowledge.

5. Each one is an authority from which there is no appeal.

6. It is a sin to question or doubt the truth of any of them, or to suggest the possibility of their containing errors.

7. Some of them were written by God, some by angels, and others by inspired men.

8. Each one points out the only safe and certain road to heaven.

9. He who is a disbeliever in any one of these holy books is an infidel.

10. Each one is to effect the salvation of the whole human race.

17

CHAPTER 5

HINDU BIBLES

I. THE VEDAS

The Vedas is considered to be the oldest sacred book of the Hindus, and is evidently the oldest Bible now extant. There is a vast amount of evidence to prove that it was written long before the time of Moses, which establishes the fact that it borrowed nothing from the Jews or Jewish writings. They purport to be the inspired utterances of very ancient and holy saints and prophets, known as Rishis, who received them directly from the mouth of the great God Brahma about nine thousand years ago, after they had existed in his mind from all eternity. These "holy men," by their devout piety and unreserved devotion to the cause of God and religion, it was believed, had attained to true holiness and heavenly sanctity. The Vedas treat of the attributes of God, and his dealings with the human race; his invisibility and spirituality; his unchangeableness, omniscience, omnipotence, and omnipresence; the nature and binding force of his laws; the doctrine of future rewards and punishments; frequent and wonderful displays of divine power, called miracles, etc. It contains, likewise, many noble, lofty, and beautiful moral precepts. It also treats, to some extent, of astronomy, medicines, and government.

The May number of "The New York Tribune" for 1838 contains a very interesting account of the recent translation of the Vedas into the English language, from which we will make a few extracts: "The whole of the Vedas is now being published for the first time by the East-India Company, by which the reader will learn that most of the odious things which have been charged to it are false. They are not found therein. They are Christian forgeries, such as the burning of widows on the funeral pile of their husbands, the marriage of children, the doctrine of caste, etc. None of these things are taught or countenanced by the Vedas. The man who believes in the Vedas approximates to a Christian." (Mark this statement, Christian reader!) Mr. Greeley further says: "The highest authority for the religion of the Brahmins is the Vedas. The most elaborate arguments have been framed by its devout believers to establish its divine origin and absolute authority. They constantly appeal to its authority, and, in controversy with Muhammadan and Christian missionaries (Muhammadans have missionaries among them, observe), they invariably fall back on the Vedas—referring to it with great confidence in support of anything they wish to establish as divine. There is no doctrine of Christianity which has not been anticipated by the Vedas." What is that you say, Mr. Greeley? "They have all the doctrines of Christianity!" Is that possible? All the holy and inspired doctrines of Jesus Christ, the great divine Lawgiver and Savior of the world, found in an old heathen Bible, written more than two thousand year before a single line of the doctrines of Christ was penned! Here is one of the most astounding announcements ever made to the world.

The reader, perhaps, will suppose that Mr. Greeley was an infidel; but here, again, is something most astonishing: Mr. Greeley was up to this time a sound member of a Christian church, and withal a truthful writer. Such an announcement ought to have startled the whole Christian world, and set them to investigating the matter. But, like the disciples of all the heathen religions, they are immovably fixed in the errors of their faith, and turn a deaf ear to all criticism, and all honest inquiry relating to the truth of its claims. Such is the tenacity of their inherited convictions of being right, their assumption of infallibility, their aversion and opposition to investigation that, if every line of their Bible was a falsehood, but few of them would find it out.

There are four works that come under the name of Vedas, known as the Rig-Veda, Yajur Veda, Sama Veda, and Atharva Veda. Each of these Bibles is constituted of various books, probably the work of different writers. Each Veda is accompanied by psalms or hymns, known as the "Samhita," and also by a sort of prose treatise or commentary, called the "Brahmana," which possesses a ritualistic or didactic character—all of which were believed to be inspired. "Never has the theory of inspiration," says Mr. Amberly, "been pushed to such extremes as in the case of the Vedas. They were believed by some to be the direct creation of Brahma," while the hymns which accompany them were claimed to be the inspired productions of holy men and prophets (Rishis). The Vedas was the standard authority in all cases, and any doctrine, opinion, or statement at variance with the Vedas was to be rejected as false. "And as for a contradiction in the Holy Book," says Mr. Amberly, "the thought was not to be entertained for a moment as possible." Such a conclusion they ascribed to the reader's wrong interpretation of its language. Such was the extreme veneration in which the book was held that every text, word, and even syllable was counted. A Brahmin was not allowed to marry until after he had devoted several years to studying the Holy Book; and, to attain to complete holiness, the disciple must commit the Rig-Veda to memory, or read it through on his bended knees. The Vedas represent God as being "one and indivisible," and "merciful to sinners." And Brahmins and Buddhists, when they pray for sinners or for their enemies, manifest a spirit of kindness and forgiveness not equalled by Christians.

The Buddhists had many churches and many priests, who taught the people to lead virtuous lives, and to avoid the commission of every species of crime, including the use of intoxicating drinks. And in no other system

19

was ever benevolence and charity, and also chastity, more emphatically enjoined, or more consistently practiced. The Vedas teach that every good act has its reward, and every bad act its punishment. Its disciples are taught that many saviors (Avatars) have appeared on earth at different periods to suffer and die for the people; the last of which was Salavahana, contemporary with Christ. God Sakia is of great veneration amongst them, and prayers are often addressed to him. Many tales are told of his goodness, self-denial, suffering, and sacrifice for the people, which leads to the conclusion that he was a pure, holy, and unselfish being. He gave utterance to many noble and morally exalting precepts. His principal precepts were comprised in six commandments: 1. "Not to kill any living creature"; 2 "Not to steal"; 3. "Not to commit unchastity"; 4. "Not to lie"; 5. "Not to drink intoxicating drinks"; and 6. "Not to lay up treasures upon earth." These are a few of his leading precepts, and which he himself practiced. In the observance of the last precept, he and his followers have excelled almost every Christian on earth, as their Bible contains the same precept, but none of them try to practice it. Hence, the Hindus are in this respect much better Christians than the Christians themselves.

Here it may be noted that the Hindus, like the disciples of the Christian faith, have had various ecclesiastical councils to settle the canon of their Bible or some controverted doctrinal questions. One of the most noted of these councils was called under the reign of King Asoka in the year 246 B.C. It was constituted of seven hundred "learned and accomplished priests." But they could not stop the progress of infidelity, as they essayed to do. It continued to increase until another council was called under the reign of King Kanishka, and another revision of the sacred text took place. But, as in Christian and Muhammadan countries, it tended rather to unsettle than to settle the popular faith. Nothing can arrest the intelligence and growth of progressive minds. Skepticism and infidelity will continue to increase whenever the mind is unfettered by priestcraft, until the last credal institution is swept from the face of the earth, and ceases to curse the human family.

II. THE CODE OF MENU

"The Code of Menu," or "Institutes of Menu," constitutes another sacred book of the Hindus. The Rev. Mr. Allen says of it: "It is a code of religious and civil laws, and makes a part of the Hindu Scriptures." It is in many respects similar to the Vedas, and is almost equal to it in age; and, like the Vedas, it is a standard of faith and a guide for moral action. Hindus call it *Menu Darma Shastra,* "the ordinances of God." "As these ordinances, or divine laws," says Mr. Allen, "profess to be of divine origin, kings have no authority to change them. Their duty was to administer their governments according to their teachings." All classes of people were required to live up to them. "In these respects," says Mr. Allen (p. 366), "they resemble the laws given by Moses, and contained in the Old Testament." These Institutes treat on the subject of creation, the doctrine of future rewards and punishments, and also define many of the duties of life.

III. THE RAMAYANA

With respect to age, the Ramayana is generally ranked next to the Code of Menu, and is equally adored as a holy and inspired book, and "may be classed," says Mr. Allen, "with the Hindu Scriptures." It treats of the war in Heaven, in which the dragon, or serpent-devil, was cast to the earth. To put an end to his ravages here, the Savior and incarnate God Krishna was sent down. Christ, we are told, "came to destroy the devil and his works." Col. Sherman tells us, in his "Recollections of an Indian Official," that "the people (Hindus) assured us this Bible was written, if not by the hand of the Deity himself, at least by his inspiration; and, if asked if any absurdity that may be pointed out in the book be true, they reply with great *naïveté*, 'Is it not written in the Holy Book? and how could it be there, and not be true?'"—exactly the same defense that is often set up for the Christian Bible by its educationally warped admirers. It is believed the great Hindu prophet, Vyasa, wrote much of this Bible, or "Inspired Poem," as some call it.

IV. THE MAHABHARATA

The origin of this sacred book is considered to be very nearly co-eval with that of the Ramayana. It has an appendix, or epistle, called the *Bhagavad-Gita*, which, on account of its high tone of spirituality, has attracted much attention in Europe. The Hindus believe the Mahabharata is highly inspired, and that every event noticed in it was recorded before it took place; thus making it in the highest degree prophetic. "Its author, they claim," says Mr. Allen, "is no other than the incarnate God Krishna, of whose life it treats." That profound Oriental scholar, Mr. Wilkins, thinks this and the other sacred books of India are more than three thousand years old, as is evidenced by sculptures in solid rocks.

V. THE PURANS OR PURANAS

Some Hindu Holy Scriptures, when arranged together in one book, are known as the *Barta Shastra,* of which the Puranas constitute a part. The last-named work treats of the creation of the world, and its final destruction and future renovation, the "great day of judgment," Divine Providence, etc.; also the ordinances and rules for worship, etc.

ANALOGIES OF THE HINDU AND JEWISH RELIGIONS

Brahminism and Judaism are each old forms of religion. Each was superseded by a new and improved form of religion. Each has a story of creation. Jehovah and Brahma both created the sun, moon, and stars (so believed by millions).

1. The spirit of both moved upon the face of the waters.
2. The world is spoken into existence by both Jehovah and Brahma.
3. The Hindus had an Adimo and Iva, the Hebrews an Adam and Eve.
4. In each case, everything is to produce after its kind.
5. Man is in each case the last and crowning work of the whole creation.
6. Both stories set man as a ruler over subordinate creation.
7. Light in each case was spoken into existence.
8. Jehovah and Brahma each occupied six days in the work of creation.
9. There is a primitive paradise and state of moral purity in each story.
10. A tree whose fruit produced immortality is noticed in each cosmogony.
11. A serpent figures in each, and outwits Brahma and Jehovah.
12. Man in each partakes of the fruit of the tree of knowledge.
13. The doctrine of the fall is found in each account. The means for man's restoration is provided in each case.
14. Each sacred legend has a story of a war in heaven.
15. The soul is the breath of life, or breath of God, in each cosmogony.
16. Labor is imposed as a curse in each case.
17. A moral code of ten commandments is found in each system. Not to kill is a command in each decalogue. Stealing is interdicted in each decalogue. Adultery is condemned in each. Bearing false witness is forbidden by each.
18. Both Brahmins and Jews lost their "Holy Law," or "Laws of God." One had a Hilkiah, and the other a Bishen, to find the law.
19. Each had an established order of priesthood. The priesthood was hereditary in each case: a tribe or family furnished the priests in each case.
20. Both claimed to be God's pet and holy, or peculiar, people; and both styled other nations barbarians or aliens.
21. Both holy nations were forbidden to marry with others, and both were too holy to eat with barbarians.

22. Each had a ceremonial law prescribing numerous rites. The church ceremonies were performed by priests in each.

23. The priests were forbidden to eat meat in both cases.

24. Both Jews and Brahmins worshipped by bloody sacrifices. Both had their favorite sacred animals. Animal sacrifices were by each to arrest public calamities.

25. One interdicted beef, and the other pork, as food.

26. Both prescribed purification after touching dead bodies, and each religion had a law of purification. Bathing was a mode of purification in each religion.

27. Each has its "holy" places, times, days, cities, mountains, rivers, etc. India, as well as Judea, was considered a holy land.

28. Each had its holy ground. Both drew off their shoes on entering upon holy ground or holy places.

29. Both had their holy days, and the same in most cases.

30. Mount Mera was no less holy than Mount Sinai or Mount Horeb. Jordan was a sacred river in one case, and Ganges in the other. Jerusalem was a "holy" city with the Jews, and Benares with the Hindus.

31. Holy fasts and feasts were a part of each religion. Both made a holy feast at full moon.

32. Each had its holy fires.

33. Both had their holy mysteries kept sacredly guarded.

34. Each prepared and kept holy water for ceremonial purposes.

35. Both anointed themselves with "holy ointment."

36. Each claimed to have the only true and "holy faith."

37. "Holy temples" were familiar terms to each. Their temples were constructed in a similar manner. Each had a "*sanctum* sanctorum," or "holy of holies." Only the holy priest of both entered the interior sanctum.

38. Both had their drink-offerings (called *turpin* by the Hindus).

39. Both sprinkled their door-posts with blood.

40. One had a scape-goat, and the other a scape-horse.

41. Both taught that the sins of the father were visited upon the children.

42. Religious pilgrimages were practiced by each.

43. Both acknowledge and teach one supreme God. Inferior deities, or angels, are believed in by each. God's omniscience, omnipotence, and omnipresence are taught in both Bibles.

44. God is represented to be invisible by each. And "God is a spirit," and infinitely wise and good, is taught in each.

45. To love God supremely is recommended by each.

46. Both taught that God was a God of power, and assisted them in their battles.

47. Both taught that a knowledge of God is essential.

48. Silent meditation upon the Lord is recommended by each.

49. God was to each a refuge in danger and trouble.

50. The government of each was a theocracy, God the executive.

51. Both religions were constituted largely of external rites. In each, the priest was the expounder of the holy books and laws. Patriarchs "was one of the sacred orders of each system. Holy "prophets" figure conspicuously in each system. Both priests and people were in each case believed to be inspired.

52. And each had its witnesses to prove the truth and fulfillment of its prophecies.

53. Both held their Holy Bibles as an inspired guide of right and wrong.

54. One Bible was from Jehovah, and the other from Brahma.

55. Ezra was inspired to compile the Jewish Bible, and Vyas the Brahmin.

56. Each religious order had a holy ark containing something sacred.

57. A story of a deluge is found in the Bible of each.

58. The corruption or wickedness of society caused the flood in each case.

59. The Brahmins had their patriarch Satyavrata, answering to Noah.

60. Each was forewarned of the flood.

61. Eight persons were saved in each case.

62. In each story a large vessel is prepared. Animals were saved by pairs in each case. A rainbow is spoken of in each flood story.

63. For Shem, Ham, and Japhet, the Hindus have a Sherma, Charma, and Jyapheta.

64. Charma was condemned to be "a servant of servants," like Ham.

65. Human life was in each traditionally spun out to nearly a thousand years.

66. One day a thousand years with God, in each system.

67. Both have stories of persons ascending to heaven.

68. Buddha was cast into the fiery furnace like the three holy children.

69. Musavod was a giant in strength like Samson.

70. Rhambha was changed to a pillar of stone, like Lot's wife to salt.

71. Mahendra was carried through the air like Habakkuk.

72. A story of Buddha answers to that of Daniel in the lions' den.

73. Idolatry is discouraged, but occasionally practiced by each.

74. Witchcraft was believed in by each.

75. Here are presented eighty-eight striking analogies.

ANTIQUITY OF INDIA

Having presented a long list of analogies between the Hindu and Jewish religions, we will proceed to prove the prior existence of the Hindu system, and leave the reader to deduce his own inferences. "In times coeval with the earliest authentic records," says a writer, "the Hindus calculated eclipses, and were venerated for their attainments in some of the arts and sciences." According to the learned astronomer Baily, their calculations in astronomy extended back to the remote period of seventeen hundred years before Moses; and some of the ancient monuments and inscriptions of India bespeak for its religion a very remote antiquity. Some of our modern learned antiquarians have expressed the opinion that the Sanskrit language of the Brahmins is the oldest language that can be traced in the history of the human race. They also state that this language was extant before the Jews were known as a nation; and neither it nor their religion has *ever* been known to *change*. These facts are sufficient to establish the existence of the Brahmin and Buddhist systems of religion long prior to the earliest records of the Jewish nation.

Note: Here we desire to call the attention of the reader to the very remarkable statement of Col. Dow in his "History of India." He tells us that "the Hindus give a *very particular account* of the *origin* of the religion" (pref. v.). They say that a pious Hindu by the name of Rajah Tura apostatized from the faith, for which he was banished to the West, where he established a system of religion, which became afterwards known as the Jewish religion. Tura only needs a change of one letter to make Tera, the father of Abraham. Let the reader make a note of this.

CHAPTER 6

THE EGYPTIAN BIBLE — THE "HERMAS"

The sacred books, the "Hermas," or "Books of Hermas," were believed by the Egyptians to have been dictated by the God Isis, and inspired by him. In their collected capacity they constituted the Egyptian Bible, and were believed to contain "the sum total of human and divine wisdom." Their great age is undisputed. They treat of the creation of the world, the attributes of God, and the theogony of the inferior deities, which answer to angels in the Christian system, as they hold the same office, and are apparently the same kind of beings. The "Hermas," like all other Bibles, recognize but one supreme God, whom it declares to be just, holy, morally perfect, invisible, and indivisible, and whom it recommends to be worshipped in silence. This "Holy Book" contains some lofty and soul-inspiring moral sentiments and useful precepts.

ANALOGIES OF THE EGYPTIAN AND JEWISH RELIGIONS

Modern archaeological researches in Egypt have disclosed a very striking resemblance between the ancient Egyptian religion and that found in the Jewish Old Testament, which, with the evidence of the greater antiquity of the former, has fastened the conviction upon the mind of every impartial reader of history that the Jewish religion was constructed from materials obtained in Egypt and India; and this conclusion is corroborated by the Bible itself, which tells us Moses was skilled in all the wisdom and learning of Egypt, and was by birth an Egyptian. When we compare the doctrines, precepts, laws, and customs of the two religions, we find but little difference between them. Even to the ten commandments there is a striking resemblance. The account of the creation and the order of its development is essentially the same in both.

1.   The Egyptians had a leader filling the place of Moses by the name of Hermes; and his writings were held in similar estimation, as they were believed to be inspired and dictated by Infinite Wisdom.

2.   The Egyptians had a priesthood of wealth and power, and possessing the same sacerdotal caste as those of the Jews.

3.   And the priesthood, Mr. Pritchard tells us (Debate 116), was hereditary, and confined to a certain tribe, as was that of the Jews. According to Diodorus Siculus, and also Mr. Wilkinson, nearly all their ceremonies were essentially the same.

4.   And their religious temples were constructed upon the same model, with an outer court and an inner court—a *sanctum sanctorum.*

5.   The Egyptians had numerous prophets like the Jews.   And Herodotus says, "The art of predicting future events came from the Egyptians."

6.   The Egyptians had an ark, or shrine, which served as an oracle, and was carried about on a pole by a procession of priests, as the ark of the covenant of the Jews was by the Levites. The Rev. John Kendrick, in his "Ancient Egypt," acknowledged that he believed "the ark of the covenant of the Hebrews was constructed on the model of the Egyptian shrine."

7.   Kitto, in his "Cyclopedia," says the Egyptian sphinxes explain what is meant by the cherubims of the Jews.

8.   In their selection of animals for sacrifices, we find the same rules were adopted. Each was controlled by the singular fancy of choosing a red heifer.

9.   Each had their scape-animals to carry away their sins—the Egyptians an ox, and the Jews a goat.

10. Both practiced circumcision.   And we have the authority of Herodotus for saying the Jews and Phoenicians borrowed the custom of the Egyptians.

11. Both Jews and Egyptians took off their shoes when approaching a holy place, which, with the Egyptians, was in the temple.

12. Both believed in one supreme, overruling God, and many subordinates, known either as angels or deities, which, in their character and their offices, were essentially the same.

And a hundred other analogies might be pointed out, which indicate the Oriental origin of Judaism.

ANTIQUITY OF EGYPT

As a full comparison will show that the religion of ancient Egypt and that of the Jews were essentially alike, not only in their general features but in their most minute details, with respect to most of their doctrines, precepts, and customs, the question arises, How came this resemblance? It is out of the question to consider it merely fortuitous: that one grew out of the other, or both were derived from a common source, we are compelled to admit. To determine which was the parent system we have only to ascertain which possesses the greater antiquity. This question is very easily settled. A large volume of facts is at our command which tend to prove that the Egyptians were in a high state of civilization before the Jews were known to history.   The Bible itself partially recognizes this fact by its frequent allusion to Egypt as a wise and powerful nation, able at all times to exercise superior sway over the Jews, and whose wise men, or magicians, could compete with not only the Jews, but their God, in the performance of miracles; that is, with the Jews and their God to help them in achieving the most astounding feats. They could make anything that Jehovah could, with

27

the exception of lice. The remote antiquity of Egypt can be proved by a few facts.

The Egyptians have a carefully preserved list of sixty-one kings, who ruled the empire between Menes and Amasis, with names and ages given, whose aggregate reign comprises a period of more than seven thousand years. Herodotus says they computed with great care and accuracy. Manetho tells us Menes reigned seven thousand seven hundred years ago, which places him more than seventeen hundred years before Adam. Engravings on monuments, and writings on papyrus, confirm the statement of Manetho. And then hieroglyphics on the pyramids of Egypt, with names, dates, and figures which have recently been deciphered, enable us to trace the antiquity of Egypt back eight thousand years, when she is shown to have been in a high state of civilization. Another fact: Layard and Rawlinson, who recently visited Egypt as commissioners or agents of the British Government, state that fragments of pottery have been recently found by digging in the Valley of the Nile, which, by counting the successive layers or deposits made by the annual overflowing of the river, are shown to be not less than eleven thousand years old. Such facts amount to demonstration, and cannot be set aside. And Mr. Wilkinson, in his "Manners and Customs of Ancient Egypt," adduces another kind of evidence to show the impossibility of Egypt having obtained her religion from the Jews. He says, "The first glimpse we obtain of Egypt shows us a nation far advanced in the arts and customs and institutions of civilized life." And this was six or seven thousand years ago; while the most conclusive evidence can be adduced to show that no essential change has been made in her religion since the inscriptions were made on the monuments, some of which bear evidence of being eight thousand or nine thousand years old. If there has been no essential change in her religion for eight thousand or nine thousand years, it is *prima facie* evidence that she did not borrow any of her religious tenets from the Jews. Such facts settle the question more conclusively than the most elaborate argument could do.

CHAPTER 7

PERSIAN BIBLES

I. THE ZEND AVESTA

The Persians, properly speaking, had two Bibles, or Testaments, regarded as inspired and of divine authority—the *Zend Avesta* and the *Sadder,* which may be denominated their Old and New Testaments. With these may be classed other sacred books of Persia, known as the *"Desatur"* (or Revealed Will of God), the *"G. Javidan"* (or Eternal Wisdom), and the *"Sophi Ibraham"* (Wisdom of Ibraham). Hyde, in his "Biography of Britain," eighth chapter, pronounces the *G. Javidan* older than the writings of Zoroaster, which were penned 600 B.C.

The Zend Avesta presents a detailed account of creation in six *kappas,* or indefinite periods of time; the temptation and fall of man, and his final restoration; the immortality of the soul, etc.

II. THE SADDER

The Sadder depicts "the war in heaven," in which the great dragon, or devil, Ahrimanes, is finally slain. This sacred book, as well as the Zend Avesta, contains many beautiful precepts. The Persian sacred writings are all full of prayer and praise to God. One portion addresses him as *Ormuzd,* another as *Ahura Mazda.* None of their Holy Books countenance or show any favor either for idolatry or polytheism. The Persians have always opposed the making and worship of devil images; and they worship but one God, with the above names. One of their prayers, as a specimen, will show this: "O Ahura Mazda, thou true and happy being! Aid us to think and speak of thee, and do only those things which promote the true welfare of body and soul. I believe in thee as the just and holy God, thou living Wise One! Thou art the author of creation, the true source of light and life. I will praise thee, thou holy Spirit, thou glorious God Mazda! Thou givest with a liberal hand good things to the impious, as well as to the pious." In that portion of the Zend Avesta called the "Yacna," constituting seven chapters, it is declared, "We worship Ahura Mazda, and pray for the spread of his religion. We praise Mazda's religion, and the pure brotherhood which it established. From the holy Spirit Mazda proceeds all good, and he is the source of perfection and immortality." Here let it be noted that Cyrus of Persia was teaching the doctrine of immortality of the soul, while Moses seems never to have thought of such a thing: he is silent on the subject. Zend Avesta means "The Living Word of God." It has also been called by its disciples "The Revealed Word," and Ahura Mazda has been called the "God of gods," as the Jews called Jehovah. Who is to settle this counter-claim?

Sin, repentance, and forgiveness are all recognized in the sacred books of the Persians. This is evinced by a devout disciple, when he says, in prayer, "I repent, O Lord, of my wicked deeds in thought and words. Forgive, O Lord: I repent of my sins." A writer says, "Upon the really fundamental duties of man, the Zend Avesta upholds a high standard of morality and honesty, and seeks to inculcate the immense importance of leading an upright and virtuous life—such a life alone as can be pleasing to God and useful to man." A text in this sacred book reads, "You can not be a worshiper of the one true God and of many gods at the same time," which is a very explicit avowal of the belief in but one God. This Persian Bible declares that one way to advance God's kingdom on earth is to confer benefit upon the poor. Its spirit of kindness and sympathetic regard for suffering extends even to the brute creation. It forbids cruelty to any class of beings, and enjoins kindness to all. Its psalms, hymns, and liturgies breathe forth a spirit of deep piety. A compliance with the divine law is urged as a means of saving the sinner from future punishment. The stern moral fortitude of the great teacher and moral exemplar Zoroaster, in resisting, like Christ, the temptations of the Evil One, evinces a high appreciation of true virtue. As a whole, the sacred books of the Persians, like those of other nations, contain a considerable amount of golden truth mixed with much rubbish and superstition.

ANALOGIES OF THE PERSIAN AND JEWISH RELIGIONS

Doctor Pocoke says, "Many things taught in the sacred books of the Persians are the same as those taught in the Pentateuch of Moses, and other parts of the Bible. They also contain many of the psalms erroneously called by the Jews and Christians the Psalms of David." Sir William Jones, in his "Asiatic Researches," says, "The primeval religion of Iran (Persia) is called by Newton the oldest, and it may justly be called the noblest, of all religions." It teaches "a firm belief that one supreme God made the world by his power, and governs it by his providence. It inculcates a pious fear, love, and adoration for God; also a due reverence for parents and aged persons, fraternal affection for the whole human species, and a compassionate tenderness even for the brute creation." Can as much as this be said of the Christian religion? Mr. Goodrich, after stating that the ancient Hebrews evidently had no idea of astronomy as a science, says, "The Chaldeans appear to have made observations on eclipses earlier than the commencement of written history" ("History of All Nations," p. 25).

The Chaldeans and Persians have a story of creation essentially the same as that of the Jews. It represents Ormuzd as creating the world through the word in six kappas, or periods of time. Previous to that period, nothing but chaos, or darkness, and water had existed. Ormuzd created, first, the heavens and the earth; second, the firmament; third, the seas and waters; fourth, the sun, moon, and stars; fifth, birds, reptiles, quadrupeds, etc.; sixth, man. The Persians and Chaldeans have also a story of a deluge, in which Xisuthra, being warned in a dream, built an ark, in which he saved himself, his wife and daughter, and the pilot, and a pair of every species of animals, reptiles, and birds. After the rain had ceased, he sent out a pigeon, which, finding no resting place, came back to the ark. The second time, it came with mud in its bill, which was a better evidence that the waters had subsided than the leaf which Noah's dove returned with, as that might have been picked up while floating on the waters. They had a giant in strength (a Gaza) answering to that of Samson. They had a story of a lofty tower designed to reach to heaven, but the gods destroyed it, and confounded the language of the builders. The Persians had their priests, their prophets, their angels, their twelve patriarchs, their holy fires, holy water, and rites of purification, like the Jews, also their ordinance of water-baptism. Their holy mountains, holy rivers, and holy waters, their animal sacrifices, and their sacrament or ceremony of bread and wine, were all similar to those of the Jews. They had a Soleimon and a Soleimon's temple. Their religion was a theocracy, and was violently opposed to idolatry; but, unlike the Jewish religion, it taught the doctrine of the immortality of the soul, and the lofty idea that the human mind is an emanation from the divine nature. We find the principal elements of the Christian system also mixed up with the doctrines and principles above set forth; such as two primary principles of good and evil (Ormuzd and Ahrimanes), termed by Christians God and the Devil—two Gods with their two kingdoms, which were always at war with each other, to moderate which stands Mithra the Mediator, who was born, like Christ, of an immaculate virgin. For a further elucidation, see "The World's Sixteen Crucified Saviors."

ANTIQUITY OF PERSIA

The historical facts to establish the existence of the Persian religion long prior to that of the Jews are numerous, cogent, and unanswerable. They have calculations in astronomy which, scientists admit, must have been made four hundred years anterior to the time of Moses. According to Berosus, fragments of their history have been found which extend it back fifteen thousand years; and he tells us it is computed with great care.

CHAPTER 8

CHINESE BIBLES

The Chinese have various sacred books, the principal of which are the Five Kings. They have also four Holy Books, known as Shoo, and one called Tao-te, though the word King is a term applied to all their sacred books. Some of these Holy Bibles are attributed to Confucius, one of them (Ta-heo, the Great Learning) to his grandson, and others to his disciples. Some of the sects recognize thirteen Kings, or sacred books, others only seven, and the principal sect but five. Some of these Holy Books bear a resemblance to the Christian Gospels, others to the Epistles; and one of them bears a considerable resemblance to Paul's Epistle to the Hebrews. They are believed to be divinely inspired; and all are regarded as authority in matters of faith, doctrine, and practice. All of them inculcate virtue, and condemn vice and immorality. I will present merely a brief exposition of a few of the leading books.

I. THE TA-HEO, OR GREAT LEARNING

This book forms the basis of the religious sect known as the Tao-ists. It treats principally of doctrines, but enjoins many important duties, such as family government, the cultivation of the natural faculties, the acquisition of knowledge, the duty of being honest and sincere and rectifying the heart, and the moral obligation of having good rulers and a righteous government as means of making all peaceful and happy.

II. THE CHUN YUNG, OR DOCTRINE OF THE MEAN

This book contains the Golden Rule: "What you do not like others to do to you, do not so to them." It recommends a state of harmony in the mental faculties as the path of duty and the road to happiness and to heaven. It teaches that people should follow the dictates of their own consciences, and cultivate and fully develop their natures. On the whole, it admonishes a system of moral perfection. It declares that spiritual beings are constantly around us, and we do nothing without them, though we do not see or hear them. Pretty good spiritualism!

III. THE BOOK OF MANG, OR MENCIUS

Mang, or Mencius, the philosopher, lived about two hundred years after Confucius. This Holy Book of his was not admitted into the Chinese canon until several centuries after it was written. Up to that date it was regarded as apocryphal, but is now held in high veneration as an inspired book. It affirms the essential goodness of human nature, instead of the Christian doctrine of "total depravity." It teaches that all men are possessed of more or less goodness by nature, but are often corrupted by bad example and bad governments. It argues the moral right of the people to choose their own rulers.

IV. THE SHOO KING, OR "BOOK OF HISTORY"

This work is constituted of fifty-eight books. It throws much light on the history of the Chinese Empire, and bears evidence of having been written in a very remote age, but was compiled about 500 B.C. It argues that people are not bad by nature, and that it is the duty of governments to bless the good and punish the wicked. Otherwise they need not expect the blessing of heaven, or the favor of the people. It relates the case of an emperor who was reformed by reading the Holy Book.

V. THE SHEE KING, OR "BOOK OF POETRY"

This book is about as devoid of moral instruction as the Books of Ruth and Esther in the Christian Bible. It is principally a display of human emotions and social feelings. Yet almost every Chinese has committed portions of it to memory. Being gotten up in the style of a poem, it is well calculated to enlist the feelings of the devout disciple.

VI. THE CHUN TSEN, OR "SPRING AND SUMMER"

This is principally a historical record, and is interpreted as representing spring and summer. It is held in high estimation as being the production of the "Great Divine Man" Confucius; and it is wonderful with what ingenuity its commentators and teachers have succeeded in extracting from its dry details about wars, marriages, deaths, travels, eclipses, battles, etc., the most profound lessons in morals. Like the admirers and expounders of other Holy Books in all ages and countries, they bestow the most recondite spiritual meanings on texts containing nothing but nonsense, senseless verbiage, or immoral teachings.

VII. THE TAO-TE KING, OR DOCTRINE OF REASON

"Tao" means *absolute*, and "Te" means *virtue*, which indicates that it teaches *absolute virtue.* Of all sacred books this is the most philosophical. It seems to constitute both a revelation and system of philosophy. It displays considerable wisdom and beauty, but is not free from those gross and repulsive elements which characterize the Christian and some other Bibles. It declares that God created, cherishes, and loves all the world. It has no angry God, but one enjoining love and benevolence, and the return of good for evil, upon all the human race. It declares God made all beings: his essence formed them, his might preserves them, his providence protects them, and his power perfects them. It condemns war and weapons of death: it says that Tao does not employ them, and all good men abhor them. It also condemns the possession of worldly wealth as being in opposition to a spiritual life, and as denoting the absence of good from the soul. Modesty, mercy, benevolence, and contentment are recommended as the highest of human virtues. An extensive commentary, written by a Chinese saint about 160 B.C., goes with this book to explain it, as all "divine revelations" have to be revealed over again by the priests, who seem to assume that Infinite Wisdom is too ignorant of human language to dictate a book that can be understood. Must it not be mortifying to him to have his blunders thus exposed?

ANALOGY OF THE CHINESE AND JEWISH RELIGIONS

The Christian historian, Mr. Milne, expressed a fear that he might be condemned for furnishing proof that, before Jesus wan born, a morality as pure was inculcated in the celestial empire (China). As in the Hindu, Egyptian, and Persian religions, we find the Jewish and Christian religions here amalgamated together. The Chinese had a cosmogony, or story of creation, similar in some respects to those already noticed. These sacred books speak of a primitive paradise, in which were a tree of knowledge and a tree of life; also of a deluge and an ark. Baptism, the cross, and the miter are emblematical rites of their religion. They also taught the doctrine of the eucharist and the trinity, and practiced circumcision.

The Chinese have a story or tradition of an Incarnate God, Natigai, who, like Christ, was both creator and mediator. His system of religious faith taught the doctrine of special providences, future rewards and punishments, a general judgment day, the duty of humility or self-abasement, and the moral and religious obligation to observe strict temperate habits, and to devote our whole lives to God, etc.

The Chinese religion inculcates many beautiful and sublime moral precepts, which we have not space to notice here.

ANTIQUITY OF CHINA

The historical books of China, comprising a hundred and fifty volumes, and called "The Great Annals," and recently translated by a scientific Frenchman, have a regular chronology, beginning nearly two thousand six hundred years before the period assigned for the creation of Adam. And they have calculations in astronomy at that remote period. The learned men of Europe have decided that they made the calculation of an eclipse about seven hundred years before the time of Moses. These facts are sufficient to prove the existence of their religion long anterior to the time of Adam.

Chinese Bibles

CONCLUDING INFERENCE

In addition to the facts and authorities we have cited to show that the Hindu, Egyptian, Persian, and Chinese religions were all established prior to that of the Jews, there are other facts which demonstrate the absolute impossibility of any of these religions obtaining any of their religious elements or doctrines from the Jews.

1.   We find both the Jewish and Christian doctrine interwoven into each one of those Oriental systems.   Hence, if they borrowed one, they borrowed both.   But that is impossible: the Christian system is known to be much younger.

2.   Those Oriental religions are all conservative in character; so that there has been scarcely any perceptible change in their doctrines during the thousands of years of their known existence.   Hence, their very nature would preclude them from borrowing any new doctrines.

3.   On the contrary, the Jewish mind has been very vacillating.   A disposition to change their religion has been constantly manifested through their whole history.   Such facts as these settle the question.

CHAPTER 9

SEVEN OTHER ORIENTAL BIBLES

I. THE SOFFEES' BIBLE — THE MUSNAVI

The Bible of the Soffees, the "Musnavi," teaches that God exists everywhere and in everything; that the soul of man, and the principle of life throughout all nature, are not *from God*, but *of* God, and constitute a part of his essence; that nothing exists essentially but God; and that "all nature abounds with Divine Life." Mr. Malcom, in his "History of the Moguls" (p. 269), says: "The Soffees are incessantly occupied in adoring the Almighty, and in a search after truth." They are passionately fond of poetry and music (two essential elements of civilization). Their Bible teaches many beautiful moral lessons.

II. THE PARSEES' BIBLE — THE BOUR DESCH

The Parsees' Bible is entitled "Bour Desch," which means "Genesis, or the Beginning of Things." Its cosmogony is similar to that of Moses, though more definite, and probably written at an earlier period. Its Eden, or primitive paradise, lasted three thousand years before Kipo (the Devil) entered, plucked the fruit, handed it to the woman, and thus caused her downfall, and, after her, that of the whole human race.

We have space for but little more than the titles of other Bibles.

III. THE TAMALESE BIBLE — THE KALIWAKAM

The Tamalese "Holy Book" was known as the "Kaliwakam," and contains some excellent moral precepts.

IV. SCANDINAVIAN BIBLE — THE SAGA

Saga, meaning "Wisdom," is the name of the Scandinavian "Inspired Volume," so called because it was believed to have emanated from the fountain of divine wisdom.

V. THE KALMUCS' BIBLE — THE KALIOCHAM

The "Kaliocham," the Kalmucs' Bible, was believed to contain in repletion "all the wisdom of God and man."

VI. THE ATHENIAN BIBLE — THE TESTAMENT

The ancient Athenians had what they claimed to be a "Holy and God-derived Book" called "The Testament." Dinarchus alludes to it in his speech against Demosthenes. It was read with deep, solemn awe and devoutness.

Seven Other Oriental Bibles

VII. THE CABALISTS' BIBLE — THE YOHAR

Yohar, or "Book of Light," the Bible of the Cabalists, relates some wonderful cures and miracles performed by that sect.

CHAPTER 10

THE MUHAMMADAN, MORMON AND SHAKERS' BIBLES

I. The Muhammadan Bible — The Koran

The Koran, or Alkoran, is the most modern in its origin of 22 in the list, having been penned six hundred years later than the Christian Bible. It differs from most other Bibles in being the production of a single author, and, for this reason, possesses more uniformity of style and fewer contradictions than most other Bibles. Muhammad did not claim to be its author, and did not write it, but merely dictated it to his secretary Zaid. Like the founder of the Christian religion, and nearly all the other great religions of the world, he was very illiterate. Incarnate Gods and religious chieftains possess no aspiration to become scholars, and no taste for science. They were governed by feeling and the impulse of religious enthusiasm, which have no affinity for science. Muhammad, however, did not profess to be a God, but merely a prophet. The Koran, having originated in a later and more enlightened age than the Christian Bible, possesses some superior features and, of course, is superior to still older Bibles. It is more consistent in its teachings on the subject of temperance, as it does not, like the Christian Bible, both sanction and condemn the use of intoxicating drinks; it uniformly forbids the use of it, and even prohibits the manufacture of it. It also shows more respect for the rights of woman by providing for her maintenance by dowry. It levies a tax on its disciples of two and one-fourth percent for the support of the poor. It enjoins not only kindness and respect for enemies, but a careful provision for their wants.

The disciples of the Koran were taught and believed that the Holy Book was originated in heaven, and had long been preserved there by its divine author Allah, and, in the fullness of time, was handed down, chapter at a time, by the angel Gabriel to the prophet Muhammad, and his scribe Zaid recorded it. The leading doctrines of the Koran are: the Unity of the Godhead, and the perfection of his attributes; the joys of paradise, and the terrors of hell; the awful fate of unbelievers in the Koran. The Day of Judgment is held up as a terror to evildoers and skeptics, and an encouragement to the faithful. Skeptics, or unbelievers in the Koran and the Muhammadan religion, are repeatedly consigned to the same terrible fate (the fires of hell) that Christ consigns the unbeliever in the Christian religion, and the same as that to which the founders of other religions doom those who reject or disbelieve their pretended revelations. The Koran abounds in precepts of a high moral tone.

Muhammad holds out the idea that Christ was created like Adam, and therefore was but a man, though a true servant of God. This, he asserts, was the view of Christ himself. The doctrine that God could have a son, or that there could be more than one person in the Godhead, was to him profanity, infidelity, and downright blasphemy. It is repeatedly denounced in strong terms in the Koran. All prayer and praises to God are addressed to him in the singular number. I will cite a few texts in illustration: "Praise be to God, Lord of all worlds, the compassionate and merciful King. Thee only do we worship, and to thee only do we cry for help. Guide us in the right path"; "The sun is God's noonday brightness; the moon followeth him: the day revealeth his glory; and the night enshroudeth him"; "He built the heavens, and spread forth the earth"; "And whoso shall fear God, and do good works, no fear shall come upon them, neither shall they be put to grief. But those who turn away from him, he will consign to eternal fire"; "To those who believe (the Koran), and do things which are right, hath God promised forgiveness and a noble recompense."

II. THE MORMON BIBLES

The Book of Mormon

This sacred book is claimed to have been found inscribed on gold plates, situated several feet below the surface of the earth, in Wayne County, New York, in the year 1823, by Joseph Smith, a pious youth, then only fourteen years of age, who declared he received information with respect to the existence of the plates and their locality from an angel of the Lord, with whom he had had frequent intercourse for several years. The following is a description of the plates and original records composing the book, as furnished by Orson Pratt, one of the "Latter-day Apostles" of Jesus Christ: "The records were engraven on plates which had the appearance of gold. Each plate was not far from seven by eight inches in length and width, being not quite as thick as common tin. They were filled on both sides with engravings in Egyptian characters, and bound together in volume as the leaves of a book, fastened at one edge with three rings running through the whole. This volume was something near six inches in thickness, a part of which was sealed. The characters, or letters, upon the unsealed part were small and beautifully engraven. The whole book exhibited many marks of antiquity in its construction, and skill in its engravings. With the records was found a curious instrument called by the ancients 'Urim and Thummim,' which consisted of two transparent stones, clear as crystal, set in the two rims of a bow. It was used in ancient times by persons called seers, by means of which they received revelations of things past or future."

Mr. Smith finally succeeded, with the aid of a profound linguist in New York City by the name of Anthon, in translating the whole work into the

English language. Several writers testify that the ground out of which the records were dug was solid, and covered with a thick and solid growth of grass, presenting no appearance of having ever been disturbed. The sect now constitutes about three hundred thousand disciples. The following testimony to the truth of the story is a voluntary offering by three witnesses:

Testimony of Three Witnesses

Be it known unto all nations, tongues, kindred, and people unto whom this work shall come, that we, through the grace of God the Father, and our Lord Jesus Christ, have seen the plates which contain this record, which is a record of the people of Nephi, and also of the Lamanites. Men, brethren, and also of the people of Jared. And we also know that they have been translated by the gift and power of God; for his voice hath declared it unto us: wherefore we know of a surety that the work is true. And we also testify that we have seen engravings which are upon the plates; and they are shown unto us by the power of God, and not of man. And we declare with words of soberness, that an angel of God came down, and that he brought and laid before our eyes, and we beheld and saw, the plates and the engravings thereon. And we know it is by the grace of God and our Lord Jesus Christ that we beheld and bare record that these things are true, and it is marvelous in our eyes. Nevertheless the voice of the Lord commanded that we should bear record of it. Wherefore, to be obedient to the commandments of God, we bear testimony of these things. And we know, that if we are faithful in Christ, we shall rid our garments of the blood of all men, and be found spotless before the judgment-seat of Christ, and shall dwell with him eternally in heaven. And the honor be to the Father and the Son and the Holy Ghost, which are one God. Amen.

Oliver Cowdery
David Whitmer
Martin Harris

The Book of Doctrines and Covenants

In addition to the Book of Mormon, Joseph Smith originated and partly composed a Book of Doctrines and Covenants, purporting to be a direct revelation from heaven relative to the temporal government of their church. It enjoined the support of the poor, the taxation of members, the establishment of cities and temples, the education of the people, the emigration of saints, etc. This book has been venerated by the Mormons as a "holy revelation from God," and hence is, in a strict sense, a Bible. Its title sufficiently indicates its character. As much as Christians ridicule the idea of Joseph Smith receiving a revelation from God, it comes to us with exactly the same authority as the claimed-to-be revelation of Moses. The evidence in each case is the same.

III. THE SHAKERS' BIBLE — THE DIVINE ROLL

The Bible of the Shakers is entitled "A Holy, Sacred, and Divine Roll from the Lord God of Heaven to the Inhabitants of the Earth, Revealed in the Society of New Lebanon, Columbiana County, New York, United States of America." The testimony of eleven mighty angels is given, who are said to have attended the writing of the Roll. A copy of the Holy Book has been sent to every king and potentate on earth. Its contents and style bear some resemblance to the Christian Bible, and it contains texts which appear to have been drawn from that book, and then altered. It should be borne in mind that the Shakers also profess to believe in the Christian Bible, with their own peculiar construction of the book, like other sects.

CHAPTER 11

THE JEWISH BIBLE

In a practical sense, there are other books beside the Old Testament which go to make up the Jewish Bible. The Talmud, or rather the two Talmuds—the Jerusalem Talmud (comprising the Mishna, or Second Law), compiled about 150 B.C. by a Jewish rabbi, and the Babylonian Talmud, compiled about six hundred and fifty years later—are regarded by the Jews as equally inspired and equally binding in their moral requisitions as that of the Old Testament. In fact, they compare the former to wine, and the latter to water, when speaking of their relative value. Some "tall stories" are found in these Jewish revelations, such as these: it tells of a bird so tall that the water of a river in which it stood came only to its knees, though the water was so deep that it took an ax, thrown into it, seven years to reach the bottom; and of an egg of such enormous dimensions that, when broken, the white of it glued a whole town together and a forest of three hundred cedar-trees. These are but specimens of their miracles. Such is the character of the Jewish sacred writings, emanating from the same source as the Old Testament; and consequently of equal authority and reliability, and equally entitled to our belief.

CHAPTER 12

THE CHRISTIAN BIBLE

The Christian Bible, as now accepted by Protestants (for it must be borne in mind that it has been altered and amended on various occasions, thus altering the canonical Word of God), is composed of thirty-nine books in the Old Testament department, and twenty-seven in the New; the whole constituting a multifarious collection of old oracles, obsolete dogmas, Oriental legends, ancient myths, religious reveries, beautiful precepts, poetry, heart-touching pathos, wild fancies, perceptive admonitions, martial exploits, domestic regulations, broken, disjointed narratives, ritual rules, and spiritual ideas; including also cosmogony, history, theocracy, theology, annals, romance, prophecy, rhapsody, psalmody, mythology, allegory, dreams, tradition, legislation, ethics, politics, and religion, all jumbled together without arrangement, division, classification, or order; committed to writing in various ages and nations and countries, and by various writers, extending over a period of several thousand years, including nearly every form of composition known to human ingenuity—gay, grave, tragical, logical, philosophical, religious, and romantic—emanating from Gods, angels, men, and devils; recorded, some of it in mountains, some of it in caves, some of it on the banks of rivers, some of it in forests, some of it in deserts, and some of it under the shadow of the Pyramids. It commenced on Mount Horeb, and ended in the isle of Patmos. From such circumstances we are not surprised to learn that its chronology is unreliable, chimerical, and incorrect; its history contradictory and incredible; its philosophy fallacious; its logic unsound; its cosmogony foolish and absurd; its astronomy fragmentary and childish; its religion pagan-derived; its morals defective, sometimes selfish, often extravagant, and in some cases pernicious. Its government, both temporal and spiritual, is, to some extent, both barbarous and tyrannical, while its theocracy is mere brute force. It presents us with narratives without authorities, facts and figures without dates, and records without names. We find no order in its arrangement, no system in its subjects or the manner of presenting them, and no connection in its paragraphs, and often no agreement in its statements, and no sense in its logic.

It seems to teach nearly everything upon nearly every question of morals that it touches. It apparently both sanctions and condemns nearly every species of crime to which it refers, and pours fulsome laudations upon the heads of some of the most bloody-minded and licentious men—such as David, Solomon, etc.—and holds them up as examples of true practical morality. It is often dark, ambiguous, and mysterious, as well as contradictory, not only in its lessons of morality, but in its account of the simplest occurrences, thus rendering it comparatively worthless as a moral guide; inasmuch as it is much easier to find out what is right and what is not without going to the Bible, than it is to find out what the Bible teaches upon the subject, or what it intends to teach in any given case. With respect to war, slavery, polygamy, and the use of intoxicating liquors, for example, it is much easier to determine whether they are right or wrong by the moral fitness of things than whether they are scriptural or anti-scriptural; while it is silent upon many crimes which now infest society. If we are compelled to determine the character of some actions without going to the Bible, why not that of all other moral actions and duties? Edmund Burke says of the Bible, "It is necessary to sort out what is intended as example, and what only as narrative; what is to be understood literally, and what figuratively, where one precept is to be controlled and modified by another; what is temporary, and what of perpetual obligation; what is appropriate to one state or set of men, and what is the general duly of men in all ages." Now, who cannot see that all this must require a quality of mind capable of determining or learning moral principles and moral duties without recurrence to the Bible? And it must require a vast amount of time to accomplish this task, all of which is lost, inasmuch as it is consuming time in making the Bible conform to what you have already learned of right outside its pages—time that might be much better employed. Such are the moral aspects of the Bible.

But it also has its beauties, which we need not occupy much space in depicting, as we have fifty thousand clergymen in this country who attend faithfully to that matter. Suffice it to say that portions of it are characterized by a high-toned spirituality, other portions by a deep, heart-stirring pathos. And then we have manifested in other parts the most devout piety, while the books of the prophets often breathe forth a spirit of the most elevating poetry. And there is scarcely a book, or even a chapter, in the whole Bible that does not evince a spirit of religious devotion, and an effort for the right, though often misdirected. Taken as a whole, the Bible may be regarded as an exposition of the condition of science, morals, religion, government, and domestic policy of the era in which it was written, and suited to the temporal and spiritual wants of the people of that age, for whom it was written, *but not for this age.* When regarded in this light, and as simply a human production of the best minds of the age and times in which it was written, many portions of it can be read with interest and instruction. But when read, as it has been for centuries, as a perfect, divine composition, designed for all time and as a finality in faith and practice and moral progress, it becomes a stumbling block in the path of progress, an embargo upon free thought, a fetter upon the soul, a fog of bewilderment to the mind, and a drag-chain to the moral and intellectual reformation of the world.

44

CHAPTER 13

GENERAL ANALOGIES OF BIBLES

From the foregoing brief analysis of the characters of the Bibles of various nations, it will be observed that they are, in their main or leading features, essentially alike, including the Holy Books of Jews, Christians, and pagans; that they are alike in their ends and aims and main characteristics; that all inculcate the same fundamental doctrines; that all impart and enjoin the observance of intrinsically the same moral lessons, the same perceptive aphorisms. All teach substantially the same superstitions, the same kind of miraculous feats performed by Gods, angels, and men and devils, the same marvelous stories and achievements overruling and overriding the great laws of nature, often checking or stopping the ponderous wheels of the machinery of the universe. The revelations on the pages of each are claimed to be God-derived, and to have been inspired through prophets, oracles, angels, apostles, or "holy men"; or to have issued directly from the mouth of God, and descended from his immaculate throne to earth, without the intervention or employment of a medium. Each puts forth similar notions and traditions concerning Gods, deities, or angels, genii, demons, or evil spirits, priests, prophets, patriarchs, prayers, sacrifices, penances, ceremonies, rituals, Messiahs, redeemers, intercessors, sin-atoning, crucified Saviors, sons of God, etc. All recognize the doctrine of atonement for sin; all, or nearly all, approximate in their, modes of propitiating the favor of an offended Deity by oblations, sacrifices, and offerings of animals, men, or Gods, or sons of God. Each has its cosmogony; each proclaims the doctrine of one supreme God, the doctrine of the immortality of the soul, of post-mortem rewards for "deeds done in the body"—endless bliss for the righteous, and punishment for the wicked. Each attests the truth and divine origin of its religion by the record of a long array of the most astonishing miracles, confirmed and ratified by the fulfillment of numerous prophecies. Most of them teach the doctrine of the primeval innocence and moral elevation of man, and of his fall, and of his prospective subsequent restoration; and also of the necessity of a "change," or "being born again," in order to a full reconciliation with God and a perfect state of righteousness. In a word, all had essentially the same religious institutions, and the same ecclesiastical orders of priests, pilgrims, monks, and missionaries; the same or similar prayers, liturgies, sermons, hymns, and sacrificial offerings; similar holy orders of saints, angels, and martyrs. All had their "holy days," their "holy fasts and feasts," "holy rivers," "holy mountains," and "holy temples," etc.; and nearly all preached essentially the same doctrines relating to a spiritual birth, regeneration, predestination, and a future life, rewards, and punishments, and a final judgment, etc. All furnish a religion cut and dried (the great end of all Bible creeds) so as to save the intellectual labor and mental toil of discovering the rule of right and the road to duty by an investigation of the great laws of cause and effect, the nature and constitution of the human mind, and the moral fitness of things. As a finale to creation, and a final consummation and triumph of their peculiar faith, each imagines and portrays a great prospective millennial epoch, at which juncture the heavens are to be "rolled together as a scroll"; the oceans, seas, lakes, and rivers to make fire, and be reduced to ashes; "the New Jerusalem to descend from God out of heaven"; and peace, righteousness, and happiness unalloyed to rule and to reign thenceforth and forever. Hence, all Bibles and religions are of divine origin, or none.

Note: Sir William Jones says the ancient religions borrowed from each other.

SUPERIOR FEATURES OF HEATHEN BIBLES

There is not one Oriental Bible in all the number but that is superior in some respects in its teachings to the Christians' Bible. None of them sanctions so explicitly every species of crime; none of them contains so much obscene language. On the contrary, the Chinese Bible, as Mr. Meadows says, "*contains not one sentence but that may be read with propriety in any drawing-room in England.*" Strikingly different from that of the Christian Bible, as shown in chapter 23. The Muhammadan Bible is quite superior in its teachings, with respect to both intemperance and the treatment of women. It forbids both the use and the traffic in intoxicating drinks, and also the manufacture; while the Christian Bible, although condemning one, sanction both (see chapter 48). With respect to women, it contains some commendable precepts. It not only enjoins husbands to treat their wives properly, and provide for them, but provides for their divorce in case this is not done; while the Christian Bible, by the authority of Christ, allows divorce for no crime, abuse, cruelty, or inhuman treatment on the part of tyrannical, wicked, or drunken husbands, but that of fornication (see Matt. v. 32). The Koran also enjoins a tax of two and one-fourth percent on its disciples to support the poor; while the Christian Bible says, "Thou shalt not countenance a poor man in his cause" (Exod. xxiii. 3), though it is true it contains counter-precepts. These examples are sufficient to lead to the conclusion that nothing would be gained to the cause of practical morality by supplanting any of the Oriental Bibles with the Christian Bible.

CHAPTER 14

THE INFIDELS' BIBLE

We find the remarkable admission in the Christian Bible that the moral guide adopted by infidels is superior to that book which Christians have adopted for a guide. Paul, in his Epistle to the Romans, says, "The Gentiles, who have not the Bible, do by nature the things contained in the Bible." An astonishing Bible concession, truly! He, however, uses the word "law" for Bible; but commentators tell us the law is contained in the Bible, and some writers make "law" and "Bible" synonymous terms. We therefore give the sense more fully by rendering it "Bible" instead of "law." It is here admitted by Paul that the great Bible of Nature, written upon man's consciousness, and inscribed upon everything around him, which is the infidels' Bible and revelation, is superior to any printed Bible. If man learns by nature the moral lessons taught by the Bible or moral law (that is, by nature's laws, as learned by observation and experience, which is the infidel's sole reliance for learning the great lessons and duties of life), then this *natural* revelation, which Paul commends so highly, is superior to any *written* or printed revelation. If, as Paul teaches, the ignorant, illiterate Gentile can learn by this *revelation* of nature, or *law* of nature, the duties of life, the great truths of salvation, and the right road to heaven, then it must be *greatly* superior to the Christians' Bible. For it is admitted by Christians themselves (foreign missionaries) that, with all the aid that priests and commentators can render, there is a considerable portion of their Bible which the heathen cannot learn or be made to understand. But not so, according to Paul, with God's natural Bible and the revelation inscribed on man's moral nature, and learned by the exercise of his common sense, natural judgment, and the experience of mankind in general. Hence, we have a Bible which is not only easily read and easily understood by even the unlettered heathen, but a Bible which possesses many advantages over all printed Bibles, some of which I will mention.

In the first place, it is a Bible always open. It cannot be kept closed under lock and key, as the Christian Bible has been in past ages. Second, it is a Bible that needs no translation in any language, for it is already written in the languages of all the nations of the earth. Third, it is a Bible, thank God! that all, whether high or low, learned or unlearned, can read and understand. Fourth, its glorious truths are easily read; for they are plainly and legibly inscribed upon every leaf and page of the soul of every human being. Fifth, hence this revelation needs no priest to expound it, and no church to unravel its mysteries, by voluminous commentaries. Sixth, no concordance is needed to enable its readers to find its golden gems, which glitter and sparkle upon every page. They are what the Quakers call "the light within." Seventh, neither moths nor mice can destroy this glorious Bible. Fire cannot consume it, nor water wash it away. It is imperishable and eternal. It is a Bible into which no errors have ever crept, either by printers, transcribers, or translators. And (soul-cheering thought!) it is a Bible which contains all the important doctrines, principles, and precepts which can be found in any perishable paper-and-ink Bible, and all the grand truths that God ever vouchsafed to man. They can all be found in this golden-leaved Bible, this eternal, soul-saving revelation of God.

Jesus refers to this natural Bible, or revelation, again when he says, "Know ye not of yourselves what is right?"—that is, by the Bible planted in your own souls, the revelation stereotyped upon your own moral sense or moral nature. Hence, the virtual acknowledgment by Jesus (who is Bible authority), that there is no necessity of running to any printed or pasteboard Bible to learn the truths of the gospel or the duties of life; for he teaches the important lesson, that we may learn them in our own inward selves. We can "know of ourselves what is right." And there are other texts which admit that God's first revelation, and his last and only revelation, to the human race, is far superior to that of any books of human origin; and which admit that this glorious revelation cannot be found in the Christian Bible, or any other perishable book, but existed for ages before any paper-and-ink Bible was ever thought of. I will quote one other text to prove these statements, and in further confirmation of the proposition that the Christian Bible itself admits that the infidels' Bible, direct from the hand of God, is greatly superior to it in all the essential features and principles of a Bible.

Paul concedes this when he says, in his Epistle to the Romans, "The invisible things of God are clearly seen and understood by the things that are made, even his eternal power and Godhead" (Rom. i. 20). Now, here it is proved, if anything can be proved by the Bible, that everything that can be learned about God and religion can be found written upon the tablets of nature, and inscribed upon everything that is made. For it is declared that even the "invisible things of God"—that is, the *great spiritual truths* of the kingdom—can be seen and learned by the revelations, or lessons, written upon things "that are made." A wonderful admission, truly! It is stated, they can not only be seen, but "*clearly seen* and understood," by studying the things "that are made," and learning their important lessons. If, then, they can be "clearly seen and understood," there is not the shadow of a doubt left upon the mind as to their truth or meaning: you are not annoyed with that perplexity, uncertainty, and painful anxiety about the meaning of moral lessons they teach, as you are with respect to hundreds of texts you find in the Christian Bible. This is a grand revelation and declaration and benefit, truly. And "even his eternal power and Godhead"—that is, God's character and attributes—we are here told, can be learned by reading and studying this beautiful and easily comprehended Bible, written by the finger of God upon every leaf and page of nature. Was there ever a more important, more pleasing, or more beautiful revelation made to the world than this of Paul's? And is it not surprising that Christians have never noticed this most important admission? It is an important moral lesson that throws their pen-and-ink Bible into the shade, and shows we would be better without than with it by substituting God's eternal and universal Bible.

It will be observed, then, that it is shown by different texts of the Bible, that the "Holy Book" which came directly from the hands of God is greatly superior to that which came through the hands of man. And the fact that it is the only Bible, or revelation, that can now be found in all countries, and the only Bible that can be read by all nations, kingdoms, tongues, and people, and that not one man, woman, or child in a hundred, take the world over, can read any other Bible but this, is very nearly prima *fade* evidence that it is the only Bible God ever designed for the human race, and that he never did impart, and never will impart, any other revelation to the world; that no other Bible is necessary for the moral, religious, and spiritual welfare of the race, or to point the road to salvation. Hence, it is the only Bible we would recommend for the reading of the young. It is the only Bible we are certain they can understand. It is the only Bible we are certain is free from errors. It is the only Bible we are certain has never been altered or mistranslated. It is the only Bible we are certain teaches no immoral lessons. It is the only Bible which we are certain contains no vulgar or obscene language, calculated to raise a blush on the cheek of modesty, and outrage every feeling of decorum, as many of the texts found in the Christian Bible do. It is the only "Holy Scripture" we can be certain was given forth by divine inspiration, and the only sacred volume or "Holy Word" which has the full seal and sanction of Almighty God. Read, then, and study well, this open and widespread Bible which infolds the universe.

All the Bibles and religions of the past claim to have been authorized by a *direct* revelation or inspiration from God. But we are satisfied that no such revelation has ever been given forth to any nation in any age of the world. For inspiration is now known to be a universal law of the natural mind; an inborn principle of the human soul, which all ages and nations, and every human being, have possessed a greater or less share of. And the amount of true inspiration possessed by each individual depends upon his or her moral, intellectual, and spiritual elevation of the soul or mind into the higher enjoyment of spiritual bliss where it becomes *en rapport* with all that is lovely, inspiring, and beautiful in God's universe; where it can take cognizance of great moral problems and spiritual truths; and where it can look through the long vista of futurity, and behold the events of corning years rolling up toward the threshold of time. This is true inspiration, and the spirit of true prophecy. But it is the work of our own minds, and not of Deity, and is not confined to any age, nation, or religion. It depends upon the culture of the moral and intellectual faculties and the spiritual aspirations of the individual, and not upon his creed or religious belief.

As for a divine revelation, it cannot be found in any book of human origin. It could not be incorporated into a book, nor could all the books in the world contain it. It is inscribed all over the face of nature. We read it upon the outstretched earth and upon the shining heavens; we read it upon

> "Every bush and every bower,
> Every leaf and every flower."

Here, then, we have a Bible with a revelation as broad as the universe. Its lids are the heavens above, and the earth beneath. Its golden-leaf pages are spread out at our feet; its lessons of wisdom, its truths of salvation, and its soul-inspiring beauties, are inscribed upon the soul, and written all over the face of nature. Read and study it, O man! and become "wise unto salvation."

CHAPTER 15

ONE HUNDRED AND TWENTY-THREE ERRORS
IN THE JEWISH COSMOGONY

As the Old Testament possesses no order, no arrangement, and no distinct system of either morals or religion, and no regular connection in its history, we have to treat it in the same unsystematic order in which we find it, and to expose many foolish errors and stories which seem almost beneath the dignity of any respectable writer to notice. But, as they constitute a large portion of the Old Testament, we have got to deal with *them* or *nothing.* And, although trifling in *themselves,* they have done much mischief. Hence, we deem it of greater importance to expose their evil influence than to trace them to their heathen origin, as we originally designed doing.

1. The first text in the Bible is evidently an error. "In the beginning God created the heavens and the earth" (Gen. i). No geologist and philosopher at the present day believes in either a creation or a creator. The assumption involves two impossibilities. First, a creation could not take place without something to create from: *"Ex nihilo nihil fit"*—"Out of nothing, nothing can come." Second, to account for the origin of the earth, sun, moon, and stars by assuming the existence of a creator, is throwing no light on the subject. We have made no progress towards solving the problem, for we are equally puzzled to account for the origin of the creator himself. It is as easy to assume that matter always existed as to assume that the creator always existed. Hence, there would be no creation possible, and none needed. This is now regarded as a settled scientific problem.

2. It is a scientific error to assert that matter had a beginning, as the Bible assumes. Many scientific facts have been developed to establish the conclusion that all beings and objects on earth were eliminated from its elements, and all the planets we can recognize were an outgrowth from some other worlds. The proposition is not only susceptible of much proof (which I have not space here to present), but is very beautiful and satisfactory. It "composes our reason to peace." All we lack of comprehending it is the capacity to grasp eternity and infinity, which finite mortals cannot do.

3. If God "created the heavens" (Gen. i. 1), and heaven is his "dwelling-place" (see 1 Kings viii. 30), then where did he dwell before the heavens were made? Here is a very puzzling question, and involves an absurdity equal to that of the Tonga-Islanders, who teach that the first goose was hatched from an egg, and that the same goose laid the egg. An idea equally ludicrous is involved in the assumption that God created the heavens and the earth about six thousand years ago; so that, previous to that

era, there was nothing on which he could stand, sit, or lie, but must have been suspended in mid-air from all eternity.

4.   If nothing existed prior to six thousand years ago, then there was nothing for God to do, and nothing for him to do it with. Hence, he must have spent an eternity in idleness, a solitary monarch without a kingdom.

5.   As we are told God created the light (Gen. i. 3), the conclusion is forced upon us that, prior to that period, he had spent an eternity in darkness. And it has been discovered that all beings originating in a state of darkness, or living in that condition, were formed without eyes, as is proved by blind fishes being found in dark caves. Hence, the thought is suggested that God, prior to the era of creation (six thousand years ago), was perfectly blind.

6.   "God saw the light that it was good" (Gen. i. 4). Hence, we must infer that God had just got his eyes open, and that he had never before discovered that light is good. Of course, it was good to be delivered from eternal darkness.

7.   "And God divided the light from the darkness" (Gen. i. 4). Hence, previous to that period, they must have been mixed together.   Philosophy teaches that light and darkness never can be separated, anymore than heat and cold, as one is only a different degree of the other.

8.   "And God called the light Day, and the darkness he called Night" (Gen. i. 5). And to whom did he call them as no living being was in existence until several days afterwards. Hence, there was no need of calling them anything; and, as we are told Adam named everything, he could as easily have found names for these as for other things.

9.   The Bible teaches us that day and night were created three days before the sun. Every schoolboy now knows that it is the revolution of the earth upon its axis that causes day and night; and, but for the existence of the sun, there could be no day and night. If Moses' God was so ignorant, he had better never have wakened out of his eternity of darkness.

10. The Bible teaches that the earth came into existence three days before the sun, but science teaches us that the earth is a child or offshoot of the sun. Hence, it could be equally true to say a son was born three days before his father.

11. "And the earth was without form, and void" (Gen. i. 2); but philosophy teaches that nothing can exist without form, or when void. The declaration brings to mind the Scotchman's definition of "nothing"—"a footless stocking without a leg." We have an idea of a thing which does not exist.

12. "And the Spirit of God moved upon the face of the waters" (Gen. i. 2). Here we are taught that the original state of the earth was that of water.

But geology teaches its original constituent was fire or fusion; that water did not exist, and could not exist in it, or on it, for millions of ages. Professor Agassiz says our earth was once in a state of igneous fusion, without water, without rain, and even without an atmosphere ("Geological Sketches," i. 2). And even the pious, God-fearing Hugh Miller says that, "the solid earth was at one time, from center to circumference, a mass of molten matter ("Lectures on Geology," 256). Here we have geology against theology.

13. God spent a day making a firmament, by which he "divided the waters from the waters." If it had then stated that he spent a day in making moonshine, or one day in making breath for Adam, it would have been as sensible; for the firmament is as truly a part of the earth (being eliminated from it) as our breath is a part of our bodies.

14. "Divided the waters from the waters." Here is disclosed a belief which prevailed in various Oriental and heathen nations, that the earth exists between two large lakes, or sheets of water; and that the firmament is a solid floor, which holds the water up, and prevents it from falling, and inundating the earth; and, being supplied with doors and windows, when God wants it to rain he opens the windows (the Bible says "the windows of heaven were opened," see Gen. vii. 11). He pours it down by opening the windows, and stops it by shutting them up. "The windows of heaven were stopped" (Gen. viii. 2). How fully is the heathen tradition disclosed here!

15. We are told that God gathered "the waters under heaven together unto one place" (Gen. i. 9). How ignorant he must have been of geography! He evidently had not studied the science, or had not traveled much, or he would have known the waters under heaven never have been "gathered together unto one place," but exist in many places, as the two hundred large lakes prove.

16. The Bible tells us that, when God created the vegetable kingdom, he ordered each species of vegetation to "bring forth after its kind" (Gen. i. 11). Can we suppose that apple-trees would have borne buckeyes, or mullein-stalks produced pumpkins, or anything foreign to their nature, if the command had not been given for each to bring forth after its kind?

17. According to the Bible, the vegetable kingdom was created before the animal; but the learned geologist Hitchcock, although a Christian by profession, in his "Elements of Geology" says, "An examination of the rocks shows us that animals were created as early as vegetables" (and he might have said much earlier). And yet the Bible says vegetables were created on the third day, and animals on the fifth (see Gen. i.).

18. The Bible represents vegetables as coming into existence before the sun, but philosophy teaches that they could neither germinate nor grow without the warming and vivifying influence of the sun.

19. The Bible tells us that "God made two great lights, the greater light to rule the day, and the lesser light to rule the night; and God set them in the firmament to give light to the earth" (Gen. i. 16, 17). That is, he made two round balls, and then stuck them into a hole scooped out of the firmament for the purpose. This seems to be the idea. Here is disclosed the moat egregious ignorance of astronomy. Think of that stupendous solar luminary, as much larger than this pygmy planet as a man is larger than a mouse, being hung up or stuck up above us for our sole accommodation! How sublimely ridiculous!

20. The Bible represents the great world-builder, the almighty architect, as spending five days in plodding and toiling at this little mole-hill of ours before he got it finished up to his notion, and then made such a bad job of it that he repented for having undertaken it.

21. But when he came to make the countless worlds, the vast suns, and systems of suns, which roll their massive forms in every direction around the earth, these were all made in a few hours. "And he made the stars also." This text tells the whole story of the origin of the boundless planetary system, comprising millions of worlds larger than our planet. What superlative ignorance of astronomy Moses' God manifests!

22. Moses is awarded great credit by Bible believers for opposing polytheism, and teaching the existence of but one God, but it would have been more to his credit if he had stuck to a belief in a plurality of Gods; for it would take a million of such Gods as his imagination has created a thousand years to make such a universe as astronomers have brought to light since he wrote.

23. The language, "Let us make man in our own image" (Gen. i. 26), seems to imply that there was an association of gods—a company of almighty mechanics, who had formed a partnership to do up a big job.

24. If man was made in the image of God, why was he cursed for eating the fruit of the tree of knowledge in order to be like God?

25. According to the Bible, God became so tired in the business of world-making that he had to take a rest of a whole day (and perhaps took a nap also) when the job was completed; but geology and philosophy both teach that creation never was begun, and never will be finished, but is going on all the time. Hence, new species of animals and vegetables are constantly coming into existence.

26. The Bible represents the entire universe as being created less than six thousand years ago, but science teaches us that it has been in existence for millions of years.

27. A large volume of scientific facts has been accumulated by scientists, showing that even our earth, one of the youngest of the planets, is at least several hundred thousand years old. Look at a few of the facts which go to prove it. The coral reefs of Florida are estimated by Professor Agassiz to be one hundred and thirty-five thousand years old. Charles Lyell estimates the delta of the Mississippi Valley to be at least one hundred thousand years old. Four growths of cypress trees far below the surface of the ground, and situated one above another, have been discovered near New Orleans, whose successive growths must have occupied a period of at least one hundred and fifty thousand years. So much for the agreement of geology and Bible chronology

28. But we are told that a day in the Bible means a thousand years. Then, as the sabbath day constitutes one of the days spoken of in the Bible, and was provided as a day of rest, Christians and Bible believers should rest a thousand years at a time; and, as God rested a whole day (a thousand years), he must have been as tired of resting as he was of world-making. Why do the figures "4004 B.C." stand at the top of the first page of the Bible, if a thousand years mean one day?

29. The Bible teaches that whales, fishes, and birds were made on the same day, but geology assures us that fishes came into existence long before fowls.

30. The Bible teaches that beasts and creeping things were all made on the fifth day of creation, but geology tells us that reptiles and creeping things crawled upon the earth millions of years before beasts came into existence.

31. The Bible represents man as coming into existence about six thousand years ago, but human bones have recently been discovered in the vicinity of New Orleans which Dr. Dowler estimates to be at least fifty thousand years old.

32. A deity who becomes so tired and physically exhausted with six days' labor as to be compelled to stop and rest, physiology teaches would be liable to physical disease; and, if physically diseased, it might terminate in death, and thus leave the world without a God (Godless).

33. The Bible tells us "the Lord God formed man of the dust of the ground" (Gen. ii. 7), but philosophy teaches that dust possesses no vital properties, and that it would have been less difficult to make man of a stone or a stump, owing to their possessing more adhesive properties. One writer suggests that the negro must have been made of coal-dust.

34. According to the Bible, a serious blunder was made by Jehovah in the work of creation, by exhausting all the materials in the process of world-making and man-making, so that nothing was left to make a "helpmeet" for Adam; and this blunder caused the necessity of robbing Adam of one of his ribs.

35. But common sense teaches us that a small crooked bone but a few ounces in weight could not furnish half the material necessary to constitute a woman. The Parsees, with a little more show of sense, tell us that the rib was used merely as a back-bone, around which the woman was constructed; which revives in memory Erin's mode of making cannon, which consisted in "taking a round hole, and pouring melted metal round it." The Tonga-Islanders have a tradition about as sensible as that of Moses with respect to the origin of the first woman. Their God made the first man with three legs, and amputated one of them to make a "helpmeet for him." This is an improvement, as a leg can be better spared when there are three than a rib: it also possesses more material than a rib.

36. The Bible teaches that man was created upright, but fell. If it means physically, it can be easily accounted for, and must be ascribed to his creator; for depriving him of one of his ribs would leave him in an unbalanced condition, so that he would be liable to fall.

37. The Bible imparts to us the strange intelligence that "the Lord God brought all the beasts and birds to Adam to see what he would call them" (Gen. ii. 19). What an idea for Omniscience or Infinite Wisdom to engage in the business of chasing bears, lions, tigers, elephants, and hyenas, and all manner of beasts great and small, and all manner of birds, also hissing, crawling, biting reptiles, and every living thing which he had created, and taking them to Adam "to see what he would call them"! Not having sufficient intelligence to find names for them himself (pardon the thought), his curiosity was no doubt aroused to see what an ignorant being of his own creation, who had not sufficient intelligence to clothe himself, would call the innumerable host of beasts, birds, etc., before any language was known, or even a single letter was invented to spell names with. (We are very far from desiring to wound the feelings or encroach upon the reverence that any man or woman may cherish for "a God of infinite love, wisdom, and goodness," but let it be kept constantly in mind we are not presenting the history of such a being here, but the mere imaginary God of Moses and the Bible.)

38. As the Bible teaches that Adam named all the beasts, animals, and birds, it must have occupied a great number of years for the Lord God of Moses to have caught and taken the several hundred thousand species to

Adam to receive names in all the three thousand languages, and then convey them back to their respective climates.

39. The question naturally arises, Why should Adam give them names by saying, "This is a horse, that is an ass, the animal yonder shall be called a hippopotamus," etc., when there was nobody present to hear it and be benefited by it? And nobody could have remembered half the names had they been present. Here we wish to call the attention of the reader specially to the fact that all the thoughts and language we have so far cited as being either that of God or Moses sounds like the utterance of ignorant children, and unworthy the dignity of an intelligent and sensible man, much less that of a God.

40. The Bible teaches that "God made man in his own image." The reverse statement would have been true, "Man made God in his own image," for this is true of all nations who believe in a God.

41. Here let it be noted the Bible contains two contradictory accounts of creation, one found in the first chapter of Genesis, the other in the second. In the first, animals are created before man; in the second, after man.

42. The first chapter of Genesis says, "Let the earth bring forth plants" (Gen. i. 11); the second says, "God created every plant ... before it was in the earth" (Gen. ii. 9). A contradiction; and neither statement is true, there being no creation.

43. The first chapter has the earth created several days before the firmament, or heaven; the second chapter has it created on the same day (Gen. ii. 4).

44. The first represents fowls as originating in the water (Gen. i. 20); the second has them created out of the water.

45. After the first chapter says, "God created man in his own image" (Gen. i. 27), the second says, "there was not a man to till the ground" (Gen. ii. 4).

46. The first chapter represents man and woman as being created at the same time (Gen. i. 27); the second represents the woman as being created after the man.

47. The first implies that man has dominion over the whole earth; the second restricts his dominion to a garden. Which is the inspired story of creation?

48. The Mexicans claim that the first man and woman were created in their country. The Hindus aver that the original progenitors of the race (Adimo and Iva) first made their appearance amongst them. The Chinese claim a similar honor. The Persians contend that God landed the first

human pair in the land of Iran. And, finally, the Jews affirm that Jehovah created the first pair in Eden.

Moses tells us God planted two trees in Eden, one of which he called "the tree of the knowledge of good and evil." This tree bore fruit which nobody was allowed to taste (Gen. ii. 9).

49. Why the tree was planted, or why its fruit was forbidden to be used, are problems which the Bible does not solve, and which set reason at defiance.

50. And then it looks like a senseless act to create a tree for the purpose of bearing fruit (as we can conceive of no other purpose for which it could have been created), and then decree that it should all go to waste.

51. It was worse still to create human beings with an appetite for this fruit, and place it in their sight, and then forbid them to taste it on penalty of death. Nothing could be more opposed to our ideas of reason and justice.

52. Did God create beings in his own image, and then treat them as if he wished to tantalize them and render them unhappy?

53. It would seem that he created man for no other purpose than to tease and torment him, and quarrel with him.

54. Common sense would suggest it to be the act of an ignoramus or a tyrant to implant in man the desire to eat fruit which he did not allow him to eat.

55. And would it not be unjust to punish Adam and Eve for doing what he himself had implanted in them the desire to do?

56. God must have known they would eat the fruit, if he were omniscient.

57. If he were not omniscient, he was not a God in a supreme or divine sense.

58. God must have had the power without the will to prevent the act of disobedience, which would make him an unjust and unmerciful tyrant.

59. Or else the will without the power, which would make him a weak and frail being, and not a God.

(For a full elucidation of these points, see chapter 69.) We will notice a few other points.

60. As God declared eating the fruit would make Adam "like one of us," that is, Godlike (and all men are enjoined to become Godlike), was not Adam, therefore, justified in eating the fruit in order to become Godlike?

61. In chapter 69 it is shown that, as Adam and Eve got their eyes open by eating the inhibited fruit, the act of disobedience turned out to be a great blessing, inasmuch as it saved the earth from being filled with a race of blind human beings.

62. And, as this blessing was obtained through the agency of the serpent-devil, we must admit "the father of lies" was a great benefactor of the human race, as shown in chapter 69.

63. As Adam could not very well exercise "dominion over every living thing that moveth upon the earth" (Gen. i. 26) while shut up in a little eight-by-ten garden, we can observe here another practical benefit of the act of disobedience which drove him from the garden.

64. Is it not a strange piece of moral incongruity to set Adam to tilling the soil in the garden as a *blessing,* and then doom him to till it *outside* as a curse? (Gen. iii. 23.) He first embarked in the business as a blessing, and then as a curse. How the same act could be both a blessing and a curse is a "mystery of godliness" which swamps us.

65. The Jews tell us the original tempter was a serpent (Gen. iii. 1); the Mexicans say it was a demon; the Hindus call him a snake; the Greeks declare it was a dragon; Josephus supposes it was an ape; some of the East-India sects speak of him as a fish; but the Persian revelations make it a lizard. Which is right?

66. The Mosaic or Hebrew cosmogony represents the serpent as dealing out the fruit to the *genus homo*, while the Mexicans, the Egyptians, and the Persians set the serpent or "evil genius" to guarding the tree to protect the fruit. Which is right?

67. When God Jehovah announced to the trinity of Gods, "Behold, the man has become as one of us to know good and evil" (Gen. iii. 22), exactly as the serpent had predicted, instead of dying as Jehovah had predicted, does it not prove that the serpent was the best and most reliable prophet?

68. As Adam and Eve could know nothing of the nature of right and wrong until they attained that knowledge by eating the fruit, does not this fact prove it to be a justifiable if not a righteous act?

69. How could Adam and Eve know that any act was sinful before an act of any kind had been committed by which they could learn the character or consequences of human conduct?

69. Is it not a logical conclusion that, if God created everything, he can control everything, and hence, strictly speaking, is alone responsible for the right performance of everything?

70. The Christian Bible tells us the first pair of human beings sewed fig-leaves together for clothing, but the Chinese revelation says palm-leaves. Which is right? Who can tell?

71. As it is declared the voice of God was heard "walking in the garden" (Gen. iii. 8), we beg leave to ask, what kind of a thing is a "walking voice"?

72. We also beg leave to ask, who took charge of "the house of many mansions" while Jehovah was down among the bushes hunting and hallooing for Adam?

72. And who took charge of creation, and kept the machinery of the universe running during the thousand years' rest of God Almighty, if the one day he rested means a thousand years?

73. Was it necessary for an omnipresent God to come down from heaven to find Adam when he hid among the bushes? And what would have been the result if he had not been found?

74. Must we not conclude that the command to "multiply and replenish the earth" was rather superfluous, inasmuch as nations who never heard of the command perform the duty faithfully?

75. If the River Gihon, one of the four rivers of Paradise, "encompassed the whole land of Ethiopia" (Gen. ii. 13), which is in Africa, how did it manage to cross the Red Sea, so as to get into Eden, which is in Asia?

111. As Bishop Colenso shows the territory lying between the four rivers in Eden, as mentioned in Gen. ii., comprised an area of several hundred miles, we would suggest that father Adam, while in Eden, had rather a large garden to cultivate.

112. How could fig-leaves be sewed together for clothing before needles were invented? (See Gen. iii. 7.)

113. How did Eve see the tree as stated in Genesis ("she saw the tree") before she ate the fruit which caused her eyes to be opened?

114. Is it not calculated to destroy all ideas of justice in the minds of man and woman to believe that God cursed and ruined the happiness of the whole human race merely for one simple act prompted by a being destitute of moral perception or moral accountability?

115. And what should we think of a being who would suffer a grand scheme, on which is predicated the happiness of his innumerable family for untold ages, to be defeated by the wily machinations of a brainless creature of his own creation?

116. Why should Adam hide from God because he was naked, when, if God made him he must have become accustomed to seeing him in that condition?

117. If God in the morning pronounced everything good, and in the evening everything bad, does it not imply not only a serious blunder in the job, but a serious mistake in his views either in the morning or in the evening?

118. As we are told "the Lord God made clothing for Adam out of goat-skins," the question naturally arises, Who caught and killed the animals, and

dressed the skins? Does it not imply that God was both a butcher and a tanner? Rather plebeian employment for a God.

119. And the statement that "the Lord God planted a garden eastward in Eden" (Gen. ii. 8) seems to imply that he was a horticulturist also.

120.It is pretty hard to believe that Adam could sleep while God Almighty (Moses' God) was digging amongst his ribs, as stated in Gen. ii. 21.

121.How could Adam know what the word "die" meant before there had been any deaths in the world, when the Lord told him he should *die* if he ate the forbidden fruit?

122.As Eve was pronounced "the mother of all living" when there were no human beings in existence but she and Adam, the inference seems to be that she was the mother of herself, her husband, and all the animal tribes.

123."In the image of God created he them" (Adam and Eve, see Gen. i. 27). If Adam and Eve were both created in the image of God, it would seem to follow that he was constituted of two genders, male and female.

In concluding this section, we ask the reader to think of an infinitely wise God being defeated in his grand scheme of creation or salvation by a crawling serpent, and a frightful hell and all its horrors originating from this act. How sublimely ridiculous is the thought!

THE SCIENTISTS' ACCOUNT OF CREATION

1. Millions of years ago the sun in its revolution threw off, as it had done on previous occasions, a sort of fire-mist, or nebulous scintillations, which floated and rolled through space for countless ages, gradually accumulating from the atmosphere in its revolution, thus swelling in size until it became a conglomeration of gas; and, continuing to grow and progress, it ripened into a fiery, liquid mass possessing the most intense heat.

2. After innumerable ages, this fiery liquid mass began to cool and finally formed a crust upon its surface.

3. As its interior elements began to evolve or emanate from its bosom, it formed a dense, heavy, murky atmosphere, almost as heavy as water, in which no living thing could have breathed or lived for a moment.

4. This atmosphere contained moisture, which in the course of time became condensed into globules forming drops, which descended to the earth in the shape of rain.

5. This rain, descending to the earth, cooled its surface, and eventually filled its vast cavities with water, and thus formed lakes, seas and oceans. The boiling, heaving mass in the bowels of the earth made it very irregular in shape.

6.   As soon as the surface of the earth became sufficiently cool, small swellings began to appear upon its surface, presenting the appearance of blisters, or boils. These outgrowths finally began to exhibit vegetable life; but for a long period of time they presented the appearance of rocks or stones.

7.   In the meantime, the washings from the surface of the earth were deposited in the seas and oceans and, sinking to the bottom, in the course of time formed rocks.

8.   These rocks, as they hardened, gave off an element of life, which in the course of time supplied the waters with various forms of animal or finny life, and thus originated mollusks, fishes, etc.

9.   As the surface of the earth cooled and grew thicker, the elements of life diffused through the liquid mass finally made their appearance on the surface in the character of the lowest forms of vegetable life, such as mosses, lichens, ferns, etc.

10. As the surface of the earth thickened, and consequently accumulated the elements of vitality, it gave forth higher and still higher forms of vegetable life, until finally the most matured forms of matter began to exhibit animal life.

11. The first species was the zoophite, a compound of vegetable and animal life, but possessing scarcely any of the functions of animal life except those of absorption and respiration, and these functions were but slightly manifested.

12. Succeeding the zoophite came the mollusks and various hard-shelled animal forms, which at first clung to the rocks, then fed on seaweed and other vegetable substances, absorbing also from the atmosphere.

13. In this way various species of animals and birds and reptiles sprang up, ran their course, and then perished, to give place to higher forms.

14. And finally, when all the elements of life became sufficiently matured, they formed a combination, and turned loose upon the earth the animal man, who at first was nearly as ugly, clumsy, and awkward as a baboon, possessed of but little more sense or intelligence.

15. Each one of these changes and outgrowths of the new forms of vegetable and animal life constituted an epoch of innumerable ages, thus showing the age of our planet to be beyond computation. We submit to the reader whether this is not a more rational, beautiful, and satisfactory solution of the great problem of mineral, vegetable, animal, and human existence than the jumbled-up medley presented by Moses.

CHAPTER 16

NUMEROUS ABSURBITIES IN THE STORY OF THE DELUGE

If there were no other errors or absurdities in the Bible, our faith in it would diminish at every step in the investigation of the ark and flood story as related in the sixth chapter of Genesis. The avowed purpose of the flood, the means employed, and their failure to accomplish the end desired, are all at war with our reason and our moral sense.

1. The first question that naturally arises in considering this story is, Why should so many millions of innocent beings—men, women, children, animals, birds, etc.—perish as a penalty for the sins of a few thousand people?

2. The reason given for this wholesale destruction was the wickedness and moral depravity of the human race. But is it true that the whole human race was in that state at that period? According to Manetho and Herodotus, Egypt was in a state of high civilization and moral culture at the time; and, according to Dr. Hulde, China was also far advanced in the arts of civilization and in morality. Col. Dow and other writers represent India as being in a similar condition. There could, therefore, be no justice in drowning all these nations in order to punish a few thousand rambling Jews: it was too much like "burning the barn to destroy the rats."

3. An enlightened moralist of the present day would decide that it was a species of injustice to destroy all the land animals and let the fishes and aquatic animals live. It looks like partiality.

4. But God, having discovered that he made a signal failure in the work of creation, acknowledged that it "grieved him at his heart," and that he "repented" having undertaken it. However, he issued a proclamation, stating that "the end of all flesh is come: every thing that is in the earth shall die."

5. "I, even I, do bring a flood of water upon the earth to destroy all flesh" (Gen. xi. 6). The language seems to imply that somebody else had undertaken, or was about to undertake, the business.

6. But "Noah found grace in the eyes of the Lord," and was placed at the head of this grand scheme; being, as was assumed, although a drunkard, the most righteous man that could be found.

7. The Lord instructed him to build an ark five hundred and fifty feet long, twenty feet wide, and fifty-five feet high—about the size of an eastern warehouse. Think of putting into this two of every species of animal, and seven of every species of clean beast, and fowls of the air!—there being one hundred and fifty thousand, or, as some make it, five hundred thousand species of animal, one hundred and twelve thousand kinds of bird, and fifty thousand species of insect.

8.   And God ordered to be taken into this ark food sufficient to supply these millions of mouths.   This alone would have required forty such vessels.

9.   As It was declared that God destroyed every living thing from the face of the earth, it would have been necessary to have food enough stored away to last several years, until the earth could have time to be replenished with a new crop of grass and vegetables to serve as food for the granivorous and herbivorous species, and animals for the carnivorous tribes.   The weight of such a cargo would have been sufficient to sink the whole British navy!

10.   Consider for a moment what amount of food would be required for each species of animal.   The four elephants (two of each species) would consume a ton of hay in two days, making more than one hundred and fifty tons in twelve months.   The fourteen rhinoceroses would consume one thousand and fifty tons.   And then the horses, cattle, sheep, goats, asses, zebras, antelopes, and other mammals, would require at least two thousand tons more; making in the aggregate three thousand two hundred tons.   This alone would have filled every inch of the vessel.

11.   The seven hundred and eighty-four thousand birds (one hundred and twelve thousand species) would require grain, which would make it necessary to store several thousand bushels.

12.   The three thousand flesh-eating animals, including lions (one lion could eat fifteen pounds a day), cats, dogs, jackals, hyenas, skunks, weasels, crocodiles, snakes, eagles, hawks, buzzards, etc., would require about forty wagon-loads to be slaughtered and fed to them each day; for all would require fresh meat but the buzzards.

13.   And otters, minks, gulls, kingfishers, spoonbills, storks, etc., would require fish for food, which must either be preserved in tanks for the purpose, or one hundred and fifty persons would have to be employed all the time in catching them; and there were only four men to do this and perform all the other labor—sufficient for five thousand hands.

14.   There were nine hundred species of fly-catchers—those that feed on flies, beetles, and other insects.   We are not informed whether flies were included in the registered list or not; but they would, of course, be impudent enough to take their quarters in the vessel without invitation.

15.   About two hundred and fifty birds known as bee-catchers would have to be supplied with this kind of insect: this would be, to say the least, rather stinging business.

16.   Many cans of cockroaches must have been saved to feed the birds-of-paradise.

17. There are several kinds of ant-eaters also, which would have required much time to be spent in searching for ants in the cracks of the vessel, or in collecting them off the water.

18. The four hundred and forty-two monkeys would require fresh fruit; and it is not probable anybody had the forethought to can it for them.

19. Sixty-five species of animal feed on insects; and it would have been necessary for several persons to spend most of their time in crawling after millipedes, fleas, wood-lice, etc.

20. There would have been work for fifty boys in providing leaves and flowers (if there were any possibility that they could be obtained while merged in twenty-seven feet of water) for the animals that feed on these things.

21. Besides food, fresh water must have been stored up for most of these animals, as they could not have endured the salty water of the briny deep.

22. Noah and his family must have studied ornithology and natural history many years to know what kind of food to save for the various kinds of birds and animals.

23. Naturalists estimate that there are fourteen different climates, each with animals adapted only to the temperature and natural growth of that locality. How, then, could they all endure the change of being removed to the vicinity of Mount Ararat? Animals from the frigid zones must have felt like fish out of water in the warm climate of Armenia.

24. And think of the immense labor required to obtain this innumerable collection of animals! In the first place, either Noah or his God must make a trip to the polar regions to obtain the white bear, the reindeer, the polar dog, etc.

25. And then the Rocky Mountains must be scaled to find and catch the grizzly bear. Some time and labor must have been required to obtain the rattlesnakes, copperheads, vipers, cobras, snapping-turtles, etc., of the torrid zone.

26. And a great deal of strategy must have been employed to catch the fox, the deer, the antelope, the gazelle, the chimpanzee of the temperate zone; also the eagle, hawk, buzzard, etc.

27. To do all this hunting and catching and conveying to the ark, of the million and a half birds and animals, would have required a larger number of persons than Napoleon or Xerxes ever commanded; for, as the whole thing is related as a natural occurrence, we cannot assume that they made the journey of their own accord.

28. The Bible commentator Scott supposes that angels were employed to aid in this business of storing away the animals in the ark; but it is

certainly derogatory to that elevated order of beings to suppose they would stoop to such groveling work as bug-hunting, skunk-catching, snake-snaring, etc.

29. And how could this immense multitude of respiring and perspiring animals live and breathe in a vessel with but one little twenty-two-inch window, and that in the third story, and shut up most of the time to keep the rain out, especially if some giraffe had been disposed to monopolize it when it was open by thrusting his head out? How could they be kept thus for a whole year without breeding pestilence and death?

30. All animals require light; and total darkness must have reigned in the two lower stories, and only a partial light supplied the third story—just what could come through a twenty-two-inch window.

31. The chorus of voices in the ark—consisting of bellowing, baying, howling, screaming, hissing, neighing, snorting, roaring, chattering, buzzing, etc.—suggests that deafness would have been a blessing to the human beings present.

32. We are told that "fifteen cubits upward did the water prevail, and the mountains were covered." Fifteen cubits (twenty-seven feet) would not cover nine-tenths of the buildings now on the earth. Ararat is seventeen thousand feet, and Everest twenty-nine thousand feet high.

33. Several scientists have shown by actual experiment that the atmosphere could not contain the fourteen-hundredth part of the water that is represented to have fallen in the time of the flood.

34. Who or what conducted the ark to Ararat when the waters subsided? In the Brahminical flood story, a fish is said to have performed this feat, and dragged it to Mt. Hinavat; but Noah and Moses are silent on this point.

35. The peak of Ararat is perpetually covered with snow and ice; hence, it must have been rather difficult and dangerous for the biped and quadruped cargo to descend from it.

36. And what was there to prevent the nine hundred carnivorous animals from devouring the sheep, hogs, poultry, rabbits, minks, hedgehogs, etc., as they tumbled pell-mell down the mountain together.

37. The same catastrophe must have ensued from the act of turning them loose upon the earth together, with nothing to subsist upon but the flesh and blood of each other.

38. Many Oriental nations have traditions of a flood, and some of them of several floods. Xisuthrus of Chaldea built a ship, in which he saved himself and family during a mighty flood which overflowed the world; also Fohi of China, Menu of the Brahmins, Satravarata of India, and Deucalion of Greece. Hence, it appears there were several families saved besides that

66

of Noah's. Egypt and India have stories of two floods occurring at different periods—one ninety-five hundred years ago. All these stories are evidently older than that recorded in the Christian Bible.

39. Geologists and archeologists have collected a whole volume of evidence, which shows that such a deluge could never have taken place as is embodied in the traditions of several nations. The fresh water of the lakes, and the salt water of the seas and oceans, would have been so mixed as never again to be separated as they are now. Egyptian monuments and sculpture can be traced to a much earlier period than that assigned for Noah's flood.

40. Lepsius has traced the existence of several races or tribes of negroes up to a period within forty-eight years of Noah's flood; this would seem to indicate that some of Noah's family were negroes, and must have "multiplied and replenished" very rapidly to start several races in forty-eight years.

41. The dynasties of Egyptian kings can be traced back several thousand years beyond Noah's time.

42. It is true Jesus Christ and the apostles endorsed the truth of the flood story (Matt. xxiv. 37), but that is evidence against their intelligence, instead of being a proof of the truth of the story.

43. And the assumed divine author of the flood admitted it was an utter failure—that it entirely failed to accomplish the end intended; for it was declared but a few centuries after that "the imagination of man's heart is evil, and only evil, continually," which is an evidence that the wicked folks were not all drowned by the world's inundation.

44. With respect to the many difficulties and impossibilities I have enumerated as lying in the way of carrying out this experiment of the flood, it is sometimes argued in defense that, as the whole thing was in the hands of God, such obstacles would not be a straw in his way. But such persons have failed to notice that it is nowhere stated or implied that it was to be accomplished by miracles. A miracle could have destroyed all the wicked inhabitants of the earth in a moment, without any flood or other means.

45. With regard to its being only a partial deluge, as argued by some Bible defenders, we will say that it is only necessary to examine the language of the Bible to settle this matter. It is declared over and over again that the whole earth was covered with water, and *every living thing destroyed.* If it had been only a partial deluge, all that would have been necessary for Noah to do to save himself and family would have been to migrate to some dry country; and the doomed sinners might have saved themselves in this way.

46. I will note here that the rainbow was for more than a thousand years looked upon both as evidence that there had been a universal deluge, and also that there never would be another. It is only at a recent period that the study of philosophy has disclosed the fact that the rainbow is caused by the reflection and refraction of the rays of light upon the falling rain, and the error thus exploded.

47. One thing in connection with this flood story is not clearly explained in the Bible: Methuselah's time was not out until ten months after the flood began, according to Bible chronology. Where was he during this ten months?

CHAPTER 17

MORAL DEFECTS OF THE TEN COMMANDMENTS

These commandments have always been regarded by Bible believers as being a remarkable display of infinite wisdom, and as being morally perfect beyond criticism; and consequently they have passed from age to age without examination, when a little investigation would have shown any logical mind that they contain palpable errors both in logic and morals.

First commandment: "Thou shalt have no other Gods before me" (Exod. xx. 3); that is, as commentators have interpreted it, "Thou shalt prefer no Gods to me." And why not? What harm can it do? Supposing the people prefer a golden calf, as the Jews did under the leadership of Aaron, in the name of reason how can it injure either God or man? If not, where is the objection? The feeling of devotion is the same in all cases, whatever may be the object worshipped. Hence, the worshiper is as much benefited by worshipping one object as another. On the other hand, it would be a slander upon infinite wisdom to suppose he can desire the homage, adoration, and flattery of poor ignorant mortals, and desire them to crouch at his feet. It would make a mere coxcomb of him to suppose he can be pleased with such adulation, or that he desires such homage. We worship no such God.

Second commandment: The second commandment prohibits our making "the likeness of any thing that is in heaven above, the earth beneath, or the waters under the earth" (Exod. xx. 4). Let us look, in the first place, at the effect of this prohibition, and then at the character of the act. It effectually cuts off the use of photographs, portraits, and pictures— illustrations of every description—for all these are likenesses of something. Hence, thousands of cases of the violation of this commandment take place every day in all Christian or civilized countries. Books are issued every day containing likenesses of something in the heavens above or the earth beneath; especially are schoolbooks illustrated with the likenesses of all kinds of living beings, and often with inanimate objects, by which children learn. The second commandment is utterly disregarded and trampled underfoot by all Christendom.

Third commandment: This commandment prohibits our bowing down to and worshipping any other God but Jehovah, because "I, the Lord thy God, am a jealous God" (Exod. xx. 5). As for "jealousy," it will make any being hateful and despised, according to William Penn. But why not worship other Gods (that is, beings supposed to represent or resemble God)? Can any serious evil result from such an act, either to God or his worshippers? If so, what is it? Let us assume, for the sake of the argument, that the heathen who bows down to images of wood and stone supposes them to be the veritable living and true God (which, however, is not true), yet it would be the very climax of folly to suppose that an infinite being, of such infinite perfection that it places him at an infinite distance beyond human flattery, can take the slightest offense at such an act. It is childish to entertain such a thought. A thousand times more sensible is the doctrine of the Hindus' Vedas, which makes God (Brahma) say, "Those who worship other Gods worship me, because I hear them, and correct their mistake." We will illustrate:

A rebel soldier (son of a doctor) was wounded near his father's house in Kentucky, during the war, in which he immediately sought refuge. As he entered the hall (it being evening twilight), he observed some person at the farther end whom he supposed to be his father, and exclaimed, "Father, I am wounded! Can you aid me?" His father, being in the room above, overheard him, and responded, "Yes, sir." Had he had the vanity of Jehovah, he should have replied, "No, sir. You mistook the servant in the hall for me; therefore I will not assist you, but punish you, and kill you." Remember, Jehovah is represented as killing the worshipers of other Gods (Deut. xiii. 6). If an illiterate heathen in like manner should, in his ignorance, call upon idols or mere imaginary beings for aid, would not his heavenly Father, "in the room above" or the heaven above, hear him and reply, "You are mistaken. I am here, not there; but no difference, the mistake is not important: your intention was good, and your motives honest; therefore I will grant your request"? This would be sensible. But Jehovah is represented as saying, "If thy brother or son or daughter, or even the wife of thy bosom, shall say, let us go and serve other Gods, thou shalt not pity nor spare, but kill them" (Deut. xiii. 6). Here is the most shocking cruelty, combined with supreme nonsense. We are commanded to kill wives, sons, and daughters if they entertain a different view of God from ours, no matter how honest they may be; and there is no question but that all worshipers are honest. They cannot be otherwise. And yet there is no sin more frequently or more fearfully denounced in the Christian Bible than that of worshipping other Gods. Who cannot see that it all grew out of the bitter sectarian bigotry of the Jews, which engendered feelings of animosity toward all nations who refused to subscribe to their creed? This has been the fault of all creed worshipers. As "no man hath seen God at any time" (John i. 18), it must be a matter of imagination with every human being as to what is the form, size, and character of God. And therefore it can make no difference what God, or what kind of God, we call upon in our prayers. We would be equally heard and answered, if there were a God answering prayer. The third commandment, therefore, is devoid of sound sense.

Moral Defects of the Ten Commandments

Fourth commandment: "Thou shalt not take the name of the Lord thy God in vain" (Exod. xx. 7). The word "vain" is defined to mean "worthless, fruitless"; that is, attended with no good results. And we cannot conceive that it can be any more sinful to take the name of God in vain than that of a human being, or of any other object. It is not rational to suppose God, while superintending the movements of eighty-five millions of worlds, pays any attention to the manner in which the inhabitants of this little planet use his name, or that he cares anything about it. And then, how is it possible for us to know when we are using his name in vain, and when we are not?

Fifth commandment: "Remember the sabbath day to keep it holy." This commandment is universally laid aside by all Christendom. Nobody keeps the sabbath but the Jews. And as God himself does not keep the sabbath, but lets all nature run and work (her laws operate the same on that day as on all other days of the week), we cannot believe the sabbath was instituted by him.

Sixth commandment: "Honor thy father and mother" (Exod. xx. 12). Pretty good, but the reason assigned for it is devoid of sense—"That thy days may be long upon the earth." We have never learned that long-lived persons have been more dutiful to parents than others.

Seventh commandment: "Thou shalt not kill" (Exod. xx. 13). If the word "not" were left out, we would concede this commandment has been faithfully obeyed. His "holy people" were killing nearly all the time; and their successors (the Christians) have inundated the earth with blood by a constant violation of this command. What good, therefore, we would ask, has resulted from this commandment?

Tenth commandment. The tenth commandment forbids us to covet our neighbor's house, wife, or servant, or any of his property (covet, "to desire earnestly"). We cannot conceive how there can be any moral turpitude in the act of desiring to possess any of our neighbor's property, or even his wife, if no improper means are used to obtain them. The command was doubtless issued to keep the poor man from aping the rich, and to make him content with his own lot and condition.

The above will be understood to be the true exposition of "the holy commandments of the Lord," "the ten glorious laws of God," when people become accustomed to use their reason in matters of religion.

CHAPTER 18

TEN FOOLISH BIBLE STORIES

I. TALKING SERPENTS AND TALKING ASSES— GEN. III, NUM. XXII

The laws of nature appear to have possessed but little force, permanency, or reliability in the days of Moses, as they were often brought to a dead halt, and set aside on the most trivial occasions, according to Bible history; and nothing could be learned of the character, habits, or natural powers of animals by their form or physical conformation, if they possessed, as represented, minds and reasoning powers supposed to be peculiar to the human species. Hence, the study of natural history must have been useless. When naturalists at the present day find animals without the organs of speech, they assume they do not possess the ability to talk and reason. But the absence of the vocal organs in the days of Moses appears to have furnished no criterion, and interposed no obstacle to becoming a fluent speaker and an able reasoner, as is illustrated in the case of a serpent and an ass talking and arguing like a lawyer. Hence, natural history could have possessed no attraction, as nothing certain could have been learned by studying it.

1.   It is a singular reflection that the Christian plan of salvation is based on a serpent, and with about as little show of sense as the Hottentot tradition of the earth resting on the heads of four turtles.

2.   The idea of God creating a serpent to thwart and defeat his plans and designs, or permitting him to do it, is absolutely ridiculous.

3.   If God knew, when he created the serpent, that his machinations would bring "death and sin and all our woe" into the world, the act would prove him to be an unprincipled being.

4.   And, if he did not know it, he must have been ignorant and short-sighted, and not fit to be a God.

5.   It would imply that he made a wonderful mistake in creating a being that "turned right round," and made war on his own kingdom, crippled it, and defeated its success.

6.   To assume that God could be outwitted by a serpent is to place him lower in the scale of intelligence than a snake.

7.   It would seem that the serpent was superior to Jehovah either in knowledge or veracity; for his statement relative to the effect of eating the fruit proved to be true, while that of Jehovah proved to be false (Gen. iii. 3).

8.   And, as we have shown in chapter 53, he was a greater friend and benefactor to the human race than Jehovah, as a number of benefits and blessings were conferred upon Adam and Eve and their posterity by yielding to his advice instead of obeying the mandates of Jehovah.

9. It would doubtless be a source of gratification to naturalists of the present age to learn what species of snake that was which possessed such a remarkable intellect and reasoning faculties and powers of speech; and also whether Hebrew was its vernacular.

10. Why is it that ladies of the present day possess none of the nerveless intrepidity and moral courage of old mother Eve, who could stand and listen to a serpent talking without any signs of fainting, and with a perfect *nonchalance,* when our modern ladies would probably scream or run if a snake they should meet should assume the liberty to address them even in the most polite manner? Mother Eve must have been familiar with oddities.

11. If serpents and asses could talk in the days of Moses, why not now? Why have they lost the power of speech?

12. The species of serpents and asses which furnished such distinguished reasoners and orators should have been preserved, both as natural curiosities and on account of their practical benefits. It would be a source of instruction as well as amusement for a traveler, while journeying astride the back of an ass, to be able to enter into a friendly chitchat and exchange views with him, especially if the ass should be well posted on the topics of the day.

13. It seems singular that the heathen prophet Balaam should be able to enlighten infinite wisdom when he called on him for information concerning Balak, King of Moab, or that he should have been better posted in the matter.

14. The circumstance of Jehovah advising Balaam to go at the call of Balak to curse Israel, then becoming very angry at him because he did go, and employing an ass to intercept his journey, evinces him to have been a fickle-minded and changeable being (Num. xxii. 20, 22).

15. It appears that, with all of Balaam's superior intelligence, he was inferior in spiritual discernment to that of his ass, as she could see the spirit standing in the road when he could not.

16. It has been contemptuously suggested as a slur on spiritualism, that perhaps the ass was a spiritual medium. But the fact that asses (of the biped species) can now be found endowed with the power of speech, renders the conclusion more rational that the ass talked without the aid of a spirit.

Such are some of the ridiculous features of these ridiculous stories. The expedient of disposing of these foolish stories as allegories, as some have attempted, will not avail anything: for such figures are too low and groveling to be employed even as metaphors; and there is no hint in the Bible that they are to be understood in an allegorical or metaphorical sense.

II. THE STORY OF CAIN

1.   Did not Eve dishonor God when, at the birth of Cain, she said, "I have got a man from the Lord" (Gen. iv. 1), inasmuch as he turned out to be a murderer?

2.   Did not God know that Cain would become a murderer? If he did not, he is not an omniscient God.

3.   And, if he did know it, would it not make him accountable for the murder?

4.   Why did God set a mark on Cain that "whosoever should find him would not slay him" (Gen. iv. 15), when there was no "whosoever" in existence but his father and mother? And it cannot be supposed they would have to hunt to find him, or that they would kill him when found.

5.   And how could "whosoever" know what the mark meant?

6.   Where did or where could Cain have gone when he "fled from the presence of the Lord" (Gen. iv. 16), as David says he is present everywhere, even in hell?

7.   How could Cain find a wife in the land of Nod (see Gen. iv. 17), when he himself had killed the whole human race excepting his father and mother? There were then no women to make wives of.

8.   Why did Cain build a city (see Gen. iv. 17), when there was nobody to inhabit it?

9.   As there were "workers of iron and brass" in this city, does it not furnish evidence that there was a race of people who had attained a high state of civilization before Adam was made?

10. And as brass is not an ore, but a compound of copper and zinc, does it not furnish evidence that the mining business and the mechanic arts were carried on long before Adam's time?

11. If Cain did find a wife in the land of Nod, is it not evidence that some ribs had been converted into women before Adam's time?

12. Where did Cain find carpenters and masons to build his city, if his father and mother constituted the whole human race?

13. Did not Jehovah know, when he accepted Abel's offering and rejected Cain's, that he was sowing the seeds of discord that would lead to murder?

14. And did he not set a bad example by showing partiality, as there is no reason assigned for preferring Abel's offering?

15. Had not Cain just ground for believing that his offering of herbs would be accepted, inasmuch as Jehovah had ordered Adam to use herbs for food?

16. Must we conclude that Jehovah had a carnivorous appetite, which caused him to prefer animals to vegetables for sacrifices?

17. What sense was there in dooming Cain to be a vagabond among men, when there was but one man in the world, and that his father?

III. THE ARK OF THE COVENANT — 1 SAM. CHAP. VI

We find no case in any history of superstition reaching a more exalted climax than that illustrated in the history of the Jewish ark of the covenant. It appears that up to the time of Solomon the Jews had no temple for their God to dwell in, but for some time previous hauled him about in a box, about four feet long by thirty inches deep, known as the "ark of the covenant." Let it not be supposed that we misrepresent in saying that Jehovah was supposed to dwell in this box; for it is explicitly stated that he dwelt between the cherubims, which constituted a part of the accouterments of the ark. (See 1 Sam. iv. 4.) One of the most singular and ridiculous features connected with this story is that Jehovah, in giving instructions for the construction of the ark, told the people they must offer, among other curious things, badger-skins, goat's hair, and red ram's skins (i.e., ram's skins dyed red). What use God Almighty could have had for the hides and hair of these dead animals is hard to conjecture. Could superstition descend lower than this? As minute a description is given of the whole affair by Jehovah and Moses as if there were some sense in it.

The box was hauled about by two cows; and it was enjoined that those selected by the Philistines should be cows that had never been worked or harnessed, and that their calves should be shut up and left at home. This is descending to a "bill of particulars." The calves must have suffered, as their dams were driven far away, and then slaughtered. What became of the calves is not stated, but we are told that the cows kept up a continual bellowing, or "lowing." Perhaps this was designed as a kind of base or tenor for the music which accompanied them, and this accounts for the calves being left at home. It is curious to observe that the cows were not yoked to the cart on which the ark was drawn, but tied to it—probably by their tails. The Jews did not seem to possess sufficient mechanical skill or genius to invent an ox-yoke. Another singular part of this singular story is that the Philistines constructed six golden mice to accompany the ark; and yet we are told that the Jews were not allowed to have images of anything (Exod. xx. 4).

The most serious consideration connected with this affair was the vast destruction of human life. In the first place the Philistines, in a battle with the Lord's people, slew thirty thousand of them, and captured this box, as we must presume, with the Lord in it. It seems strange that, when Jehovah had fought so many successful battles, he would allow himself to be captured. It was some time, too, before he was recovered from the

75

Philistines. When this was effected, as the ark was being conveyed back under the superintendence of David, with a company of thirty thousand people, while passing over some rough ground, the cart jostled, and the ark came near being thrown off, with the Lord Jehovah in it, who would probably have been considerably bruised by the fall. But a very clever man by the name of Uzzah clapped his hand upon the cart to prevent this awful catastrophe; and, although probably actuated by the best and most pious motives, he was immediately killed for it. This part of the story has a bad moral. On another occasion, on the arrival of the ark at Bethshemesh, because one or two persons attempted to gratify a very natural curiosity by looking into the ark, Jehovah became so much enraged that he killed fifty thousand of the people of Bethshemesh. Here is another of the many cases in which thousands of innocent people were punished for the sin of one man or a few persons. How can any good grow out of the relation of such unjust, unprincipled, and superstitious doings recorded in a book designed for the moral instruction and salvation of the world?

We are told that at every place to which this box was carried, while in the hands of the Philistines, it caused death and destruction, or some other serious calamity. At Ashdod, it produced disease and destruction among the people to an alarming extent; and similar results followed while the ark was at Ekron. Assuming that there is any truth in the story, the thought is here suggested that the box might have been affected with some malarious disease. While at Dagon it caused the God of that place to fall down in the night from his resting-place; on the second night he lost both his hands.

Who that is acquainted with Jewish history cannot see that this circumstance is related to show that the God of the Jews was superior to other Gods, as he excelled them in working miracles in Egypt and other places? That it was a borrowed tradition is quite evident from the fact that the Hindus and Egyptians had practiced similar rites and customs anterior to that period. The Hindu ark was carried on a pole by four priests; and, wherever it touched ground, it wrought miracles in the shape of deaths and births, or the outgushing of springs of water. The Egyptian ark was constructed of gold, which probably made the box more valuable than the God within. All such wooden or metal Gods were supposed to operate as a talisman, or protection against evil. When will the believers in divine revelation and divine prodigies learn that all such superstitious customs and inventions were the work of men, and not of God?

IV. KORAH, DATHAN, AND ABIRAM — NUM. CHAP. XVI

These three leading men of Israel, growing tired of the tyrannical usurpations of Moses, concocted a mutiny, in which they succeeded in enlisting some two hundred and fifty persons. When Moses learned what was on foot, this "meek man" became very angry, and reported the case to Jehovah, and requested him not to accept their offering when they came to make their usual oblations. The Lord took Moses' advice, and not only refused their offering, but split the ground open where they stood, so that they fell in, and were seen no more. And, when their two hundred and fifty followers saw this, they fled, fearing they might share the same fate. But that expedient did not save them: "a fire came out from the Lord," and consumed the whole number. It must have been a fearful fire to consume so many while they were running. The fire came from the Lord; but where the Lord was at the time we are not informed—whether sitting on his throne in heaven, or standing beside the altar, as he frequently did. Hence, we cannot tell whether the fire came from heaven, as it did on some other occasions, or from below. It must have been a very aggravated case of religion, for God and Moses both got angry at once, which was something rather unusual. It was customary, when Jehovah got a angry and made severe threats of what he would do, for Moses to interfere, and intercede for his people, and try to cool him down; and, by the power of his logic and eloquence, he mostly succeeded in convincing him that he was wrong, and got him to desist from carrying his threats into execution. But, on this occasion, Moses, being angry himself, let him take his own course. But the most unjust and unmerciful act in the whole transaction was that of Jehovah sending a plague, and destroying fourteen thousand more, merely because they mourned for their destroyed friends, and ventured to complain of the course he and Moses were pursuing. It was certainly cruel to destroy them for so slight an offense. It appears that, by Aaron's standing "between the dead and the living, the plague was stayed." But for this timely interference of Jehovah's high priest, there is no knowing when or where the plague would have stopped. Now, is it not something near akin to blasphemy to charge such nonsense—ay, worse than nonsense, *cruelty*, *injustice*, and malignity—to the just God of the universe?

V. THE STORY OF DANIEL AND NEBUCHADNEZZAR

We shall not attempt to present an exposition of all the absurdities in the Book of Daniel, but will merely notice a few of its most incredible statements. The most amusing chapter in the history of Daniel is his interpretation of the dreams of King Nebuchadnezzar. It appears that on one occasion the king had forgotten his dream, which made it ostensibly necessary for Daniel, before interpreting it, to reproduce it. But who cannot see it was not necessary for him to do either to save his reputation and his life, both or which it appears were at stake? If he were possessed of an active, fertile imagination, he could invent both, and palm them off on to the king as the original, who would be perfectly unable to detect the trick, as he knew nothing about either. It is stated that one of the dreams consigned the king to the fate of eating grass like an ox for three years. In all such incredible stories which abound in the Christians' Bible, we find glaring absurdities, which a little reflection would reveal to the reader if he would allow himself to think. There is a palpable absurdity in this story which shows that the conversion of the king into an ox as a punishment could not have achieved that end. If he were converted into an ox, his reason was gone, and he was unconscious of his condition; and hence it was no punishment at all. Or, if he still retained his reason, he had nothing to do but to walk away, and find food more congenial to his appetite than grass. And thus the story defeats itself. It Is stated his hair became like eagles' feathers, and his nails like the claws of a bird (Dan. iv. 33)—a very singular-looking ox surely. It would have been more appropriate to call such a being an eagle or a dragon. Such is the careless and disjointed manner in which all Bible stories are told, as if related by mere ignorant children. The most conclusive "knock-down argument" to the truth of this story is found in the fact that no allusion to this astounding miracle can he found by any of the historians of that or any other nation. Had the king been transformed into an ox, the history of his own nation (the Persians) would abound in allusions to the marvelous fact. Its silence on it settles the question.

We will occupy sufficient space to allude to one incident in the story of "the three holy children," which we find related in the Book of Daniel. It is stated that a being who looked "like the Son of God" was seen by the king walking in the furnace. To be sure! We are quite curious to know how he found out how the Son of God looks. How long had he lived in heaven with him so as to become familiar with his countenance? What silly nonsense!

VI. SODOM AND GOMORRAH

Story of Sodom and Gomorrah. We are seemingly required by this story to believe that God keeps a manufactory of brimstone in heaven; for we are told that "the Lord rained upon Sodom and Gomorrah brimstone and fire from the Lord out of heaven" (Gen. xix.). If we credit this story, we may infer that the Lord keeps a supply of the article on hand, perhaps to be let down occasionally to replenish the bottomless pit.

The science of chemistry has demonstrated within the present century that the air is composed of nitrogen and oxygen; and it has also demonstrated that oxygen gas and sulphur or brimstone, when brought into contact are, with a moderate amount of heat, dissolved, united, and converted into oil of vitriol. Hence, if fire and brimstone rained from heaven in that climate, it is scientifically and chemically certain that the people were pelted with a shower of the oil of vitriol.

One square mile of the earth's surface in that locality would be supplied with about thirteen thousand million pounds of oxygen. The requisite amount of brimstone to convert this into oil of vitriol would be about ten thousand million pounds, making in the whole twenty-three thousand millions of pounds.

This would have been sufficient to spoil all the Sunday garments of the people, but could not have burned them up; for cold oil will not burn, and the fire and brimstone would have been converted into oil long before they reached the earth, and become too cool for the heat to injure anything.

We are told that several cities were destroyed by this divine judgment. And pray how many cities could exist in a hot and arid desert, where there was not a drop of water that a human being could drink?

VII. THE TOWER OF BABEL

Of all the stories ever recorded in any book, disclosing on the part of the writer a profound ignorance of the sciences—embracing, at least, astronomy, geography, and philosophy—that of the Tower of Babel was probably never excelled. A brief enumeration of some of its absurdities will disclose this fact.

1.   We are told (in chap. xi. of Genesis) that, after God had discovered by some means that "the children of men" were building a city and a tower to reach to heaven, he "came down to see the city and the tower" (Gen. xi. 6).   The statement that he "came down" implies that he was a local being, and not the omnipotent and omnipresent God.

2.   If he were not already present, and had to travel and descend in order to be present, we should like to know what mode of travel he adopted. It appears from the story that, if he came down, he must have returned almost immediately, and descended a second time; for, after this, he is represented as saying "Go to, let us go down, and there confound their language" (Gen. xi. 7).

3.   Who was this "us"?   The use of this plural pronoun "us" implies that there were several Gods on hand.

4.   And, if he came down, who did he leave in his place?   Must we assume there is a trinity of Gods?   But it would be superlative nonsense to assume that the three Gods could be one (as Christians claim) if one of them could leave the kingdom.

5.   How did the writer know that he or they talked in this manner, as he could not have been present in person to hear it?

79

6.   In this same chapter the "inspired writer" tells us, "'The whole earth was of one language and one speech" (Gen. xi. 1). In the preceding chapter, there is a long list of different tongues, or languages, and nations; and it is declared they were "divided in their lands, every one after his tongue, families, and nations." How contradictory!

7.   What a childish and ludicrous notion the writer entertained with respect to heaven when he cherished the belief that a tower could be erected to reach it!

8.   According to St. Jerome, the Tower of Babel was twenty thousand feet high. A Jewish writer says it was eighty thousand. In the first case it would be nearly four miles in height; in the other, over fifteen miles— nearly three times the height of the highest mountain on the globe! No method has ever yet been discovered for elevating building materials to such a height.

9.   Taking St. Jerome as authority, the hod-carriers, in ascending and descending, would have to perform a journey of more than seven miles each trip.

10.   As the air becomes rarefied in proportion to its distance from the earth, the lungs of the workmen would have collapsed, and their blood have congealed, before they climbed half-way to the top. They could not have breathed at such a height.

11.   As the earth is constantly revolving on its axis, the crazy tower-builders would only be in the direction of the point at which they aimed once in twenty-four hours, and then moving with a speed one hundred and forty times greater than that of a cannon-ball. It would require dexterous springing to leap into the door of' heaven as they passed it.

12.   And as the earth, in its orbit, moves at the rate of sixty-eight thousand miles an hour, it would soon carry them millions of miles beyond any point they might be aiming to reach.

13.   After all, we cannot see any possible objection Jehovah or any other God could have had to such an enterprise.

14.   If the Babelites had succeeded in climbing into heaven, what of it? Was Omnipotence afraid they would dispossess him of his throne, and seize the reins of government? If not, what could have been the objection?

15.   And then it would not have taken the "heavenly host" fifteen minutes to tumble them out, as they did Michael and the dragon.

16.   The truth is, the imaginary God of the Jews was a suspicious, cowardly, and jealous being. He was constantly getting into hot water. He appeared to live in perpetual fear day and night that some other God, or some of his own creatures, would encroach upon his rights. In this case he seemed to be alarmed for fear those ignorant, deluded tower-builders and

wild fanatics would succeed in reaching the heavenly home, perhaps bind him, and cast him out of his own kingdom. What superlative nonsense is the whole story! And yet millions believe it to be divinely inspired, and many thousands of dollars have been spent in printing it, and circulating it over the world.

VIII. STOPPING THE SUN AND MOON

Of all the stories that ever taxed the brain or credulity of a man of science, that of Joshua stopping the sun and moon stands preeminent. Think of bringing to a stand-still that magnificent and immense luminary which constitutes the center of a solar system of one hundred and thirty worlds, all of which move in harmony with it. Such a catastrophe would have broken one hundred and thirty planets loose from their orbits, and dashed them together in utter confusion, and would thus have broken up our solar system. The shock produced upon this earth would have thrown everything on its surface off into boundless space.

For a puny man, on a little planet like this, to command the mighty sun, which is fourteen hundred thousand times as large as the earth, to stop in its grand career, would be comparable to an ant saying to a mountain, "Get out of my way."

And, when we look at the cruel and wicked purpose for which this stupendous miracle is said to have been wrought, we are shocked at the demoralizing effect such lessons must have upon the millions who look upon it as the work of a just and righteous God.

It savors too much of blasphemy to assume that a God of infinite justice would perform an act attended with such direful consequences, merely to allow the little, bloody-minded Joshua more time to blow out the brains and tear out the hearts of his enemies, guilty of no crime but that of believing in a different religious creed. Farewell to reason, justice, and morality, if we must subscribe to such moral lessons as this!

And why did he have the moon stopped at midday, when it could not be seen, and was, perhaps, on the opposite side of the globe? Egypt, India, Greece, and Mexico all have traditions of the sun stopping, but, in most cases, have too much sense to stop the moon. Fohi of China had the sun stopped eight hundred and fifty years before Joshua, the son of Nun, ever saw the sun. Bacchus and other God-men of Egypt had it stopped four times. While in Greece Phaethon was set after it to hurry it up, and increase its speed. A "poor rule that will not work both ways!" The Chinese annals state that the sun stopped ten days during the reign of the Emperor Yom. Argoon of India stopped it several days for his own accommodation.

The Bible of Bibles

But, unfortunately for the cause of religion, or rather religious superstition, no man of science, in any of these countries, has as much as noticed these world-astounding phenomena; and no writer, but one religious fanatic in each case, has spoken of them—a circumstance of itself sufficient to render them utterly incredible.

IX. THE STORY OF SAMSON

Were the story of Samson found in any other book than the Christian Bible, it would he looked upon by Bible believers as one of those wild and incredible legends of heathen mythology with which all the holy hooks of that age abound. But it is accepted as true because it is found in the Bible; and the Bible is considered to be true, partly because it tells such marvelous stories. It is assumed that they prove each other. Perhaps it is upon the presumption that "it is poor rule that will not work both ways."

1. We are told (Judg. chap. xiii.) that an angel appeared to the wife of Manoah, and promised her a son; and Manoah seemed to be as well pleased about the matter as his wife, and seemed to care but little whether the father was a man or an angel or a God, and we are left in the dark as to which it was.

2. It is rather a notable circumstance that the Jewish God and his angels seemed to have a great deal to do in trying to accommodate and aid old women in becoming mothers, as in the case of Abraham's wife and Manoah's wife, also Elizabeth and Mary in the New Testament, and other cases.

3. The man or angel or God, whichever it was (for he is called by each name), that appeared to Mrs. Manoah, advised her to abstain from strong drink, and to eat no unclean thing. Very good advice to be observed at any time, but it seems to imply that she was in the habit of using such pernicious articles.

4. And, when her child was born, he was called Samson, and was remarkable for his great strength, which is said to lie in his hair. The mighty denizens of the forest interposed no obstacle to his march; and houses were but playthings, to be tossed in the air like balls. He is reported to have seized a lion and slain him when yet a boy, without a weapon of any kind. It would have been well if this mighty hero had been present when Jehovah had a battle with the Canaanites (Judg. i. 19), as he would not probably have been defeated so easily because they had chariots of iron. Those vehicles of iron would have been mere straws for Samson. If their respective histories be true, he excelled Jehovah, both with regard to strength and courage, in a severe contest.

5.   It is stated that, a short time after this young bachelor-hero had slain the king of the forest, as he was returning home from a visit to his lady-love, he observed that a swarm of bees had taken possession of the carcass, and filled it with honey.   Those bees must have been very much less fastidious in their tastes and habits than the bees of modern times; for the latter shun a carcass as instinctively as death.

6.   Another remarkable circumstance connected with this case is that the long-haired bachelor thrust his hands through the bees, and tore out the honey, regardless of their stinging mode of defending their rights. His skin must have been as remarkable for toughness as his muscles for strength.

7.   One of the most cruel, ungodly, and fiendish acts of this young hero was that of murdering thirty men to get their garments, as a recompense to those thirty persons who solved his riddle; thus massacring thirty innocent persons in order to strip them of their garments—an unprovoked and wanton murder.   And yet it is declared, "the spirit of God was with him."   What shocking ideas of Deity!

8.   Samson was evidently a "free-lover," as he had intercourse with a number of women of doubtful character.

9.   His next great feat consisted in chasing and catching three hundred foxes, and tying their tails together, and making a firebrand of them.   It must have been a good time to raise poultry after so many foxes had disappeared, but certainly not before that event, if foxes were so numerous.

10. It seems strange that these "tail-bearers" of fire did not take to the woods, instead of running through all the fields in the country, and setting them on fire.

11. The next feat was the breaking of two strong cords, with which his arms had been bound by three thousand men.   (See Judg. xv. 4).   It is difficult to conceive how three thousand men could get to him to tie them, as it is intimated they did.   His mode of being revenged after he had snapped the cords was to seize the jaw-bone of an ass, and slay a thousand men; and, after he had killed these thousand men with the bone, there was enough of it left to contain a considerable amount of water.   It is related that the Lord clave a hollow in it, and there came out of it water to quench Samson's thirst.

12. Asses seem to figure quite conspicuously in Bible history. Sometimes they talk and reason like a Cicero, as in the case of Balaam; and they serve other important ends in the histories of Abram and Job (who had a thousand) and Samson, and also that of Jesus Christ, who is represented as riding two at once.   In the hands of Samson, the jawbone of an ass was more destructive than a twenty-four pound cannon, besides furnishing him with water sufficient to supply his thirst.

13. Another feat of this young Hercules was that of carrying away the gate and gateposts of the city of Gaza, in which the keepers had shut him up while lodging with a harlot. Most of his female companions seem to have been licentious characters; and yet "the Lord favored him"!

14. It is said "the spirit of the Lord moved Samson" (Judg. xiii. 25). It would seem that the spirit of the Devil did also, for he had a terrible propensity for lying. He lied even to his own wife three or four times. He once deceived her by telling her that his strength could be overcome by tying him with green withes; and yet he snapped them like cobwebs. He then virtually confessed to her that he had lied, but told her that new ropes would accomplish the thing; and yet he was no sooner bound with them, than he freed his limbs as easily as a lion would crawl out of a fish-net. The next experiment in lying and tying appertained to his hair. He told his sweet Delilah that, if she would weave his seven locks of hair into the web in the loom, he would be as weak as another man; but he walked off with the web and the whole accouterments hanging to his head, as easily as a wolf would with a steel trap dangling to his foot. Why did not the hair pull out by the roots? He then told her the truth, as was assumed, but which was evidently the biggest falsehood he had uttered—that his strength lay in his hair, and that his strength would depart if his hair were to be shorn off. But if there were any physical strength incorporated in the hair, so that it would flow into the brain and down into the muscles when wanted to be used, men would not frequent barber-shops, as they now do, but let it grow two feet long if necessary.

15. The last great act in this drama of physical prowess was that of overthrowing a house with three thousand people on the roof. (Modern architecture does not often produce a roof large enough or strong enough to sustain three thousand people. This feat would require more strength than to conquer the battalion armed with chariots of iron!

16. And in all this unholy and wicked business of lying, cheating, and murdering, "the Lord was with him." This is a slanderous imputation upon Divine Perfection and Holiness.

17. No good that we can discover, but much evil, was accompanied by the practical life of this extraordinary man. He was ostensibly raised up to redeem Israel; and yet, immediately after his death, the Philistines gained a complete victory over the Israelites, and took prisoner the ark of the Lord, and reduced them to a worse condition than they were in before.

18. We cannot escape the conviction that such stories have a demoralizing effect upon those who read them, and believe they have the divine approval.

19. For seeming to treat the subject in a spirit of ridicule, I will cite a Christian writer as authority, who says, "He who treats absurdities with seriousness lowers his own dignity and manhood."

20. Such stories as the foregoing can certainly do nothing toward improving the morals of the heathen by placing the book containing it in their hands.

X. THE STORY OF JONAH

The history of Jonah is so much like numerous stories we find in heathen mythology that we are disposed to class it with them. Its absurdities are numerous, a few of which we will point out:

1. It represents Jonah as claiming to be a Hebrew, but as it says nothing about the Jews or Hebrews, and treats entirely of the heathen or Gentiles, that is probably its source, and it was perhaps intended as a fable.

2. The ship he boarded, when making his escape, was a heathen vessel, which implies that he had some affinity for that class of people.

3. It seems very singular, that if Jonah did not believe Jehovah to be a mere local personal deity, rather than the Infinite and Omnipresent God, he should entertain the thought of running away from him or escaping from his presence by flight.

4. The heathen who had charge of the vessel were evidently possessed of more humanity and more mercy than either Jehovah or the leading men of Israel, who seem to have made it a point to kill nearly all the heathen they could lay their hands on; as did Abram, Moses, Joshua, etc. For it is stated that, after they had cast lots to find who was the cause of the storm which overtook the ship, and in this way discovered it was Jonah, they strove with all their might to get the vessel to the shore, rather than resort to the desperate expedient of throwing Jonah overboard. This bespeaks for these heathen a feeling of mercy and humanity.

5. We learn by the language these heathen used in their prayer to stop the storm; "We beseech thee, O Lord," etc., that they believed in one supreme God. Where, then, is the truth of the claim of the Jews that they alone believed in one God, or the unity of the Godhead? In this way, their own Bible often proves this claim was false; that the nations they had intercourse with believed in one supreme and overruling God.

6. It is stated that, after Jonah was thrown overboard, and was swallowed by a fish, he prayed to the Lord. How was this discovered? Did he pray loud enough to be heard through the sides of the whale? Or did the fish open its mouth for his accommodation?

7.   As for the prayer, it appears to have been made up of scraps selected from the Psalms of David without much connection or relevancy to the case.

8.   It is stated that the Lord spake to the fish, and it vomited Jonah upon the dry land. It must have been a very singular fish to understand Hebrew or any human language.

9.   In another respect the whale must have been a peculiar one, or of peculiar construction. The throat of an ordinary whale is about the diameter of a man's arm. It must therefore have been very much stretched to swallow Jonah, or Jonah must have been very much compressed and elongated.

10.   The gourd that sheltered Jonah must also have been of a peculiar species to have a vine that could grow several yards in one night, and stand erect so as to hold the gourd in a position to shelter the prophet; and the gourd would have to be as large as a cart or locomotive, or it would soon cease to afford him shade.

11.   Jonah seems to have been a very proud and selfish man, with but little of the feeling of mercy, as he preferred that the whole nation of Ninevites should be destroyed rather than that his prediction should not be fulfilled, for he became very angry when he found the Lord was going to spare them.

12.   The reason the Lord assigns for sparing Nineveh is a very sensible one—because "there are more than threescore thousand persons that can not discern between their right and their left hand." This is certainly very good reasoning, but why did he not think of this when millions of innocent persons perished in the act of drowning the whole human race, excepting four men and four women; or when Sodom and Gomorrah were swallowed up; or when seventy thousand were killed for a sin committed by David; or in the numerous cases in which a war of extermination was carried on against whole nations, with the order to slay men, women, and children, and "leave nothing alive that breathes." Why such partiality? But this is one of the two thousand Bible inconsistencies.

13.   This is a very poor story, with a very bad moral. It indicates fickleness, short-sightedness, and partiality on the part of Jehovah; and selfishness and bad temper on the part of his prophet.

14.   There are other absurdities in this story which we will bring to view by a few brief questions.

15.   Why did Jehovah care anything about the salvation or welfare of Nineveh, a heathen city, when usually, instead of laboring to save the heathen, he was plotting their destruction?

16. What put the thought into the heads of the mariners that the storm was caused by the misconduct of some person on board? Can we suppose they ever knew of such a case? If the misconduct of human beings could produce storms or a disturbance of the elements, the world would be cursed by a perpetual hurricane.

17. We are told the sailors cast lots to ascertain who was the cause of the storm. Rather a strange way of investigating the cause of natural events.

18. Is it not strange that Jehovah would bring on a violent storm on Jonah's account, and continue it for hours, and let him sleep during the time; and still stranger that Jonah was so indifferent that he could sleep in such a storm?

19. Jonah must have been the most considerate and merciful sinner ever reported in history to propose himself that he should be thrown overboard as a means of allaying the storm, and saving a set of gambling heathen. What a wonderful freak of mercy and justice! But it seems to have been all exhausted on the mariners, so that he had none left for the poor Ninevites; for he became very angry when he found Jehovah was not going to destroy them, the innocent and guilty and all together. This was inconsistent, to say the least.

20. What must have been the astonishment of the crew of the hundreds of ships sailing on the same sea to observe a sudden storm to arise and stop without any natural cause! And when they afterwards learned that the whole thing was brought about by the misconduct of one man in one of the vessels, perhaps hundreds of miles distant, they must have abandoned all idea of ever looking again for natural causes for storms after that occurrence. How repressing such events would be to the growth and cultivation of the intellect, and the study of the natural sciences!

21. How could Jonah remain three days in the whale's stomach without being digested, as fish have astonishing digestive powers? And, if he were not digested, both he and the fish must have been extremely hungry at the end of the three days' fast.

22. As a fish large enough to swallow Jonah could not swim through the shoal-water to reach the land, it becomes an interesting query to know how it got Jonah on to "the dry land." It must have required the use of a powerful emetic to inspire the fish with force sufficient to throw him fifty or a hundred feet.

23. Is it not strange that Jonah's message to the Ninevites should have had such a marvelous effect upon the whole city, when it was evidently delivered in a language that none of them understood?

24. We are told the king issued orders for everybody, including men, women and children, and beasts, to stop eating and drinking, and to be

covered with sackcloth. What sin can we suppose the beasts had committed that they must be doomed to starve, and be covered with sackcloth as an emblem of repentance? It must have required an enormous amount of sackcloth to cover two millions of people, and probably as many domestic animals. Where it all came from, the Lord Jehovah only knows. And it seems singular that all of the animals should stand quietly while such an uncouth covering was thrown upon them.

25. It is also difficult to comprehend why a nation of people, who probably never heard of Jehovah before, should all repent in sackcloth and ashes. It is the most effective missionary work we have ever read of. In modern times, it requires two hundred missionaries a whole century to make half that many converts.

26. But the most conclusive argument against the truth of the story is found in the fact that it is falsified by the testimony of history. According to her history by Diodorus, Nineveh was destroyed by Arbaces sixteen years before Jonah's time.

27. I have noticed this senseless story at some length, because Christian writers have invested it with great importance, and because it is endorsed by nearly all the New Testament writers. Even Christ himself endorses it, and compares Jonah's case to his. Their extreme ignorance is evinced by the foregoing exposition.

28. Several similar stories are found in heathen mythology, a few of which we will briefly sketch here. The Hindu sacred book, the Purans, states that Krishna was swallowed by a crocodile, and, after remaining three days in its stomach, was thrown upon dry land, much to his relief and also to that of the crocodile. A Grecian demi-God (Hercules), according to Gales, was swallowed by a dog, and remained in his stomach three days. But the story entitled to the premium is one preserved in the legends of some of the Eastern islanders. A man, for some misdemeanor on a voyage across the Indus, was thrown overboard and swallowed by a shark; but, as the fish still followed the vessel, it was finally caught, and search made for the man when, to the surprise of the whole crew, he was found sitting bolt upright, playing the tune of "Old Hundred" on a fiddle he had in his possession when he went down the throat of the sea monster. This was rather a pleasant way of putting in the time. Jonah, it appears, was not so fortunate as to have a fiddle in his possession while in the stomach of the whale.

The foregoing ten stories, from that of the serpent to Jonah, have been for hundreds of years printed by the thousand, struck off in almost every known human language, and sent off by ship-loads to almost every nation on the globe, to be placed in the hands of the heathen as being *productions* of *Infinite Wisdom,* the *inspirations* of *an All-wise God,* and calculated to *enlighten* them and *improve their morals.* What sublime nonsense! What egregious folly! And what a deplorable and sorrowful mistake has been thus committed by the blinded disciples of the Christian faith!

CHAPTER 19

BIBLE PHOPHECIES NOT FULFILLED

Having devoted a chapter to this subject in "The World's Sixteen Crucified Saviors," we shall treat the subject but briefly in this work. The Old Testament has been thoroughly searched for prophecies, and more than a hundred texts selected, by various Christian writers, and assumed to be prophetic of some future event. But a critical and impartial investigation of the subject will show that not one of them is, strictly speaking, a prophecy; most of them refer to events either in the past, or events *naturally* suggested by the circumstances under which the writer was placed. And in many cases the text has no reference whatever to the event which Bible commentators assume they refer to. In treating the subject briefly, we will show:

1. That if one-fourth of the texts from Genesis to Revelation were prophecies, and it could be shown that every one of them has been fulfilled to the letter, it would not prove that there was any divine inspiration or divine aid in the matter; because many facts show that prophecy, or the power to discover future events, is a *natural,* and not a supernatural, gift.

2. Many cases are reported in history of the prediction of future events by pagan or heathen seers, and also by persons not claiming to be inspired nor even religious. I will cite a few cases: Josephine, wife of Napoleon, relates that she had all the important events of her future life pointed out to her by an ignorant, illiterate fortune-teller, long before they occurred; such as her marriage, her unhappy life, and the death of her husband—all of which were fulfilled to the letter. An astrologer predicted the great fire in London. Rousseau foretold the French Revolution. Cicero made a remarkable prophecy, which was realized in the discovery of America and the history of George Washington, by consulting the Sibylline oracles. These, and many other cases that might be cited, furnish satisfactory evidence that the capacity for foretelling the occurrence of future events is a natural and inherent power of the human mind, and hence can do nothing toward proving the divine origin of any religion, or the divine illumination of any prophet. Therefore, any further argument in the case would be superfluous.

We will only briefly review a few of the Jewish prophecies (or texts assumed to be prophecies) to show that the Jewish nation occupied a lower moral plane, and possessed less of the gift of prophecy, than some of the contemporary heathen nations. Hence, Christian writers are wrong in assuming that the Jews alone possessed this power, while they possessed it in a less degree than some of the Oriental prophets. Prophecies (assumed to be) relating to Babylon, relating to Damascus, relating to Tyre, relating to the dispersion of the Jews, relating to the advent of Christ, etc., have been quoted time and again by Christian writers and clergymen, and dwelt upon at great length in attempts to show their fulfillment, in order to deduce therefrom the argument and conclusion that the Jewish nation were divinely commissioned to furnish the world with a true system of religion and morals. But we are prepared to show that *every one* of these prophecies so called has *utterly failed* of any fulfillment in the sense that writers and preachers assume. As it would require a large work to treat this subject fully, we shall only briefly refer to one or two cases as samples of the whole. As Babylon and Tyre are the most frequently referred to, and are regarded as the strongest cases, our attention will be confined to them.

Relative to Babylon, Isaiah says, "It shall not be dwelt in from generation to generation; neither shall the Arabian pitch his tent there" (Isa. xiii. 19); but he says, "It shall be inhabited by wild beasts of the desert and satyrs and dragons"—not one of which predictions has ever been realized. It is still inhabited, though its name has been changed to Hillah, which has now a population of about nine thousand. So far from the "Arabian not pitching his tent there," it is the very thing they have done, and are now doing daily. Mr. Layard, who recently visited the place, says in his work ("Nineveh and Babylon"), "The Arab settlement showed the activity of a hive of bees." What a singular rebuff to Isaiah's prophecy, and also to that of Jeremiah, who says it should become a "perpetual desolation" (xxv. 12), and that it should not be dwelt in by man nor the son of man! (Jer. i. 40.) Isaiah declared, "Her days shall not be prolonged" (Isa. xiii). And thus the prophecies have all failed which refer to Babylon.

Speaking of Tyre, Ezekiel says it should be taken by Nebuchadnezzar, and trodden down by his chariots and horses; and "thou shalt be built no more, and thou shalt never be found again." And yet Tyre never was destroyed by Nebuchadnezzar, nor by any power; and, although it has suffered like other Eastern cities, it is still a flourishing city with a population of about five thousand. St. Jerome spoke of it in the fourth century as being "the most noble and beautiful city in Phoenicia." And this was more than a thousand years after Ezekiel's predictions were pronounced against it, which declared it should be destroyed, and never be rebuilt. True, it has been partially destroyed several times—and what ancient city has not?—but it has been rebuilt as often.

We have, then, before us two illustrative cases of the failures of Jewish prophecies pronounced against neighboring cities and kingdoms, probably prompted by a spirit of envy and animosity because they had either overruled the Jewish nation, and subjected it to their power, or outstripped it in temporal prosperity. The Jewish prophets were continually fulminating their thunders and curses upon those powers and principalities which had overpowered them, and held them in subjection. This was very natural; and occasionally an unpropitious prediction may have been realized. But it is a remarkable fact that more than forty disastrous events, which the Jewish prophets declared the Lord would inflict upon Egypt (the nation they so much contemned and envied because it held them in slavery for four hundred years), have never been realized in the history or experience of that nation. Some of these cases are noticed in "The World's Sixteen Crucified Saviors," as also the prophecies and failures in regard to Damascus and other cities, to which the reader is referred for a further elucidation of this subject.

CHAPTER 20

ERRONEOUS BELIEF IN BIBLE MIRACLES

Having treated the subject of miracles at some length in "The World's Sixteen Crucified Saviors," we shall give it but a brief notice in this work, and will comprehend the whole thing in a few points.

1. The history of miraculous achievements by Gods and men form a very large chapter in the "inspired writings" of nearly all the ancient religious systems which have flourished in the world; and to notice all these cases would require volumes enough to make a library.

2. Almost the only evidence we have in any case of the actual performance of a miracle is the report of the writer who relates it.

3. St. Chrysostom declares that "miracles are not designed for men of sense, but only for sluggish minds." It will be understood, therefore, that what we write here on the subject will not be designed for persons of sense, but only for the ignorant and superstitious.

4. Many things in the past which were set down as miracles are now known to be the result of natural causes; such as the rainbow, most cases of sickness, and, in fact, nearly every phenomenon of nature. And, as every age develops new light on natural causes, it has made the list of miracles not already explained so small that we may reasonably conclude that they will all yet be explained and understood in this light, excepting those fabricated without any basis of truth.

5. As God appears to have regulated everything in the beginning by fixed laws, if he should break one of those laws by the performance of a miracle, it would throw everything into chaos and confusion, and prove that he is not a God of order and stability.

6. If God, as we are told, made everything perfect, then the performance of a miracle must make them imperfect, or prove that they have always been imperfect.

7. The performance of a miracle would prove that God is an imperfect being in not having everything regulated by the laws of nature.

8. If the performance of miracles can authenticate the truth of one religion, then it must prove the truth of all religions; for all report miracles of some kind, and furnish, in most cases, the same kind of evidence that these miracles were performed.

9. There is not a miracle related in either the Old or New Testament that has not a parallel reported in the Bibles or sacred writings of the Orientals; such as curing the halt and blind, raising the dead, crossing streams in a miraculous manner, etc. Many cases are reported of the Hindu Savior and Son of God, Krishna, raising dead persons who had been drowned, murdered, or died a natural death. According to Tacitus,

Vespasian performed a number of miraculous cures, such as curing the lame, restoring sight to the blind, etc., just as is related of Jesus. According to Josephus, Alexander with his army passed through the Sea of Pamphylia in the same miraculous manner that Moses did through the Red Sea. As Alexander's army was engaged in the work of human butchery, we may assume that, if God could have had anything to do with it, he would have embraced the opportunity to drown them, and wash them all away.

10. *Jewish Miracles.* The Jewish Talmud speaks of birds so large that they darkened the sun, and shut out the light of the sun from the earth. Probably they supposed, like Moses, that nearly all the earth was located between Dan and Beersheba. Another kind of bird was so tall that, when walking in a river seventy feet deep, the water only reached its knees. This is a tall story, but it should be remembered that it is related by the same people who tell us about sticks being converted into serpents, water into blood, dust into lice, etc., and a man (Samson) overturning a house with several thousand people in it, etc. Hence, all these stories are equally reliable or unreliable.

11. *Muhammadan Miracles.* Muhammadans bear off the palm in miraculous prodigies. For instance, a cock is spoken of so large that the distance between its feet and head was five hundred days' journey. What a pity Barnum could not obtain it! Another example: an angel so large that the distance between his eyes was seventy thousand days' journey. The head of this tall ghost must have been among the planets. The earth would have been too small to furnish him with a seat, and the attempt to use it for that purpose would probably have thrown it out of its orbit.

12. *Christian Miracles.* The early Christians seem to have had the whole miracle-making machinery of heaven under their control. Their miracles were prodigious and numerous. They claimed they could cast out devils, call the dead from their graves, and make ghosts walk about either end up. We are told that when a Mr. Huntington was reduced to great poverty and suffering, and prayed for divine assistance, fishes came out of the water to him, and larks and leather breeches from heaven, to serve as food and clothing. It is difficult to conceive how leather breeches came to be stored in heaven. With these few specimens, selected at random, we will stop. They are too large even to excite our marvelousness. The most ignorant and superstitious nations have always had the longest creeds and the tallest miracles.

13. We have stated that the only evidence of the performance of any miracle in most cases is the simple narration of it by the writer who records it. The Roman Catholics, however, claim to have the testimony of thousands of reliable witnesses to attest to the performance of some

extraordinary miracles which they have reported the history of; such as a picture of the Virgin Mary, hanging on the walls of the church, opening and shutting its eyes daily for six or seven months, which they declare was witnessed by sixty thousand people, including Pope, cardinals, bishops, etc.—leading men of the Church.

14. There is as much evidence that Esculapius raised Hypolitus from the dead (as related by the Roman historian Pausanias), as that Elijah or Christ raised the dead; as much evidence that the serpent's egg inclosed in gold (as related by Pliny in his "Arguinum Ovum") swam up stream when thrown into the river, as that Elisha raised an ax to the surface of the water by casting a stick into it (2 Kings vi. 6); as much evidence that Muhammad opened a fountain of water in the end of his little finger, as that Samson found a spring of water in the jaw-bone of an ass; as much evidence that Muhammad's camel talked to him, as that Balaam's ass was endowed with human speech; and as much evidence that Esculapius cured the blind with spittle, as that Christ performed such cures. All stand upon a level: all lack the proof.

15. Here let it be noted that many of the miracles recorded in the Christian Bible as susceptible of an explanation upon natural principles; such as the shadow going back on the dial of Ahaz, as the phenomenon has been witnessed in some of the Eastern countries of the shadows appearing to recede when the sun is near the solstice, once in the forenoon and once in the afternoon. The story of the devils entering the hogs may be explained by assuming the devils to have been frogs, for they are described as being like frogs. (See Rev. xvi. 13.)

The resurrection of Lazarus may be explained by assuming him to have been in a state of coma, or trance; for Christ once declared, "This sickness is not unto death," but he sleepeth" (John xi). The bloody sweat of Christ, and his transfiguration, can also be explained on natural principles; also Paul's conversion, and his miraculous cures with a handkerchief. Dr. Newton, the great healer, has cured hundreds of cases in a similar manner. And the time will come when all real occurrences, now called miracles, will be accounted for and understood as the operation of natural causes.

CHAPTER 21

ERRORS OF THE BIBLE IN FACTS AND FIGURES

A spiritual or metaphorical interpretation, if allowable in any case, cannot avail anything towards either removing, explaining, or mitigating, in the least degree, the numerous palpable Bible errors represented by *figures*. "*Figures never lie*," and admit of no construction. The almost innumerable errors, therefore, of this character which abound in the Bible utterly and forever prostrate it as a work possessing any authority, reliability, or credibility in matters of history, science, or even theology. Bible writers, when they have occasion to refer to numbers which they are interested in making *appear* very large, seem to make almost a lawless use of figures. I will present some examples, stated in brief language, commencing with the Pentateuch.

The author of these five books, in speaking of the genealogy, population, armies, etc., of his own tribe, makes use of figures which are not only incredible, but utterly impossible. The number of valiant fighting men, for example, among the Israelites, is frequently stated to be about six hundred thousand, and never less. (See Exod. xii. and xxxviii.; Num. xxvi., etc.) This number, as Bishop Colenso demonstrates, reaches far beyond the utmost limits of truth. If the regular army had been six hundred thousand, then the whole population (women and children included) could not have been less than two millions—a number which many facts, cited by the Bible writer himself, demonstrate to be impossible. I would ask, in the first place, how Moses could address all this immense congregation at once, as he is often represented as doing. (See Exod. xxiv. 3; Lev. xxiv. 15; Num. xiv. 7, etc.) Joshua makes "all the congregation" to include women and children. But how could Moses address this vast multitude of people, some of whom must have been at least ten miles distant, unless he used a speaking-trumpet or a telephone, neither of which, however, had then come to light? The writer of Deuteronomy says, "Moses spake unto all Israel" (Deut. i. 1). But not one in a hundred could have heard it; therefore, it was very nearly "labor lost." And Joshua says Moses wrote out his commandments, and he read them "before all the congregation of Israel" (Josh. viii. 35). But it would have required a voice as loud as thunder to make "*all*" of them hear. And it should be borne in mind that the people on these occasions were assembled in the tabernacle—as we infer from many texts—a building one hundred and eight yards square, and capable of holding about five thousand people, which would be just one to four thousand of the congregation; so there were five thousand people inside, and one million nine hundred and ninety-five thousand outside. These last, we are told, occupied the outer court, which was just eighteen feet wide. This would place the most distant hearers twenty miles off. How comforting the thought that, when Moses called them to the temple to worship (see Josh. viii. 35), they could get within miles of him and "the tabernacle of the Lord"! The Lord had built a tabernacle for them to worship in, but only one or two in six thousand could get inside of it. This small number only could enjoy seeing and hearing Moses and the Lord. The rest—one million nine hundred and ninety-five thousand—were *outside*, waiting for admission.

Bishop Colenso estimates the size of the camp of Israel at about twelve miles square. This camp was situated in a desert of Sinai for at least a year; and the business of keeping this camp in order, waiting upon the people, and removing also the remains of the daily sacrifice of two hundred thousand oxen, sheep, etc., devolved upon three priests—Aaron, Eleazar, and Ithamar. It would be quite an improvement of the sacerdotal order if the priests of today could be subjected occasionally to some such healthy exercise; but they have managed to get the rule reversed. They now have the people to wait upon them. But those three priests of the Israelites must have achieved a herculean task to wait each one upon three hundred and thirty-three thousand people daily, and, after preparing their food outside the camp, travel twelve miles to supply each one of this vast multitude with food and water. If they carried provision for only one person at a time, they would have had to perform this journey of twelve miles five thousand five hundred times an hour, which would have required them to be rather fleet on foot. And, besides the labor of carrying away every day, to the distance of six or seven miles, five hundred cart-loads of the offal of the dead animals, there would be at least one pound of victuals to be carried to each person, making, in the aggregate, five thousand five hundred pounds. They must have enjoyed good health, if abundant exercise would produce it. They could not have been much troubled with dyspepsia or liver complaint, as many of that order are nowadays.

1.   We are told that Moses gave notice to the children of Israel at midnight that they must take their departure from Egypt the next morning for the promised land (Exod. xii.); but, if they constituted the immense number represented, they would have made a column two hundred miles long, arranging them five abreast, so it would have taken several days for all to get started. How, then, could they all start the *next morning*? And how did they keep their two millions of sheep and cattle alive for several days while passing over a sandy desert too poor to produce dog-fennel? And it is strange how the whole tribe of Israelites, if two millions in number, could live forty years in a wild, barren desert and keep their immense flocks and herds alive.

2.   The number of first-born male children over a month old, on a certain occasion, is set down at twenty-two thousand two hundred and

ninety-three, which would make about eighty-eight children for each mother. This was "replenishing" rapidly. But their little tents, like the tabernacle of the Lord, would not accommodate one-fourth of that number. This would necessitate the mothers to leave most of their children "out in the cold." The number of the children of Israel that went down to Egypt, according to Exod. i. 5, was seventy souls; and they remained there during four generations, represented by Levi, Kohath, Amram, and Moses, making a period (as marginal notes state) of two hundred and fifteen years; though Exod. xii. 40 gives it at four hundred and thirty years. But this is another case of incredible exaggeration. Four generations of ordinary length, in that age, would not exceed the marginal calculation of two hundred and fifteen years; and for those seventy souls to increase to two millions in that short period of time of four generations, would have required each mother to have had twelve or fifteen children at birth.

3. Dan, in the first generation, had but one son (Gen. xlvi. 23), yet in the fourth generation he had increased to sixty-two thousand seven hundred, or, according to Num. xxvi. 43, to sixty-four thousand, which would have required each son and grandson to have had about eighty children apiece. This would have been "multiplying and replenishing" on a rapid scale.

4. Aaron and his two sons had to make all the offerings, and on an altar only nine feet square; and an offering had to be made at the birth of every child, which would require about five hundred sacrifices daily; and then there were thirteen cities where these offerings had to be made, and only three priests to do it. (See Lev. i. 11.) And, besides, the priests had to eat a large portion of the burnt offerings (see Num. xviii. 10); and, as these offerings consisted of five hundred lambs and pigeons, it would subject them to the task of eating enormous quantities daily.

5. At the second passover, an offering had to be made for every family (Exod. xii.), which would require the slaughter of about one hundred and fifty thousand lambs. The three priests had to sprinkle the blood of these lambs, and it had to be done in about two hours (1 Chron. xxx. 35). The lambs had to be sacrificed at the rate of about one thousand two hundred and fifty a minute, and each priest had to sprinkle the blood of more than four hundred lambs per minute with their own hands, which would make the affair rather a bloody business, if it were not wholly impossible, and therefore an incredible story.

6. If we could credit the statements of "the inspired writer" of the book of Numbers (see chapter xxxi.), we should have to believe twelve thousand Israelites, in a war with the Midianites, after selecting out thirty-two thousand young damsels, killed forty-eight thousand men, eighty thousand women, and twenty thousand boys; burned all their cities, and

captured all their stock, amounting to eight hundred and eight thousand, and all this without the loss of a single man. Each Israelite would have had to conquer seventy-five resisting enemies, including men, women, children, and stock. It is a story too incredible for serious reflection. We are told that the clothing of the Israelites lasted forty years "without waxing old" (see Deut. xxix. 5)—another story too incredible to be entertained for a moment.

7.   In Deuteronomy the priests are always called sons of Levi, or "Levites," but in the other books of the Pentateuch, they are always called "the sons of Aaron," which is an evidence they were not written by the same hand. Contradictions. According to Exod. xviii. 25, Moses appointed judges over Israel before the giving forth of the law; but (Deut. i. 6) we are told that the appointment took place after the law was issued at Sinai.

8.   According to Deuteronomy, chap. x., "the Lord separated the tribe of Levi" after the death of Aaron; but according to Numbers, chap. iii., the separation took place before his death.

9.   According to Exodus, God instituted the sabbath because he rested on that day; but according to Deuteronomy, it was because he brought the Israelites out of Egypt "by a stretched-out arm." In Deuteronomy, chap. xiv., every creeping thing that flieth is declared to be unclean, and is forbidden to be eaten; but in Leviticus, chap. xi., every creeping thing, including four kinds of locusts, is allowed, and is prescribed as a part of their food.

10. In Exodus, chap. vi., God is represented as saying, "By my name Jehovah was I not known to them" (the patriarchs). But he was mistaken, for that name occurs frequently in Genesis. In 1 Sam. chap. viii., we are told the name of Samuel's first-born was Joel; and the name of his second, Abiah; but in Chronicles, vi. 28, we are told the name of Samuel's oldest son was Vashni. Which is right?

11. *Bad Bible Morals.* Persons mutilated by accident, or otherwise in helpless condition, were excluded from the congregation of the Lord, while the guilty culprits who caused this mutilation were allowed free access to the holy sanctuary. (See Lev. xxi.) We consider this bad morality. Innocent base-born children were also excluded from the temple, while the guilty parents were allowed free admission.

12. By the law of Moses and the will of God, as is claimed, parents were required to stone rebellious children to death; and yet the parents were often the cause of this rebellious disposition, and tenfold more guilty than the children, having corrupted them by bad influences. (See Deut. xxi.) This is a specimen of Bible justice and Bible morality.

13. *The Jews not Civilized.* The Lord's chosen people possessed so little of the element of civilization, they had to go to the King of Tyre to

hire artisans and skilled workmen to build their temple. (See 2 Chron. ii. 3, and 1 Kings v. 6.)

14. It is stated that it took one hundred and fifty-three thousand men seven years to build Solomon's temple—and heathen at that. (See 2 Chron. ii. 17, 18.) Strange, indeed, when it was only a hundred and ten feet long, thirty-six feet wide, and fifty-five feet high! (1 Kings vi. 2.) Some of our modern churches are much larger buildings, and generally erected in less than a year by less than a dozen workmen. It is certainly very damaging to the exalted pretensions of "the Lord's peculiar people" that they possessed minds and intelligence so far below the heathen, that no workmen could be found amongst them, and they had consequently to go to these same heathen to hire workmen to build the Lord's house. Such facts sink the reputation both of them and their God.

CHAPTER 22

TWO HUNDRED AND SEVENTY-SEVEN
BIBLE CONTRADICTIONS

It is difficult to conceive how any real benefit or any reliable instruction can be derived from a book which contains statements with respect to doctrines or matters of fact that are contradicted on the next page, or in some other portion of the book; because it not only confuses the mind of the reader, but renders it impossible for him to know, as he reads a statement in one chapter of the book, that it is not contradicted and nullified in some other chapter, until he has sacrificed sufficient time to commit the whole book to memory; and but few persons have ever achieved that herculean task. Hence, it must be an unreliable book as an authority. We know it has been stated by many admirers of the "Holy Book" that it contains no conflicting statements when properly understood. But who is to decide when it is properly understood? Here, again, is a conflict of ideas. All words have certain specific meanings attached to them by common consent. And certainly any man of good sense would not attempt to attach any other meaning to them, without stating the fact and clearly defining his new meaning, if he expects any reader to understand him, or any two readers to understand him alike; and if he writes without giving a hint that he has invented or employed new meanings for the words he uses, we are compelled to assume that his words and language have the ordinary and universally adopted signification. With this view of the case (as the writers of the Bible have given no hint that they employed new meanings), it is false to assume or say there are no contradictions in the Bible, when, if we accept language with its ordinary and established signification, an honest and unbiased investigation will show that it contains several thousand statements which conflict with each other or with science, history, or moral truth, and hence must be totally unreliable as an authority. To prove this, we will now enter upon the unpleasant task of arranging and classifying a large number of these contradictions found both in the Old and New Testaments.

CONTRADICTIONS IN MATTERS OF FACT AND IN DOCTRINES

1. Was it death to eat the forbidden fruit? Yes: "In the day thou eatest thereof thou shalt surely die" (Gen. ii. 17). No: "And all the days of Adam were nine hundred and thirty years" (Gen. v. 5).

2. Can a woman, according to scripture, ever speak on religious matters? Yes: "The same man had four daughters—virgins—who did prophesy" (Act. xxi. 9). No: "I suffer not a woman to teach, but to be in silence" (1 Tim. ii. 2).

3.   Should a man ever laugh? Yes: "There is a time to weep and a time to laugh" (Eccles. iii. 4). No: "Sorrow is better than laughter" (Eccles. 3). Yes: "I commend mirth, because a man hath no better thing under the sun than to eat, drink, and be merry" (Eccles. vii. 15).

4.   What is our moral duty relative to trimming the hair on our head? "There shall no razor come upon his head, ... let the locks of his head grow" (Num. vi. 5). "If a man have long hair, it is a shame unto him" (1 Cor. xi. 14).

5.   Is there any remedy for a fool? Yes: "The rod of correction will drive it far from him" (Prov. xxii. 15). No: "Though thou bray a fool in a mortar, yet will his foolishness not depart from him" (Prov. xxvi. 6).

6.   Should we pay a fool in his own coin? Yes: "Answer a fool according to his folly" (Prov. xxvi. 5). No: "Answer not a fool according to his folly" (Prov. xxvi. 6).

7.   Is man's life threescore years and ten? Yes: "The days of our years are threescore years and ten" (Ps. xc. 10). No: "His days shall be a hundred and twenty years" (Gen. vi. 3).

8.   Is it desirable to be tempted? Yes: "Count it all joy to be tempted" (Jas. i. 2). No: "Watch and pray, that ye enter not into temptation" (Matt. xxvi. 41).

9.   Which is the tempter, God or the devil? The devil: The devil tempted Christ and Judas. (See Matt. iv. 1.) God: God tempted David (2 Sam. xxiv. 1).

10. Does the Lord ever tempt man? No: "Neither tempteth he any man" (Jas. i. 13). Yes: "And God did tempt Abraham" (Gen. xxii. 1). No: "He blinded their eyes, and hardened their hearts" (John xii. 40).

11. Can God be tempted? No: "God can not be tempted" (Jas. i. 13). Yes: "They have tempted me, the Lord, ten times" (Num. xiv. 22).

12. It anything good? Yes: Everything (1 Tim. iv. 4). No: "Every thing is corrupt" (Gen. vi. 12).

13. How many Gods are there? One: "The Lord our God is one Lord" (Deut. vi. 4). Several: "Let us make man in our own image" (Gen. i. 26). Three: "There are three that bear record in heaven, Father, Son, and Holy Ghost:" (1 John v. 7).

14. Is God omnipresent? Yes: David declares the Loud is everywhere, in heaven and earth, and even in hell (Ps. cxxxix. 7). No: "The Lord came down to see Sodom"(Gen. xviii. 20). Yes: "There is no place where the workers of iniquity can hide themselves" (Job xxxiv. 22). No: "Adam and Eve hid themselves from the presence of the Lord" (Gen. iii. 8). No: "Cain fled from the presence of God" (Gen. iv. l6). Yes: "Man can not get out of his presence" (Ps. cxxxix. 7).

Bible Contradictions

15. Is God omniscient? Yes: "He knoweth the hearts of all men" (Acts i. 24). No: "The Lord had to prove the Israelites, and also Abraham, to know what was in their hearts" (Deut. viii. and Gen. xxii).

16. Is God omnipotent? Yes: "With God all things are possible" (Matt. xix. 26). No: "He could not drive out the inhabitants of the valley, because their chariots were made of iron" (Judg. i. 19).

17. Is God unchangeable? Yes: With him "there is no variableness, neither shadow of turning; I change not" (Mal. iii. 6). No: "And the Lord repented of the evil he said he would inflict upon the Ninevites" (Jon. iii. 10).

18. Is God a merciful being? Yes: "The Lord is very pitiful, and full of mercy" (Jas. v. 11). No: "I will not pity nor spare, nor have mercy, but destroy" (Jer. xiii 14). Yes: "His tender mercies are over all his works" (Ps. cxlv. 9). No: "Have no pity on them, but slay both man and woman, infant and suckling" (Sam. xv. 2). Yes: "His mercy endureth forever" (1 Chron. xvi. 34). No: "I have taken away my loving-kindness and mercies" (Jer. xvi. 3).

19. Does God ever hate? No: "God is love" (1 John iv. 16). Yes: "He hated his own inheritance" (Ps. cvi. 40).

20. Is God's anger perpetual? No: "His anger endureth but a moment" (Ps. xxx. 5). Yes: "Mine anger shall burn for ever" (Jer. xvii. 4).

21. Is God the author of evil? Yes: "I make peace, and I create evil" (Isa. xiv. 7). No: "Out of his mouth proceeds not evil" (Lam. iii. 38).

22. Is God in favor of war? No: "He is the God of peace." Yes: "The Lord is a man of war" (Exod. xv. 3). No: "He is not the author of confusion, but of peace" (1 Cor. xiv. 33).

23. Is the spirit of God for peace? Yes: It is "love, peace, joy, gentleness, and goodness" (Gal. v. 22). No: "The spirit of the Lord came upon him, and he slew a thousand men" (Judg. xv. 16). Yes: "The spirit of the Lord begets love, peace, and goodness" (Gal. v. 22). No: "By the spirit of the Lord Samson slew thirty men" (Judg. xiv. 19).

24. Has any man seen God? Yes: "Moses, Aaron, Nadab, and Abihu, and the seven elders of Israel" saw the God of Israel (Exod. xxiv. 9). No: "No man hath seen God at any time" (John i. 18). Yes: "I have seen God face to face, and my life has been preserved" (Gen. xxxii. 30). No. "There shall no man see me, and live" (Exod. xxxiii. 20). Yes: "I saw also the Lord standing upon the throne" (Isa. vi. 1). No: "Ye have never seen his shape" (John v. 37).

25. Can any man hear God's voice? Yes: "I heard thy voice in the garden" (Gen. iii. 9). No: "Ye have never heard his voice at any time" (John v. 37).

26. Does God dwell in light? Yes: "He dwelleth in light which no man can approach to" (1 Tim. vi. 16). No: "The Lord said he would dwell in thick darkness" (1 Kings viii. 12).

27. Does God dwell in temples? Yes: "I have chosen this [Solomon's] temple for a house" (2 Chron. viii. 16). No: "The Most High dwelleth not in temples made with hands" (Acts xvii. 24).

28. Does God ever tire? Yes: "God rested, and was refreshed" (Exod. xxxi. 17). No: "God fainteth not, neither is he weary" (Isa. xl. 28).

29. Is God a respecter of persons? No: "There is no respect of persons with God" (Rom. ii. 11). Yes: "And God had respect to Abel and his offering" (Gen.).

30. Can God always be found? Yes: "Those who seek me early shall find me" (Prov. viii. 17). No: "They shall seek me early, but shall not find me" (Prov. i. 28).

31. Does the Lord believe in burnt offerings? No: "I delight not in the blood of *bullocks* or of lambs or of he-goats" (Isa. i. 11). Yes: "Thou shalt offer every day a *bullock* for a sin-offering" (Exod. xxix. 36).

32. Does the Lord believe in animal sacrifices of any kind? No: "Your burnt offerings are not acceptable, nor your sacrifices sweet unto me" (Jer. vi. 20). Yes: "Burnt sacrifices are sweet unto the Lord" (Lev. i. 9).

33. Does God believe in human sacrifices? No: For he condemned the human sacrifices of the Gentiles. (See Deut. xii. 30.) Yes: "For his anger was abated by David's hanging his five sons of Michal in the hill before the Lord." (See 2 Sam. xxi. 8 and Judg. xi. 30.)

34. Does God ever repent? Yes: "It repenteth the Lord that he had made man" (Gen. vi. 6). No: "The Lord is not a man that he should repent" (Num. xxiii. 19).

35. Is all scripture given by inspiration of God? Yes: "All scripture is given by inspiration of God" (2 Tim. iii. 16). No: "I speak it not after the Lord" (2 Cor. xi. 17).

36. Is war and fighting right? No: "They that take the sword shall perish with the sword" (Matt. xxvi. 52). Yes: "He that hath no sword, let him sell his coat and buy one" (Luke xxii. 36). No: "Beat your swords into plowshares, and your spears into pruning-hooks" (Mic. iv. 3). Yes: "Beat your plowshares into swords and your pruning-hooks into spears" (Joel iii. 10). Yes: "Cursed be he who keepeth back his sword from blood" (Jer. xiviii. 10).

37. Shall nation war against nation? Yes: "Nation shall rise up against nation" (Matt. xxiv. 7). No: "Nation shall not rise up against nation" (Mic. iv. 3).

38. Shall we love our enemies? Yes: "Love your enemies" (Luke vi. 27). No: "Bring my enemies, and slay them before me" (Luke xix. 27).

39. Is hatred right? No: "Whosoever hateth his brother is a murderer" (1 John iii. 15). Yes: "You must hate father and mother, brother and sister, etc., or ye can not be true followers of Christ" (Luke xiv. 26).

40. Is anger commended? Yes: "Be ye angry, and sin not" (Eph. iv. 26). No: "Anger resteth in the bosom of fools" (Eccles. vii. 9).

41. Is it right to steal and rob? No: "Thou shalt not steal" (Exod. xx. 15); "Neither rob" (Lev. xix. 13). Yes: The Israelites took from the Egyptians "jewels of silver and jewels of gold, and raiment, and they spoiled the Egyptians" (Exod. xii. 35).

42. Is it right to kill? No: "Thou shalt not kill" (Exod. xx. 13). Yes: "Kill every male child amongst them." Yes: "Go ye out and slay every man his companion, and every man his neighbor, and every man his brother" (Exod. xxxii. 27).

43. Is it right to lie on any occasion? No: "All liars are to be punished with fire and brimstone" (Rev. xxi. 8). Yes: "Go put a lying spirit into the mouths of all the prophets" (1 Kings xxii. 21). No: "Lying lips are an abomination to the Lord" (Prov. xii. 22). Yes: "The harlot Rahab lied, and was justified by works" (Jas. ii. 25). No: "Say nothing but the truth" (2 Chron. xviii. 15). Yes: "If the truth of God hath more abounded through my lie for his glory, why am I adjudged a sinner?" (Rom. iii. 7).

44. Is God in favor of lying and deception? No: "Thou shalt not bear false witness" (Exod. 20). Yes: "If a prophet is deceived, I the Lord deceived that prophet" (Ezek. xiv. 9).

45. Is a pious life a happy life? Yes: "Come unto me, and I will give you rest" (Matt xi. 28). No: "In this world ye shall have tribulation" (John xvi. 33).

46. Will righteousness make a man happy? Yes: "There shall no evil happen to the just" (Prov. xii. 21). No: "It is through much tribulation the righteous enter the kingdom of heaven" (Acts xiv. 21). Yes: "The righteous shall flourish"(Ps. xcii. 12). No: "The righteous shall perish" (Isa. lvii. 1). Yes: "The prayer of the righteous availeth much" (Jas. v.16). No: 'There is none righteous; no, not one" (Rom. iii 10). Yes: The righteous to be slain with the wicked (Ezek. xxi. 3). No: The "righteous not to be slain" (Exod. xxiii. 7).

47. Can we live without sinning? Yes: "Those born of God can not sin" (1 John iii. 9). No: "There is no man that sinneth not" (1 Kings viii. 46). Yes: "He that committeth sin is of the devil" (1 John iii. 8). No: "There are none that doeth good, and sinneth not" (Eccles. vii. 20).

48. Does wickedness shorten a man's life? Yes: "The years of the wicked shall be shortened" (Prov. x. 27). No: "The wicked live, and became old" (Job xxi. 7).

Shall we resist evil? Yes: "Put away the evil of your doings" (Isa. i. 16). No: "Resist not evil" (Matt. v. 37).

49. Who can know whether the golden rule a right or wrong? Right: "Whatsoever ye would that men should do unto you, do you even so unto them" (Matt. vii. 12). Wrong: "Spare them not, but slay both man and woman, infant and suckling" (1 Sam. xv. 3).

50. Is wisdom desirable? Yes: "Happy is the man that findeth wisdom (Prov. iii. 13). No: "Much wisdom is much grief, and he that increaseth knowledge increaseth sorrow" (Eccles. i. 18). Yes: "Get wisdom with all thy getting" (Prov. iv. 7). Yes: "Be wise as serpents" (Matt. x. 16). No: "The wisdom of the wise shall be destroyed" (Cor. i. 19).

51. Shall we aim at a good reputation? Yes: "A good name is better than riches" (Prov. xxii. 1). No: "Woe unto you when all men speak well of you" (Luke vi. 26).

52. Are riches desirable? Yes: "The rich man's wealth is his strong City" (Prov. x. 15). No: "Woe unto you that are rich" (Luke vi. 24). Yes: "Blessed is the man that feareth the Lord, ... wealth and riches shall be in his house" (Ps. cxii.). No: "Blessed be ye poor, for yours is the kingdom of God" (Luke vi. 20).

53. Can a righteous man be rich, or a rich man be saved? Yes: "In the house of the righteous is much treasure" (Prov. xv. 6). No: "It is easier for a camel to go through the eye of a needle, than for a rich man to enter the kingdom of God" (Matt. xix. 24).

54. Does the Lord believe in riches? Yes: "The Lord blessed Job with fourteen thousand sheep, and six thousand camels, and a thousand yoke of oxen," etc. (Job xiii. 12). No: "A rich man can not enter into the kingdom of heaven" (Matt. xix. 24). Yes: "Wealth and riches shall be in the house of the man that feareth God" (Ps. cxii. 1). No: "Lay not up for yourselves treasures on earth" (Matt. vi. 19).

55. Shall we use strong drink? No: "Wine is a mocker, and strong drink is raging" (Prov. xx. 1). Yes: "Give strong drink to him that is ready to perish" (Prov. xxxi. 6).

56. Should we ever use wine? No: "Do not use wine nor strong drink" (Lev. x. 9). Yes: "Use a little wine for the stomach's sake" (Tim. v. 23). No: "Look not upon the wine when it is red" (Prov. xxiii. 31). Yes: "Give wine to him that is of heavy heart" (Prov. xxxi. 6).

57. Is it right to eat all kinds of animal? Yes: "There is nothing unclean of itself; eat every moving thing" (Gen. ix. 3). No: "Swine, hares, and camel are unclean; ye shall not eat of their flesh" (Deut. xiv. 7).

58. Is it good to eat flesh? Yes: It is good to eat flesh (Deut. xii. 20). No: It is not good to eat flesh (Rom. xiv. 21).

59. Is man justified by works? Yes: "Abraham was justified by works" (Jas. ii. 21). No: "A man can not be justified by works" (Gal. ii. 16).

60. Is man saved by faith? Yes: "Man is saved by faith without works" (Rom. iii 28). No: "Man can not be justified by faith without works" (Jas. ii. 24).

61. Should our works be seen? Yes: "Let your light shine before men" (Matt. v. 16). No: "Do not your alms before men" (Matt. vi. 1).

62. Is public prayer right? No: "Enter into thy closet, and shut thy door" (Matt. vi. 6). Yes: "Solomon prayed before all the congregation" (1 Kings viii. 22).

63. How can it be a moral duty to pray, there being no certainty of an answer? "Every one that asketh receiveth" (Matt. vii. 8). "They that seek me early shall find me" (Prov. viii. 17). "Then shall they call upon me, but I will not answer; they shall seek me early, but shall not find me" (Prov. i. 28).

64. Is man to be rewarded in this life? Yes: Both the righteous and the wicked are to be rewarded on earth (Prov. xi. 31). No: They are to be rewarded after death (Matt. xvi. 27).

65. Are children punished for the sins of their parents? Yes: "The iniquities of the father are visited upon the children" (Exod. xx. 5). No: "The son shall not bear the iniquity of the father" (Ezek. xviii. 20).

66. Should marriage be encouraged? Yes: "Marriage is honorable to all" (Heb. xiii. 4). No: "It is good for a man not to touch a woman" (1 Cor. vii. 1).

67. Is divorce wrong according to the Bible? Right: "If thou have no delight in her (thy wife), then thou shalt let her go" (Deut. xxi. 11). Wrong: "Whosoever shall put away his wife, saving for the crime of fornication, causeth her to commit adultery" (Matt. v. 32).

68. Is it right to marry a brother's widow? Yes: "If a man die childless, his brother shall marry his widow" (Deut. xxv. 5). No: "To marry a brother's widow is an unclean thing" (Lev. xx. 21).

69. Is it ever right to marry a sister? No: "Cursed shall he be who does so" (Deut. xxvii. 22). Yes: "Abraham married his sister, and was blessed" (Gen. xx. 2).

70. Does the Bible allow adultery? No: "Whoremongers and adulterers God will judge" (Heb. xiii. 4). Yes: "The Lord commanded Hosea to takes a wife of whoredom" (Hos. i. 2).

71. Is fornication sinful? Yes: "You should abstain from fornication" (1 Thess iv. 3). No: "Every woman who hath not known man by lying with him, save for yourselves" (Num. xxxi. 18).

72. Should we always obey kings and rulers? Yes: "To resist [them] is to resist the ordinance of God" (Rom. xiii. 3). No: "Whether it is right to obey God or man, judge ye." Yes: "Submit yourselves to every ordinance of man for the Lord's sake" (1 Pet. ii. 14). "Whatsoever they bid you observe, that observe and do" (Matt. xxiii. 3). No: "We ought to obey God rather than man" (Acts v. 29).

73. Is the obedience of servants a duty? Yes: "Servants, obey your master" (Col. iii. 22). No: "Be ye not the servants of men" (1 Cor. vii. 23).

74. Is slavery right? No: "Be not called master"; "Break every yoke" (Isa. lviii. 6). Yes: "Ye shall buy of the children of the stranger, etc., and they shall be your possession" (Lev. xxv. 46). No: "Proclaim liberty throughout all the land" (Lev. xxv. 10).

75. Who can tell if baptism is an obligatory ordinance? Yes: "Go ye and teach all nations, baptizing them" (Matt. xxviii. 19). No: "Christ sent me not to baptize, but to preach the gospel" (1 Cor. i. 17).

76. Is image-making right? No: "Ye shall make no image of any thing" (Exod. xx. 4). Yes: "Moses made an image of a serpent" (Num. xxi. 9).

77. Is circumcision right? Yes: Except ye be circumcised after the manner of men, ye can not be saved" (Acts xv. 1). No: "If ye be circumcised, Christ shall profit you nothing" (Gal. v. 2). Yes: "Ye must be circumcised" (Acts xv. 24). No. "Circumcision is nothing" (Cor. vii. 19).

78. Is it right to swear? No: "Swear not at all" (Matt. v. 35). Yes: God swore eleven times, says the Bible.

79. Why was the sabbath instituted? Because "God rested on the sabbath day" (Exod. xx. 11). Because "he delivered his people on that day" (Deut. vi. 15).

80. Is it right to observe the sabbath? Yes: "Remember the sabbath day to keep it holy." No: "Your new moons and your sabbaths, … I can not away with. It is iniquity" (Isa. i. 12).

81. Is it right to judge? Yes: "Judge righteous judgment" (John vii. 24). No: "Judge not, that ye be not judged" (Matt. vii. 2).

82. Can a man work miracles without divine aid? No: "No man can work such miracles except God be with him" (John iii. 2). Yes: "The Egyptians did in like manner with their enchantments" (Exod. vii. 10).

83. Can any man ascend to heaven? Yes: "Elijah ascended in a chariot of fire" (2 Kings ii. 11). No: "No man hath ascended up to heaven" (John iii. 13). Yes: "All men must see death" (Heb. ix. 27). No: "Enoch did not see death" (Heb. xi. 5).

84. Should we fear death? Yes: "Christ walked not in Jewry because the Jews sought to kill him" (John vii. 1). No: "Fear not them that kill the body" (Matt. x. 28).

85. Will the earth ever be destroyed? Yes: "The earth also shall be burned up" (2 Pet. iii. 10). No: "But the earth abideth for ever" (Eccles. i. 4).

86. Does the Bible teach a future life? Yes: "They shall go away into everlasting punishment" (Matt. xxv. 46). No: "For that which befalleth men befalleth beasts; ... as the one dieth, so dieth the other," etc. (Eccles. iii. 19).

87. Does the Bible teach a future resurrection? Yes: "The dead shall be raised" (Cor. xv. 52). No: "They shall not rise" (Isa. xxvi. 14). Yes: "The saints came up out of the ground" (Matt. xxvii. 52) No: "Those who go down into the grave never come up again" (Job vii. 9).

88. Are the actions of men ever to be judged according to the Bible? First, "The Father judgeth no man" (John v. 22). Second, "I [Jesus Christ] judge no man" (John viii. 15). So there is to be no judgment.

89. No: "God saw every thing was corrupt" (Gen. vi. 11). Yes: "God saw every thing he had made was good" (Gen. i. 31).

90. Yes: "God forgives the sinner" (Jer. xxxi. 34). No: "God kills the sinner" (Ezek. xviii. 20).

91. Yes: "God justifies the ungodly" (Rom. iv. 5). No: "God will not clear the guilty" (Exod. xxxiv. 7).

92). Yes: "Man is justified by the law" (Rom. ii. 13). No: "Man can not justified by the law" (Gal. iii. 11).

93. Yes: "Many have sinned without the law" (Rom. ii. 12). No: "Where there is no law there is no transgression" (Rom. iv. 18).

94. Yes: "Heaven is a kingdom that can not be moved" (Heb. xii. 18). No: "I will shake heaven and earth" (Heb. xii. 26).

95. Yes: "Every thing is afraid of man" (Gen. i. 28). No: "The lion is not afraid of man" (Prov. xxx. 30).

96. Yes: "Every man in his own tongue" (Gen. x. 5). No: "The whole earth one tongue" (Gen. xi. 1).

97. Yes: "All things are become new" (2 Cor. v. 17). No: "There is nothing new under the sun" (Eccles. i. 9).

98. Yes: "You shall make a likeness of a serpent and a cherubim" (Exod. xxv. 18). No: "Make no likeness of any thing in heaven above or the earth beneath," etc. (Exod. xx. 4).

99. Yes: "Deborah the prophetess judged Israel" (Judg. iv. 4). No: "A women is not to judge or rule a man" (1 Tim. ii. 12).

100. Yes: "God's people shall be ashamed" (Hos. x. 6). No: "God's people shall never be ashamed" (Ps. xxxvii. 19).

101. Yes: "Blessed are the fruitful" (Gen. i. 28). No: "Blessed are the barren" (Luke xxiii. 29).

102. Yes: "Edom being thy brother, do not abhor him" (Deut. xxiii. 7). No: "He slew of Edom ten thousand" (2 Kings xiv. 7).

103. Yes: "Bear ye one another's burdens" (Gal. vi. 2). No: "Every man must bear his own burden" (Gal. vi. 5).

104. Yes: "Labor not for meat" (John vi. 27). No: "He that labors not shall not eat" (2 Thess. iii. 10).

105. In Genesis vi. 5, God declared he would pour out his curses because "the imagination of man's heart is evil, and only evil continually." In Genesis viii. 21, he gives the same reason for not cursing the world.

And these are mere specimens of a vast number of similar kind. Kings and Chronicles especially are full of such discrepancies of dates, numbers, names, etc. In one case, the author of Chronicles makes a son two years older than his father, the father being forty and the son forty-two. For proof, compare 2 Chron. xxi. 20 with xxii. 1, 2. And observe, the author of 2 Chron. xvi. 1 has Baasha, King of Israel, fighting against Judah ten years after the author of 1 Kings xvi. 8 has him dead and buried. But we have not space to spare to continue the list, as it would comprise a large chapter. Let the reader compare the names and numbers of the leaders, families, tribes, etc., of the children of Israel, as recorded by Ezra (chap. ii.), with those of Nehemiah (chap. vii.), and he will find more than a dozen discrepancies and contradictions; the difference amounting in some cases to thousands. He will also find a difference with respect to the coronation, period of rule, and termination of the reign of various kings, and wide differences tracing genealogic families, tribes, etc., if he will compare Kings, Chronicles, Samuel, Ezra, Nehemiah, etc. Such are the verbal discrepancies of the "Word of God"; such is arithmetic when "inspired."

Two questions upon the above: 1. How much older can a son be than his father according to scripture, basing the inquiry upon Chron. xxi. and xxii.? 2. How long can a man continue to fight after he is dead and buried, as is illustrated in the case of Baasha, King of Israel? (See contradictions 142, 143, and 144.)

Bible Contradictions

CONTRADICTIONS IN HISTORY

106. When was man created? Gen. i. 25 says after the other animals. Gen. ii. 18 says before the other animals.

107. Were seed-time and harvest to be perpetual? Yes: "Seed-time and harvest shall not cease" (Gen. viii. 22). No: "There was neither earing nor harvest" for five years (Gen. xiv. 6).

108. Did Eve see before she ate the forbidden fruit? Yes: "Woman saw before she ate the fruit" (Gen. iii. 6). No: "Her eyes were opened by eating the fruit" (Gen. iii. 7).

109. When did the earth become dry after the flood? "In the first month the waters of the flood were dried up" (Gen. viii. 13). "In the second month the waters of the flood were dried up" (Gen. viii. 12).

110. How old was Abraham when he left Haran? The eleventh chapter of Genesis makes him one hundred and thirty-five years old, but the twelfth says he was only seventy-five.

111. Did Abraham know where he was going? Yes: "He went forth to go into the land of Canaan" (Gen. xii. 5). No: "He went out, not knowing whither he went" (Heb. xi. 8).

112. Did God give Abraham land? Yes: "I give it to thy seed for ever" (Gen. xiii. 15). No: "Abraham had none inheritance in it, not so much as to set his foot on" (Acts vii. 5).

113. Did Moses fear Pharaoh? Yes: "Moses fled, fearing Pharaoh" (Exod. ii. 14 and 18). No: "Moses did not fear Pharaoh" (Heb. xi. 21).

114. Who hardened Pharaoh's heart? "The Lord hardened the heart of Pharaoh" (Exod. ix. 12). "Pharaoh hardened his heart" (Exod. viii. 15).

115. How many fighting men in Israel? Samuel says eight hundred thousand (2 Sam. xxiv. 9). Chronicles says one million one hundred thousand (1 Chron. xxi. 5).

116. How many fighting men in Judah? Samuel says five hundred thousand (2 Sam. xxiv. 9). Chronicles says four hundred and seventy thousand (1 Chron. xxi. 5).

117. Who moved David to number Israel? God: "The Lord moved David to number Israel" (2 Sam. xxiv. 1). The devil: "Satan provoked him to do it" (Chron. xxi. 1).

118. Did David sin more than once? Yes: "I have sinned greatly in numbering Israel" (2 Sam. xxiv. 10). No: "He sinned only when he killed Uriah" (1 Kings xv. 5).

119. How many years of famine was David to suffer? Chronicles says it was three years (1 Chron. xxi. 11). Samuel says it was seven years (2 Sam. xxiv. 13).

120.How many horsemen did David capture? Samuel says it was seven hundred (2 Sam. viii. 4). Chronicles says it was seven thousand (1 Chron. xviii. 4).

121.What did David pay for his threshing-floor? Samuel says fifty shekels of silver (2 Sam. xxiv. 24). Chronicles says six hundred shekels of gold (1 Chron. xxi. 25).

122.Was David's throne to come to an end? No: "It shall be established for ever" (Ps. lxxxix 4). Yes: "It was cast down to the ground" (Ps. lxxxix. 44).

123.Was David really a man after God's own heart? Yes: "David was a man after God's own heart" (Acts xiii. 22). No: "David displeased the Lord" (2 Sam. xi. 24).

124.Was it a man or God that Job wrestled with? "Jacob wrestled all night with a man" (Gen. xxxii. 24). "Jacob wrestled all night with God" (Gen. xxxii. 30).

125.How many were there of Jacob's family? "Jacob's family was only seventy souls" (Gen. xlvi. 27). "Jacob's family was seventy-five souls" (Acts vii. 14).

126.How long was Israel in Egypt? "Israel was four hundred and thirty years in Egypt" (Exod. xii. 41). "Jacob was only four hundred years in Egypt" (Acts vii. 6).

127.Did they see what the Lord did in Egypt? Yes: "You have seen all the Lord did in Egypt" (Deut. xxix. 2). No: "You have seen nothing he did in Egypt" (Deut. xxix. 4).

128.Who was the father of Salah? Arphaxad (Gen. xi. 12). Cainan (Luke iii. 35).

129.Had Michal any children? No: "Michal had no children unto the day of her death" (2 Sam. vi. 23). Yes: "The five sons of Michal" (2 Sam. xxi. 8).

130.Where was the law written? Exodus says it was written on Mt. Sinai. Deuteronomy says it was written on Mt. Horeb.

131.How many died of the plague? Numbers says it was twenty and four thousand (Num. xxv. 9). Corinthians says three and twenty thousand (1 Cor. x. 8).

132.When did Zachariah begin to reign? "In the thirty-eighth year of Azariah" (2 Kings xv. 8). But a comparison of 2 Kings xiv. 29 and xv. 1 makes but fourteen years.

133.How many stalls for horses had Solomon? We are told in 1 Kings iv. 26 he had forty thousand. But according to 2 Chron. ix. 25, it was only four thousand.

134. How much oil did Solomon give Hiram? According to King v. 11, it was twenty measures. But according to Chron. ii 10, it was twenty thousand.

135. Of what tribe was Solomon's artificer, who came from Tyre? According to 1 Kings vii. 14, he was of the tribe of Naphthall. But according to 2 Chron. ii. 14, he was of the tribe of Dan.

136. How long were the two pillars of Solomon's porch? According to 1 Kings vii. 15, they were eighteen cubits long. But according to 2 Chron. iii. 15, they were thirty-five cubits long.

137. How many baths were contained in the brazen sea? According to 1 Kings vii. 26, it contained two thousand. But according to 2 Chron. iv. 5, three thousand.

138. How many mothers had Abijah and who was she? According to 1 Kings xv. 2, she was the daughter of Abishalom. But 2 Chron. xi. 20 says she was the daughter of Absalom; and 2 Chron. xiii. 2 says she was the daughter of Uriel.

The chronology of the kings of Judah and Israel are a mass of confusion.

139. Where was Ahaziah killed, and how often? According to 2 Chron. xxii. 8, he was killed at Samaria; and according to 2 Kings ix. 27, he was killed again.

140. How many did Jashobeam kill? "Jashobeam slew eight hundred at one time" (2 Sam. xxiii. 8). No: It was only three hundred he slew (1 Chron. xi. 11).

141. Who killed the Amalekites? Samuel says "Saul utterly destroyed them" (1 Sam. xv. 3). But according to chapter twenty-seven of the same book, David killed them all, "left neither man nor woman" (1 Sam. xv. 13). And yet it appears they were not well killed; for, forty years after, they fought a battle with Ziklag (see 1 Sam. xxx. 18), and they were all killed again, "save four hundred young men," and Simeon afterwards slew them. (See 1 Chron. iv. 3). And yet, although destroyed three times, Josephus says he was a descendant of the Amalekites. They must have been a live people.

142. When did Baasha fight a battle with Judah? According to 2 Chron. xvi. 1, it was in Asa's thirty-sixth year. But according to 1 Kings xvi. 8, in the twenty-sixth year of Asa, Baasha died, or, at least, vacated the throne— a difference of ten years.

143. How did Asa and Baasha stand toward each other? "There was war between Asa and Baasha all their days" (1 Kings xv. 16). But according to Chron. xiv. 1, they were at peace ten years.

144.How long did Baasha reign? "Baasha reigned over Israel twenty-four years" (1 Kings xv. 33). But according to 1 Kings xvi. 8, it was twenty-three years.

145.How long did Elah reign? According to 1 Kings xvi. 8, Elah reigned two years, commencing in Asa's twenty-sixth year.

146.When did Ahaziah begin to reign over Judah? Kings says it was the eleventh year of Joram (2 Kings viii. 16). Kings also says it was the twelfth (2 Kings viii. 25).

147.When did Omri begin to reign? "In the thirty-eighth year of Asa began Omri to reign" (Kings xvi. 15). But as Zimri only reigned seven days, and began in Asa's twenty-seventh year, Omri must also have commenced in his twenty-seventh year.

148.When did Ahab commence his reign? "In the thirty-eighth year of Asa began Ahab, son of Omri, to reign" (1 Kings xvi. 29). How can that be if Omri reigned twelve years? (See 1 Kings xvi. 23.)

149.When Jehoram, son of Ahab, begin to reign? "In the eighteenth year of Jehoshaphat, King of Judah, began Jehoram to reign" (2 King. iii. 1). Impossible, if his son Ahaziah commenced in Jehoshaphat's nineteenth year (see 1 Kings xxii. 51), and reigned two years: seventeen and two are nineteen. And, according to 2 Kings i. 17 and 1 Kings, it was twelve years later, if Jehoshaphat reigned twenty-five years. (See 1 Kings).

150 When did Azziah, or Uzziah, begin to reign? In the twenty-seventh year of Jeroboam, according to 2 Kings xv. 1. But according to 2 Kings xvi. 17 and 23, it was only sixteen years.

151.How long did Jehu reign over Israel? "Jehu reigned over Israel twenty-eight years" (2 Kings x. 36). But according to 2 Kings xiii, 1, he reigned thirty years.

152. How long did Jehoabaz reign? Jehoabaz reigned seventeen years (2 King. xiii. 1). But according to 2 Kings xiii. 10, it was twenty years.

153.How old was Ahaz when he began to reign? Twenty years (2 Kings xvi. 2). According to the text (2 Chron. xxiv. 2), his father was about eleven years old when he was born.

NEW TESTAMENT CONTRADICTIONS

There is a continual conflict in the statements of Christ's biographers with respect to the various events of his life as compared with each other; and in some cases they contradict themselves. We will present some examples:

154.Who came to worship Christ when he was born? Matthew says, "wise men from the East" (Matt. ii. 5). Luke says they were shepherds of the same country (Luke ii. 8).

114

155.How were they led? Matthew says they were led by a star (Matt. ii. 6). Luke says by an angel (Luke ii. 3).

156.What did the parents of Jesus do when he was born? Matthew (ii. 13) says they fled into Egypt. But according to Luke (ii. 26), they stayed there forty-one days.

157.To whom did God speak at Christ's baptism? To him: "Thou art my beloved son" (Luke iii. 22. To the bystanders: "This is my beloved son" (Matt. iii. 17).

158.Where did Christ go after being baptized? Mark says he went immediately into the wilderness, and was there forty days and (Mark i. 12). John says three days after he was in Cana (John ii. 12).

159.Where was John while Christ was in Galilee? "John was put in prison" (before that) (Mark i. 14). "John was baptizing in Aenon" (John iii. 23).

160.Where was Christ when he called Peter and Andrew? Matthew and Mark say, "walking by the Sea of Galilee." Luke says, "sitting in their ship" (Luke v. 10).

161.Where were Peter and Andrew at the time? Matthew and Mark say, "in their ship, fishing." Luke says, out "washing their nets" (Luke v. 2).

162. How came Peter and Andrew to follow Jesus? Matthew and Mark say he "called them." But according to Luke the draught of fishes caused them to go.

163.Where did Christ heal the leper? Matthew says at the mount, after the sermon (viii. 2). Mark says when preaching in Galilee.

164.Who told Jesus the centurion's servant was sick? Luke says he sent the elders of Israel to tell him (Luke vii. 3). But Matthew says the centurion went himself (Matt. viii. 5).

165 Where did Christ go after curing Peter's wife's mother? Matthew says beyond the lake, and drowned a herd of swine (viii. 18). Luke says to Nain, and raised the dead (Luke vii. 11).

166.Where did Christ drown the swine with devils? Matthew says in the country of Gergesenes. Mark and Luke say in the country of Gadarenes.

167.Where did the devils remonstrate against going? Mark (v. 10) says against being sent out of the country. Luke (viii. 31) says it was against going into the deep.

168.Were Christ's disciples allowed to use staves? Yes: "Take nothing … save a staff only" (Mark vi. 8). No: "Take neither shoes or yet staves" (Matt x. 9).

169. When did Christ pluck the ears of corn? Matthew (xii. 1) says after he had appointed his twelve disciples. But Luke and Mark make it before that event.

170.What woman interceded for her daughter? "A woman of Canaan ... cried unto him" (Matt. xv. 22). The woman was a Greek (Mark vii. 26).

171.How great was the multitude that Jesus fed with seven loaves and a few fishes? Matthew says four thousand, besides women and children (xv. 38). Mark says four thousand in all (viii. 9).

172.How long was it after Christ was transfigured that he took James and John up into the mountain? Six days after (Matt. xvii. 4). Eight days after (Lake ix. 28).

173.How much power did Jesus say faith as big as a grain of mustard-seed can impart? Matthew (xvii. 20) says enough to remove mountains. Luke says (xvii. 6) enough to pluck up trees by the roots. Both large jobs for one man.

174.Who asked seats in the kingdom for Zebedee's children? Matthew says (xx. 20) it was their mother. Mark says (x. 35) they asked it themselves. Why did he refuse them two seats when he promised them, with the other ten disciples, twelve thrones? (Matt. xix. 28.)

175.How many blind men did Jesus restore near Jericho? Matthew says (xx. 30) two blind men. Mark and Luke say only one, Bartimeus.

176.Where did he perform this miracle? Matthew says as he was going away from Jericho. Luke says as he was coming into the city (xviii. 35).

177.When did Christ drive out the money-changers? Matthew and Luke say the day he rode into the city. Mark says not until the next day (xi. 11).

178.What did Jesus tell his disciples about the ass? Matthew says (xxi. 2) he told them they would find an ass and colt tied. Mark and Luke say they found tied only a colt. And John says it was a young ass, and Jesus found it himself (xii. 14). Mark and Luke say he rode the colt. But Matthew (xxi. 7) represents him as riding both the ass and the colt.

179.Who answered Christ's question in the parable of the vineyard? Matthew says (xxi. 41) his disciples answered the question. Mark and Luke both say he answered it himself.

180.When did Christ tell the truth about Lazarus? He first said his sickness was not unto death, but afterwards said he was dead.

181.When did the anointment of Christ take place? Matthew says (xxvi. 2) it was two days before the passover. But John says it was six days after (John xii. 1). And Luke makes it much later (viii. 36 and xxii. 1).

182. Where did the anointment take place? Matthew says (xxvi. 6) in the house of Simon the leper. Luke says (vii. 36) in the house of a Pharisee. But, according to John, it was in the house of Lazarus (xii. 1).

183. Where was the ointment poured? Matthew and Mark say on his head. But Luke and John say on his feet.

184. When did Christ say one of his disciples would betray him? Matthew says (xxvi. 21) while they "did eat supper." But according to Luke (xxii. 20), it was after supper was over.

185. Where did Jesus go after supper? John says "over the brook Cedron" (xviii. 1.). But the other three evangelists say to the Mount of Olives.

186. When did Judas betray Christ? John says (xii. 27) after supper he went out and made the bargain. But the other three say it was before supper he made the bargain.

187. Where and to whom did Peter first deny Christ? John says (xviii. 17) to the damsel at the door. The other three say to the men in the hall.

188. To whom was the second denial made? Matthew and Mark say to a maid. Luke says to a man. John says to those who stood by the fire (xviii.).

189. To whom was the third denial made? Matthew and Mark say to those who stood by. John says (xviii.) to the servant of the high priest.

190. Where was Christ crucified? John says at Calvary. The other three say at Golgotha.

191. .At what hour was Christ crucified? Mark says (xv. 25) it was the third hour. But according to John (xix. 14), it was after the sixth hour.

192. How was Christ dressed for the crucifixion? "And put on him a scarlet robe" (Matt. xxvii. 28). "They put on him a purple robe" (John xix. 2).

193. What was the drink offered to Christ at the crucifixion? Mark says it was wine mixed with myrrh (xv. 23). Matthew says it was vinegar mingled with gall. But Luke represents it as being only vinegar (xxiii. 36). Matthew says Christ tasted it; but according to Mark, he did not.

194. Who bore Christ's cross? Matthew says Simon of Cyrene (xxvii. 32). But John says Jesus bore it himself (xix. 17).

195. Which of the thieves reviled him? Mark says both of them (xv. 29). Luke says (xxiii. 39) only one of them, and the other reviled him for it.

196. What were the words of the superscription on the cross? "This is Jesus, the King of the Jews" (Matt. xxvii. 37). "King of the Jews" (Mark xv. 26). "This is the King of the Jews" (Luke xix. 18). "Jesus of Nazareth, the King of the Jews" (John xix. 19). But only one of these can be right.

197.Was it lawful for the Jews to put Christ to death? Yes: "We have a law by which he ought to die" (John xix. 7). No: "It is not lawful to put any man to death" (John xviii. 31).

198.Who came to Christ's sepulcher? Matthew says (xxviii. 1) Mary Magdalene and another Mary. According to John, it was Mary Magdalene only (xx. 1). But Luke says the two Marys and Joanna (xxiv. 10).

199.Was it daylight when they came to the tomb? No: "They came while it was yet dark" (John xx. 1). Yes: "They came at the rising of the sun" (Mark xvi. 2).

200.Whom did the women see at the tomb? Matthew says (xxviii. 1) an angel sitting. Mark says (xvi. 5) a young man. Luke says (xxiv. 4) two men. John says (xx. 12) two angels.

201.Did any of the women enter the sepulcher? Yes: They entered in (Mark xvi. 6). No: They did not (John xx. 2).

202.Who looked into the sepulcher? According to Luke, it was Peter (xxiv. 12). According to John, it was another disciple (xx. 4).

203.Did Peter go into the sepulcher? John says he did go in (xx. 6). According to Luke, he did not (xxiv. 12).

204.Did those who visited the tomb relate the case to anyone? According to Luke, they told the eleven disciples (xxiv. 27). But Mark tells us they said nothing to any man (xvi. 8).

205.To whom did Christ appear after his resurrection? Matthew says to the two Marys (xxviii. 9). Mark says to Mary Magdalene alone (xvi. 9). According to Luke, it was to two of his disciples at Emmaus.

206.When did Christ first appear to his disciples? Matthew says it was at Galilee (Matt. xxviii. 16). Luke says it was at Jerusalem (Luke xxiv. 33).

207.How did Christ's disciples feel when they met him? Luke says they were terrified (xxiv. 37). But John says they were glad (xx. 20).

208.How often did Christ show himself to the disciple? John says, "This is now the third time." But according to the other three, it was the sixth time.

209.Where did Christ part from his disciples? Mark says (xvi. 14) it was at Jerusalem. But according to Luke, it was at Bethany.

210.When did Christ ascend? According to Luke, it was the day of his resurrection (Luke xxiv. 18). John says it was nine days after (John xx. 26). But according to Acts i. 3, it was forty days after.

211.From what place did Christ ascend? Luke says (xxiv. 6) it was from Bethany. Acts says (i. 5) it was from Mount Olivet.

212.Did Christ bear witness of himself? Yes: "I am one that bear witness of myself" (John viii. 18). No: "If I bear witness of myself, my witness is not true" (John v. 21).

213.Could man bear testimony for Christ? Yes: "Ye also shall bear witness" (John xv. 26). No: "I receive not testimony from man" (John v. 23).

214.Did Christ come on a mission of peace? Yes: "To preach glory to God, ... and on earth peace" (Luke ii. 13). No: "I came not to send peace but a sword" (Matt. x. 34).

215.Did Christ have a dwelling-place? No: Matthew says (viii.20), "He had not where to lay his head." But John says he had a house, and his disciples saw it (i. 34).

216.Was Christ the savior? Yes: "Christ is the savior of all men" (1 Tim. iv. 10). No: "Beside me [Jehovah] there is no savior" (Isa. xliii. 11).

217.Was Christ omnipotent? Yes: "I and my Father are one" (John x. 30). No: "My Father is greater than I" (John xiv. 28).

218.Was Christ equal to God? Yes: "He thought it no robbery to be equal with God" (Phil. ii. 6). No: "My Father is greater than I" (John xiv. 28).

219.Was Christ supreme God? Yes: "He was God manifest in the flesh" (1 Tim. iii. 16). No: "He was man approved of God" (Acts ii. 22).

220.How did Judas die? Matthew says he went out and hanged himself (Matt. xxvii. 5). The Acts says he went out and fell headlong (Acts i. 18).

221.Did the men at Paul's conversion hear a voice? Yes: "Hearing a voice, but seeing no man" (Acts ix. 7). No: "They heard not the voice" (Acts xxii. 9).

222.Did John see a book? Yes: "I saw ... a book written within," etc. (Rev. v. 1). No: "No man in heaven or earth could look on the book" (Rev. v. 3).

223.Was John the Baptist Elias? Yes: "This is Elias which was to come" (Matt. xi. 14). No: "And he said I am not Elias" (John i. 21).

224.When did Herodias ask for the head of John the Baptist? Matthew says before Herod's great promise to her; but Mark says it was after (Mark vi. 24).

225.Is the law of Moses superseded? Yes: "We are delivered from the law" (Rom. vii. 6). No: "I came not to destroy the law" (Matt. v. 17).

226.Who was the father of Joseph? "And Jacob begat Joseph, husband of Mary" (Matt. i. 16). "He was the son of Heli" (Luke iii. 23).

227.Who purchased the potter's field? "Judas, with the reward of iniquity" (Acts i. 18). "The chief priest took the sliver, and bought the potter's field" (Matt. xxvii. 6).

228.Yes: "The spirit led Christ to Jerusalem" (Acts xx. 22). No: "The spirit forbade him to go" (Acts xxi. 4).

226. Yes: "I go to prepare a place for you" (John xiv. 2). No: "It was prepared from the beginning" (Matt. xxv. 34).

230. Yes: "The mission of the gospel began at Jerusalem" (Luke xxiv. 47). No: "It began at Galilee" (Acts x. 37).

231. Yes: "I beseech you as strangers" (1 Pet. ii. 11). No: "You are not strangers" (Eph. ii. 14).

232. Yes: "Christ died for his enemies" (Rev. x.). No: "For his friends" (John xv. 13).

233 Yes: "I write unto you, fathers" (1 John ii. 13). No: "Call no man father" (Matt. xxiii. 9).

234. Yes: "I am with you always" (Matt. xxviii. 20). No: "It is expedient for you that I go away" (John xvi. 7).

Total 277, including double contradictions.

We will not attempt to argue that these conflicting statements prove that no such events as here referred to ever transpired, and that the whole thing is a fabrication. We only argue that it proves the writers were not inspired by infinite wisdom, or they would have told the exact truth in all cases, so that there could have been no mistakes. It also proves that we never can know the real facts, or arrive at an accurate knowledge or the exact truth, with respect to any of those doctrines, duties, or events the contradictions appertain to; and, as these contradictions refer to almost every doctrine, precept, and event of any importance, it thus sinks all Bible teaching into a labyrinth of uncertainty. Hence, not *one single statement* in it can be set down as absolutely true without corroborative evidence.

Note: The reader will observe, from the contradictions in the foregoing list with respect to all the duties of life, as well as all the crimes of society—such as war, intemperance, slavery, theft, robbery, murder, falsehood, swearing, lying, etc.—that it is *absolutely impossible* to learn our moral and religious duties from the Bible.

CHAPTER 23

TWO HUNDRED CASES OF
OBSCENE LANGUAGE IN THE BIBLE

No person of refinement and good morals, who has not been warped and biased by education or religious training in favor of the Christian Bible, can read that book through without being often shocked and put to the blush by its obscene and vulgar language. Indeed, there are more than two hundred texts calculated to raise a blush on the cheek of modesty. Many of them are so obscene that we would not dare copy them into this work. It would not only outrage the feelings of the reader, but it would render the author liable to prosecution. A law has been recently passed by Congress prohibiting the publication and circulation of obscene literature; and many persons have already been prosecuted under that law—some of them for merely selecting and publishing some of the obscene texts of the Bible. But, without being influenced by these considerations, we will, in order to spare the feelings of the reader, merely state the import of some of these texts.

1.   Omitting the history of Adam, in which we find some not very refined language, we will commence with Noah. We are told that Noah became so drunk as to strip off all his clothing, and one of his sons, to avoid seeing him in that situation, walked backward, and covered him; for which act his father cursed him. Thus, it appears that Noah, although "a righteous man," was not a very modest or decent one. And such a man being held up as a righteous example must have a demoralizing tendency upon those who accept him in this light. (See Gen. ix.)

2.   The story of Abraham and Sarah, and the account of Abraham's illicit intimacy with his servant-maid Hagar, as related in Genesis (chap. xvi.), and his and Sarah's gossip over the affair, is anything but modest.

3.   The "holy man" Lot: The story of Lot's incest with his daughters, as set forth In Genesis (chap. xix.), is both immodest and disgusting.

4.   Rachel and Bilhah: The tea-table talk of Jacob and Rachel, about the act of Jacob in seducing their maidservant Bilhah, must be morally repulsive to all only Bible believers.

5.   The story of Leah and Zilpah is not much better. (See Gen. xxx.)

6.   The bargain between Leah and Rachel about Reuben's mandrakes (Gen. xxx.) is too immodest to relate or contemplate.

7.   Jacob's trick of using peeled sticks and poplar-trees among his cattle is something more than a descent from the sublime to the ridiculous. And were it not deemed "divine revelation, heavenly instruction," it would have been left out (Gen. xxx.).

8.   The account of Rachel's stealing her father's images, and then telling an indecent falsehood to hide it, is not very suitable for a "Holy Book" (Gen. xxxi.).

9.   The story of the defilement of Dinah we will not attempt to describe, as we cannot do it without offending decency. (See Gen. xxxiv.)

10. The story of Reuben and Bilhah, in the next chapter, may be instructive to the pious, but is not so to persons of refined taste.

11. If you read the narratives of Judah, Onan, and Tamar, as related in the thirty-eighth chapter of Genesis, for humanity's sake keep it out of the hands of your children, and use your influence to prevent its circulation among the heathen; for it must have the effect to sink them still deeper in moral depravity and mental degradation.

12. The disgusting story of Absalom's familiarity with his father's concubines, as related (2 Sam. xvi. 32), is so disgusting that we will barely allude to it.

Having referred to twelve cases more, we shall pursue the repulsive subject no further, except merely to indicate the chapter and verse where a long list of such cases may be found and examined by those who may need more evidence that the Bible is an obscene book, not fit to be read in decent society.

13. Vulgar language is used in representing men as acting like dogs. (See 2 Kings ix. 8.)

14. Job describes disgusting conduct toward a woman (Job xxxi. 9).

15. Solomon's Song of Songs contains much that is obscene language from the first to the eighth chapter.

16. Isaiah makes revolting suggestions relative to stripping women. (See Isa. xxxii. 2.)

17. Ezekiel is represented as eating disgusting food (dung) (Ezek. iv. 12).

18. Jehovah's command to Hosea to marry a harlot is of immoral tendency.

19. Isaiah frequently makes use of vulgar language. One case may be found in chap. lxvi. 3.

20. Another case in Hosea, describing horrible treatment of women and children. (See chap. xiii. 16.)

21. The conduct of Sechem towards certain women, as told in Gen. xxxiv. 4, is loathsome.

22. 'The conduct of parents toward their daughters, as described In Deut. xxii. 15, and as enjoined by the Mosaic law, is disgusting and shocking in the extreme.

23. And language no less disgusting, relative to the treatment of men, as prescribed by law, is found in Deut. xxiii.

24. The account of Paul's conversion, as described in Acts ix., is extremely vulgar.

The above-cited cases are mere samples of hundreds of similar ones to be found in God's Holy Book in the use of indecent language, calculated to make any person blush to read in private, much more if read in public. Indeed, no person dare read them to a company of decent people. Look, then, how the case stands. Look at the mortifying condition in which every devout Bible believer in Christendom is placed. Here is a book which, it is claimed, emanated from a pure and holy being; which contains so many passages couched in such obscene and offensive language, that any person who attempts to read the book to a company must be constantly and critically on his guard, and is liable to be kept in a state of fearful anxiety (as the writer knows by his own experience), lest he stumble on some of these offensive texts. What an uncomfortable situation to be placed in when reading a book which is claimed to be perfect in every respect! We have seen a Bible class in school stopped suddenly by the teacher, with orders to close their Bibles, because he had observed, by looking ahead, that the chapter contained language which would bring a blush to every cheek if read. In the same school we saw a modest boy, of refined feelings, burst into tears because he was required to read to the school a certain passage in the account of the conversion of Paul. The teacher being a devout Christian, whose piety overruled his decorum, attempted to enforce the reading by a threat of punishment, but failed. We have also seen the offer of one hundred dollars' reward, standing in a paper for a considerable time to any person who would read a dozen texts to a company of ladies, which the gentleman offering the reward might select, but no person dared to disgrace himself by accepting the offer.

And what is the moral, or lesson, taught by these things? Why, that the Bible is a very unsuitable book for a refined nation of people to read habitually, or for a morally elevated and enlightened age of the world, though it was probably adapted to the age and to the people for which it was written. They had not attained to the present standard of morality and refinement. We cherish no disposition to censure them. They were probably honest, and lived up to their highest idea of right. If anybody deserves censure in the case, it is the professedly enlightened Christians of the present age for going back to a savage, unenlightened age and nation for their religion and morals.

The Bible of Bibles

A PARTIAL LIST OF THE OBSCENE PASSAGES OF THE BIBLE

The following figures point to texts, many of which are too vulgar to be described in any kind of language:

Gen. xvii. 2, very disgusting; xix., 8, 33, 35, a shocking case; xx. 18; xxv. 23, disgusting; xxx. 3, very obscene; xxx 15, 16; xxxi. 12; xxxiv. 2, 7, 16, 22; xxxviii. 9, loathsome; xxxviii. 29; lix. 25; Exod. i. 16; xix. I5; xx. 2; xxii. 16; xxxiv. 15, 16; Lev. xii. 15; xviii. 7, 19, 20, 22, 23, 24; xxi. 7, 20, extremely vulgar; Num. xiv. 33; xix. 5, disgusting; xxv. 1; xxxi. 35; Deut. xxi. 11; xxii. 15, 21; xxii. 22, 23, 25; xxiii. 1, very disgusting, xxiii. 13, 17, 18; xxv. 5, 7,10; xxxi. 16; Judg. xi. 37; xix. 2, 25; Ruth i. 11, 12; iii.; iv 13; 2 Sam. vi. 20, 22; vii. 12; xi. 4, 11; xii. 11, 12, very disgusting; xiii. 11, 12, 14, 20, 22, 23; 1 Kings i. 4; iii. 16, 17, 26; xi. 3; xvi. 11, very filthy; xxi. 21; 2 Kings xviii. 27, very filthy; 2 Chron. xxi. 13, 15; Esth. ii. 12, 14; Job iii. 10; xvi. 15; xxi. 24; xxxi. 10, very disgusting, and 15; xxxii. 19; xi. 16; Ps. xxii. 10; xlviii. 6; cxxxix. 13; Prov. xxiii. 27; xxx. 16, 19; Eccles. iv. 11; xi. 5; Sol. i. 13; iii. 1; vi. 8; vii. 2, 3; viii. 8; Isa. iii. 17; xxvi. 17, very nasty; xlvii. 2; xlix., very obscene; xlvi. 7; Jer. ii. 20; iii. 1, 2, 6, 9, very filthy, and 13; iv. 31; xiii. 27; xiv. 17; xvi. 3, 4; xxix. 8; xxx. 6; xxxi. 8, 27; Lam. ii. 13; vii.; Ezek. iv. 15, 16, 17, 18, 19, 20, 21, 22, 25, 28, 33, 35; xviii. 6; xix. 2; xxii. 11; xxiii. 2, 3, 5, 7, 8, 10, 11, 14, 17, 18, 19, 20, 21, 29, 43; xliv. 25; Hos. i. 2; ii. 2, 4, 5; iv. 14, 18; vii. 4; ix, 1, 14; Mic. i. 2; iv. 10; Nah. iii. 4; Hab. ii. 16; 2 Esd. viii. 8; ix. 43; xvi. 38, 49; Jud. ix. 2; Wisd. of Sol. iii. 13; iv. 6; Eccles. xx. 4; xxvi. 9; xxxviii. 25; xiii. 10; Bar. vi. 29; 2 Macc. vi. 4; Matt. i. 25; xxiv. 19; xxv. 10; Luke i. 15, 24, 31, 36, 41, 44, 49; ii. 6, 7, 23; xi. 27; John xvi. 21; Acts ii. 30; Rom. i. 26, 27; iii. 28; 1 Cor. vii. 1; 2 Cor. vi. 12; Heb. xi. 11; 2 Pet. ii. 2; Rev. xii. 2; xvii. 1; xviii.4.

CHAPTER 24

CIRCUMSION — A HEATHEN CUSTOM

Circumcision is a very ancient rite, and of heathen origin, though we are told in Genesis that it was a command of God to Abraham, and it was nationalized by Moses. It was considered by the Jews a very important religious rite, and has been practiced by them from their earliest history. So highly was this ordinance esteemed amongst them, that it was in some cases performed twice. According to Herodotus and Diodorus, instead of the Jews getting the command direct from God, they borrowed the custom of the Assyrians; and Josephus silently assents to its truth. J. G. Wilkinson says, "It was established in Egypt long before Joseph was sold into that country," which furnishes evidence of its existence before the time of Moses. Among the Jews, this rite was performed on the eighth day after birth: all converts to their religion, and all servants, had to submit to the ordinance.

Jerome says that in his day a majority of the Idumaeans, Moabites, Ammonites, and Ishmaelites were circumcised. The ancient Phoenicians also observed this rite, and the aboriginal Mexicans likewise. The Muhammadans also practice it; and, although the Koran does not enjoin it, it has been practiced wherever that religion has been adopted. The rite is performed on both sexes in Arabia. This rite was practiced by the early Christians. Even the wise Paul gave practical sanction to this ordinance in the case of Timothy. The Coptic and Abyssinian Christian churches still observe the custom. A circumcision festival was established in the Church, and kept on the 1st of January in commemoration of the circumcision of Jesus.

The toleration of this rite by the Jews and Christians shows that they were dwelling on the animal plane—that they had not risen to that high state of spirituality which would lead them to abandon such heathenish ordinances and customs. It is so repulsive to refined society, that some civilized nations have enacted laws interdicting the custom. Yes, this senseless, cruel, heathenish rite has to some extent been abandoned, and must ere long entirely disappear from the earth. It cannot withstand the lights of science and civilization: it is a childish, senseless, obscene, vulgar, heathenish, cruel, and disgusting superstition.

FASTING AND FEASTING IN VARIOUS NATIONS

A total ignorance of the laws of health is indicated as existing amongst the disciples of all the ancient religions by the alternate extremes of fasting and feasting. The latter is injurious to health, and the former also, if long continued, as was frequently the case. But the subject of health did not occupy the minds of religious enthusiasts. They knew nothing of the laws of health, and cared less if possible. Fasting is reported, in some cases, as extending to an incredible period of time, continuing in some cases for months. Hindus often fasted for a week, and in some cases, if reports are true, for several weeks. Pythagoras of Greece fasted, it is said, forty days. Both the fasts and the feasts were generally held to signalize or celebrate some astronomical epoch, such as the changes of the moon, changes in the seasons, etc. The ancient representatives of the Christian faith were much given to fasting, as were also some of the Jews; but, at the present day, Christians, with others, are more addicted to feasting than fasting, although fasting is enjoined by the Bible both by precept and practice. In this respect, modern Christianity bears no resemblance to ancient Christianity.

CHAPTER 25

HOLY MOUNTAINS, LANDS, CITIES AND RIVERS

I. HOLY MOUNTAINS

Those who have read the Christian Bible are familiar with the fact that the ancient Jews and early Christians had their holy mounts and holy mountains, and that they are often referred to in the Bible. Mount Sinai and Mount Horeb were to the Jews consecrated spots. They called forth their highest feelings of veneration; they occupied a place in their devout meditations, similar to that of heaven in the mind of the Christian worshiper. It may be said to have been a substitute for heaven with the Jews; for they knew no other heaven, and dreamed of no other in their earlier history. And Mount Zion was a place equally sacred in the devout meditations of the early Christians. All the Oriental nations had their holy mountains before the Jews were known to history: Merau was the holy mount of the ancient Hindus; Olympus, of the Greeks; Athos, of the Egyptians. It is therefore evident that the founders of the Christian religion borrowed the idea of attaching sacredness to mountains. Several of Christ's important acts were represented as having been performed on mountains. His sermon was delivered on a mount; his march into Jerusalem was from the "Mount of Olives." Luke says he went and abode in the Mount of Olives (xxi. 87). The Devil took him up into an exceeding high mountain, and showed him all the kingdoms of the world; and, finally, his earthly career culminated on Mount Calvary. "Holy hill," holy mount, and holy mountain—the most important of which was Mount Zion—are terms often used in the Old Testament. History discloses very fully the origin of the custom of attaching sacredness to hills and mountains. One writer says it was partly from the conviction that the higher the earth ascends, the nearer it approaches the residence of the Gods; and consequently they would the more certainly hear the prayers and invocations of mortals. Prophets, seers, and anchorites were accustomed, from these considerations, to spend much time on the hills and mountains. In view of these facts, we may conclude that all persons acquainted with history will acknowledge that the Jews and Christians derived the tradition of regarding hills and mountains as "holy" from the Orientals, and that it is consequently a heathen tradition.

II. HOLY LANDS AND HOLY CITIES

Jerusalem was the principal holy city of both Jews and Christians, and Palestine was their holy land. Here, again, we find them anticipated by heathen nations. Thebes was the holy city of Egypt, Ida the holy city of India, Rome the holy city of the Greeks and Romans, Mecca the holy city of the Muhammadans. And, like the early Christians who spent much time in visiting Jerusalem, the Muhammadans make frequent pilgrimages to Mecca. Syria was the holy land of the Chaldeans and Persians, Wisdom the holy land of the Hindus, and Benares the principal "holy city." And these holy places they visited very frequently, going in large companies, singing hymns and reciting texts from their holy books as they traveled. And Christians in the time of Constantine spent much time in traveling to and from Jerusalem and the Holy Land, prompted by the same superstitious notions and feelings. Here we observe another analogy in the religious customs of the Jews, Christians, and heathens, all of which were derived from ancient India.

III. HOLY RIVERS

Holy rivers were quite numerous among the devotees of the ancient religions. The Ganges in India appears to have been the first river invested with the title of "holy." Its waters were used for the rite of baptism, and were supposed to impart a spiritual life to the subject of immersion. Jordan and the Euphrates were regarded as sacred by the Jews, and the former was the chosen stream for the rite of baptism by that nation. Even Christ appears to have believed he could receive some spiritual benefit by being dipped beneath its waves. The Nile was a sacred river in Egypt, and many repaired to it for spiritual benefit. Thus, the origin of holy rivers and holy waters is plainly indicated to be of heathen origin.

CHAPTER 26

CHARACTER OF JEHOVAH

The Old Testament is principally a history of the Jews and their God Jehovah—a narrative of their trials, troubles, treachery, quarrels, and faithless dealings toward each other. No other God ever had so much trouble with his people; and no other nation ever showed so little respect for their God, or so little disposition to obey him, or live up to his commands. There appears to have been almost a natural antipathy between them, so that they were constantly repelling each other. The relationship appears to have been a forced one, possessing but few of the adhesive ties of friendship.

Both parties were apparently happier when separated, as they were several times—on one occasion for a long period (Lam. v. 20). And yet, according to the biblical history of the case, they got along as well, were as moral and as happy, as when their God was with them. Hence, it is evident, if he had never returned, they would have sustained no serious loss or disadvantage in any way. The case furnishes an argument in favor of that class of people who are frequently denounced by the priesthood for "living without God in the world." If "God's own people" could get along without him, why can not men and women of this intelligent age? And the reason he assigns for remaining with them as much as he did shows it was not from natural affinity or affection for them, but because he had "promised" to do so. Did he not know that "a bad promise is better broken than kept?"

Another circumstance which implies that Jehovah cherished but little respect for his people, and cared but little about them is that, from his neglect (as it seems most natural to attribute it to this cause), they were literally broken up while he was apparently with them. One portion of them fell into the lands of Shalmaneser, King of Assyria, and the other portion into the hands of Nebuchadnezzar, King of Babylon; and they were never able to regain their political power as a nation afterwards. And, to cap the climax, ten out of the twelve tribes were lost entirely, thus leaving Jehovah almost childless, and destitute of worshipers. And a search for them for several thousand years has failed to bring them to light. This circumstance is entirely irreconcilable with the idea that the Jews were the special favorites of God. Indeed, it prostrates the assumption entirely beyond defense. It proves, also, that Jehovah's promise never to leave or forsake them was not adhered to. (See 1 Sam. xii. 22.) And the language and conduct of the God of the Jews on several occasions imply that, if he ever did make choice of them as his pets, he was disappointed in them, and repented of the act.

1. When he exclaimed, "I have nourished and brought up children and they have rebelled against me" (Isa. i. 2), he virtually confesses he had

been shortsighted, or that he had erred in judgment in selecting the Jews as special favorites. Certainly, this is the language of vexation and disappointment, and want of judgment or foresight.

2. We are told "he hated his own heritage" (Jer. xii. 8). Here is evinced again a feeling of hatred, vexation, and disappointment that no sensible being should manifest, much less a God.

3. "He gathered unto him the children of Ammon and Amalek, and went and smote Israel" (Judg. iii. 13). This was a traitorous act, calculated to discredit any being. Hence, it could not have been the act of an all-wise and benevolent God. Think of such a being getting into a squabble with his own children, and having to invoke the aid of heathen tribes to subdue them, and get him out of the difficulty! One day he heads an army composed of his "peculiar people" to fight the heathen, with the avowed determination to exterminate them, and "leave nothing alive that breathes." The next day he gets out of patience with their stubbornness and iniquity; his fury gets up to fever heat; and he traitorously abandons them, and joins those same enemies to fight them, and reduce them to slavery. It is scarcely necessary to say we do not believe such a God ever existed, excepting in the imagination of ignorant people.

4. Again: Jehovah is represented as selling his people several times to the neighboring heathen tribes, which again leads to the conclusion that he was disappointed in them, tired of them, and wished to get rid of them. He sold them once to Jaban, King of Canaan (Judg. iv. 2), and twice to the Philistines. Wonder what he got, and what he did with the money! The first time he sold them to the Philistines, he told them he never would deliver them again: but he seems either to have forgotten his promise, or forgot there is a moral obligation to stick to the truth, for he delivered them several times after that, if his own biographer and inspired writer tells the truth. Here is more evidence that he is fickle-minded and unreliable, or that the Bible writers have misrepresented his character.

5. If we could assume there is any truth in the Bible history of Jehovah, we should not wonder that the Jews preferred worshipping a golden calf to paying their devotions to such a God, and, on the other hand, it is not surprising that he should manifest his displeasure toward them, and frequently steal away from them, and often confess grief, vexation, and regret for having made choice of such an ignorant, rebellious set of rambling nomads, who subsisted by war and plunder.

6. Jehovah's jealousy of. other Gods, which he so frequently manifested and so often confessed, and which is one of the most objectionable traits of his character, must be attributed to his own moral defects; for he acted in such a manner as to cause his own people to prefer

other Gods to him. He frequently scolded and punished them for worshipping other Gods—a circumstance which furnishes evidence that other Gods were better, and therefore more worthy of being worshipped. What else could have caused them to prefer other Gods? He should have acted in such a loving and fatherly manner that other Gods could not have been more venerated and sought after. Then he would not have been so often vexed, harassed, and perplexed at the idolatrous proclivities of his worshipers, and so often resorted to retaliation by forsaking them, selling them, enslaving them, or delivering them into the hands of the spoiler. In Judges ii. 14, it is declared, "The Lord delivered them into the hands of the spoiler;" and in Judges vi. 1, we are told he delivered them into the hands of Midian for seven years. This looks like an attempt to spoil his own plans, and to falsify his own promises to be with them, and protect them at all times.

7.   Much of Jehovah's dealings with his people seemed to be by way of experiment, as in the case of trying Abraham's faith by requiring him to offer up his son. What an idea for an all-wise and omnipotent God, of whom it is said, "Known unto him are all his works"!

8.   But many circumstances prove that Jehovah was not the God of the universe, but only a family or national God. 1. His acknowledgment of the existence of other Gods (Deut. vi. 14); 2. his jealousy of other Gods (Exod. xxxiv. 14); 3. his traveling on foot, lodging in tents, having his feet washed, eating veal and cakes (Gen. xviii.), etc., all tend to prove this; and 4. the fact that he could not know what was going on in other nations, and not even his own until he visited the spot in person (as in the case of the Tower of Babel), is proof he was not the God of the universe.

9.   We cannot concede that the "Creator of unnumbered worlds" is (like Jehovah) an angry, malevolent being, addicted to feelings of revenge and retaliation, which seemed to banish the feeling of love and goodness entirely from his mind, and who is represented as being frequently thwarted in his designs and purposes by the caprices of his weak and ignorant children, who, so far from answering his expectations of being the best, turned out to be the worst of his human heritage. Such ideas would be derogatory to Deity.

And this is the God the "American Christian Alliance" is trying to obtain a recognition of in the Constitution of the United States. What a moral calamity such a step would be!

CHAPTER 27

CHARACTER OF THE JEWS

As the Jews are reputedly "the chosen people of God"—chosen by him out of all the nations of the earth to be the special recipients of his favors; the chosen instruments through which to communicate his will and his laws to the whole human race, and chosen to be a moral example for all mankind, for that age, and for all future generations—it becomes a matter of great importance to know their real character for morality, for intelligence, for honesty, and for reliability. And that we may, in the effort to present a brief sketch of their character, furnish no ground for suspecting any misrepresentation, we will present it in the language of Jewish and Christian writers of established reputation. It may reasonably be presumed that their own writers would be more likely to overrate than underrate their virtues. Hear, then, what one of their leading prophets says of them. Isaiah thus describes them (Isa. lix.): "Their hands are defiled with blood, and their fingers with iniquity; and their lips speak lies; their tongues mutter perverseness. None of them call for justice; none of them plead for truth. They trust in vanity, and speak lies; they conceive mischief, and bring forth iniquity, and the act of violence is in their hand. Their feet run to evil, and they make haste to shed innocent blood. Their thoughts are thoughts of iniquity; wasting and destruction are in their paths." Such is a description of God's holy people by one of their number. And David completes the picture by declaring, "There is none righteous; no, not one."

And Christ calls them "a generation of vipers." Rather a shocking picture of God's peculiar people! "Peculiar" they were, if Isaiah's description of them was true—peculiar for defective character. It is rather strange that Jehovah should have selected such moral outlaws as lawgivers and moral examples for the whole human race. There were, at the time, several nations superior to the Jews in morals and intelligence, and much further advanced in civilization. The Greeks, Egyptians, Chaldeans, and a portion of the Hindus were in advance of the Jews.

The Rev. Mr. Hilliard, in a sermon preached in New York in 1861, says of the Jews, "They were by nature, perhaps, the most *cruel* and *blood-thirsty,* as well as idolatrous, people in the world." And yet he says in the same sermon, "that the Lord chose the Israelites because of their adaptedness of character to the carrying out of his divine ends of mercy to the race." What cogent reasoning! Why not select the Devil at once, if beings the most *cruel* and *blood-thirsty* were best calculated for "carrying out his divine ends of mercy to the race"? Here is more proof of the evil effects of preaching, or adhering to, a religion which is so full of errors, absurdities, and immoral elements, that it blinds the moral vision, and weakens the reasoning faculties to give it a place in the mind, and leads to a system of false reasoning, and often corrupts the natural judgment.

We have more orthodox testimony to show the defective morals of the Lord's chosen people. Dr. Burnet (a Christian writer), in his "Archaeologia Philosophie," says, "They were of a gross and sluggish nature, not qualified for the contemplation of natural things, nor the perception of divine ones. And consequently," he tells us, "Moses provided nothing for them of an intellectual nature, and promised them nothing beyond this life—did not teach a future state of existence." Lactantius says, "They were never visited by the learned men of other countries, because they were never famous for literature." St. Cyril says, "Moses never attempted to philosophize with the Jews, because they were 'grossly ignorant,' and addicted to idolatry." Dr. Burnet further says, "They were depraved in their manners and discipline, and almost bereaved of humanity. If I may speak the truth, ... they were a vile company of men—an assembly of slaves brought out of Egyptian prisons, who understood no art but that of making bricks." Josephus, being a Jew, was their friend and defender; and yet he says, "They were so illiterate, that they never wrote anything, or held intercourse with the learned." St. Cyril says, "Some of them adored the sun as a deity; others, the moon and stars; and others, beasts, and birds." One writer says, "They hated all nations, and were hated by all nations," and they seemed determined to exterminate all nations but their own. They might also have used the language of an ancient Christian sect, which declared, "We are the friends of God, and the enemies of all mankind."

Let it be borne in mind that the testimonies here cited are not from infidel writers, but all from Jews and Christians, who, we should presume, could have no motive for exaggerating their moral defects, but rather inducements for concealing them. Other similar testimony might be presented. Some of the laws which Moses adopted for the government of the Jews corroborates still further the statement that they occupied a very low position in the scale of morals as well as intellect; for the laws of a nation are a true standard of their character. Hence, the law of Moses prohibiting uncleanness (Lev. xv.), the law against incest (Lev. xviii.). Laws against bestiality, to prohibit both sexes from carnal familiarity with beasts, and various other laws of a similar character, furnish a clear implication that they were addicted to all these vile habits; and a law to compel them to wash their hands leads to the conclusion that they were inclined to be filthy in their habits. And the following law shows that they were not very particular about their food: "Ye may eat the locust after his kind, and the beetle after his kind, and the grasshopper after his kind" (Lev. xi. 22). Here were three kinds of rather repulsive insects which the Jews were expected to eat, at least licensed to use as food. Can such a nation be considered to be civilized? If so, where is a nation now existing that cannot, with equal propriety, be said to be civilized?

This portraiture of the Jewish character is not here presented in any caviling spirit, or to show that they are justly objects of either censure or ridicule. Far from it. They most probably acted up to the highest light they were in possession of. The primary motive of this exhibition of their character is to show that they possessed no qualifications and no traits of character calculated to fit them for moral lawgivers and moral exemplars for *us,* and for the *whole human race*; and we cannot assume, without really dishonoring ourselves, that such a morally and intellectually inferior nation of people were the chosen instruments in the hands of God to communicate the revelation of his will to the human family. We are under no moral obligation to believe it. A revelation from a pure, perfect, and holy God must (if we assume a revelation necessary) come through a pure and holy channel; otherwise it would be contaminated and corrupted before it reached us. If God could consent to communicate a revelation to the human race through such a channel as the Jewish nation furnished, we see not how he could escape a stigma upon his character for stooping to such ignoble means. And would not the act of familiarizing himself with such a people show that he kept bad company, and furnish a bad example to us who are enjoined to be "perfect as our Father in heaven is perfect"?

CHAPTER 28

CHARACTER OF MOSES

The history of Moses is so intimately and thoroughly interblended with that of the Jews that, to present the character of one, is to present the character of the other. We shall therefore devote but a brief chapter to a special exposition of his character, as it will be found fully set forth in the history of the Jews, and the practical illustration of their moral character. No religious chieftain ever claimed to be on more intimate terms with God, and no writer ever presented a more dishonorable exhibition of his character. He made God the author of nearly everything he said and did, no matter how wicked, how cruel, how demoralizing, or how shocking to decency or refined moral sensibilities. If some of his characteristics of God are not blasphemous, we can have but little use for the word. Some of his laws serve as an illustration of this statement.

He says, "The Lord spake unto Moses," and told him that no person with a flat nose or crooked back or broken hand, a crooked eye, or who was lame or possessing any kind of a physical blemish, should be admitted into the congregation of the Lord (Lev. xxi.). This was punishing the unfortunate for defects they could not help, thus aggravating the misfortunes of a class who, above all others, had special claims upon his kindness on account of the very defects for which they were excluded. These laws, and many others no better, sufficiently illustrate the character of the man. His penal code, which inflicted death for two hundred acts, many of them no crime at all (such as picking up sticks on the sabbath to make a fire to cook their food with), furnishes conclusive evidence that he was a cruel and unmerciful lawgiver. And the fact that he was almost constantly engaged in a bloody warfare with neighboring nations, with the avowed determination to exterminate them, and "leave nothing alive that breathes," simply because they preferred to worship some other God than the cruel Jehovah, leads to the conclusion that he was a bloody-minded warrior. Had Christ lived under the Hebrew monarchy, Moses' laws would have put him to death; and yet they both claimed to derive their moral code from the same God, the Jewish Jehovah.

A circumstance is related of Moses killing an Egyptian, and hiding him in the sand. And it is stated, "He looked this way and that way" before committing the deed, and then concealed the dead body. This implies that he felt guilty, and that it was an act of murder in the first degree. Although every chapter of Moses' history proves him to have been a cruel and bloody-minded barbarian, with a moral code possessing but a slight exhibition of the elements of mercy, humanity, and justice, yet Dr. Gaussel, in his "Theopneustia," calls him "a holy and divine man," and says, "He was such a prophet, that his holy books were placed above all the rest of the

Old Testament." The doctor furnishes us one of the many cases of the blinding and biasing effect of a perverted religious education, and an argument in favor of laboring to supersede Bible religion with something better. Here we will notice it as a curious circumstance that, after Jehovah had occupied but six days in creating eighty-five millions of worlds, and made most of them in a few hours, it should have taken him and Moses both forty days to write a law, and a very imperfect one at that. And then it would seem it took Jehovah three thousand years to make a devil, as his Satanic Majesty does not figure in the Jewish hierarchy until after the lapse of that period.

One of the most conspicuous traits in Moses' mental composition was an unbounded self-esteem. Although he claimed to be in constant consultation with Jehovah, he seldom yielded to his advice when it conflicted with his own judgment. On the contrary, he several times detected his God in error, and admonished him, and entered into an argument to convince him that he was wrong; and, of course, he always came out first best in the logical contest. Take, for example, the case of Aaron making the golden calf. It occurred while he and Jehovah were engaged in writing "the holy law" on Mount Sinai. When the case became known to Jehovah, it so disturbed and aggravated him that he at once declared he would not only punish the guilty sinner—the apostate Aaron—but would exterminate the whole race. But the better tempered and more considerate Moses began to reason and remonstrate against such a rash act. He appealed to his honor and love of approbation, and told him the Egyptians would report that he was not able to get his "holy people" to the promised land, and hence killed them to conceal the failure. "Oh, yes, Moses, you are right! I never thought of that," was the seeming reply of Jehovah. And thus Moses proved to be smarter than his God, and enlightened his ignorance.

Here we will call the attention of the reader to the resemblance between Moses and the still more ancient Egyptian Mises, or Bacchus. It is so striking that we cannot resist the conviction they were originally closely connected with each other.

1.   Bacchus, like Moses, was born in Egypt.

2.   Bacchus, or Mises, was also exposed to danger on the River Nile, like Moses.

3.   Bacchus lived on a mountain in Arabia called Nisas; Moses sojourned on Mount Sinai in Arabia.

4.   Bacchus passed through the Red Sea dry-shod with a multitude of men, women, and children, as Moses is represented as doing.

Character of Moses

5. Bacchus likewise parted the waters of the River Orontes, as Moses did those of Jordan.

6. Bacchus commanded the sun to stand still, as Moses' friend Joshua did.

7. Bacchus, with his wand, caused a spring of wine to spring from the earth, as Moses did a spring of water to flow from a rock with the "rod of God," or "the rod of divination."

8. Mises, like Moses, also engraved his laws on tables of stone.

9. Both have been represented in pictures with rays coming out of their heads, indicative of the light of the sun. Thus, it will be observed, the resemblance runs through nearly the whole line of their history.

That Bacchus figured in history anterior to the time of Moses, no person versed in Oriental history can doubt—a fact which impels us to the conclusion that the two stories got mixed before the history of Moses was written. There is one important chapter in the practical life of Moses we cannot omit to notice before we close his history, as it furnishes a still fuller illustration of his character. We allude to his deliverance of "the Lord's holy people" from Egyptian bondage. Several of the incidents in this narrative are incredibly absurd; and some of such demoralizing tendency, that it becomes the duty of the moralist to expose them to view. The conduct of his God Jehovah toward the King of Egypt in this case is so repulsive and unjust that it must call forth the condemnation of every honest-minded reader possessing a true sense of justice.

1. We are told that Jehovah, through Moses, frequently ordered Pharaoh to let his people go, and then as often hardened his heart that he should *not* let them go; and finally punished him with death because he was unwilling to let them go. It would certainly be difficult to discover any sense or any justice or any consistency in such conduct.

2. It looks like not only a strange kind of *justice,* but monstrous *injustice,* for Jehovah or any God to kill a man for doing what he had purposely *compelled* him to do. Live frogs, lice, flies, blood, vengeance, and death were poured out upon the king and his subjects, ostensibly for the purpose of compelling him to liberate the Jewish nation; and yet it was morally impossible for him to do so, because the same Jehovah had planted in his mind the determination not to let them go.

3. When Moses spake to Pharaoh in the name of Jehovah to release the Israelites, the king asked, "Who is the Lord [thy Lord] that I should obey his voice?" Here let it be borne in mind that different nations had their own Gods. And Moses' God is here the same itinerant being who had been rambling about among the bushes, hunting his lost child (Adam), eating griddle-cakes with Abraham, wrestling all night with Jacob, getting

137

whipped in a fight with the Canaanites, etc. Pharaoh was therefore justified in calling for his credentials.

4.   In nearly all the contests between Jehovah and other Gods, their power is fully admitted; and their success was only secondary to that of the God of Israel. The question was not, Shall Jehovah succeed, and other Gods fail? but Shall Jehovah be awarded the first prize in the contest, and his name stand at the top of the list?

5.   There are many texts in the Bible which go to show that Jehovah was jealous of other Gods, and perpetually in fear of being outgeneraled by them. "Ye shall know that I am the Lord," was the constant burden of his song. In the case before us he is represented as saying to Pharaoh, "In this thou shalt know that *I am the Lord*" (Exod. vii. 17). "It is true you have a God, and he is very smart and powerful; but he can't come up to me."

6.   Jehovah seems to have been actuated by an aspiration for fame and power, as well as by a sympathy for his people in this contest with Pharaoh; for he is represented as saying, "I will get me *honor* upon Pharaoh and his host" (Exod. xiv. 17). Here seems to be displayed a spirit of vanity, and a thirst for glory—the aspiration of vain rulers and petty tyrants.

7.   The magicians kept up with Moses' God in the performance of miracles until it came to making lice: here they failed. We might conjecture it was because all the dust had been already converted into lice by Jehovah, were it not that they had previously converted the water into blood just after Jehovah had performed that miracle, and left not a pint to drink.

8.   In the achievement of all the ten prodigies, there is no intimation but that the heathen magicians performed the miracles in the same manner that Moses did, and with equal success in most cases and in all the most difficult ones; thus leaving Jehovah no laurels worth boasting of.

9.   There must have been a great many thousand honest men and women in Egypt; and yet Jehovah is represented as killing the first-born of all Egyptian parents without any distinction of character, or any regard to their innocence; and even the firstborn of beasts also. In the name of justice and mercy, what sin had the beasts committed that they had to be punished?

10. We are somewhat puzzled to see how the magicians could turn all the waters of Egypt into blood, when it was already blood, having been converted into blood a short time before by Moses and Jehovah.

11. And it seems strange that Pharaoh should have horses enough for six hundred "chosen chariots" (Exod. xiv. 7) after they had all been killed three or four times by some of the plagues of Egypt.

12. It is not strange that Aaron's rod should swallow up the others as represented; for he had such a start in the business, and had made such a

large serpent, he had probably used up most of the materials, and left nothing but scraps for making others.

13. The Christian who can lay down his Bible after reading such stories as this, and not feel his natural and instinctive love of honesty, justice, and morality weakened, must be strongly fortified by nature against moral corruption.

CHAPTER 29

CHARACTER OF THE PATRIARCHS
ABRAHAM, ISAAC AND JACOB

I. CHARACTER OF ABRAHAM

A brief history of the father of the Jewish tribe will tend to illustrate and indicate the character of the whole nation, as children usually inherit the qualities of their parents.

1. We will first notice the great promise that Jehovah made to Abraham with respect to the boundless extent of his future dominion. His seed were to be as the dust of the earth or the sands of the sea for multitude (Gen xiii. 16). And how has this promise been fulfilled? Why, after a faithful compliance with the command to "multiply and replenish the earth" for more than three thousand years, his whole tribe only numbers about six million souls, which is less than one in two hundred of the entire population of the globe. It would take but a few handfuls of dust to furnish the particles to represent the number, instead of all the dust of the earth as promised or predicted.

2. Jehovah promised Abraham, in the second place, all the country "from the river of Egypt to the great river—the River Euphrates" (Gen. xv. 18). And yet, after the lapse of three thousand years, we do not find many occupying a foot of it. Another failure to execute his promise.

3. "To thee will I give it [the promised land], and to thy seed for ever" (Gen. xiii. 15). It will be observed here that the title and possession was to be perpetual—to the end of the world, *"for ever."* And yet it has been in the possession of other nations five or six times; and now not many of the Lord's holy people can be found there. Another signal failure.

4. Jehovah promised Abraham all the land "from the river of Egypt to the River Euphrates," but they have never had possession of the country within two hundred miles of the river of Egypt (Nile). A writer quaintly suggests that Jehovah could never have previously seen the country he selected for his holy people or he would not have chosen it; for all modern travelers agree in describing it as being a poor, mountainous, rocky, barren, and desolate country. One writer says, "It is a country of rocks and mountains, stones, cliffs, bounded by vast, dreary, and uninhabitable deserts." St. Jerome describes it as "the refuse and rubbish of nature." And this is the country, let it be remembered, that Jehovah promised his people as the chosen spot of the earth. How little he knew of geography!

5. Jehovah and Abraham appear to have been very intimate friends, as they ate and slept together; and the "Judge of all the earth" was often a guest in the little, narrow, mud-built hut of the patriarch to eat veal, parched corn, and griddle-cakes with him, and have his feet washed also by the old

man (Gen. xviii. 18). From such circumstances it would appear that Jehovah traveled over the country in the character of a foot-pad or "tramp," and got into the mud occasionally. It is strange that Christians can read their Bible without noticing the disparaging caricature of their God.

6. Abraham's conduct towards his servant-girl Hagar is both disgraceful and inhuman, as he first destroyed her character and virtue by criminal intimacy, and then turned her and her child into the wilderness to starve (Gen. xxi.). Such conduct is certainly very reprehensible.

7. And this is the man who is represented as being chosen by a God of infinite wisdom, infinite purity, and infinite holiness, to stand at the head of the moral regeneration and salvation of the whole human race. Such a conception is derogatory to the divine character, and demoralizing to those who read and believe it.

8. Among other immoral and disgraceful acts of "God's chosen servant," "the righteous patriarch," "the Holy man of God," was that of uttering the most shameful and unblushing falsehood. He is charged with intentional lying on two different occasions, in representing his wife as being his sister—once to Pharaoh, and once to King Abimelech—and his wife endorsed his falsehood. (See Gen. chap. xii. and xx.)

9. And yet, in the face of all these immoral deeds, God is represented as saying, "Abraham kept all my commands, all my statutes, and all my laws." (See Gen xxvi. 5.)

Hence, the inevitable conclusion that Abraham was living up to the commands, statutes, and laws of God, while committing these crimes and outrages upon humanity. What a moral, or rather immoral lesson, is this to place before the heathen of foreign countries, and the children of our own, who read the Bible! It must have a tendency to demoralize them, and encourage them in the commission of similar crimes, as certainly as they are beings endowed with human frailties. Note these facts.

10. And we find other disgraceful, as well as incredible, deeds charged to the father of "the faithful." The account of the surrender of his manhood, and the obliteration of every impulse of parental feeling required to obtain his consent to butcher his son Isaac upon the altar, imparts a humiliating moral lesson (Gen. xxii.). It matters not that he did not commit the deed. He consented to do it, and was ready to do it, which proves a state of mind calculated to make humanity shudder. The New Zealanders have been known to point the missionaries to this example as a justification of their cruel practices of slaughtering human beings. If a father in this age of civilization should do such a thing, or even attempt it as Abraham did, he would be looked upon as a monster in human shape, or perfectly insane, even if he should claim that God called upon him to perform the act. It

would have been infinitely better to disobey such a God than to disobey and outrage every parental and kindly impulse of his nature. But the case furnishes *prima facie* evidence that Abraham was under a religious delusion in supposing God required the performance of such an inhuman deed. To assume that he did would make him more of a demon than a God. Any man or woman is to be pitied whose education has misled him or her, and blinded them so that they cannot see that the reading of a book teaching such lessons must prove morally injurious to the mind.

11. The injunction on Abraham to slay his son is said to have been imposed upon him to try his faith. His faith in what? I would ask. Faith in his own humanity? faith in his love and affection for his son? Nothing of the kind! but faith in his susceptibility of rendering himself an inhuman monster. Let us suppose a father says to his son, "Richard, I want you to draw a knife, and cut your brother Robert's throat"; and afterwards explains the matter by telling him he issued this order to try whether he would obey him. But his son would evince more manhood, and a better moral character, by refusing to obey him. It is much better to obey the dictates of conscience, humanity, and mercy, than to obey a father or a God in a case like this.

12. And Jehovah is represented as saying, through an angel, "Now I know that thou fearest God" (Gen. xxii. 12); equivalent to saying, "If I had not tried this experiment, I should not have known anything about it." What blind mortals human beings can become, to suppose that a God of infinite wisdom, who "searcheth the hearts of all men," must resort to cruel and shocking experiments to find out the state of their minds!

13. But the history of the case discloses the fact that it did not effect the end desired—that of proving Abraham's faith—not in the least, unless we assume that Abraham lied in the case. For he said to the young men while on the road to the altar, "Abide here until we [myself and son] go yonder and worship, and come again to you." Here is evidence that Abraham knew he would bring his son back alive; that is, that Isaac would return with him, or that he told a falsehood in order to deceive. The reader can seize which horn of the dilemma he prefers. If he knew what the issue of the case would be, it would, of course, be no trial of his faith whatever. And yet Paul and other New Testament writers laud the act as being one of great merit and a proof of his faith.

14. We must hasten on. We can only give a passing notice of a few other acts of this illustrious patriarch, in whom "all the nations of the earth were to be blessed." Jehovah is represented as saying to Abraham, on a certain occasion, "I will go down now, and see whether they [the Sodomites] have done according to my desire. "If not, I will know" (Gen.

xviii. 21). This is one of several cases in which "the Judge of all the earth" is represented as abandoning the throne of heaven, and coming down to learn what was going on below. What a contracted and ignorant being was the Jewish Jehovah!

15. The mission of Jehovah at one time, when he called upon Abraham, was to inform him that his gray-headed wife, approaching a hundred years, was to be blessed with a son in her old age. Has it never occurred to Bible admirers that this and other similar cases represented the Almighty, whom "the heaven of heavens can not contain," as traveling over the country in the character of a fortune-teller, notifying old women that the laws of nature would be suspended long enough to allow them to be blessed or cursed with the care and perplexity of children in their old age?

16. It should be noticed that Abraham's God never reproved him for any of his misdeeds; while, on the other hand, the heathen King Abimelech called the man of God to account for his moral defects (Gen. xx.).

17. One of the most dishonorable acts recorded in the history of Abraham's God was that of bringing a plague upon Pharaoh and his household for receiving Abraham's wife, when it was brought about wholly through his treachery and misrepresentation, and when it appears that Pharaoh treated her in the most respectful manner.

18. But with all these moral stains upon the character of Abraham, it becomes a pleasant task to record one good act in his life. He seems to have presented the practical proof that he was a better man than his God; for, when Jehovah threatened the destruction of Sodom for her wickedness, Abraham remonstrated, and suggested that it would be an act of injustice to destroy the righteous with the wicked. It appears that this moral consideration had escaped the mind of Jehovah. What an inconsiderate, ruthless being Bible writers represent the Almighty as being!

19. Abraham according to his history, was a man of valor, and achieved some great exploits. For instance, with the assistance of his regiment of one hundred and eighteen servants, he chased at one time four great kings, with their mighty hosts—the King of Babylon, the King of Persian, the King of Pontus, and the King of Nations (Gen. xiv.). He drove them, we are told, more than a hundred miles, and reconvened his brother Lot from their grasp. A few such daring heroes could have put down the American Rebellion without a battle.

20. We will only observe further, that this "true servant of the Lord" was both a polygamist and an idolater; at least we have the authority of the Jewish writer, Philo, for saying that his father was a maker of images, and that Abraham worshiped them. Such is a brief outline of the character of the man who is held up as an example for us to imitate, and through whom

"all the nations of the earth are to be blessed," and the man who stands at the head of that nation through which, we are told, a revelation has been given to the world which is to effect the moral regeneration and salvation of the whole human race. Whether the means are adapted to the ends, the reader is left to judge.

II. CHARACTER OF ISAAC

1.   In accordance with the adage, "Like father, like son," we find Isaac carrying out the same spirit of fraud and deception practiced by his father. When "the men of the plain asked him about his wife, he said, she is my sister" (Gen. xxvi.), and this man Isaac was another of "the faithful servants of the Lord."

2.   If the statement is true that the Lord struck Ananias and Sapphira with sudden death for telling a falsehood, as related in Acts v., the question naturally arises, Why did Abraham and Isaac escape the same fate, as they were guilty of the same sin? Why this partiality? Manifestly, this is a bad lesson in morals.

III. CHARACTER OF JACOB

1.   "Like father, like son," is again verified in the practical life of Jacob. We find this patriarch excels, in moral defects, both his father and his grandfather.

2.   His conduct toward his brother Esau, in robbing him of his just and inherited rights, is an act that stamps an eternal stigma upon his character. When Jacob's father, old and blind, asked him, "Art thou my son Esau?" he replied, "I am" (Gen. xxvii. 24), thus telling a base falsehood, and deceiving his old father; and this deceptive and underhanded act caused his brother "to cry an exceedingly bitter cry" (Gen. xxvii. 34). What an unfeeling brother was this "true servant of the Lord"! It appears that Isaac and Jehovah both intended that Esau should inherit the blessing, but Jacob outwitted them by the aid and connivance of his mother. This is but a sample of the character and conduct of the family throughout their whole history.

3.   Jacob seems to have entertained very singular and selfish ideas in regard to his religious obligation to serve and worship his God. He made it entirely a question of *bread* and *butter,* or, rather, of *bread* and *raiment.* He proposed to strike up a trade with Jehovah relative to his future allegiance to his government, and to fix the terms of the contract *himself* (Gen. xxviii.). He kindly and condescendingly told Jehovah that if he would provide him with food and raiment, and be his constant companion in the future, "then shall the Lord be *my* God, and this *stone* shall be *God's house;* and I will

give *one-tenth* to the Lord of what he giveth me" (Gen. xxviii. 20). Here is the attempt to drive a bargain with Jehovah on the *quid-pro-quo* principle. We are not informed how Jehovah appreciated this kindly offer. This is an unfortunate omission, as every reader must feel interested in knowing whether he accepted the proposition; and henceforth he whom "the heaven of heavens can not contain" took up his abode in the patriarch's little stone hut. We are led to infer that, if Jehovah refused to accept his terms, Jacob would henceforth refuse to be a subject of God's kingdom, and thus bring him to grief. This is a sample of the childish conception entertained by the whole Jewish nation of "the God of the tinkers," if we may presume their God was anything more than a family or national deity.

4. The proneness of the Lord's holy people to falsify, cheat, and deceive is well illustrated in the case of Laban who, after Jacob had, by a fair contract, labored seven years for him for his daughter Rachel, would not let him have her, but forced his older daughter Leah upon him; and, when Jacob complained, he told him he must serve seven years more if he got Rachel; and his love for her prompted him to accept the terms. But he seems not to have been well compensated for his fourteen long years of toil for these two sisters. Their subsequent conduct indicates that he "paid dear for the whistle"; and one month's labor ought to have paid for both, even at ten cents a day, for they both turned out to be failures. They were, however, a fair specimen of the race. Rachel stole her father's images, and, when pursued and overtaken by him, she hid them, and told him a falsehood to conceal the act. The circumstance of her father *having* images, and of her stealing them, is an evidence that both were idolaters (Gen. xxxi.).

5. It is easy to see, from the foregoing facts, from what source the Jewish proclivity to idolatry and also to falsehood was derived. The latter was practically manifested by four hundred at one time. It is true the Lord was charged with putting the lie in their mouths (1 Kings xxii. 22).

6. We are told that, on a certain occasion, "the sons of Jacob answered Shechem, and Hamor his father, deceitfully" (Gen. xxxiv. 13); by which it appears the spirit or propensity to fraud and deception was still transmitted to their posterity.

CHAPTER 30

CHARACTER OF DAVID, SOLOMON AND LOT

I. Character of David

Here is one of the illustrious Bible characters who has been held up to the world for several thousand years as the "sweet singer of Israel," and "the man after God's own heart"; whose life is stained by the commission of a long list of crimes of the blackest character, some of which would send him to the State prison for life if committed in this morally enlightened age.

1.   One of his first acts of moral delinquency was that of turning traitor to Achish, King of Gath.   After the king had kindly given him a rulership over the city of Ziklag he manifested his ingratitude by waging an unprovoked war for plunder upon the king's friends and relatives, to rob them of their cattle (1 Sam. xxvii.).

2.   David, with an army, committed a similar act of aggression and spoliation upon the rights and property of Nabal, to attain his cattle by robbery (1 Sam. xxv.).

3.   David at one time turned traitor to his own nation by joining the army of Achish to fight them (1 Sam. xxix.).

4.   David obtained possession of the kingdom of Ish-bosheth by bribery and intrigue, after acknowledging him to be a righteous man (2 Sam. iii.).

5.   David robbed Mephibosheth, the son of his bosom-friend Jonathan, and a poor cripple, of one-half of his estate, upon the plea that might makes right (2 Sam. xvi.).

6.   David connived at some of the moat abominable and atrocious crimes of his sons (2 Sam.).

7.   The manner in which David obtained his first wife Michal is shocking to all who possess kind and philanthropic feelings.   Saul had proposed a hundred foreskins of the Philistines as the price of his daughter; but David, in wanton cruelty, killed two hundred for this purpose.

8.   The manner in which David obtained his beautiful wife Bathsheba, to add to his list of wives, might be tolerated in that era of barbarism; but it must be looked upon at the present time as an act of cruelty and wickedness. He said to Joab, "Set Uriah in the front of the battle ... that he may be smitten and die "(2 Sam. xi. 15); which was equivalent to slaying him with his own hands, and for no crime, but solely to get his widow for a wife.

9.   Thus, we ace, David was not only a polygamist, but he obtained his wives by fraud, murder, and intrigue.

10. David's dancing naked in public was an indecent act, although several cases are reported of "the holy" men of that age appearing in public

in a state of nudity. His wife Michal upbraided him for "uncovering himself to the eyes of the handmaids, his servants, as one of the vain fellows shamelessly uncovereth himself" (2 Sam. vi.). It is said that "David danced before the Lord with all his might." Can we suppose the Lord would fancy such sights?

11. David's treatment of the Moabites in killing two-thirds of them without any just provocation is an act that would hang any man of the present day (2 Sam. viii.).

12. The fiendish act of David in placing the Moabites under saws and harrows of iron, and under axes of iron, and making them walk through brick-kilns (2 Sam. xii.), bespeaks a heart callous with cruelty, and unmerciful as a tiger. The very thought of it is calculated to chill the blood of a person with the feelings of common humanity.

13. David's murder of five step-sons and two brothers-in-law, to gratify a malignant grudge toward the house of Saul, is another act showing the fiendish character of the man.

14. When David was so old and stricken in years that no amount of bed-clothing could keep him warm, he made this a plea for marrying another wife—and a young maid at that—to lie in his bosom, and keep him warm (1 Kings i. 1). Lust knows no failure in expedients.

15. David's advice to his son Solomon on his deathbed, to assassinate Joab and his other enemies, shows that his ruling passions—animosity and revenge—were strong in death.

16. And finally David's wicked prayer, as found in the hundred and ninth Psalm, in which he invokes a string of the most horrid curses upon his enemies, culminates his immoral history. It completes the demoralizing picture of the "man after God's own heart." Now, we ask in solemn earnest, is it not evident that a book endorsing such characters as David, placed in the hands of the heathen of other countries or the children of our own, must have a demoralizing tendency? Most certainly, if Franklin was right in saying, "The reading of bad examples will make bad morals." Remember, the perpetrator of all these crimes is said to be "a man after God's own heart." If so, then God must have approved of all his crimes. But such a God will not do for this age; and to teach children and heathen such a lesson is calculated to effect their moral ruin.

II. CHARACTER OF SOLOMON

Solomon's writings and history both show that he was a libertine, a tyrant, and a polygamist. His tyrannical monopoly of seven hundred wives and three hundred prostitutes, making him a practical "Free-lover" on a large scale, is an indelible stigma upon his character. It was a usurpation of the rights, and a trespass upon the liberties, of nearly two thousand men and women. It prevented them from filling the mission or sphere in life that God designed them to enjoy. The organization of the sexes shows they were designed to be husbands and wives and parents. And the nearly equal number of the sexes is an evidence that nearly a thousand men were deprived of wives by Solomon's monopoly of women; while, on the other hand, those women were prevented from sustaining the true relation of wives. When he could not see those women more than once in three years by calling on one of them each day, it is a farce, and an insult to reason, to call them wives. Could a woman sustain the practical relation of wife to a man she only saw as husband once in three years? The very idea is ridiculous, and a mockery of the true marriage relation. And yet this is the man who is represented as being such a special favorite of God as to receive a portion of his divine wisdom. It is a slander, if anything can be, upon Infinite Wisdom. By reading his amorous song, we can learn his motives for enslaving such a large number of women. If this "wise man" is to be accepted as authority (and he should be if he got his wisdom directly from God), then we must relinquish all hope of an immortal existence. Hear him: "For that which befalleth the sons of men befalleth the beasts: ... as the one dieth, so dieth the other; yea, they have all one breath, so that a man hath no pre-eminence over a beast" (Eccles. iii. 19). Here is a plain and unequivocal denial of man's conscious existence beyond the grave. Nor does the Old Testament writer teach the doctrine. Job denies it in still more explicit terms, if possible. (See Job xiv. 10.)

III. Character of Lot

The act of Abram's brother Lot delivering his two daughters to the Sodomites, "to do to them as is good in your eyes" (Gen. xix. 8), must excite reflections in the highest degree revolting to the mind of every father who has daughters. The act of a father voluntarily offering up his virtuous daughters to gratify the depraved passions of a mob is too shocking to contemplate. And to accept such a character as a "righteous man" must certainly weaken the faith of the Bible believer in a true system of morality, and plant in his mind a very low standard of the moral perfections of God.

We are told (Gen. xix. 26) that Lot's wife was converted into a pillar of salt as a penalty for the simple act of looking back. Several absurdities are observable in this story:

1. It is difficult to conceive how any sin or crime could be attached to the natural act of turning the head to look in any direction, especially when no injunction had been laid upon the act.

2. If there were anything so inherently wrong in the act of looking back as to be visited with such direful penalties, pillars of salt would soon become more numerous than frogs were in Egypt.

3. Reason would suggest that, to put the thing in shape to be believed by future generations, the woman should have been converted into some imperishable substance, such as granite, gold, silver, or pig-iron. A woman made of salt, or salt of a woman, would soon dissolve and disappear.

4. The Hindus relate that a woman in India was once converted into a pillar of stone for an act of unchastity; and "the stone is there unto this day." Here is a story with a better foundation: the Egyptians have the tradition of a woman being converted into a tree for the act of plucking some fruit after it had been interdicted. How many of these stories should we credit?

CHAPTER 31

CHARACTER OF THE JEWISH PROPHETS

It is a circumstance indicative of the natural moral defects of the Jewish character, that their most "holy men," who were assumed to be familiar with the counsels of Infinite Wisdom, and on terms of daily intercourse with Jehovah, yet were, according to their own history, men of such defective moral habits and moral character as to be unreliable either as examples of moral rectitude, or with respect to their prophet's utterances. We will here present a brief sketch of the character of the principal prophets, drawn from their own "inspired writings":

The leading prophet Isaac says, "The priest and the *prophet* have erred through strong drink. They are swallowed up of wine. They are out of the way through strong drink. They err in vision. They stumble in judgment" (Isa. xxiv. 7).

Here is a sweeping charge against *all* the prophets—*not one* of them excepted. If they err in vision (of course he means *spiritual* vision), then what reliance can be placed in their prophecies, especially if it is true, as he declares in chap. ix., that "the prophets teach lies"? Then we cannot confide implicitly in anything they say. This conclusion, and also the foregoing portraiture of their character, is confirmed by Hosea, who says, in chap. ix., that "the Lord will punish the *prophets for their sins and their iniquities*"; also, "The *prophet* is a *snare* in all his ways; the *prophet* is a *fool*," etc. (Hos. ix. 7, 9). Micah says that they *divined for money,* and *made* the *people err.* What confidence, we ask, can be placed in men, either for truthfulness or as moral teachers, who are thus represented by their own historians and their own friends to be almost destitute of moral principle? Each one denounces all the others. The implied meaning in each case seems to be, "Take my pills, and beware of counterfeits." Zechariah, who was one of them, declared the Lord would drive them all out of the land with the unclean spirits (Zech. xiii. 2).

We should not, however, be surprised to find them possessing such a character, when their God, Jehovah, is represented as being no better, and is on the same moral plane. They, in fact, make him responsible for all their moral derelictions and sinful acts by representing him as being the author or instigator. "If a prophet be deceived, ... I the Lord have deceived that prophet" (Ezek. xiv. 9). Here the word prophet is used in a general sense, so as to imply that none are excepted. Jeremiah takes God at his word when he exclaims, "O Lord, thou hast deceived me" (Jer. xx. 7). Here, it will be observed, the moral character of Jehovah and his prophets were all cast in the same imperfect mold.

That superstition reigned supreme in the very *highest order* of the Jewish minds, to the exclusion of science, is shown by some of the wild, superstitious freaks of the prophets. Isaiah traveled through Egypt and Ethiopia three years stark naked (Isa. xx. 3). Such a disgusting exhibition, if attempted in this age of civilization, would terminate in a few hours by the lodgment of the lunatic in the calaboose. Jehovah, it appears, first prompted the act, and afterwards spoke approvingly of it by saying it was performed by "my servant Isaiah" (Isa. xx. 3).

Ezekiel and Habakkuk both would have us believe that God seized them by the hair of the head, and carried them—the former, the distance of eight miles; and the latter, three hundred miles. How Jehovah himself traveled while performing this feat of carrying the prophets is not explained. It must have been rather an unpleasant way of traveling, and must have caused some serious perturbation of mind lest the hair-hold should slip, and precipitate them to the ground. If this mode of travel could have been continued, it would have superseded the necessity of railroads.

Ezekiel, we are told, lay three hundred and ninety days on his left side, and forty days on his right side; and then, having swallowed a roll of parchment with the aid of Jehovah (Ezek. iii. 1), he was prepared for business. We are not told what was the object in swallowing such a formidable document, or how he managed to get into his stomach an article having a diameter four times that of his throat. Jeremiah wore cords around his neck, and a yoke on his back (rather a singular place for a yoke). Hosea claimed that God commanded him twice to go and marry a whore (Hos. i. 2). This looks like a connivance at, if not a tacit endorsement of, whoredom. Ezekiel relates a "story" about being carried by "the hand of the lord," and set down among some old dry bones, which he proceeded to invest with human flesh and sinews, and then drew skins over them to hold the flesh and bones together (Ezek. xxxvii.). Having thus manufactured a new supply of the *genus homo*, he invoked the four winds to inflate their bodies with breath, when, lo! there "stood upon their feet an exceeding great army." We use his own language. Here is a story that casts all the wild and weird tales of heathen mythology in the shade. There would have been no necessity for drafting soldiers in the recent Rebellion if the country could have been blessed with such a creative genius as Ezekiel. Such stories set all logic at defiance. If the first commandment, "Multiply and replenish the earth," had been neglected so as to render it necessary to adopt another process for increasing the number of human beings, certainly a more rational and decent mode might have been invented. We will not relate anymore of the curious capers of these "inspired men of God."

Some Christian writers have disposed of such erratic conduct, and such wild freaks of fancy, by assuming them to be the garb or metaphor of some great spiritual truth. This is explained by the proverb, "Necessity is the mother of invention"; but the common mind knows nothing of these inventions of the priesthood to save the credit of the Bible. Hence, whether true or false, such an explanation does not destroy the demoralizing influence of such ideas and language upon the public mind; and then it is derogatory to the character of God to assume he would do such senseless and unrighteous things as are related in some of the above cases. We insist that it would be a serious calamity upon the country to make a book containing such moral lessons, or rather immoral lessons, "the fountain of our laws and the supreme rule of our conduct," as urged by the Evangelical Alliance; and it is a sorrowful and deplorable circumstance that such a book is circulated among the heathen by the thousand as guides for their moral conduct. We wish they would refuse to accept it, as the Japanese have done in the past.

Elijah and Elisha

There are some peculiar features in the history of these two Hebrew prophets, for which they seem to merit a special notice. They appear to have been on very familiar terms with Jehovah; and the whole machinery of heaven, we are led to conclude, was under their control, with no special reason why they should merit such divine partiality, as they were not overstocked with practical righteousness. The acts of raising the dead and controlling the elements appear to have been to them very commonplace performances. One of Elijah's greatest miraculous feats was that of "shutting up the heavens," so that there was no dew nor rain for three years (1 Kings xvii. 1). Aside from the absolute impossibility of intercepting the action of the laws that control and regulate the entire machinery of the universe, there are several considerations that render this story wholly incredible.

1. It appears, from the language used, that this drought extended over the whole earth, and all nations must have suffered the direful consequences; and yet none of their histories alludes to it. The absence of rain and dew for three years must have caused the surface of the earth to become dry and parched to a considerable depth, particularly in the torrid zone. The creeks and rivulets must have been dried up. Every spear of grass, every tree, every plant, must have withered and perished; and all the cattle must have died for want of food and drink; and the people must have shared the same fate. Indeed, not a living thing could have been left upon the face of the earth where this drought prevailed. And yet no other history makes allusion to such a calamity; and a circumstance which renders it more incredible is that the moisture which is constantly ascending from the earth could not have been held in the upper strata of the atmosphere for half

that period of time. When it ascends and accumulates, and becomes sufficiently condensed, it must fall in the shape of rain.

2. It appears that the prophet himself, in order to escape the fatal consequences of this terrible visitation of divine wrath, was instructed to flee, and hide near the Brook Cherith, which was in the vicinity of Jordan. Here, we are told, he was fed by a raven, which brought him both bread and water. The queries naturally arise here, Where did the raven obtain those articles of food? Why can not suffering and starvation be prevented at the present day by a similar expedient? Why should several millions of human beings have suffered a terrible death by starvation in India within a recent period, if ravens can be employed as messengers of mercy? Why should God be partial? The preservation of the life of the prophet could not have been of so much more importance, judging from his subsequent history, as he achieved but little good afterward; and, as nobody claims to have seen the raven but Elijah, the case looks a little doubtful.

3. The next miraculous feat of Elijah was that of increasing a widow's barrel of meal and cruse of oil after they were nearly exhausted, so that they lasted for many months. In nearly all such cases, we find incredible features, in addition to the impossibility of performing the act. No reason can be found, in the history of this case, for bestowing such miraculous favors upon this woman that would not apply to thousands of women now, some of them even in a worse state of suffering, and in greater need of divine aid. It does not appear that the miracle had the effect to convince anybody of the might and power of his God, nor that it was designed to produce such an effect. Hence, nothing was accomplished by it but the relief of the poor widow's wants, which was a very good thing; but, as we have already remarked, she mad no more claim upon the benevolence and munificence of God than thousands of poor widows and others of the present day who receive no such aid.

4. The prophet performed, we are told, another miracle for the benefit of this woman, though we do not learn that she was more righteous than other women. Her son sickened and died (perhaps the meal was not in a very healthy condition), and Elijah restored him to life. If there were any truth in the story, it could be accounted for by supposing the boy was in a state of catalepsy, or trance, as life has been revived in numerous cases in persons in this condition in modern times; and the conduct of Elijah furnishes some evidence that he understood it in this light. He took the body into an upper room, so the performance should not be witnessed by any of the company (perhaps for fear of being disturbed; and he was probably apprehensive that they would suspicion, from his actions, that the boy was not dead). In fact, the narrator does not say he was dead, but only

that the breath had gone out of him; and this could be said in any case of swooning, trance, or catalepsy.

5.   Ahab is reported as reproving Elijah for bringing so much suffering upon the people by the great drought.   The reason the prophet assigns for this divine judgment is worthy of note.   It was because Ahab and his subjects worshipped a false God (Baalim).   This explains the whole affair.   The Jews were always assuming that those who did not worship as they did were worshipers of false Gods; but there is no evidence of this, and no reason in the assumption.   As St. John (i. 18) declares, "No man has seen God at any time," it follows that each worshiper, under every system of religion, pictures out the form, size, shape, and character of God for himself; and, certainly, other nations had as much right to form their own mental conceptions of God as the Jews had, and were as likely to form a correct idea of him as they.   They could not picture out a worse God than Jehovah.   Here we have a true explanation of the reason the Jews were perpetually denouncing and making war on other nations: it was simply because they would not subscribe to the Jewish creed.   The Jews were creed-worshippers.

6.   This conclusion is confirmed by the relation, in the next chapter, of a contest between the God of Elijah and the God of the prophets of Baal. We are told that Elijah's God could kindle a fire upon the altar, while theirs could not.   Here is admitted the existence of other Gods.   The only difference between them is Elijah's God was a little smarter.   The same is aimed to be shown in numerous other contests between Jehovah and other Gods.   It is merely a trial of skill, strength, and knowledge.

7.   And because the God of the prophets of Baal fell a little and could not quite equal the achievements of Jehovah, we are told that Elijah put the prophets all to death.   Here is another circumstance tending to show that Elijah could not have been a true servant of a just God; for such a God would not sanction such cruelty.   But the story carries an absurdity upon the face of it.   To suppose that four hundred and fifty men would stand quietly, and submit to be slain by one man single-handed and alone, without any resistance, is altogether too incredible to be entertained for a moment.

8.   The next achievement of Elijah, after eating a barley cake, baked on the coals, and drinking a cruse of water (1 Kings xix. 8), was to walk forty days and forty nights, without stopping to eat or sleep.   This performance was almost equal to that of the Hindu, Yalpa, who walked round the sun in eleven hours.   One story is just as credible as the other.

9.   We are told that when Ahaziah, who succeeded his father Ahab upon the throne, got crippled by falling, and sent to consult the God of Ekron, Elijah, on hearing of it, asked why he did not consult the God of

Israel (2 Kings i. 6); and, when the king's messengers reported to him what the prophet Elijah had said, he sent fifty messengers to the prophet to invite him to come and see him, that he might consult with him. These messengers treated him very respectfully and called him "the man of God"; but the prophet, we are told, instead of complying with the king's request, called down fire from heaven, which consumed the whole number. When the king heard of the circumstance, he sent fifty more messengers, who shared the same fate, and were likewise consumed by fire from heaven. An uncivil and very wicked thing for a righteous prophet to do.

10. We are told that Elijah, in the course of his travels, came to a stream of water, and took off his mantle, and smote it. The water parted hither and thither, and permitted him to walk in the bottom of the stream. Another display of his great miraculous power; but it is void of truth.

11. The last astounding feat reported of this miraculous prophet was that of ascending to heaven in a chariot of fire, with horses made of the same material. Rather a hazardous mode of traveling. This story is contradicted both by the laws of nature, and the express declaration of the Bible itself. The former teaches us that the fire would have been extinguished for want of oxygen before he had ascended many miles from the earth; and the latter declares, "Flesh and blood can not enter the kingdom of heaven"; and also that "no man hath ascended up to heaven but he that came down from heaven"—Christ Jesus (John iii. 13).

There are several circumstances which render these marvelous achievements of Elijah wholly incredible, in addition to their setting aside the laws of nature. We cannot learn that any good was accomplished by it. It does not appear that anybody was converted to a life of practical righteousness; while we must assume that God must have had some great purpose in view to cause him to thus set aside and trample under foot his own laws. On the other hand, a great deal of bad feeling was engendered, and a great many lives destroyed. And then there is no allusion whatever to these astonishing miracles in any other history. All these circumstances and considerations warrant us in discarding the whole affair, though Christian writers attach great importance to it.

The marvelous deeds of Elisha appear to be, to a considerable extent, a mere repetition of those of Elijah. Like his predecessor, he raised a dead child to life, increased the supply of oil for a widow after it had run short, and also increased the quantity of good water for the people by a supernatural process, though not by a shower of rain, as Elijah did, after a three years' drought. There is evidently a disposition to imitate and outdo his predecessor: hence, he brings water without the process of rain. There are two or three incidents in his history worthy of notice:

1. When Elijah took his perilous flight heavenward, and left him alone, we are told he rent his garments. This act, although customary among "the Lord's holy people," was rather an insane way of manifesting his grief. A man in this age doing so would be taken to the insane asylum.

2. The second performance of Elisha, deserving particular notice, was an act of malignant revenge upon some frolicsome boys reminding him that he was bald-headed. For this simple, childish, though rude, act of calling him "bald-head," we are told he caused "two bears to come out of the woods, and tear forty-two of them to pieces." Why the other children escaped this fate, we are not told. This conduct on the part of the prophet evinces a morose, cruel, and revengeful disposition, instead of a philanthropic and benevolent one, as we should have expected the Lord's chosen prophet to manifest. If the story were a credible one, it would be a stigma upon his character while it stands on the page of history.

3. There is one circumstance related in the history of Elisha that seems to indicate that he was a man of rather gross habits. It is stated that when he killed a yoke of oxen for food, he "boiled their flesh with the instruments of the oxen," and gave the people to eat (1 Kings xix. 21). We infer, from this language, that the oxen were thrown into the cooking-vessel whole, without being skinned or cleaned. It must have been rather a rare dish, and a tough one also.

4. We will notice one more remarkable incident in the history of this remarkable prophet. We are told that, as some men were felling some trees on the banks of the Jordan, one of them, by accident, let his ax fall into the stream. On the case being reported to Elisha, he soon relieved the man of his trouble by throwing a stick into the water, which caused the ax to swim. Here is another specimen of the philosophy of the Christian Bible. Heathen mythology is full of such lawless stories. When the boat in which a Hindu was rowing capsized, and threw his dinner into the Indus, a fish was accommodating enough to arrest it in its descent, and bring it to the surface, and restore it to the hungry boatman. A very accommodating fish—as much so as the stick!

We will now take a view of the moral bearing of the stories of these great "God-chosen" and "God-favored prophets," as one Christian writer styles them. We must assume that God would not suspend the action of those laws which secure order and harmony throughout nature to perform such miracles as the prophets are represented as performing, unless some great and important end was to be accomplished by it. Well, let us see if this was the result; if not, we must assume that these miracles were never performed. According to Dr. Lardner, miracles were always designed to accomplish some great good, and generally to remove the skepticism of unbelievers, and to convince them of the mighty power of God. But we do not find that any such effects were produced by any of the miracles here reported. The performance of Elijah did not convert Ahab nor Jezebel, nor the worshipers of Baal, either to the faith or to a life of practical righteousness; nor did those of Elisha convert Naaman; nor did either of the prophets convert or reform any of the thousands of heathen in the countries through which they traveled. The contemporary kings of Judah and Israel still continued in their ungodly course as before. In a word, nobody was benefited, nobody reformed, and no good effected by any of these miracles, only to a few individuals, who could have been accommodated in the usual way, by ordinary means. On the other hand, bad feelings were engendered, many lives lost, and much suffering caused by their miraculous proceedings. We must conclude, then, that so far as any agency of God is claimed in the several cases, these miracles were never performed; and we have the negative testimony of history to prove still further that these miracles were never wrought. The history of no other nation mentions them, not even the three years of drought; yet Christ speaks of it, and endorses it with all its impossibilities and all its bad consequences, which is an evidence of his ignorance of natural law. As these stories, by their stultifying absurdities, do violence to our reason, and also to our moral faculties, on account of the cruelty, injustice, bloodshed (for it shows both prophets were murderers), we hold, from these considerations, that the influence of these stories is demoralizing, and that they should not be put into the hands of the heathen, as they are every year by the thousand.

CHAPTER 32

IDOLATRY: ITS NATURE, HARMLESSNESS AND ORIGIN

There is no act, no species, of human conduct, nothing recognized as a sin within the lids of the Christian Bible, which is perhaps more fearfully or more frequently condemned, or denounced with more awful and terrible penalties, than that of idolatry. Those who practiced it are ranked with murderers and liars (Rev. xxii. 15); and it is declared, "They shall not inherit the kingdom of God" (1 Cor. vi. 9), but "shall have their portion in the lake of fire and brimstone" (Rev. xxi. 8). Now, we propose to bestow a brief examination upon the origin, character, and practical moral effect of this ancient practice, that we may learn the nature of the custom which is thus placed at the head of the list of the acts of human depravity, and regarded as the blackest and most infamous crime ever perpetrated by sinful man.

We find it manifested under various forms, the original or most primitive aspect of which, so far as disclosed by the light of history, is known as *Fetishism*—the worship of inanimate objects. Stretching the imagination far away in the rearward of time—far back along the receding pathway of human history, over a series of many thousands, not to say millions, of years—we arrive at a period in which man is found occupying a plane of mere animal, sensorial existence, connected with which was an imperfect development of perception and reflection. In this era of his mental growth he began to perceive and recognize the motions of objects around him. He observed bright and shining bodies rolling over his head—one by day, and ten thousand more by night. At least he observed that they changed positions—being in one locality in the morning, and in the opposite direction in the evening. What conclusion from these observations could be more natural, more childlike (for, bear in mind, this was really the childhood of the race), or more reasonable than that these bodies possessed life—that they inherently possessed the power of locomotion, the same ability to move that he did himself—just as the infant, now gazing out upon the sky from the lap of its mother, fancies the darting meteor to be a bird or an animal? Wherever the ignorant, illiterate, primitive inhabitants of our globe perceived motion—whether it was displayed in the revolution of the planets, the falling tree, or the rippling stream—there they associated life and motion. And, soon learning that these adjuncts of nature possessed a power and force superior to that with which they themselves were endowed, their feelings of awe and veneration were thereby excited; and to the highest degree their deep in-wrought devotional feelings first found an outlet by bowing in humble acknowledgment to the superior greatness of the shining orbs wheeling in such majestic grandeur along the deep blue sky, and "bidding defiance to all below." This is believed to have been the first form, the first practical manifestation, of religious worship, and the first form or phase of idolatry now denominated Fetishism.

Polytheism. This word is from *polus*, "many," and *Theos*, "God," and hence is used to denote a belief in many or several Gods, which comprehends the second form and stage of idolatry. We have spoken of the early recognition by the primitive inhabitants of the earth of the motion of the heavenly bodies as giving rise to the belief that they possessed self-constituted life and volition. But progressing a step farther, their attention was turned to motion where there was no visible agent to produce it—action without a visible actor. The thunder rolled and reverberated along the great archway of heaven, the winds whistled and moaned through the thick foliage of the trees, and rushed along the valleys, oft-times with such violence as to overturn their rude tenements, and prostrate the towering oak at their feet. Yet nothing could be seen of the agent that produced these direful effects. No being, no agent, no cause adequate for their production, was visible. Hence, they very naturally concluded that they were produced by invisible beings that could wing their way through space without being seen. This assumed discovery soon gave rise to the thought that the stars might be moved by these beings, instead of possessing, as they had previously been supposed to do, an inherent power of motion of their own. And these prime movers of the planets they concluded to be Gods, or moving spirits. Thus originated the notion of a plurality of Gods, each planet having a separate ruling Deity. And the sun—being greatly superior to, transcending in magnitude, light, power, and influence, all the other luminaries, with their qualities all combined—was, with the most childlike naturalness, supposed to be ruled by the chief of the Gods, "the Lord of lords and King of kings." It was he who, every morning throwing open the magnificent portals of the Orient—the huge golden gates of the eastern horizon—slowly lifted aloft his stupendous body of light to dispel the deep dark gloom which for many hours had been spread like a pall over universal nature. It was he who, plowing his way through the heavens, despite the mist and clouds piled upon the great highway of his wonted arch, rolled down at eventide the western declivity of the cerulean causeway to give place to Luna, queen of night, realizing that,

> "Soon as the evening shades prevail,
> The moon takes up the wondrous tale";

and that

> "Ten thousand marshaled stars, a silver zone,
> Diffuse their blended radiance round the throne."

The Bible of Bibles

It was this mighty solar orb, "the king of day," who, having performed his wonted journey to the south, returned in early spring to banish the chilling blasts of the dreary cold season; to drive from off the earth the biting frosts and freezing snows of gloom-dispensing winter, and pour down, in lieu thereof, his genial and vivifying rays to waken the flowers; to call forth vegetation, and ultimately ripen the golden harvest. In a word, he dispensed heat, light, life, and blessings innumerable over all the earth. How easy, how natural, then, it was for the untutored savage to conclude that the indwelling or ondwelling spirit of the sun was "the chief of the Gods," to whom all the inferior Deities (those who presided over the stars) bowed in humble allegiance, acknowledging his superior sway, his right to rule over the boundless universe! The sun, being thus the great central wheel of all recognized power—i.e., the tabernacle or ondwelling place of the supreme, omnipotent God—became the principal object of admiration and adoration, the pivot around which clustered their deepest devotional aspirations; the subordinate Deities of the planets holding but a second place in their devout contemplations and uprising venerations. The worship of these imaginary beings, including the ruling and overruling "God of all," with his tabernacle pitched in the blazing sun, is now termed idolatry, and may be regarded as the second phase or form of this species of worship.

Hence, we may note it as a remarkable circumstance, that all the principal systems of religion now existing, as well as most of those which have passed away, exhibit very strong marks of this ancient solar worship; and it is more especially remarkable, that both Judaism and Christianity, with all their exalted claims to a supernatural origin, should be, as they seemingly are, deeply tinctured with this ancient Sabean or solar worship. Distinct traces of it are observable in the whole religious nomenclature of Christianity. It, in fact, pervades the whole system. This declaration is borne out by the fact that nearly every divine epithet, nearly every name applied to the Deity in the Christian scriptures, including those addressed to Jesus Christ, and also nearly every theological term in both the Old and New Testaments, are traceable to the ancient solar worship; that is, the words, when traced to their roots, or original form, are found to have been solar titles. We will present some samples by way of proof:

The divine title Lord, in the New Testament, is translated from the Greek *Kuros,* which is the Persian name for the sun; God is from *Gad,* an Ammonian name for the sun; Jehovah, by translation and declension, becomes Jupiter, which, according to Macrobius, is "the sun itself"; Deity is from the Latin *Deus,* which is traceable to *dies,* a day—a period of time measured by the sun; Jesus is from *Jes* or *J-es* (with the Latin termination *us*), which means "the one great fire of the sun"; and Christ is derived from *Chris*, a Chaldean term for the sun; and so on of other divine titles. And whole phrases of scripture-texts disclose the same idolatrous solar origin. Why is Jesus Christ called "the sun of righteousness"? (spelled *s-u-n*, let it be noticed), as this text, quoted from Malachi, is assumed to apply to him; and why is the term "light," so frequently used and preferred throughout the Christian scriptures, to denote the spiritual condition of man? Why are nations, whose minds are cultivated and stored with knowledge, said to be "enlightened"? Certainly, to our external vision, they are as opaque as the most grossly ignorant barbarians. But they are called enlightened when advanced in knowledge, simply because all knowledge was once supposed to be imparted by the God of the sun through its descending rays of light. Hence, light and knowledge are now synonymous terms.

David says, "The Lord is my light and my salvation" (Ps. xxvii. 1)—just what the ancient pagans used to say of the sun. Isaiah says, "The Lord shall be to thee an everlasting light" (Isa. lx. 19)—exactly such a conception as the ancient heathen entertained of the sun, to which its application is more obviously appropriate. Habakkuk says, "His brightness was as light" (iii. 4). Apply this language to the sun, and its meaning becomes strikingly significant. Christ is said to be "a light to lighten the Gentiles," "the true light," "the light of the world," etc.; and yet we cannot discover that those who have embraced his doctrines, and thus come into possession of this "true light," shed anymore light upon a devious pathway, traveled in the darkness of night, than the veriest Jewish pharisee or infidel.

The Christian reader will reply, "These phrases are mere figures of speech." To be sure, they are; we admit it. But then their derivation and origin are none the less obvious, and, when scrutinizingly examined, disclose remote traces of Oriental idolatry; and, moreover, they most unmistakably prove Christianity to be of heathen extraction with respect to its verbal habiliments, or external vestment, as well as the main drift and scope of its doctrines and teachings, as shown elsewhere. We will observe further that such conceptions (found in the Christian Bible) as "God is a consuming fire," "God is light," etc. (John i. 5), originated in the primeval ages, when God was supposed to reside in the sun; also such ejaculations as "O Lord, the Gentiles shall come to thy light, and kings to the brightness of thy rising" (Isa. lx. 3). The words "light," "brightness," and "rising" apply with striking force to the sun, and were used by the ancient Persians in such a relation, while, on the other hand, it is difficult to discover any sense or appropriateness in applying them—at least the word "rising"—to the Supreme Being; for he is represented as always occupying "the highest heavens": so there can be no higher point to rise to. We might also ask,

Why are "the Lord's day" and "Sunday" used as synonymous terms? Or why is the Lord now worshipped on the very day anciently set apart for the worship of the sun or solar Deities? Do not these facts prove that many remnants of the ancient idolatrous religions are still retained in Christian theology?

Monotheism. This word—from *monos*, one, or alone, and *Theos*, God—represents a belief in but one God. We have shown in the preceding section how a belief in a plurality of Gods originated. We will now trace the progress of this idea to a unitary conception of the Deity. It will be observed, by the study of ancient theology, that, as the human mind becomes enlightened and expanded by the discovery of the laws governing the heavenly bodies, the lesser or inferior Deities gradually fall into disbelief and disuse, and "the Supreme Holy One" proportionally becomes exalted in the devout affections of the worshipping multitude, until most religious nations become, in one view, virtually and practically monotheists. And it may be remarked here that, as neither the imaginary God nor carved images of God were objects of worship by the most enlightened classes of any nation, they cannot strictly and truthfully be termed idolaters. Hence, some writers are bold to affirm there never was a nation of idolaters; and we incline to this opinion. We are also bold to affirm that there never was, properly speaking, a nation of monotheists—believing in but one God, and no more—neither Jews nor Christians excepted; and we are likewise prepared to exhibit the proof of the animation, that every nation, reported in history making a profession of religion, has acknowledged the existence of *one supreme God.* This is true even of those who believe in a multiplicity of Gods—a circumstance which places both Jews and Christians in rather an awkward position, claiming as they do, and always have done, a monopoly of this faith; and the fact that they have long professedly labored to bring other nations to this belief, while some of those nations have, as we shall show, been much more consistent, both in the belief and practice of this doctrine, than themselves, places them, as we conceive, in rather a ludicrous aspect. The Christian Bible and the Christian world have arrogated vastly too much to themselves, and overstepped the bounds of truth, in claiming to be the only propagators of the unitary conception of a God, as the following citations from historical authorities will clearly manifest:

1. Christians have a numerous *cortege*, or retinue, of angels in their system of inspired theology, as is shown in various parts of the Bible, which, in theological parlance, must be regarded as so many secondary Gods, inasmuch as they are assigned the same duties, perform the same functions, and sustain precisely the same relation to the supernal Deity as

did the subordinate Gods of the pagans under the ancient systems. It is, in fact, only a change of name, in order to get rid of the illogical dilemma of holding to the existence of but one God, while virtually acknowledging the existence of many. We might cite many facts and testimonies from history in proof of this statement, but will restrict ourselves to one. Mr. Higgins says, "All nations believed in one supreme God, and many subordinates. The latter some termed angels; others called them Gods." More anciently than the Jews, we find that the Babylonians, Chaldeans, Persians, and Syrians all vested these subordinate beings with the properties of mere angels. "Angels," then, with Christians, we legitimately infer, is only another name for second-class Gods, or subordinate Deities of the Orientals.

2. Even if we should pass over, as unworthy of consideration, the historical facts which go to identify the Christian angels with the subordinate Deities of the ancient pagans, there is yet spread out before us a broad and tenable ground for charging Christians with being polytheists—that is, for rejecting their pretensions of worshipping and preaching a unitary God; for it is a very striking and depreciating fact that, notwithstanding their boastful and arrogating claims, there are many texts in the Old Testament which imply, in the most distinct manner, a belief in a plurality of Gods. Indeed, the first passage in the book, according to Mr. Parkhurst, would read, if correctly translated, "In the beginning the *Gods* created the heavens and the earth," thus disclosing an acknowledgment of more than one God. And we find many other passages that are made to conceal the old polytheistic idea by a wrong translation. Fortunately, however, for the disclosure of truth, there are many texts in which it comes very distinctly to the surface. As for example, in Genesis i. 26, we have the undisguised language, "Let *us* make man in *our* own image." Now "us" and "our" being plural pronouns, it would be folly and nonsense to deny that they refer to a plurality of *Gods*. "Let us make man" means, "Let us Gods make man," for no sophistry, shifting, or dodging can make sense of it with any other construction. And several times, in this and other chapters, is similar language used. We will cut the matter short by observing, upon the authority of Parkhurst, that *Aleim* and *Elohim* are the Hebrew plurals used to represent God in the Old Testament; that these are much more frequently employed than the singular forms, *Al* and *El*, thus disclosing the conception of a plurality of Gods beyond dispute.

3. And this argumentation acquires additional logical strength when based on the fact that the Jews did not claim Jehovah as the *only* God, but merely as supreme to other Gods. He was "God of Gods" and "Lord of Lords." Nor was he claimed to be a God of any but the Jewish nation. Jethro is made to say, "Now I know that Jehovah is greater than all Gods"

(Exod. xviii. 11). And in Exodus xv. 11 it is asked, "Who is like unto Jehovah among the Gods?" Just such a claim as is put forth for Jupiter by Homer in his Iliad:

> "O first and greatest God, by Gods adored,
> We own thy power, our Father and our Lord!"

Hence, it will be observed, that if there were any merit or any honor in professing faith in a unitary Deity, or any truth forming a basis for such a claim, neither Jews nor Christians could justly arrogate a monopoly of such faith, inasmuch as there is an older claim to the doctrine.

4. But we find that the professors of the Christian faith occupy still more untenable and more palpably erroneous ground than the Jews with respect to the profession of holding strictly to the unitary conception of Deity; for they not only tacitly accept the contradictory phases of this doctrine, which we have pointed out above, in the Jewish writings, but they add thereto a new installment or chapter of errors by having accepted into their creed the old Oriental doctrine of a trinity of Gods. They have "God the Father, God the Son, and God the Holy Ghost," which present us with a family of Gods as complete and absolute as the confederated union of Gods in either the ancient Hindu or Grecian Pantheon. To allege, in defense, that these three Gods were all one, while we find each in various parts of the Bible spoken of separately, and discriminated by peculiar and distinct properties and titles, instead of mitigating the error and contradiction, such a plea only aggravates it. In the same sense, the Hindus claimed that their thousand Gods were one. And all the triads or trinities of Gods swarming through the ancient mythologies were proclaimed to be each "a trinity in unity," so that such a defense only lands the professor of Christianity amongst heathen myths.

5. The absurdity of the Christian Church in professing to worship a single God, also making a profession of rising above and contemning the idolatrous, polytheistic conception of Deity, culminates in their act of embodying and incorporating the infinite deityship in "the man Christ Jesus," and declaring him to possess "the fullness of the Godhead bodily." For we thus have one *full* and absolute God perambulating the earth in the person of Christ during his temporary sojourn here, while another absolute God (the Father) occupied the throne of heaven, thus presenting us with a plurality of Gods too marked and undisguised to admit a rational defense. A profession of monotheism arrayed with such facts bespeaks folly supreme.

The polytheism of the ancient heathen is science and sense compared with such jargon. For, with all their Gods, they never paid divine honors, or prayed to but one God ("The Supreme Ruler"); while Christians, on the contrary, worship all of theirs—Father, Son, and Holy Ghost—frequently naming each one separately in their supplications to the throne of grace, thus rendering themselves more open to the charge of polytheism, and that species of idolatry which consists in worshipping several Gods, than those whom they condemn as heathen for committing similar acts. We will prove this statement. The reverend missionary, D. O. Allen, says of a large body of heathen professors, "They believe in the existence of beings whom they call Gods, but do not recognize them as possessing any qualities, or as having any agencies in human affairs, which properly make them objects of worship. They resemble the angels in the Christian system. Brahma with them is the supreme God, and all the other Gods offer him worship." It is evident, then, that they virtually worship but one God, the inferior Deities being but angels; while Christians, on the contrary, have placed two, if not three, Gods on the throne. When, then, have the best claim to be considered monotheists?

6. And what sense, we would ask, can attach to the profession of monotheism with such a God as the Bible sets forth—a limited, local, personal God. No doctrine stands out more prominently as a fundamental tenet of the Christian faith than that which makes God appear a circumscribed, finite being. He is represented in their "inspired" book as possessing those qualities, properties, faculties, and functions which only a local, organized being can possess—such as a body, head, eyes, nose, mouth, arms, fingers, feet, stomach, bowels, heart, etc.; as eating, sleeping, walking, talking, riding, laboring, resting, laughing, crying; and as getting angry and jealous, and cursing, swearing, smiting, fighting, etc., and on one occasion getting whipped or vanquished in a fight because the enemy were fortified with chariots of iron. (See Josh. xvii. 16.) And hardly was creation completed before he was down in Eden striding over the bushes, hunting for his lost child Adam—the first sample of the *genus homo*. And several times he had to leave his golden throne and descend to earth before he could be posted in human affairs.

Now it must be evident to any person possessing a moiety of common sense that such a limited, local, circumscribed being, limited in size, and restricted in powers and qualities as Jehovah is represented in the Bible to be, could neither be omnipotent, omniscient, nor omnipresent. True, Christians consider him so; but the Bible fails to make him so. And hence there would be room in infinite space for countless millions of such Gods, and the doctrine of polytheism would be perfectly consistent. Indeed, such a dwarfish and circumscribed God would need thousands of such confederates to aid him in governing the countless worlds of the vast universe; so that the polytheistic doctrine from the Christian standpoint becomes a necessity, as it does also from another plane of view. We are told in Gen. i. that the work of creation was completed in six days; that the myriads of worlds which now chase each other through the sky were all rolled out of the vortex of infinitude in a week. But it is evident to every scientific or reflecting mind that a million of years would not have sufficed for the work, especially for such a God as Moses describes and sets to the task. Hence, the period of creation should be extended, or the number of Gods increased *ad infinitum*, to save the credibility of the cosmological traditions. We would say, then, that, for the following reasons, the more Gods Christians acknowledge, the better for the consistency of their cause:

1. Their conception of the Divine Essence is that of a local, limited, anthropomorphic, organized being, in exact conformity with the notion of the ancient pagans; with which, in order to have every part of the infinite universe supplied, would require more in number than the most fertile imagination of the heathen ever created.

2. A countless host of such finite Gods would have been required to complete the work of creation in six days.

3. There is room enough for any number of such finite Gods to exist without encroaching on each other's dominions.

4. There should have been at least one such God to be assigned the creation of each planetary world, which would require many millions of creative entities.

5. And the superintendent of the endlessly complicated machinery of each planet, and the supply, specifically and individually, of the various wants of its swarming millions of diversified inhabitants, would require an infinite host more of such local Gods as Jehovah of the Jews.

6. And, as Christians already practically acknowledge the worship of three Gods, the addition of three hundred or three thousand more would only be an extension of the principle, and could not be a whit more objectionable. For it is not any specific number of Gods they object to, but a "plurality"; and three is as certainly and absolutely a plurality as three hundred or three thousand. From the above considerations, founded on views of consistency, we think Christians should ground their arms, and cease their moral warfare upon the votaries of other religions for being polytheistic or idolatrous. And "the sin of worshipping many Gods," which they declaim so much on, is all a mere phantom. We cannot see how the divine mind could possibly be offended at the simple mistake of overnumbering the Godhead. We will illustrate the case. We will suppose

a merchant in Cincinnati orders a bill of goods from New York, addressing the order to John Ap John & Co. The latter opens and examines it, then returns it unfilled, with the following quaint protest: "Sir, there is no 'Co.' attached to my address. It is simply John Ap John; and you have insulted my dignity by this mistake, thus assuming that I have not the brain and bullion to do business on my own hook, but must have partners. I therefore return it with contempt for your insolent blunder." Now, we ask if there can be a man found who would be guilty of displaying such coxcomb vanity as this. We know not. Then, why charge it upon an infinite God—an all-wise Deity—by supposing that a prayer addressed, by an innocent mistake, to a hundred or a thousand Gods would not be as acceptable to him as if addressed to him alone, or even if erroneously addressed to the Christian trinity of Father, Son, and Holy Ghost?

The Construction and Worship of Images. In Exod. xx. 4 we find the following command: "Thou shalt not make unto thee any graven image or any likeness *of any thing* that is in heaven above, or that is in the earth beneath, or that is in the water under the earth." Here, it will be observed, is a sweeping interdiction against image-making; and, as it prohibits "the likeness of *any thing* that is in heaven above or the earth beneath," it is a dead-lock upon the fine arts. All engravings, paintings, photographs, etc., with which the civilized world is now flooded, and which hold high rank among the arts and sciences, involve an open infraction of this command. And hence, this biblical interdiction being devoid of reason, and of an anti-civilizing tendency, the enlightened portion of Christendom, by common consent, tramples it heedlessly under foot. And we are bold to say that this command is both foolish and of impracticable application; for a living, thinking human being can no more avoid forming images of everything that comes within the range of his mental vision, whether situated in heaven above or the earth beneath, than he can stop the entire machinery of his thoughts, or the blood from circulating through his veins. It is as natural as eating, and as inevitable as breathing. To be sure, he does not give expression with wool, metal, or canvas to every image formed in the mind; but the nature of the act, morally speaking, is precisely the same as if he did. St. Clemens admits this when he declares it to be a sin for women to look in the glass, because they form images of themselves. All true, viewed from the Christian standpoint, which regards image making as a sin.

The most sinful or reprehensible act of image making, however, in the view of Christians, is the construction of idols or images to represent the Deity. Living in a civilized age, they would be ashamed to occupy the broad ground assumed by the command which we have quoted above, which forbids the likeness of everything that exists; yet they still hold that it is wrong to make images of the Deity—not anymore so, according to the above command, than the acceptance of engravings of animals and photographs of friends. But where is the man now living, or when did the man live, who has not formed images of the Deity, or who does not instinctively and habitually do it every day of his life? Every man makes a likeness of God, or what he supposes to be such, every time he thinks of such a being. It is impossible to make him the subject of thought without constructing a mental image of him—i.e., without constructing an image of him in the brain. And can it be more sinful to make an image of him with the hand than with the head—in other words, to construct a likeness of him externally, than to construct it internally? Certainly not. One is shaped out in the mind; the other is shaped out of a block of wood or metal; and most certainly, if the latter is idolatry, the former is also. The Christian kneels in supplication with the image of God set up in his mind; the pagan worships with the image set up in the temple or on the altar. One is externally represented with words; the other with wood. The only difference between the Christian and pagan idolatry is that, after each has sketched out a likeness of the Creator upon the tablet or dial-plate of his mind according to his conception of the form of Deity, the Christian stops short with his work but half completed, while the pagan goes on and gives practical expression to his by representing it with wood, stone, or other material, by which it is more thoroughly impressed upon the memory, and "the devout contemplation," "the remembrance of God," kept more constantly in the mind; and thus the savage is proved to be the most practically religious of the two.

We have shown that the representation and delineation upon canvas, paper, wood, or steel, of the various objects of art—of human creation—are set down as the highest marks and the most distinguishing proofs of civilization. And can it be right and laudable to thus represent or image the works of the Creator, and wrong to image the Creator himself? Not according to the above command. Or can one be pleasing to him, and the other offensive? There is neither sense nor science, logic nor lore, in such conclusions. Christian reader, do you not know that your little innocent daughter violates the command every day of her happy life by nursing, dressing, and caressing her wax doll, her *image* miniature man? For if it be true—and the Bible teaches it—that "man was created in the image of God," then these artificial human likenesses, these images of the infant man, are also images of God; and your little girl daily commits "the awful sin of idolatry," and you, too, for countenancing her in the act. It may be noticed here that the pious Christian confers upon himself an honor which he denies to the Creator when he has his photograph struck off for the

168

accommodation of a friend, while he denounces as idolatry all attempts to construct an imaginary likeness of God. But consistency is a jewel rarely found.

Image-Worship. We may be met here with the answer that "it is not the making of images, but the worship of images, in lieu of the worship of God, that constitutes idolatry." To this we reply, we have no proof that any nation or people reported in history were ever obnoxious to the charge. True, the people of many countries have been in the habit of prostrating themselves before idols in their daily worship. Yet in no case which we have examined do we find that those idols were worshipped with the thought of their being the true and living God, or of their being endowed with divine attributes, but only as types or representations of God. It is possible that some of the lower stratum of society—some of the debased and ignorant—may have been deluded into the idea that God had taken up his abode in those lifeless images. In fact, we are assured that the priest, in some cases, labored to instill this belief into their minds. Some of them may have been ignorant and pliable enough to be misled by his artful misrepresentation. But, by a large proportion of the idol-worshipers of every nation, we have the highest authority for asserting that these artificial images were not regarded as anything more than the mere representation, or outward type, of the Deity, and were venerated with the same religious conviction which Christians experience in partaking of the body and blood of Christ with the images of bread and wine, and without the suspicion of incurring the charge of idolatry. The two acts are precisely the same in spirit and essence. But the untutored denizens of the Pacific isles do not conceive that the dumb and lifeless sylvan figure before which they prostrate themselves in worship is the omnipotent, self-existent God, the Creator of heaven and earth, more truly than the Christians believe they are really eating and drinking "the body and blood of Christ" when partaking of the sacrament. They are both mere symbols, or representations, of something higher. It is irrational to suppose that beings endowed with minds believe that inanimate figures of gold, silver, iron, etc., possess omnipotent thought, power, and feeling.

That able, pious Muhammadan writer, Abel Fezzel, declares (in his "Aren Akberry") that "the opinion that the Hindus (who make many idols) are idolaters has no foundation in fact; but they are worshipers of God, and only one God." "This," says the modern traveler, Mr. Ditson of New York, "I know to be true; for I had it from the lips of the Hindus themselves." And this will apply with undiminished force to other nations habitually styled idolaters. "Even the most savage nations," says Mr. Parker, "regard their idols only as types of God." And we might quote whole pages from heathen writers to that effect. The ancient Grecian poet Ovid says, "It is Jove we adore in the image of God." "The Gods inhabit our minds and bodies," says Statius, a Latin writer, "and not the images made to represent them." Hence, it is evident they had a perception of their true character. And the missionary, Rev. D. O. Allen, tells us that even those who have been represented as worshipping the sun, moon, and stars, only contemplate these planets as symbols of the Deity, and that "their worship is really aimed to the invisible, omnipotent, omnipresent God." It appears, then, that whatever external objects the most ignorant and savage tribes have addressed, or have been supposed to worship, have been used merely as types and symbols to enhance their devotion in the worship of the true God. Though, as Cicero remarks (in his philosophical works), "A few may have been so feeble in their perceptions as to confound and identify the statues and Gods together." But another writer avers, "There is not in all antiquity the least trace of a prayer addressed to a statue." He also says, "All paganism does not offer a single fact which can lead to the conclusion that they ever adored idols; nor was there ever a law compelling them to do so." When Paul declared to the Athenians, "Whom ye ignorantly worship, him declare I unto you," he confessed most explicitly that they worshipped the true God through their idols. Where, then, is the sin of idolatry?

In one of the Hindu Bibles (the Bhagavad-Gita) God is made to say, "They who serve other Gods with a firm belief of being right do really involuntarily serve me, and shall be rewarded." How admirable, how noble, how magnanimous and merciful is this sentiment compared with the damming, death-dealing denunciations against idolatry by the Jewish Jehovah! And the Muhammadan Bible (the Koran) contains a similar sentiment to the above. Thus, we observe, both the Hindu and Muhammadan Bibles evince in this respect a higher degree of moral sense than that of the Christian Bible, whose violent interdictions against idolatry have caused many nations to be butchered, and their lands deluged with blood. "There is nothing in the Christian Bible," says Mr. Higgins, "of one-twentieth part of the value of this text of the Hindu Bible in the way of preventing a foolish persecution and bloodshed." It may be remembered here that Christians inherited their extreme hatred of idolatry from the Jews, which is fostered by the Jewish Bible, and that the Jews derived their feelings of opposition to it from the two nations under which they were long enslaved—the Persians and Egyptians—both of which, according to Herodotus, forbid the making of idols, the former interdicting it by law; as did also the Roman emperor, Numa Pompilius, 600 B.C. The Parsees of India to this day oppose idolatry; and the learned among the Chinese have always discountenanced it. Strabo and other Grecian philosophers wrote against it. "And many sects arose among the ancient heathen," says the "Hierophant," "who rejected all external symbols of the Deity." On the other hand, neither Jews nor Christians have been entirely free from this "sin" so called.

As for "the Lord's holy people," there probably never was a nation who manifested a stronger or more invincible proclivity to idolatry than they, or who indulged more eagerly in the practice of it whenever opportunity presented; and frequently did they break over all restraint to plunge into this seemingly enticing luxury, not even withholding their earrings when a molten image or golden calf was to be constructed. And even their lawgiver Moses consented to the construction of a number of imitations or substitutes for the carved images of the pagans. Their brazen serpent displayed upon a pole; their carved cherubims with the body of a man, the head of an animal, and the wings of a bird; and the ark of the covenant, which was borne about in the same manner the heathen carried their idols— were all compromises with and concessions to idolatry, and were all venerated with the same spirit and in the same fashion the heathen adored their carved or molten images. As for the holy ark, the Jews as solemnly believed that God Almighty was shut up in that little box of shittim-wood as truly as ever the pagans believed that he sometimes condescended to a transient abode in their idols; while it was death to touch it with "unholy hands," and sixty thousand were butchered because one man (the Pious Uzza), on a certain occasion, instinctively and devoutly clapped his hand on it to keep it from falling. In fact, the golden image that it contained was an idol to all intents and purposes; nor were the brazen serpent and cherubim of the altar much less so. Hence, the vindictive condemnation of other nations for making and adoring images came with an ill grace from the Jews.

Nor are the skirts of the disciples of Christ any freer from the stain of idolatry. In fact, it constitutes the very substratum of their religion. In the first place, they quote approvingly such texts as the following: "The Lord is my rock" (Ps. xviii. 2); "Who is a rock save our God?" (Ps. xviii. 31); "The shepherd the stone of Israel" (Gen. xlix. 24). Peter calls him "a living stone" (1 Pet. ii. 4). And there are a number of other similar texts, all of which disclose real fetishism, or the first form of idolatry. The ancient Laplanders, Arabians, Phoenicians, and several tribes of Asia Minor used rocks and stones as representative images of Deity. And here we find the same association of ideas in the Christian Bible. Do you reply, "They must be considered figurative"? Very well: prove that the ancient heathen tribes did not also consider them figurative.

The Bible of Bibles

But we have a much more serious and conclusive proof than this that nearly the entire retinue of Christian professors are practical idolaters, and that their "holy religion," in all its essential characteristics, comprises, in its very nature, the highest species of idolatry. Some Christian professors tell us that those who worship idols must have a limited conception of the character and attributes of the Deity; thus conceding that idolatry consists in ascribing to God a false character. Well, now, this is the very objection that we would urge as one of the first and one of the most serious charges against the Christian system. It presents us with a cramped, dwarfish, and childish conception of Deity.

In the first place, the disciples of Christianity still cling to the old tradition, which they inherited from the heathen, of investing God with the form and characteristics of a man. For if the Deity possesses the human form, as they and their Bible teach, then he must possess the human characteristics—a logical sequence, which science defies all Christendom to overturn, as it is the infallible testimony of the natural history of all time that nothing can possess the form of one being and the characteristics of another. As is form, so is and must be the character, is an axiom supported by numberless proofs of daily and hourly observation. Hence, Jesus Christ possessing, according to the scriptures, the form of a man—"the form of a servant"—must inevitably have possessed the character of a man. Hence, we are not surprised to find that, in spite of the combined efforts of his evangelical biographers to make him a God (if they are really to be understood as designing to elevate him to the Godhead), his finite human qualities are displayed in his history in every chapter. Every saying and every credible incident of his life prove him to have been a man, notwithstanding some of them are apparently set forth as *prima facie* evidence of his being a God. Therefore, the conclusion that, as Jesus Christ had the form of a man, he could not have been a God; and to worship him as such was and is idolatry in the highest and fullest sense. And, besides the form, there are other evidences of his having been a man. He walked, talked, ate, slept, wept, shed tears, etc., and finally died just as other men do. And, furthermore, he believed and taught some of the traditions and superstitions of finite, ignorant men—such as a vengeful God, an endless hell, disease produced by demons, a personal devil, the speedy conflagration of the world, etc. Thus, we have a threefold proof of his manhood, and disproof of his Godhead, and a proof that those who worship him are idolaters.

And as the primitive or primordial Bible God Jehovah is represented as possessing, as we have already shown, a comprehensible body, eyes, nose, mouth, hands, arms, legs, feet, bowels, etc., and as being a jealous, angry, revengeful, fighting God (the God of battles), and inferior in several respects to some of the men who worshipped him, such worship is consequently idolatry. We observe, then, that the Jews worshipped one idol (Jehovah), and the Christians, three ("Father, Son, and Holy Ghost")—the two former possessing the form of man, and the latter the form of a bird (a dove). There is exactly the same objection, and it is to exactly the same extent idolatry, to worship Jesus Christ as to worship Krishna, Confucius, Muhammad, or any of the wooden Gods or graven images of the idolatrous pagans. In each case it is assuming that God, instead of being eternally infinite in all his attributes, has been invested with the finite, limited, and comprehensible form of man, to say nothing of the corresponding finite qualities which his worshipers have assigned him. And this narrow, childish assumption, with its attendant conceptions, keeps the mind of the worshiper in an intellectually cramped and dwarfish condition, besides perpetuating their dishonorable and disparaging views of Deity. And herein lies the great objection to idolatry.

If any of these venerated beings could possess divine attributes, there would be less moral objection to worshipping them as Gods. The error is not in ascribing divine attributes to the wrong being, but in the conception of wrong qualities and attributes as comprehensible in a divine being. For God is not possessed of the vanity to be offended by the simple mistakes of men and women directing their prayers and devotions to another being or object instead of to him. The grand error consists in mistaking the real character and attributes of Deity; that is, in constructing false images of him—whether *mental or material is all the same.* In other words, idolatry consists in worshipping, for God, beings or objects possessing finite forms, with whom, consequently, infinite and divine attributes could not be properly associated, and through whom they could not possibly be displayed. And so self-evident was the proof that these beings, possessing the form, size, and physical outline of men, and presenting every appearance of men (as Christ, Krishna, Confucius, etc.), were nothing but men, that even those who were habitually taught to adore them as the supreme, omnipotent Deity, naturally and instinctively, in their intercourse with them and their descriptions of them, invested them with human qualities as well as divine. And thus they came to present to the world the awkward and ludicrous figure of beings displaying both finite and infinite attributes—i.e., of being demi-gods, half God and half man. This is especially true of "the man Christ Jesus." And it may be safely assumed as an incontrovertible proposition that, just so long as they are in the habit of worshipping beings in the human form, whether Jehovah or Jesus Christ, or beings possessing any conceivable form as the great "I am," just so long will they entertain, to their own injury and to the disgrace of religion, inferior and dishonorable views of God. They must learn that a finite body cannot contain an infinite spirit, nor possess an infinite attribute; and that to worship an object or being known to possess or even supposed to possess any conceivable form, size, or shape within the comprehension of man, whether the materials composing this adored object or being are gold, silver, wood, brass, iron, or flesh and blood (as in the case of Jesus Christ), constitutes the highest species of idolatry. It can make no difference what the materials are, as it is just as impossible to associate divine and infinite attributes with an image of flesh and blood or a finite body, as to associate them with an image of wood, stone, or metal. All is alike idolatry.

The Christian world has an image or idol, constructed in part of flesh and blood, restricted, as they tell us, to a spiritual body, which they call Jesus Christ, and which they place upon an imaginary throne situated in or above the clouds, and worship it as God; while the Babylonians had the same image carved from wood and metal, which they called Dagon, and set upon a throne in the temple: and, in both cases, we are told, by way of apology, that it was not the external form, or outward body, which constituted the divinity, but the spirit within. Now, as there is room in infinite space for millions of such beings (such finite Gods), there could be no moral objection to multiplying their number, and worshipping as many of them as the imagination could conjure up, or the polytheist's fancy could create. We worship none but the infinite God; the living, moving, all-pervading, and all-energizing spirit of the infinite universe, who has no finite or comprehensible body, and never had; and hence, being infinite in extent and in all his attributes, but one such being can possibly exist, and monotheism thus becomes a virtue and a necessity. We will only remark further that the man who can worship a being with the human form or any form as the infinite God, no matter if he swells his proportions by imagination to the size of the planet Jupiter or the whole solar system, yet still, as this is not one step of an approach toward infinitude or omnipresence, his conceptions of Deity are puerile, childish, belittling, and dishonorable, if not blasphemous. If there is such a thing as blasphemy, it is found here. And his ignorance of the essential characteristics of an infinite being, or the scientific view of God, is on a par with the child's ignorance of astronomy, who exclaims, "Give me the moon!"

Here we desire to apprise the reader more distinctly that we do not regard idolatry as a crime or blameworthy act in those who originated it, but actually useful when restricted to its legitimate uses. To those groveling in spiritual darkness, on the lower plane of religious development, it is as "eyes to the blind, and crutches to the lame." It is only in those, who, like

Idolatry

Christians, profess to be enlightened, that it becomes a culpable act. Several writers have shown that idols were really practically useful, in a religious point of view, in the primitive spiritual condition of mankind, and are yet so to the lower classes in various countries; that is, to those who dwell upon the sensorial plane, and whose spiritual perceptions are hence too feeble to soar to an ethereal world to find the great object of spiritual worship. The learned Hindu, Roh Mun Roy, who wrote a work against idolatry, and who condemned the Christian churches for "worshipping an idol, in the person of Jesus Christ," beautifully sets forth the true nature and purpose of idolatry when he says (after stating that idols were not made for the learned), "The Vedas [Hindu Bible] directs those who are spiritually incapable of adoring the invisible Supreme Being to apply their minds to some visible object as an external manifestation of the only true God, rather than lose themselves in the mazes of irreligion, the bane of society. As God exists everywhere, and pervades everything (even idols), such means were mercifully provided for the ignorant and untrained to lead them on to true mental adoration and spiritual worship." And thus idols were used as aids and stepping-stones to the true worship for those who were mentally incapable of raising their minds from "nature up to nature's God," as taught by this heathen writer. Thus, they served the same purpose as pictures do for children, and were equally innocent and useful. It is, therefore, no more sinful to be an idolater than to be a child. In fact, idolatry was a necessity of man's religious nature.

The Vedas make God say, "The ignorant believe me visible while I am invisible." The able, pious Abel Fezzel (a Muhammadan writer) says, in his "Aren Akberry," "The Brahmins and Hindus all believe in the unity of the God-head; yet they hold images in high veneration, because they represent celestial beings and prevent the mind from wandering." Swedenborg says in like manner, "The heathen kept images not only in their temples, but in their houses, not to worship them, but to call to mind the heavenly being they represented." Thus, it will be observed that the idol was the sanctuary where man, in his childhood, met to commune with his God, just as the Christian now seeks his spiritual presence at the communion-table or the altar. The pagan, who was a child in religious experience, was morally necessitated to have a God, or representation of God, he could see, feel, and handle. And it is remarkable that the Christian world, after two thousand years' religious experience, still occupy the same plane—are still pagans or children with respect to believing in visible external Gods, as they virtually worship two, Jehovah and Jesus Christ, who, according to the teaching of their Bible and their established creeds, were often seen in the human form, and one of them with a human body. Thus, it will be observed they have not outgrown or advanced beyond the essential principle of idolatry—that of worshipping a visible or imaginary form for an invisible God, who, the "positive philosophy" teaches, never has been and never can be seen under any circumstances, because, being omnipresent (that is, present everywhere, and everywhere alike), if he could be seen at all, he could be seen at all times and in all places. This is a self-evident, axiomatic truth.

Origin of Idolatry. Here we deem it proper to speak more directly and specifically of the primary origin of idolatry, or image-worship, than is disclosed in the preceding pages. After the primitive inhabitants of the earth had conceived the notion that the sun, moon, and stars are moved in their orbits through the heavens by beings who occupied them (as has already been shown), they were in the habit of gazing upon these tower-lights of the Elysian fields (the home of the Gods) with the most intense delight, the most reverential awe and devotion. But ever and anon this pleasing reverie was interrupted, and subjected to sad suspense, by "the departure of the heavenly host to other and distant lands." First of all, the solar God, mounted upon high-wheeled chariot drawn by his fleet steeds, after plowing his way through the deep-blue vault of the sky, was off on his swift-sped journey behind the western hills, but followed almost immediately by the whole retinue of stellar orbs (the homes of the lesser Gods), who danced along in his wake; but, ever true to the line of march, followed on apace, and were soon beyond the bounds of human vision. This left an aching void in their devout minds. Hence, the invention and construction of images as imaginary likenesses of the Gods, to serve as substitutes for them, to be venerated in their stead during their absence, as we secure the likeness of a friend when about to leave us for a journey, or to be long absent. And here we may date the primary origin of idolatry, which is nothing more nor less than the first rude germination of man's religious nature.

ALL CHRISTIANS EITHER ATHEISTS OR IDOLATERS

It seems most strikingly strange that atheism and idolatry should be considered by the orthodox representatives of the Christian faith as "the most God-defying and heaven-daring sins that man can be guilty of" (as one Christian writer represents them to be), when there is not a professor of the Christian faith, and never has been, who was not guilty most unquestionably of one of these sins. It requires but a few words to prove this statement. Nearly all the early Christian writers defined atheism to be "disbelief in a personal God" and idolatry as "image-making." How obtuse must have been their perceptions that they could not see that their definition of these terms made them all either atheists or idolaters, and that it is impossible to escape one of these charges without becoming obnoxious to the other! No person can believe in a personal God without forming an image of him in the mind; and this is just as much idolatry as though that mental image should find expression in wood or stone or brass, as shown in the preceding chapter. On the other hand, to believe in an infinite and spiritual God, instead of a personal God, is, as shown above, atheism. It will be seen, then, to believe in a personal, organized Deity is, to all intents and purposes, idolatry; while to reject this anthropomorphic and sensuous idea, and accept the belief in a spiritual God in its stead, is atheism. And thus the position is reduced to a demonstrated problem, that all Christians are either atheists or idolaters.

CHAPTER 33

NEW TESTAMENT ERRORS

DIVINE REVELATION IMPOSSIBLE AND UNNECESSARY

The Hindus, Egyptians, Persians, Chaldeans, Jews, and Muhammadans, and various other nations, claim to have had a special revelation of God's will communicated to them for the benefit of the whole human race. But the following facts and arguments will tend to show that no such revelations have ever been made, and that there is none necessary:

We will inquire, in the first place, what a divine revelation would be. Coming from a perfect being, it would of course be perfect, and perfectly adapted to the moral and spiritual wants of the whole human race. Such a revelation would be so clear, explicit, and unequivocal in its language with respect to every doctrine, principle, and precept, and every statement of fact, that no person of ordinary mind could possibly misunderstand it; and no two persons could differ for a moment with respect to the meaning of any text embraced in it. It would need no priest and no commentator to explain it; and, if any attempt should be made to explain it, it would only "darken counsel," render the matter more obscure, and would amount to the blasphemous assumption that Omniscience can be enlightened, and his works improved. And a *divine* revelation should be communicated to the whole human race; for, if restricted to one nation, it would render God obnoxious to the charge of partiality. And, in order to make it practicable to communicate it to all nations, it would be necessary to comprehend it in a universal language constructed for the purpose, or else impart it to the world through all the three thousand languages in use by different nations and tribes. But, as such a revelation has never been made or known on the earth, it is at once evident that no such revelation has ever been communicated to man by Infinite Wisdom.

REVELATION FOR ONE AGE AND NATION
NO REVELATION FOR ANOTHER

A revelation issued two or three thousand years ago could be no revelation for this age. The Rev. Jeremiah Jones admits that "a revelation can only be a revelation to him who receives it," and cannot be made use of to convince another (Canon, p. 51). Bishop Burnet admits that a revelation to one man is no revelation to another. You can neither see nor feel a revelation made to another person. You can merely see the marks on the paper on which he has recorded what he claims to have been a revelation to him. And this is all the proof you can have in the case, which is no proof at all.

New Testament Errors

A Revelation on the Brain Called Reason

I know that God has inscribed a revelation on my brain called reason, as it is ever present with me. Hence, I know that it was *designed for me.* But I cannot have this testimony with regard to a written revelation, as it was not communicated to me. Hence, as a matter of certainty and safety, I should hold to my own revelation in preference *to any other.*

I can only be certain of my own revelation. Indeed, I cannot know that any other revelation was designed for me, because a dozen revelations are brought forward by different nations for acceptance; and I cannot determine to an absolute certainty which is divine and which is human. To settle the matter, I must have another revelation made expressly to me to inform me which is the true revelation. To save this extra labor, I might as well have had the original revelation itself.

The Human Brain Superior to Any Revelation

As an idiot cannot be made to understand a revelation, it is evident that a revelation presupposes a rational mind for its reception; otherwise, the revelation would be perfectly useless. Hence, it is evident the brain must be right before the revelation is given, or it will not be able to understand it. This makes the brain superior to, and of higher authority, than revelation.

The moment we begin to reason on the revelation of the Bible, which we are compelled to do to determine which is the true one, that moment we transfer the authority of the Bible to the brain, and the brain thus becomes its judge and jury. The reason sits in judgment over the Bible, and is thus proved to be superior to it. This is realized in the experience of every man who is superior to an idiot; and thus the question of Bible authority and superiority is at once and forever settled. It is proved to be inferior to reason, and subordinate to it, and dare not advance a step beyond it.

Infallible Revelation Impossible

A Bible or revelation could only be infallible to a man or woman of infallible understanding; that is, to an infallible being. And, as no such being has ever existed, it is evident that no infallible revelation has ever been issued.

Everything Must Be Infallible

No infallible revelation could be of any practical use to any person unless all the circumstances connected with it were infallible. The language in which it is written must be infallible; the person reviewing it must be infallible; and the reader or his understanding, must also be infallible. But, as no such state of things has ever existed, it follows that no infallible revelation has ever been given to man, and is absolutely impracticable.

No Divine Revelation Without A Series of Miracles

A divine revelation must be miraculously inspired; and then it must be miraculously preserved from the slightest alteration by the translator or the transcriber, and from any error on the part of the printer. And, finally, the reader's mind and understanding and judgment must be miraculously guarded from any mistake or misunderstanding or wrong conclusions relative to every text in the book. Otherwise, there is no absolute certainty that the revelation is a true one, or superior to a mere human production.

Our Moral and Religious Duties Cannot Be Learned From Any Bible or Revelation

A critical investigation of the matter will show that our moral and religious duties are not half of them enumerated in the Bible; and to suppose that God would reveal only a portion of them, and leave us in the dark with respect to others, and compel us to find them out by chance and conjecture, is to trifle with Omniscience, and assume that he is short-sighted and imperfect.

No Moral Duty Clearly Defined By the Bible

As the circumstances of each case of moral duty differ from every other case, so our courses of action must be different. Hence, revelation, to be of any practical use, should have foreseen those circumstances, pointed them out, and instructed us how to act in the case. But this is not done in any case. We will illustrate. We are enjoined by the Bible to "bring up a child the way he should go," but that way is not pointed out or defined. We are not told which one of the thousand churches he should join; we are not told, when a man's leg is broken, how it should be mended; we are not told what means we should use to restore the sick to health, nor instructed as to the best means to be used for the preservation of health and life. And, as these are among the first and most important duties, we should have been instructed as to the best means to be used for that purpose; but these things are omitted, and left to the province of reason. There is no case in which we are not compelled to make reason our supreme judge to decide how we shall practice the duties of revelation; and thus revelation is made a servant or subsidiary agent.

Christians sometimes tell us, "Give us something better in the place of our religion before you take it from us." But the Bible tells them, "Cease to do evil [before you] learn to do well." Doom error to destruction, and truth will spring out of the ashes. What would you think of a man who should say to a physician, "Stop, sir! Before you administer that medicine to my child, I want to know what you are going to let it have in place of its pains and aches"? We do not propose or desire to destroy any religion as a whole, but only the deleterious weeds that are choking and poisoning the healthy plants. We do not wish to put down or arrest the progress of any truth.

The clergy sometimes assert that "we could not distinguish right from wrong, but for the Bible." And was nothing known to the world about right and wrong, or the means of distinguishing between them, during the two thousand years which elapsed before the Bible was written? Christians place Moses, its first writer, about fourteen hundred years before Christ, while the Bible dates back 4004 B.C. And then what about those millions of the inhabitants of the globe who never had our Bible? And millions of them never had a Bible of any kind. Are they destitute of moral perception? On the contrary, reliable authority, and even Christian writers, assure us that the morals of many of those nations will put to shame the morals of any nation professing the religion of Christ. Take, for example, the Kalaos tribe of Africa, who appear to have no formal religion whatever; and yet, as Dr. Livingstone informs us, they maintain strict honesty in all their dealings with each other, and have made considerable progress in the arts and manufactures. They have never had a Bible or revelation of any kind. Look also at the inhabitants of the Arru Islands. "These people," says Dr. Livingstone, "appear to have no religion whatever; and yet they live in brotherly peace, and respect each other's rights"—the rights of property in the fullest sense. The Rev. W. H. Clark, speaking of the Yoruba nation in Central Africa, says, "Their moral and even their civil rights in some respects would put to shame any Christian nation in the world." We might present a hundred more cases of this kind; but these three cases are sufficient to show that nations with no Bible, no revelation, and even no religion, transcend any Christian nation with respect to strict honesty and a practical sense of right and wrong. How absurd, therefore, is the idea shown to be, that a knowledge of the Christian Bible is essential to the knowledge and practice of good morals! (See chapter 50.)

OUR DUTIES ARE ALL RECORDED IN THE BIBLE OF NATURE

There is not a moral or religious duty that is not inscribed on the tablet of man's soul or consciousness which he would not soon learn if his attention were not constantly directed to, and his mind occupied with, the erroneous theories of the dark, illiterate ages. The God of nature has endowed every human being with two sensations—one of pleasure, and the other of pain—which serve as guides in all his actions, both physical and moral. They stand as sentinels at the door of his soul to warn him of the approach of evil of every kind. The moment their kingdom is invaded, they raise an alarm, which he soon learns he must heed or suffer a penalty. If he drinks intoxicating drinks, or improperly indulges his appetites and propensities in any way, he learns, by suffering, that is the penalty affixed to the violation of the law of health, and that he cannot escape it, and that no one can suffer for him, or make any "atonement for his sins." If he attempts to handle fire, he is soon apprised that he is meddling with something that will injure him; if he commits a moral wrong against a neighbor, it reacts upon himself in various ways, as explained in chapter 46. It thus acts as a two-edged sword, which cuts both ways, punishes both the victim and the perpetrator. Man learns by experience that crime will not only injure him, but, in many cases, will destroy him. On the other hand, when he practices virtue, she greets him with her smiles, and fills his soul with pleasure. Let me illustrate: The bells in some city toll the alarm of fire at midnight. In a few minutes, thousands of men and boys are congregated on the spot, many of them half-dressed, and without hats or shoes, in order to aid a fellow-being in rescuing his dwelling from the all-devouring element. What prompts them to this act? It is not an injunction of their Bible. No: it was the well-spring of philanthropy leaping up through their souls that prompted to the deed, and not a written Bible. Again: why is a mother's loving, watchful care ever exercised for the protection and welfare of her child? She will endure almost any hardship or privation that its welfare requires. Why does she do this? Her Bible is silent on the subject. It is the impulse of nature welling up from the fountain of maternal affection that prompts to these acts of loving care—to this moral duty. And this is true of all the other moral duties of life. They are all imbibed at her fountain—at the fountain of Nature. A man with a good moral development needs no revelation to teach him what is right, no Bible to prompt him to the performance of his duties. We rejoice "with joy unspeakable" that the world is fast learning this moral axiom. The Bible truly teaches us that our moral duties are revealed in the book of nature (chapter 14). And Christian writers also admit this. Tertullian says, "Why pain yourselves in searching for a divine law while you have that which is common to mankind, and engraven upon the tablet of nature?" This is a wonderful admission for a Christian writer to make, as it virtually concedes there is no moral or religious necessity for a written Bible or revelation.

New Testament Errors

A Divine Revelation Adverse to Human Progress

One argument against the belief in a divine revelation is found in the fact that it would tend to paralyze human effort, and thus make man a mental sloth. If a man could find all his moral and religious duties "cut and dried," and laid out before him, he would be thus robbed of the motive to study and learn his duties by the exercise of his mental powers. And having no incentives to healthy, energetic action, he would become a drone and mental sloth. We cannot believe God ever made such a blunder as this.

A Divine Revelation Would Imply Imperfection on the Part of Deity

It is admitted that no revelation was ever given to man for more than two thousand years after creation. This would imply that it was forgotten by Infinite Wisdom, or else the moral necessity for it overlooked. Either assumption would make God an imperfect and shortsighted being. It would appear like an after-thought. After man had lived so many years upon the earth, it just occurred to God that he had not given him a written revelation instructing him what to do and believe. The assumption of a divine revelation presupposes such a blunder as this on the part of Omniscience, and is therefore derogatory to his character.

Now, we ask seriously, Do not the foregoing facts and arguments show that there is no moral or religious necessity for a divine revelation to man? Let the believers in the necessity of the Bible, or a divine revelation, show their fallacy, or for ever abandon the old mythological assumption that it is necessary.

Another conclusive argument: A mind that could comprehend a truth divinely revealed could originate that truth. We will give an illustrative proof: A teacher works out a mathematical problem on the blackboard for the benefit of his school. Now, every teacher and every logical mind will admit that every pupil, possessing the mental capacity to understand the mathematical truth thus revealed, could, by his own unaided powers, have developed it himself sooner or later. In like manner, the mind that could comprehend a truth revealed from God, could originate it without the aid of revelation. Hence, revelation would be worse than useless, as it would furnish a pretext for mental or intellectual sloth, and thus have a tendency to stop human progress by doing for us what we could and should do ourselves. A logical investigation of the case will show that we possess the mental capacity to discover *every truth we need,* whether it be scientific, moral, or *religious;* and such exercise furnishes the only means to keep the mind in a healthy condition. And thus the problem is proved again.

CHAPTER 34

PRIMEVAL INNOCENCY OF MAN NOT TRUE

The tradition so universally prevalent among the disciples of all the Oriental systems of religious faith, as well as those of a more modern origin, and which is still a conspicuous element of the Christian system—that man commenced his career in a state of moral perfection—is so obviously at war with every principle of anthropology, and every page of human history tending to demonstrate the moral character of the primitive inhabitants of the earth, that I shall employ but little time and space in exposing its absurdity and falsity.

1. All the organic remains of the *earliest* types of the human species that have been found demonstrate conclusively that man started on the animal plane with animal feelings, propensities, and habits, almost totally devoid of moral feelings, and consequently a victim to his passions, propensities, and lusts. Where, then, were his moral purity and angelic holiness? The idea is a mere chimera.

2. It is now a settled problem in mental science that the character of every species of animate being corresponds with its organization; that the organic structure of the being, whether dead or alive, always indicates its true character. If it possesses the form and type of the tiger, it will always be found with the disposition and habits of the tiger; or, if it is a sheep in form, it will be a sheep in character. There is no deviation from this rule. Hence, when we find the bones of the early types of the human species resembling those of the lower order of animals, there is no escaping the conclusion that they possessed an analogous character.

3. Look, then, at the fact that the skulls and facial bones of human beings, found embedded in the rocks of Gibraltar, belonging to a race which naturalists have decided existed upon the earth sixty-five thousand years ago, closely approximate those of an animal. They possessed retreating foreheads, prognathous jaws, extremely coarse features, and skulls nearly an inch in thickness; hands resembling those of a monkey, feet resembling those of a bear, and cranial receptacle showing a very small amount of moral brain. Now, it is evident that this early race, with such a gross, brutal organization, could not have possessed fine moral sensibilities and lofty virtue, purity, and perfection.

4. And we find that nations whose organizations indicate a higher moral character are of more modern origin, as shown by their organic remains being found in more recently formed strata—the tertiary formation. It is thus scientifically demonstrated that man's tendency toward moral perfection is inversely to the remoteness of time—that the nearer we retrace his history to his origin, the lower position he occupies in the scale of morals.

5.　We will cite one more historical fact to establish this theory.　The existence of a tribe of negroes has been traced (as stated in chapter 16) to near the date of Noah's flood, whose organization indicates a very near approach to the animal; thus showing that, if they are descendants of Adam, he himself must have possessed an inferior or defective moral organization and character.

6.　Let the reader, after noting these facts, read the history of the practical lives of the earliest races or nations whose deeds have been recorded, and he will find they sustain the same proportion; that their defective moral character corresponds (*ceteris paribus*) to the remoteness of the era in which they lived.　The history of the Jews themselves illustrates and corroborates the proposition, as the character of the modern Jews is far superior to those of the era of Abraham and Moses.

7.　Once more: The fact that the moral character of nearly all nations is constantly improving, proves beyond question that man once occupied a much lower plane, and that, instead of falling from a state of moral purity, he is constantly ascending toward that condition.

8.　The current belief of man's primitive moral perfection is easily traced to its origin.　Nearly all the Oriental nations had a tradition of a "golden age," when the most sublime and unalloyed bliss was the lot and enjoyment of the *genus homo*.　But the serpent that beguiled Eve to eat of the forbidden fruit in Eden, the serpent who stole the recipe of immortal life in Assyria, the entering of Typhon into the golden paradise of Osirus in Egypt, the opening of Pandora's box in Greece, the piercing of the evil egg by Ahrimanes in Chaldea, the machinations of the snake in India, of the lizard in Persia, and the demon in Mexico, seem to have all had an agency in defeating the omniscient designs of Deity, and placing the reins of government in the hands of the world's omnipresent, omnipotent, and omniscient evil genius, thus prostrating forever the great and glorious plans of Infinite Wisdom.

CHAPTER 35

ORIGINAL SIN AND FALL OF MAN NOT TRUE

Having shown that man commenced his earthly career on a low moral and intellectual plane, and that therefore the assumption of his original moral perfection is a fallacy, the correlative dogma of his fall into a state of moral depravity falls to the ground of its own weight. It would be a work of supererogation to attempt to show that man never fell in a moral sense, after having shown that he never occupied an elevated moral position to fall from. It is self-evident that he could not fall if there was no lower position for him to fall to; and this has been shown. Nevertheless, we will expose its absurdity from other logical standpoints. According to the Westminster Catechism, "God placed man in the garden of Eden, and forbade him to eat of the fruit of the tree of knowledge; and, because he disobeyed, he became the victim of God's eternal wrath, an accursed and totally depraved being." Such doctrine is not only morally revolting, but replete with logical absurdities. We will recount some of them:

1. God formed and fashioned man, according to the Bible, after his own image, the product of his Infinite wisdom; and if he had not possessed infinite wisdom, which must enable him to do everything to perfection, he had had an eternity to study the matter, and get it fully matured, so as to make everything work in harmony, and endow every sentient being with happiness.

2. And, as happiness is the highest end and aim of every living being, it is hence evident that, where there is a want of happiness, there is a want of perfection in the being who established such a state of things; and such a being could not by any possibility be infinitely good and infinitely wise.

3. A few points considered will show very clearly that, if man sinned and fell, God has to sustain the responsibility of it. We are told that God made man; and, being all-wise, he would, of course, endow him with exactly such faculties and inclinations and appetites as were best adapted to his situation, and calculated to make him happy. But, according to orthodoxy, God had planted a tree near the spot where he placed Adam, furnished it with some beautiful and luscious fruit, and planted in man an appetite and relish for it, and, as if to tantalize him with perpetual hunger, forbade him to eat the fruit; and apparently, for fear Adam would obey his command and abstain from eating the fruit, he created a serpent-devil to persuade him (or rather his wife) with bland smiles (assuming that a snake can smile, which is rather doubtful) to partake of the fruit, and satisfy their appetites. All this appears to have been the work of their Creator, and not theirs. But the conspicuous features of the absurdity do not stop here.

4.　We are told that the prohibition to eat the fruit was issued to Adam before Eve was released from her imprisonment in Adam's side, or from performing the functions of a rib-bone, before she became a woman and a wife; and it is not even implied that it was intended to extend to her. Why, then, in the name of God, should such curses be heaped upon her devoted head for eating the fruit when she had not been forbidden to do so? And it does not appear to have been wrong in any sense, only that Jehovah had issued an order forbidding it.

5.　Jehovah professed great sympathy for Adam's lonely condition, and made a help meet for him; and yet the first meat she helped him to, it would seem, damned him and his posterity forever. In view of this fact, it is probable Adam would have preferred to let her remain a bone in his side.

6.　Here let it be noted that Adam and Eve were ignorant and inexperienced beings. They had had no experience in anything and hence could not know that such an act, or any other act, was wrong and sinful.

7.　Nor could Adam know what the word "die" meant when Jehovah told him he would die the day he ate the fruit, as he had seen nothing die.

8.　It may here be said in reply, that they should, in their ignorance, have obeyed the command that was given them. To this we reply, they did obey the command of one being. God told them not to eat, and the serpent told them to eat, the fruit; and, not having lived within or had any experience with either of those omnipresent beings, how could they know what would be the consequence of obeying or disobeying either of them? This question of itself is sufficient to settle the matter. They could not possibly know, with no experience in either case, that the consequence would be more serious or more fatal in disobeying Jehovah than the serpent.

9.　And as they got their eyes open by eating the fruit, and did not die as Jehovah told them they would (while the serpent told them they would not), it is not to be wondered at that ever after they and their posterity should be more inclined to serve the serpent-devil than Jehovah, seeing that all the happy consequences which the former predicted as the result of eating the fruit were realized, while those of Jehovah were falsified. For proof, see chapter 53.

10. The most artful sophistry cannot disguise the fact that the doctrine of moral depravity is a slanderous imputation upon divine mercy, goodness, and justice, and challenges not only his goodness, but his good sense.

11. And every page of history and every principle of science demonstrate it to be both false and demoralizing.

Man *fell up*, and not *down*.

187

CHAPTER 36

MORAL DEPRAVITY OF MAN A DELUSION

It is alleged by the orthodox world that man's moral nature and reasoning faculties both became depraved by the fall. "Totally depraved" has been the doctrine; but the gradual expansion and enlightenment of the mind by progressive science have modified the doctrine with some of the churches, and they have substituted "moral depravity" for "total depravity." But neither assumption can be scientifically or logically sustained. The assumption that our reason is depraved is made the pretext for urging the superiority of revelation, and making reason subordinate to it. We are told that, as our reason is depraved, we cannot safely rely upon it to judge and criticize the Bible or the doctrine of the churches.

Mr. Moody recently exclaimed, in a religious controversy, "I never reason on religion. None but the disciples of devils reason. It is dangerous to reason on religion." Unconscious of his ignorance, Mr. Moody assumed a very ludicrous position. By the *exercise* of his reason on religion, Mr. Moody came to the conclusion that it is *wrong* to reason on religion, thus committing the very sin he condemns in others. He *reasons* on religion to convince people that it is *wrong* to reason on religion, and thus violates his own principles. His case is analogous to that of the town council which attempted to keep the prisoners of the county in the old jail while they erected a new jail with the timbers of the old one—rather a difficult task to achieve, but not more so than Mr. Moody's attempt to keep his reason in chains while he is trying to exercise it. Or, rather, he insults his auditors by saying to them virtually, "I will use *my* reason on matters of religion, but you must not use *yours*." As a reasoning being he reasons with reasonable beings, and addresses their reason to convince them they ought not to reason on certain subjects. He uses logic to prove that logic is dangerous, and should not be used. By reasoning against reason he pulls *both ways*, like the Scotchman who attempted to lift himself by his ears. He commits logical suicide when he attempts to show there is any case in which reason should not be used.

The truth is, a person cannot *think* on the subject of religion without beginning t*o reason* on it, because his *reasoning faculties* and his *thinking faculties are both one.* He *thinks* with his intellect, and he *reasons* with his intellect; and the very moment *he begins* to *think, he begins* to *reason.* And therefore, if it is *wrong* to *reason on religion, it is wrong* to *have any religion.* We should not allow it to occupy our thoughts for a single moment, and thus we would banish religion from the world; which, however, would be no great loss if it is too absurd to bear the test of reason. And, if it is wrong to *reason on religion,* it is wrong to *reason on any*

Moral Depravity of Man

subject. The more *important* the subject, the more *necessary* to use reason upon it, that we may make no mistakes in regard to it. The truth is, reason is the *only faculty* with which a man can comprehend religion, revelation, or the Bible. This would prove again that it is *wrong* to *have any religion,* if it is wrong to submit it to the judgment, and test it by our reasoning faculties. Reason is the principal faculty which distinguishes us from the brute; and, therefore, to discard it is to approximate to the condition of the brute. What a pity Mr. Moody had not been consulted in his creation that he might have had his reasoning faculties *left out!* Then he would not be under the necessity of *sinning* daily by exercising his reason in his attempts *to stop* its exercise.

And then there are other serious difficulties growing out of the reverend gentleman's position. His *reason being "depraved,"* we can place no confidence in its *exercise* or *decision* in this case, so as to assume that his judgment and conclusions are correct when he declares against reason. If he reaches his conclusions through a depraved reason, they can be of no account. The verdict cannot transcend the judge or court that makes it. The *reasoner* being depraved, his *reasoning* and *decision* in the case must be depraved *also,* and therefore *worthless.* Verily the gentleman is in a bad position, and rather a serious quandary; and every struggle to get out only sinks him deeper. He is in the predicament of a dog running round after his tail. And then we should like to ask the gentleman, If our reason is not to be depended upon in *matters* of *religion,* how is it to be depended upon *in any case?* And how does he know, or how *can* he know, but that, his reason being depraved, it has lead him off the track, in this case, in his attempts to put it in chains? Will the reverend gentleman furnish a rule by which we can know in what case our reason can be trusted, and in what cases we are to doff our moral manhood, and lie prostrate in the dust with the brute? And then the rule, being the product of a depraved reason, could not be relied upon. Really, the reverend gentleman is in an inextricable quandary. The case furnishes an illustrative proof of the extent a man can make a fool of himself when he attempts to shipwreck his reason, and a proof that orthodoxy is a conglomeration of absurdities, and is entirely out of place in an age of progressive thought, and an age of reason and science. The only evidence we have ever had of the truth of the depravity of human reason is found in the fact that men professing to have common sense and reason can believe it to be true. And the fact that our *moral sense* instinctively *repels* the doctrine of *total* depravity or *moral* depravity, and our *reason rises* up in rebellion against it, is proof positive of its absurdity.

The thought is here suggested that, if God could not get along without the adoption of an expedient calculated to corrupt our moral nature and deprave our reason, he *should not* and *would not* have implanted in us such an instinctive horror to the doctrine. This natural feeling of repugnance is alone sufficient to condemn it, and prove that it is a slander upon Infinite Wisdom, and a libel upon human nature, to assume its existence. And such doctrine is evidently calculated to demoralize society. An old Roman proverb teaches us, "Call a man a dog, and he will be a dog." *Call* a child depraved, and it will *feel* depraved, and, *feeling* so, it will *act* so. On the other hand, teach the child he possesses the grand principle and feeling of an inherent nobility, and he will rise to the dignity of moral manhood. Such is the difference in the moral value of the two doctrines.

CHAPTER 37

FREE AGENCY AND MORAL
ACCOUNTABILITY ERRONEOUS

One of the cardinal doctrines of the Christian faith is the free agency of man, but the very term is a logical contradiction. An agent must act in accordance with the will and wishes of his employer, or he will be called to account, and perhaps dismissed. Where, then, is his moral freedom? It may be assumed that the employer licenses him to take his own course, but this must be with certain conditions, or else he will act for himself, and be no agent at all. Certain alternatives are placed before an agent, which he is privileged to choose; but that does not make him free in any rational or practical sense. If he does not act as required or desired, he will be either punished or dismissed. That is a singular kind of freedom. It is the freedom of a slave, which is no freedom at all; and this is exactly the kind of freedom orthodoxy grants to the sinner, and to the whole human race. It marks out the road to heaven, and says, "This is the road to eternal bliss; and you must walk in it, or eternal misery will be your portion." To escape such a terrible doom, millions tremblingly travel the road impelled and propelled by fear. And this painful alternative Christians are pleased to term free agency, or moral freedom. It is simply the freedom of a slave to clank his chains. It is a perversion of language to apply the term "free agency" to such a case. The orthodox give us our choice to accept their terms of salvation or reject them; but they attach to the consequence of rejecting them the most awful penalties. We will illustrate:

A father says to his son some sabbath morning, "John, I am going to leave you free today either to go to church or go a-fishing." He instantly darts away to the river or the lake with the glee of a humming-bird, and is seen no more until nightfall. As he approaches the door, his father says to him, "John, where have you been today?" — "Why, father, I have been fishing, to be sure." — "Well now, John, I am going to give you one of the most terrible floggings you ever had in your life for not going to church." — "Why, father, you told me I might take my choice, and go either to church or go a-fishing." — "That is true, .John; but it was with the implied understanding that, if *you did not choose* to go to church, I would give you an unmerciful whipping." This is free agency indeed! It is the free agency of orthodoxy illustrated, and applied to practice. Free agency coupled with a penalty is moral slavery and moral tyranny. There is no moral freedom about it. You are simply free to take your choice between two systems of slavery and two systems of punishment or suffering. A hare pursued by a hound enjoys a similar kind of freedom—the freedom to stand and be caught, or the freedom to run.

The Bible of Bibles

Of all the absurdities that ever entered the brain of a human being, that of setting God and the Devil both after man, as orthodoxy does, and then calls him a free agent, is not excelled. We are told that we cannot think a thought of ourselves. All our good thoughts and actions are prompted by a good being; and all our bad thoughts and actions by a bad being (God and the Devil). Where, then, is our moral freedom or our moral accountability, if neither our thoughts nor our actions are our own, as they cannot be if they are prompted by other beings? When a man performs a good act, it is assumed that God is the author of it; and he is told that he must give God praise for it. On the other hand, all wicked actions are assigned to the Devil. He is thus a target between these two cross-fires. Such an assumption sweeps away the last vestige of free agency and moral accountability. Some Christian professors accept the doctrine of free agency to escape the dreaded alternative of assuming man to be a mere machine, which they call fatality. But here you have fatality to repletion. If to place man between two all-powerful beings, and have them both trying to direct his actions at once, don't make him a machine, then we have no use for the word.

It is strange that Christian professors have never discovered that, according to the teachings of the Bible, God himself is not a free agent. A free agent is one who can have things as he wills or wishes, so far as he has the power to make them so. Look, then, at the fact that, according to their own Bible, God himself does not enjoy this desirable boon. It is declared by that book that "God wills not the death (destruction) of the sinner, but that all shall be saved." And it is elsewhere declared that "strait is the gate, and narrow is the way, that leadeth unto life; and few there be that find it." According to the first text, God desires to save all; but, according to the second, he succeeds in saving but very few. Hence, not having things as he desires or wishes them to be, it is evident he is not a free agent, according to the orthodox or technical sense of that term. Why, then, talk of men being free agents, if a being with infinite power cannot be a free agent?

To make man a free agent strictly or truly, he should have been consulted beforehand as to how, when, and where he would be born, or whether he would be born at all or not. Douglas Jerrold significantly remarks that, "if I had foreknown that a portion of mankind would be born to be damned, I'll be d——d if I would have been born at all." This expression, although profane, contains a good moral. Certainly, nothing could be more preposterous or unreasonable than to hold one being accountable to another when the former had no agency in creating his mind or originating his inclinations, out of which all his actions grow. True accountability can only appertain to beings who created their own natural inclinations, or consented to receive those they are in possession of. This is clear and unanswerable logic. If man was made by God, or Infinite Wisdom, as Christians affirm, then common sense would teach that God alone is accountable for his actions. The man would be a fool who should blame a watch for not running right, knowing that the maker conferred upon it all the properties and powers it possessed. The maker of the watch alone is held responsible for all its perfections and imperfections. And, if man has a maker, it is a very clear case that that maker is equally responsible for his running wrong. There is no resisting this conclusion. The true assumption in the case is that man has no creator in the orthodox sense, and is only responsible to himself, and to society so far as he is a voluntary member of it. But orthodoxy makes his salvation depend not only upon his resisting the natural inclinations implanted in his system, but also upon the position of his birth. As an argument in favor of sending the Bible to the heathen, they declare that millions perish every year because they have not the opportunity of reading that "Holy Book," and learning the name of Jesus. This makes their salvation depend upon the locality of their birth; as some sections furnish the opportunity, and others do not, of becoming acquainted with their Bible, and the name of their Savior.

We must imagine, therefore, in "the day of judgment" every human being will have a geographical question to answer. After being interrogated as to their conduct and practical lives, the next question will be, "Where were you born?" If the answer is, "In Arabia," the reply of the judge will be, "Oh, yes! You are a Muhammadan. Our religion only saves those born in Christian countries. I must therefore set you aside among the goats." If the applicant is from India, he will be rejected from the kingdom, and consigned to perdition, because he is a "heathen." And thus Christianity is shown to be a geographical system of salvation, and makes a man's eternal destiny depend upon whether he is born in this country or that country, which strips it of all claim to either justice, impartiality, or good sense. The doctrine of free agency and moral accountability is one in a long list of theological absurdities, which originated in an age of scientific ignorance, when nothing was known of the natural powers, or the philosophy of the human mind, or the laws which control its action.

Moral Accountability. What is it and where is it? It is certainly one of the greatest moral puzzles ever submitted to a philosopher, as to how a being, forced into existence by an omnipotent creative power, without his consultation or consent, can be responsible to that creative power for his conduct, when he had no agency and no volition in his own creation, and no power of resisting it, or in shaping its conditions. If God possesses omnipotent power and infinite wisdom, and *is a creator*, he could and should have made man to act just as he wished him to act; and, if he did not do so, common sense would suggest that it was his own fault. It will be seen from the force of this logic, that Christians must either give up the doctrine of a voluntary personal creator, or that of moral accountability. The two doctrines *cannot* be made to harmonize together.

CHAPTER 38

REPENTANCE: AN ERRONEOUS DOCTRINE

Having treated this subject somewhat lengthily and critically in "The World's Sixteen Crucified Saviors," we shall devote but brief space to its elucidation here. Nearly all religious nations have attached great importance to the act of repentance; but such an act does not repair the injury or wrong repented of. The repentance of a murderer does not restore his murdered victim to life; nor does the repentance and tears of the incendiary rebuild the dwelling he has destroyed by fire. What, then, is its practical value?

We would ask, also, what moral value or merit can attach to an act of repentance when it is not claimed to be an act of the sinner, but "the power of God upon the soul"? (Luther) It appears, then, according to orthodox logic:

1.   That God won't save the sinner unless he repents.

2.   That he can't repent only as God moves him to do so. This places him in a bad predicament. Hence, when he does repent, it is an act of God.

3.   And then God saves him because he makes him repent. Here is a jumble of logical incongruities and moral contradictions that can find no lodgment in a scientific mind. A few brief questions will set the doctrine of repentance in its true light.

4.   Repentance consists in merely a revival of early impressions, that may be either right or wrong, true or false, and almost as likely to be one as the other.

5.   Whoever knew a person to embrace more rational doctrines, or become more intelligent, or have a stronger taste for scientific pursuits, by repentance?

6.   Is it not a fact that repentance usually causes a person to cling more tenaciously to the errors and superstitions in which he was educated?

7.   Whoever knew a person by repenting, in either health or sickness, to condemn one wrong act which he had erroneously been taught to believe was right? If not, does it not prove that repentance always conforms to education, whether that education is right or wrong, and hence does nothing toward enlightening the convert or anybody else?

8.   On the contrary, when a man repents with his mind full of religious errors, is it not evident that the act of repentance will have the effect to rivet these errors more strongly upon his mind, and thus effect a moral injury instead of a moral benefit?

9.   If a man may abandon some of his immoral habits, which he has been taught to believe are wrong, by an act of repentance, are not the good effects to some extent counterbalanced by his clinging more strongly to his religious errors?

10. Whoever knew a person to abandon a false religion by repentance? Does a Hindu or Muhammadan ever embrace Christianity by repenting?

11. Whoever knew a Roman Catholic to become a Protestant, or a Protestant a Catholic, by repentance? And yet orthodox Christians will cite the belief and testimony of a dying man as an evidence of the truth of their doctrines.

12. How can an act of repentance do anything toward proving what is right and what is wrong in any case, when one person repents for doing what another repents for not doing? We have such cases recorded in history.

We have known a Campbellite to leave his dying testimony in favor of water baptism, and a Quaker to leave his dying testimony against it. Does one case prove it to be wrong, and the other right? If not, why do Christians cite such cases? What do they prove?

For a further illustration of this subject, see "The World's Sixteen Crucified Saviors."

DEATH-BED REPENTANCE

If there is any class of people who need to repent for misspent time, and for leading false and foolish lives, it is the colporteurs who travel over the country distributing pious tracts, containing doleful accounts of death-bed repentance, which, whether right or wrong, prove nothing.

Such cases of repentance as are reported do not appertain to the moral conduct, but to the religious belief, of the sinner. It is the abandonment and condemnation of his past creeds, and not of his past conduct, which makes the tract so valuable. Such a case contains no moral instruction whatever.

If his early education was Muhammadan, his repentance will establish that religion again in his mind; but if Mormonism was the religion of his childhood, he would again have full faith in that religion. What nonsense!

Whoever knew repentance to divorce or emancipate a man from all or any of the religious errors of his past life, and plant in his soul a better and more rational religion, or lead him to advocate any religion only that in which he had been educated! Such repentance is worth nothing, and absolutely foolish. Let us assume that the numerous cases of death-bed repentance published in religious tracts are all true; and what would it prove? Why, simply this: that the converts had all been educated to believe in Christianity, and had gone back to that religion. Had Buddhism or Muhammadanism been their early religion, they would have returned to that. It is merely old errors and old truths revived and re-established in the mind.

196

Repentance

But many facts afterwards gathered by honest investigation, appertaining to some of these cases, show that they have either been manufactured or greatly exaggerated. As for example, the case of Thomas Paine is proved to be without foundation. His close was calm and peaceful. Many times has it been declared, in the pulpit and elsewhere, that "Tom Paine repented, and died a miserable death." And yet we have the testimony of those Christian professors who were present with him almost constantly during his last illness, that he never manifested the least compunction of conscience, or the least disposition to condemn anything he had said or written in opposition to Christianity or the Bible. Take, for example, the testimony of Willet Hicks, a reliable Quaker preacher. On being interrogated by a neighbor of the author of this work as to the truth of the statement that he repented, he replied, "I was with Paine every day during the latter part of his sickness, and can affirm that he did not express any regret for having written 'The Age of Reason,' as has been reported, nor for any thing he had said or written in opposition to the Bible, nor ask forgiveness of God. He died as easy as anyone I ever saw die; and I have seen a great many die." And yet this Mr. Hicks was in hopes he would repent. Other similar testimony might be adduced, but this is sufficient. The story of Ethan Allen's daughter calling upon her father during her last illness, and asking him if he would recommend her to die in his religious belief, and his feeling so conscience-smitten by the question, that he exclaimed, "No, die in the belief of your mother!" (who was a Christian) has gone the rounds of the Christian pulpits. And yet we have the statement of his nephew, Col. Hitchcock, that he had no daughter to die during his lifetime. There is not one word of truth in the report. These two cases furnish samples of the manner in which a dying cause will grasp at straws.

We will subjoin here the testimony of a clergyman, in proof that infidels are not more likely to die in a state of mental distress than Christians. The Rev. Theodore Clap, in his autobiography, says, "In all my experience I never saw an unbeliever die in fear. I have seen them expire without any hope or expectation of the future, but never in agitation from dread or misgiving as to what might befall them hereafter. We know that the idea is prevalent that this final event passes with some terror or agony of soul. It is imagined that, in the infidel's case, the pangs of dissolution are greatly augmented by the upbraidings of a guilty conscience, and by the reluctance of the spirit to be torn from its mortal tenement, and hurried into the presence of an avenging Judge; but this is all a superstitious fancy. It is a superstitious fear, from a false education, that causes any one to die in fear."

The Bible of Bibles

The Rev. W. H. Spenser, of the First Parish Church (Massachusetts), says, "Some of the men most bitterly stigmatized as infidels have been among the most brilliant and useful minds the world has ever known, and, when dying and suffering from calumny and scorn, have only to wait for time to do them justice, and place them in history with the world's benefactors or saviors. There is not to be found on record one purely infidel man, in the sense now referred to, whose death-bed was attended by recantations and remorse." Thus testifies a clergyman.

We will now show from reliable authority that the most ardent faith in Christ and the Bible, and the most rigid and conscientious observance of their doctrines and precepts, do not guarantee permanent acquiescence or satisfaction, or protect the mind from the most violent mental perturbation in the hour of death. John Calvin stood in the first ranks of the Church militant in his time, and was considered by many the leading clergyman in Christendom. Hear what Martin Luther, his co-laborer, says with respect to his mortal exit: "He died forlorn and forsaken of God, blaspheming to the very end.... He died of scarlet fever, overrun and eaten up by ulcerous abscesses, the stench of which drove every person away. He gave up the ghost, despairing of salvation, and evoking devils from the abyss, and uttering oaths most horrible, and blasphemies most frightful." Then tell us no more about infidels recanting and dying unhappy, after reading this case. Yet all the cases and evidences cited above only tend to show that no forms of religious belief have anything specially to do with the condition of mind in the hour of mortal dissolution, except so far as that belief has been invested with groundless, superstitious fears. Hence, persons who distribute death-bed tracts are in rather small business. We like the answer of a liberal-minded man, who, when in his dying moments he was asked by a priest if he had made his peace with his God, replied, "We have never had any unfriendly words." We do not believe there can be a case found in all Christendom of an infidel repenting whose parents were unbelievers, so that he was not educated and biased in favor of any form of religious faith or belief.

CHAPTER 39

FORGIVENESS FOR SIN: AN ERRONEOUS DOCTRINE

The doctrine of divine forgiveness for sin is another illogical and immoral doctrine of the orthodox school, as well as that of heathen nations, which a logical analysis and the practical experience of nearly all religious countries show has been pernicious in its effects upon the morals of society. A little reflection must convince any unbiased mind that, while men and women are taught to believe that the consequences of sin or crime can be arrested or mitigated by an act of forgiveness by the divine Law-maker, they will feel less restrained from the commission of crime and wickedness. They naturally look upon it as a sort of license for the indulgence of their passions and propensities. They are taught that none of the evil consequences of wrong-doing can follow them to another world if they repent in time, and ask forgiveness. This they accept as a broad license to take their swing in vice and villainy. Thus, they are partially demoralized by the doctrine.

Much more rational is the doctrine of the Swedenborgians and Harmonialists that every sin or wrong act we commit makes its impress upon the soul, or immortal spirit, which will be carried with it to the life eternal, and will there long operate to impair the happiness, and retard the spiritual growth, of every person who in this life indulges in crime or immoral conduct. They teach us that the character we form for ourselves on this plane of existence will be carried with us to the spirit-world, and that our character undergoes no radical change by merely passing through the gates of death. Hence, whatever defective moral qualities we permit to be incorporated into our characters here will operate to sink us to a lower plane of happiness in the after-death world. This is a plausible and rational doctrine, to say the least, and can have no effect to demoralize the community, as the sentiments breathed forth by some of the orthodox hymns have evidently done.

> "There is a fountain filled with blood,
> Drawn from Immanuel's veins;
> And sinners plunged beneath that flood
> Lose all their guilty stains."

Could any doctrine be more demoralizing than that here set forth—that the deep-dyed stains of a life of crime, debauchery, and wickedness can all be wiped out by the simple act of plunging into a pool of blood, or rather by believing that the atoning blood of Christ will cleanse from all sin? The same idea is incorporated into Watts's well-known hymn:

The Bible of Bibles

"While the lamp holds out to burn,
The vilest sinner may return."

The idea here set forth is shocking to the moralist, as well as demoralizing in its effects on the community. "The vilest sinner" must feel very little concern about "returning" to the path of virtue, or abandoning his wicked deeds, while the conviction is established in his mind that he is losing nothing by leading such a life, and will have nothing to do at the end of a long life of the most shocking crimes, villainies, and vices, to escape entirely their legitimate punitive consequences, but to take a dip in "the blood of Jesus." Every scientific moralist can see very plainly that the world can never be reformed while such license for sin and wickedness is issued from the Christian pulpit.

Practically speaking, God could not forgive a sin. An act of forgiveness implies that the legitimate consequence of the evil deed or sinful act can be set aside and escaped. The principles of moral science teach us that this is impossible. It demonstrates that the moral law is a part of our being; and, consequently, an act of forgiveness for the violation of that law could not suspend its operation, or stop the infliction of its penalty upon the perpetrator. It could then, of course, effect nothing. Hence, it will be seen that no sin can be forgiven, but must work out its legitimate consequences.

Scientifically speaking, the law is the cause, and the penalty the effect: when the cause is set in operation, the effect must follow. It would be as easy to arrest the thunderbolt in its descent from the clouds as to evade the penalty of this law. God could not if he would, and would not if he could, forgive the violation of his laws. He could not, because he has wisely arranged those laws to operate without his interference. On the other hand, he would not if he could, because it would encourage their future and further violation. And then a God, who would confer on us an inclination to commit certain acts, and then require us to ask his forgiveness for committing them, would not be a very consistent being.

Forgiveness is, theologically speaking, "a free ticket to Heaven." Buy a through ticket of the priest, and you can go on "the strait-line" road, direct to the orthodox "house of many mansions," without having to switch off at any station to unload your burden of sins. "All is well that ends well" is their motto. The orthodox clergy tell the most vile and debauched villain and bloody assassin, after he has inhumanly butchered and murdered his innocent and virtuous wife, can, by an act of repentance and forgiveness, swing from the end of the hangman's rope directly into a heaven of pure and unalloyed bliss, and, with his fingers all dripping with human blood,

200

join the white-robed saints in shouting, "Glory hallelujah to the Lord God and the Lamb forever and ever!" Spare me, oh, spare me, from ever believing in such a demoralizing religion as this!

CHAPTER 40

AN ANGRY GOD: EVILS OF THE BELIEF IN

All Bibles, and nearly every religious nation known to history, have taught that God often gets angry at the creatures of his own creation. But in the light of modern science, nothing could be more transcendently absurd, or more absolutely impossible, than that a being possessing all knowledge—a being infinite in power, infinite in wisdom, and filling all space throughout the boundless universe—should be a victim to the weakness and ungovernable impulse of passion. The very idea is revolting and blasphemous, and presents to every reflecting and unbiased mind a self-evident impossibility. The emotion of anger can only be the weakness of finite and imperfect beings. It is self-evidently impossible for a being possessing infinite perfection, and consequently infinite self-government, to cherish the feeling of anger for a moment, as the following consideration will show:

1. The modern study of mental philosophy has demonstrated anger to be a species of moral weakness; and hence it could not, for a single moment, occupy a mind possessing infinite perfection. A being, therefore, who is assumed to possess such weakness is self-evidently not a God, but merely an imaginary being, fit only to be worshipped by ignorant slaves.

2. The practical experience of every person demonstrates anger to be a species of unhappiness, and often of absolute misery; and the indulgence of this passion not only makes the possessor unhappy, but destroys the happiness of everyone around him. If, therefore, God were an angry being, instead of heaven being a place or state of happiness, it would be the most miserable place imaginable; for God is represented by the Christian Bible as getting angry every day (see Ps. vii. 11), and so angry that the "fury comes up in his face." As a Yankee would say, "He gets mad all over." I frankly confess I don't want to live in such a heaven, or with such a God. Indeed, it would be no heaven at all for anybody; for heaven is a state of happiness.

3. In the third place, the modern study of the science of philosophy has discovered that anger is a species of disease, which may result in mental and even physical suicide if carried far enough. It produces a congested state of the blood-vessels of the brain, which, if not arrested in its progress, will produce death. Dr. Gunn, in his work on domestic medicine, reports several cases in which an inquest was held over a dead body by a coroner's jury, and the verdict rendered, "Came to his death in a fit of anger." However irreverent, the thought forces itself upon us that such a verdict might be given over the dead body of Jehovah if we were compelled to believe all we read of his getting angry; for it is a scientific deduction that cannot be resisted that, if anger can produce death in one being, it may in all beings subject to its influence.

An Angry God

4.   Again: as the result of the study of mental philosophy, anger is now known to be a species of insanity. It deranges, more or less, all the faculties of the mind, and often disqualifies the possessor for doing anything right, or acting rationally, while under its influence. It often causes him to act without reason or judgment, and is liable to drive him to the commission of crime. As well think of entering the cage of a tiger as to take up our abode in a heaven ruled by such a God—a heaven controlled by a God bereft of reason by the ungovernable action of his own passions. We could not be happy in such a heaven: we should be constantly under the influence of fear and apprehension, lest he should become enraged, and his vengeance falls upon us. Where there is fear there is no heaven or happiness. If, as the Bible tells us, he is liable to repent, he might experience this mental perturbation at any time, and repent for having admitted us into the heavenly kingdom, and consequently expel us. Under such circumstances our motives would be very much weakened for laboring to reach such a heaven, not knowing that we should be permitted to remain there a single hour.

How supremely ridiculous, when logically analyzed, is the conception of an angry God! It is entirely behind the age, and adapted only to the lowest stages of barbarism; and yet thousands of Christian clergymen preach this demoralizing doctrine from the pulpit every sabbath day. It is demoralizing, because no person can believe in an angry, sin-punishing God, without cherishing such feelings in his own bosom. It is impossible for him to avoid it. Indeed, he has no motives for trying to avoid it; but, on the contrary, he possesses the strongest motives for cultivating such feelings. For Archbishop Whately says, "Religious people always try to be like the God they worship." They consider it not only their privilege, but also their duty, to imitate him.   Hence, if they believe he gets mad occasionally, and pours out his vengeance upon his offending children (his disobedient subjects), they will naturally feel like following his example, and be cruel and revengeful to those who excite their anger. This preaching the doctrine of an angry God has a tendency to foster vengeful and vindictive feelings amongst the people; when, if the clergy would preach only a God of infinite love, infinite goodness, infinite perfection in all his attributes, we should soon see a marked change in society. Kindness, love, and good-will would be manifested between man and man; and cruel, vengeful, and vindictive feelings would gradually die out, and be numbered amongst the things which have been and are not. Then would the kingdom of peace be established on earth, and the millennium be ushered in. But we cannot expect the priests to be better than their God, nor the people to be better than their priests. "Like God like priest, and like priest like people."

The Bible of Bibles

The priest deals out damnation upon the people to be like his God; and the people follow in his footsteps, and exercise cruel and revengeful feelings toward each other. It seems astonishing that such an immoral and blasphemous doctrine should have been so long and so extensively tolerated in professedly enlightened countries, as it is evident it must have had a bad effect; and past experience proves it has had a demoralizing effect upon the people where the doctrine has been preached. It furnishes an illustration of the omnipotent power of custom.

CHAPTER 41

ATONEMENT FOR SIN: AN IMMORAL DOCTRINE

Having appropriated a portion of two chapters in "The World's Sixteen Crucified Saviors" to an exposition of the doctrine of the atonement, we shall treat the subject but briefly in this work.

1.   It is shown in the work above mentioned that the doctrine of the atonement is of heathen origin, and that it is predicated upon the assumption that no sin can be fully expiated without the shedding of blood. In the language of Paul, "Without the shedding of blood, there can be no remission for sin." A barbarous and bloody doctrine truly! But this doctrine was almost universally prevalent amongst the Orientals long before Paul's time.

2.   Christians predicate the dogma of atonement for sin upon the assumption that Christ's death and sufferings were a substitute for Adam's death, incurred by the fall. But as Adam's sentence was death, and he suffered that penalty, this assumption cannot be true.

3.   If the penalty for sin was death, as taught in Gen. iii., and Christ suffered that penalty for man, then man should not die; but, as he does, it makes the doctrine preposterous. It could not have meant spiritual death, as some argue, because a part of the penalty was that of being doomed to return to dust (Gen. iii. 19).

4.   If crucifixion was indispensably necessary as a penalty, then the punishment should have been inflicted either upon the instigator or perpetrator of the deed: either the serpent or Adam should have been nailed to the cross.

5.   We are told in reply that, as an infinite sin was committed, it required an infinite sacrifice. But Adam, being a finite being, could not commit an infinite sin and Christ's sacrifice and sufferings could not be infinite unless he had continued to suffer to all eternity. Therefore, the assumption is false.

6.   An all-wise God would not let things get into such a condition as to require the murder of his only son from any consideration whatever.

7.   And no father, cherishing a proper regard and love for his son, could have required him to be, or consented to have him, put to death in a cruel manner; for the claims of mercy and paternal affection are as imperative as justice.

8.   To put an intelligent and innocent being to death for any purpose is a violation of the moral law, and as great a sin as that for which he died. Hecatombs of victims cannot atone for the infraction of the moral law that is engraved upon our souls.

9. If it were necessary for Christ to be put to death, then Judas is entitled to one-half the merit of it for inaugurating the act, as it could not have taken place without his aid; and no one who took part in it should be censured, but praised.

10. It is evident that, if everybody had been Quakers, atonement would have been made, as their religion is opposed to bloodshed.

11. The atonement is either one God putting another to death, or God putting himself to death to appease his own wrath; but both assumptions are monstrous absurdities, which no person distinguished for science or reason can endorse.

12. Anger and murder are the two principal features in the doctrine of the atonement, and both are repugnant to our moral sense and feelings of refinement, and indicate a barbarous and heathen origin.

13. The atonement punishes the innocent for the guilty, which is a double, or twofold crime, and a reversal of the spirit of justice. If a father should catch four of his children stealing, and the fifth one standing by and remonstrating against the act, and should seize on the innocent one and administer a severe flagellation, he would commit a double crime: first, that of punishing an innocent child; second, that of exonerating and encouraging the four guilty children in the commission of crime. The atonement involves the same principle.

14. No persons with true moral manhood would consent to be saved on any such terms, but would prefer to suffer for his own sins, rather than let an innocent being suffer for them. And the man who would accept salvation upon such terms must be a sneak and a coward, with a soul not worth saving.

15. Who that possesses any sense of justice would want to swim through blood to get to the heavenly mansion? I want neither animals, men, nor Gods murdered to save my soul.

16. If there is any virtue in the atonement in the way of expiating crime, then there is now another atonement demanded by the principles of moral justice to cancel the sin committed by the first atonement—that of murdering an innocent being, "in whose mouth was no guile"; and then another atonement to wipe out the sin of this atonement, and so on. And thus it would be atonement after atonement, murder after murder, *ad infinitum*. What shocking consequences and absurdities are involved in this ancient heathen superstition!

17. It seems strange that any person can cherish the thought for a moment that the Infinite Father would require a sacrificial offering for the trifling act of eating a little fruit, and require no atonement for the infinitely

greater sin of murdering "his only-begotten son." Another monstrous absurdity!

18. The advocates of the atonement tell us that man stands toward his Creator in the relation of a debtor; and the atonement cancels the debt. To be sure! How does it do it? We will illustrate. A man says to his neighbor, "I owe you a thousand dollars, but I won't pay it." — "Very well," says the creditor, "I will tell you what I will do. I will forgive the debt by seizing on my own son, strip him of all he has, and then put him to death. The claims of justice will then be satisfied." A monstrous idea of justice!

19. The Jewish and Chaldean law of atonement required the offender to place his hand on the head of the beast while being consumed in sacrifice; and this was accepted as an atonement for his transgressions. Such a conception is both senseless and demoralizing. He was thereby taught that he would escape the legitimate consequences of his crime. And the Christian atonement is no better. The sin-atoning offering of Christ furnishes an open door through which the sinner escapes the just punishment of law. It is at least a partial liquidation of his sins. When one being is punished for another, this is, to the latter, an immunity from punishment; and the ends of justice are thus completely thwarted, and the moral law broken and trampled under foot. If a culprit were sentenced to the penalty of death for murder, and the punishment of another man were accepted in his stead, every court in the civilized world would decide that two wrongs were committed—the punishment of the innocent, and the pardon of the guilty. Such doctrines are repugnant to all ideas of justice, and are most certainly demoralizing.

20. The wrong-doer should be taught that he is just as guilty, and just as certain of punishment for his crime, as if all the Gods in heaven were put to death to atone for his sin; the penalty being inseparable from the act.

21. What would be thought of the government that should punish the law-maker instead of the law-breaker? This is exactly what the atonement amounts to; so that the law-maker falls a victim to the penalty of his own laws. It is God the law-maker dying for man the law-breaker. Such ideas and such doctrines are monstrous, and completely overthrow every principle of civil jurisprudence.

22. A God who could resort to such desperate expedients to appease his anger, and satisfy the demands of justice, is not a God, but merely an imaginary being which was conjured up in an age of ignorance and superstition. The belief in such a God is, nevertheless, demoralizing.

We will here relate an anecdote, showing that such ideas of the Supreme Being are repulsive even to the unenlightened heathen. In Smith's "Gulf of Guinea" it is stated that, as a Christian missionary was presenting the doctrine of the Christian religion to Pepples, King of Bonny, and told him that God gave his only-begotten son to die for us—to be put to death for our sins—the king stopped him by saying, "Do you think me a fool to believe such palaver as that—that God would kill his own son to please himself; get mad at man, and then kill his own son, instead of killing him? Never, never can I believe such fool palaver as that! It is big fool lie." "I tried," says the missionary, "to impress upon his mind that nothing would satisfy divine justice but such a sacrifice; but he cut me short by exclaiming, 'That will do; that will do: I have got enough of such fool palaver.'" Quite a sensible "heathen" was King Pepples.

CHAPTER 42

SPECIAL PROVIDENCES: AN ERRONEOUS DOCTRINE

All the holy books, and nearly all holy men who have figured in the world, have cherished a belief in what is termed "special providences"—a doctrine which teaches that God individually and personally superintends the affairs, not only of all nations, but of each individual human being, *now* amounting in number to about fourteen hundred millions. It seems strange that the striking absurdity of such an assumption has not struck every mind possessing the power to reflect or investigate. The thought of his looking after the affairs and happiness of fourteen hundred millions of human beings at a time, besides running several thousand millions of worlds, far excels any of the astounding feats of the evil genii of Gulliver. In the sublimity of its absurdity and impossibility, it stands without a rival. It expands beyond the utmost stretch of human credulity. Like all the other doctrines of the popular creed, it sprang up in an age of the world when the human mind accepted everything presented to it without investigation—when nothing was rejected on the ground of its being too absurd to be believed. And an absurdity, when once established, no matter how monstrous or how stultifying to the intellectual or reasoning faculties, can bid defiance to the efforts of the few men of the world whose minds are too much expanded and enlightened to accept such gross absurdities. There are several objections to the doctrine of "special providences," both of a logical or scientific character, and also upon moral grounds, which shows that it should have no place in an age of scientific intelligence.

One of these objections is the one just brought to notice—that of its extreme absurdity and practical impossibility. It does not require a great mind, but only a reflecting one, to see that no rational conception of the Supreme Being could render it practicable for one mind, however boundless in knowledge and infinite in power, to be so divided as to look after the interest of each individual of a countless number, scattered over a world of more than a hundred and seventy-five thousand millions of miles in extent. A scientific investigation of the operations of nature has settled the conviction in every scientific mind that the life, actions, and destiny of every human being are under the control of fixed and immutable laws, which need only to be studied and observed to guard him effectually from personal accidents, and those physical disasters to which he often falls a victim through ignorance of the proper means of avoiding them.

It is now patent to all critical observers that the serious disasters and numerous causes of physical suffering to which the larger portion of the human family were so frequently subjected in past ages, have largely diminished, and are constantly decreasing as the march of science dispels the ignorance of the people—such as the sinking of ships, attributable to imperfect mechanical construction; pestilential diseases, caused by the general ignorance of the causes of and means of preventing; the explosion of steam-boilers on rivers, railroads, etc. And, from the present rates of improvement in these respects, we may reasonably calculate that the time is not far in the future when such disasters will be unknown. Then we will have no need of "special providence" to save the people from the fatal consequences of their ignorance.

The conviction seems now to be generally established in the public mind that when a boat is wrecked, or a locomotive strays from the track, and a few persons escape with their lives from the general wreck and ruin, it is to be ascribed to the interposition of the hand of Providence. But common sense would suggest that, if Providence had anything to do with it, he should have commenced a little sooner, and put some more brains or common sense into the heads of the managers of these cargoes of human beings, or kept the whiskey out of their stomachs until they reached their point of destination. In the thousands of cases annually reported of Providence interposing his aid to save some reckless mariners, or some heedless passengers on a pleasure-boat, from a watery grave, or rescuing a few persons from the wreck of a railroad bridge, or some similar calamity, the disasters might all have been avoided by Providence simply acting upon the wisdom of the proverb, "An ounce of prevention is worth a pound of cure." It would be considered an act of criminal neglect on the part of a father who could stand by and see his children, from ignorance of the danger of such a situation, fall from a precipice, and get crippled: for which his diligence in taking care of them, and trying to heal their bruises, would by no means excuse him, as he should have commenced sooner, and prevented the accident from taking place. And nearly all the cases of providential interposition are liable to the same objection: the assistance is too long delayed.

A collisions of two ships recently occurred on the Atlantic, by which both vessels were reduced almost to wrecks; but "providentially but few lives were lost," though most of the passengers were injured. Now the question naturally arises, Why did not God, when he perceived the vessels were approaching each other, impose his providential care and prevent the disaster? He either could not, or would not; and, in either case, he is not infinite in all his attributes, according to the general ideas of the matter. If he could not, he is either not omnipresent or not infinite in power; and if he could and would not, he is not infinite in kindness and benevolence, or he would have put forth his hand and saved his children from such a terrible fate. It is time mankind would learn that God governs the universe by general laws, fixed and unalterable, and ever harmonious, and that he never interferes immediately or personally in the affairs of men.

That finite human spirits do, in many cases, aid in human affairs by warning of danger, etc., is fully believed by many persons. If this be true, their interposition would be liable to be mistaken for that of the Infinite Spirit. But that any being can perform millions of finite acts at once, or that God should suspend the operations of his laws, which control the universe, for the purpose of attending personally to the wants and prayers of each and every individual the world over—many of the petitions running counter to, or in direct conflict with, each other—is an idea too absurd to find lodgment in any truly enlightened mind. But we entertain the pleasing thought that men are beginning to learn that God governs by general laws, and not by personal or special agency. These laws are so perfect in their operations that no special laws or personal interference is necessary in any case. A critical investigation of any case of special providences would satisfy any scientific investigator that it was governed entirely by natural causes; but such scrutinizing investigations are seldom made.

The great mass of pious people in all past ages have been so ignorant, and so little accustomed to reasoning or observation, that they have never observed that, although many cases are reported of Providence interfering to save the life of a child who fell from the window of a basement-story, none are recorded of his saving a child that fell from the fifth story. Why is this? Does not this fact suggest a scientific lesson? But the heads of the great mass of the people have been so filled with creeds and catechisms that they have no room for science. It will be time enough to talk about special providences after a case is known of a man escaping with his life after a cannonball has passed through his head, or a bullet through his heart. The belief in special providences, is calculated to paralyze human effort in times of danger, and thus suffer the consequences to be more frequently fatal. Let a man believe, while a ship is being wrecked in a storm, dashing against rocks and billows, and her deck overflowed with water, that there is a Providence in the case, and he will naturally labor with less zeal and effort to save the vessel. If the case is in the hands of God, and it is his good pleasure that they should be lost, it is of but little use to work the pumps; and if it is his will that they should be saved, they will be saved without much effort on their part. There can be no doubt but that millions of pious people have been restrained on various occasions from putting forth their strongest efforts to arrest a threatening disaster, from the conviction that the hand of God was in it, and that no human efforts could change the fate he had decreed for them. And thus the doctrine, in its practical consequences, has been pernicious. But in this age of reason and scientific illumination, men are beginning to learn that, in cases of threatening danger and destruction, muscle is more necessary than "Providence"; that, when a ship is sinking in mid-ocean, pumps are more efficacious than prayers; and, when a building is on fire, they can better do without the assistance of Providence than without water, firemen, and engines.

CHAPTER 43

FAITH AND BELIEF: BIBLE ERRORS RESPECTING

"Faith" and "belief" seem to be among the most important words in the Christian New Testament. No words are much more frequently used. They occur in nearly every chapter, and are used more than two hundred times. The following is a specimen of the manner in which these words are used:

"He that believeth and is baptized shall be saved; but he that believeth not shall be damned." This text, and the sentiment it contains, have caused more misery, cruelty, and more butchery than all the edicts of any king that ever sat on the throne of England. Never did a more delusive and fatal error find lodgment in the human mind than the idea couched in this text. Terrible have been the denunciations, punishments, and cruelties poured upon the unbelievers in the popular creed, though that creed has been one thing one day, and something else the next. No matter how honest, how upright, how benevolent, or how righteous a man proved himself in his practical life, he was doomed to the dungeon, the fagot, and the halter, if his creed was not conformable to the orthodox faith then in power. Men and women have been condemned and punished for assuming the right to doubt the truth of any doctrine of the popular creed—an egregious mistake, showing a profound ignorance of the nature of the human mind. All persons versed in the science of mental philosophy now know that a man has no more control over his doubts and beliefs than he has over the blood that courses through his veins; for, without evidence, he cannot disbelieve; and with it, he cannot disbelieve, as everyone will find who will examine this matter critically. Consequently, it is as unreasonable to condemn a man for his belief or disbelief, as to condemn him for the color of his hair. Doubt, so far from being restrained, should be cultivated, as being the first step toward the attainment of knowledge and progress; for a man never makes any advancement or improvement in his views on any subject until he begins to doubt the correctness of his present views, or, at least, doubts their being perfect, or being incapable of improvement.

Who, then, cannot see that to threaten a man for disbelief is tyranny and injustice inasmuch as it has a tendency to make him a slave, and to repress the growth of his mind? Condemning a man for disbelief is virtually offering a premium for hypocrisy, as it has the effect to make thousands *profess* to believe doctrines which they do not, and which their consciences really condemn, in order to avoid the frowns and ill-will of their neighbors. And, as hypocrisy is a greater evil in its practical effects upon society than unbelief, it can be seen that the practice of erecting a standard for belief and disbelief is wrong, and mischievous in its effects.

The Bible of Bibles

The Bible declares that "faith is the gift of God." It is evident that, if this be true, no responsibility can attach to faith or religious belief; but all responsibility rests with the being who gives it.

Two great blunders have been committed by faith-dealers: First, in assuming that belief is of the nature of a coat, which can be put on and off at pleasure—i.e., that a man can believe what he pleases or wishes to believe. The second is that knowledge and belief are synonymous terms, which is very far from being true. Knowledge begins where faith and belief end. Belief is that uncertain state of the mind which is experienced in the absence of knowledge; and, when that knowledge is obtained, the belief may prove to have been entirely erroneous. Belief implies *uncertainty*; knowledge implies *certainty*. There is this wide difference between them. We believe a thing when we do not know whether it is so or not; consequently, the belief may be true or false. How egregious, then, the blunder of the orthodox world in condemning for disbelief! Belief, then, is a state of guessing. We will illustrate the position of orthodox Christendom: A boy throws up a copper coin, and cries, "Heads, or tails?" A bystander, believing from its construction that "heads" will come up, cries out, "Heads!" Now, according to the logic of the orthodox, if he guesses wrong, he should be damned eternally for it.

When you say to a man, "You shall believe this, or you shall believe that," you bind his soul in chains, and reverse the wheels of his progress, and push him toward the "dark ages."

The fear that it would be a sin to doubt, causes religious ignorance; and a man will never abandon his religious errors and superstitious while he fears to doubt their truth. A man's belief and creed grow shorter as his knowledge increases. And the time is not far distant when philosophers and men of science will have no religious belief: all will be knowledge.

It can be seen from the above exposition that it is folly and consummate ignorance to attach so much importance to religious belief, inasmuch as it is impossible to know whether it is right or wrong. As the doctrine that belief is a virtue, and unbelief a crime has inundated the world with persecution, misery, and blood, it is time to abandon it.

Those Christians who assume that belief is under the control of the will can settle the matter by trying the following experiment upon themselves: Let them try to believe, for only five minutes, that Muhammad was a true prophet, and Jesus Christ was an impostor. If they can do this, it will settle the question, and prove that man is responsible for his belief: otherwise, he is not.

Some persons adhere to the Bible upon the plea that "it is safest to believe it, and unsafe to disbelieve it." But he who can believe an error or absurdity, or, rather, profess to believe it because he is afraid to disbelieve it, has not a soul big enough to be saved, and will be certain to miss it; or, if he could be saved, no man of sense would want to live in heaven made up of such moral cowards and moral dwarfs. Besides, the only way to make a safe thing of being saved on this ground is to swallow all the two thousand systems of religion in the world—six hundred Christian creeds, and fourteen hundred heathen traditions; and, to do this, a person must have a very capacious stomach.

CHAPTER 44

A PERSONAL GOD IMPOSSIBLE

Most of the Bibles, and nearly all the religious teachers of the world, have represented God as being a personal being, and, at the same time, an infinite spirit. But that is another of the "thousand and one" absurdities that have been taught and believed in the name of religion. A personal being must, in all cases, be an organized being. This is so self-evident as to need no argument; and that an organized being cannot be an infinite being is almost equally self-evident. An organized being must be a finite being. The word "finite" is used to express the opposite of "infinite." To assume, therefore, that a finite being, or a being with a finite body, can also be infinite, is equivalent to assuming that a thing can be white and black, large and small, long and short, light and heavy, etc., at the same time, which is a self-evident absurdity. A personal being must be constituted of different parts or numbers—as a head, heart, body, feet, etc.; and, if such a being could be infinite, then each member must be infinite. But as it is self-evident that a being to be infinite must fill all space, and that nothing can be infinite unless it does occupy all space, it can be seen at once that, if one member were infinite, it would occupy all space, which would preclude the possibility of another member being infinite. Thus, we are completely swamped at the first step toward making a personal God infinite. Here let it be noted that the God of the Bible is represented as possessing all the members of the human body—eyes (1 Pet. iii. 12), ears (*Ibid.*), nose (Isa. lxv. 5), mouth (Isa. xlv. 23), feet (Rev. i. 15), arms (Isa. xxx. 30), hands (Exod. xiii. 3), fingers (Exod. viii. 19), head (Dan. vii. 9), heart (Isa. lxiii. 4), lips (Ps. xvii. 4), etc. Now, it is evidently impossible that such a being could be infinite. We may be told that these members are all to be taken in a spiritual sense. Granted, and the thing is equally impossible; for they must still be separate members. There could be no possible sense in applying all those terms to the whole being. They must apply to separate parts; and the moment we use terms which imply the existence of more than one part, we concede the impossibility of such a God being infinite; for only one part, one being, or one thing can be infinite. There cannot be two infinite beings—self-evidently not.

And there are other logical difficulties in the way of admitting the existence of an infinite personal God. If there could be such a thing as an infinite personality or organized being, it is evident that only one such being could exist. What, then, becomes of the Father, Son, and Holy Ghost, and also the Devil? They are all spoken of in the Bible as being omnipresent. Hence, they must all be infinite, which is another self-evident impossibility. We could as easily conceive of two Gods wearing the same hat at the same time, as two such beings being infinite. If one of them is infinite, the others

A Personal God Impossible

cannot be; and yet each is represented as being omnipresent, which would make them infinite. And thus we fail in every attempt to make a personal God infinite. David, in speaking of the God Jehovah, says, "If I descend into hell, behold thou art there." Then he would not find the Devil there; for two infinite beings could not be found there. And, if God's dwelling-place is in hell as well as in heaven, it can make but little difference which of the two places we go to, as we are told our happiness will consist in being in his presence.

The defenders of a personal God sometimes have recourse to an illustrative argument. They tell us that the sun is a local, circumscribed body, and yet shines to a boundless extent. It is here assumed that the rays of the sun are a part of the sun; but this is not true. They once constituted a part of the sun, it is true; but to assume that they are still a part of the sun, after they have left it, is as absurd as to assume that the breath is still a part of the human body after it has escaped from the mouth. Thus, every argument and every illustration fail to establish the self-evident absurdity of a personal God of the orthodox world being an infinite being; or, in other words, of their conception of a God conforming to the teachings of science and good sense.

Those who assume the existence of a personal God must hold him accountable for all the crime and all the misery existing in the world. For such a God could not be controlled or circumscribed in his actions by any arbitrary laws; and hence could and should, by personnel interference, put a stop to all the crime, misery, suffering, and wrong of every description existing on earth; and the fact that he does not do it we hold to be *prima facie* evidence that there is no personal God, but that everything is governed by fixed, immutable laws, which control God himself, and which no God can alter.

Note: We have shown in the twelve preceding chapters that all the leading doctrines of Christianity are wrong—from that of a belief in divine revelation to that of the conception of a personal God. Hence, a better religion is needed for this age.

217

CHAPTER 45

EVIL, NATURAL AND MORAL, EXPLAINED

The problem of the origin of evil has been the great theological puzzle to all theologians and with all religious systems, and has turned the hearts of more good people, and sent more devout Christians to the lunatic asylum, than any other theological question, excepting that of endless punishment; and yet modern science, which furnishes the principles for solving all the "holy mysteries" and miracles embodied in the religious creeds and Bibles of the past ages, shows the question to be quite simple and easily understood. The true signification of the word *evil*, in a moral sense, can be expressed in a few words. It is only another name for *imperfection* or *negation.* It is the negative pole of the *great moral battery*; and without it the battery could not be run. And without it there could be no morality, no moral principle or accountability, while man exists upon the present animal plane. In fact, morality without evil would be an unmeaning word. Evil is a state of imperfection running through every vein of nature, from the igneous rock to the brain of man.

Some writers attempt to discriminate between natural and moral evil, but there is no dividing line. Moral evil is as natural as any phenomenon in nature, and is, strictly speaking, the phenomenal action of the brain. Moral evil is governed as rigidly by natural laws as physical evil, because (as science demonstrates) it has its basis in man's moral nature. And, practically speaking, there will be neither natural nor moral evil when nature (now in a crude state) grows to a state of maturity. Evil or imperfection, which now characterizes everything, diminishes in its ratio to goodness or perfection as we ascend from inanimate matter to man—the crowning work of nature.

The theological world assumes that man alone bears the impress of imperfection, and that his imperfection is restricted principally to his moral action. "Man alone is imperfect: all else bears the mark of divine perfection." So says Archbishop Whately. But the converse assumption is nearer true: Man is the crowning work of nature, and his moral attributes constitute the keystone of the arch. He is occasionally erratic, and often wicked, but not universally and continually so, like some of the lower animal tribes.

The hyena will murder at all times when opportunity offers; but man only occasionally, and when driven to it by the pressure of circumstances. All monkeys are thieves; but only a small portion of the *genus homo* are such. Man derives all his propensity to evil and wickedness from the lower animals. His propensity to rob is exhibited in the eagle; his inclination to steal, in the monkey; his disposition to murder, in the hyena, alligator, rattlesnake, etc.; his disposition to enslave, in the red ant, which makes a slave of the black ant, as has often been observed by naturalists. Such was the wickedness among the lower animals in their earlier stage of development that, by theft, robbery, and murder, they effected the entire extinction of many species of animals.

And if we descend still lower, and learn the practical history of the mineral kingdom, we shall find that its operations are marked by a still more ruinous and destructive form of evil. The hideous and devouring earthquake; the heaving and overflowing volcano, burying whole cities beneath its deep and merciless waves of running fire; the roaring and furious tornado, destroying hundreds of dwellings, and dooming the inmates to a terrible death; and the swift-sped lightning, which, with no note of warning, strikes down hundreds of people every year—all these violent operations of nature are the manifestation of evil, and a proof that imperfection exists everywhere.

Man is the last and least manifestation of this multifarious destructive outburst of nature, and he will never outgrow it and escape its operation entirely until all nature arrives at manhood. While nature is imperfect, man will be imperfect; for he is a child of nature, and all things move forward in correlated order. He can, however (and it is a necessity of his nature that he should), battle with opposing forces, and modify the circumstances around him. His nature impacts him to this, as naturally as it urges him to eat food when hungry; but as at present constituted and situated, it will be the work of time to rid the earth of moral evil.

The only way to accomplish the extinction of evil is to labor for the elevation of the whole race. We are only rowing against the current in attempting to put down evil with our present system of moral ethics, which treats the criminal as a wicked being instead of an unfortunate, sin-sick brother. He should be sent to a moral hospital instead of to the gallows, the jail, and the dungeon. He should be treated as an unfortunate brother, rather than as a being to be spurned from society as a viper. He should be treated kindly, not cruelly; fed, and not starved. His moral nature should be warmed by affection, and not congealed by frowns. His instinctive respect for virtue should be developed by a sound moral education, and not crushed by pursuing him with a malignant spirit. Moral evils must be treated as the fruit of the imperfections of our nature and not as the product of sin-punishing devils, who first originate and stimulate crimes, and then join with God in punishing the criminal with fiendish cruelty; then applying a remedy which is a thousand times worse than the disease.

The science of phrenology explains most beautifully the cause and nature of sins or crime, and demonstrates that it is simply the perverted or unbalanced action of the natural faculties of the mind. Combativeness,

219

when excessively developed or unduly excited, prompts to quarrels and fighting; destructiveness, under similar circumstances, leads to war and bloodshed; amativeness, when not properly restrained, leads to the various forms of licentiousness; over-active acquisitiveness is the main-spring in most cases of theft and robbery, and all crimes committed for the acquisition of property or money. And other crimes are prompted by the over-active condition of these and other mental faculties unrestrained by the moral faculties. Every act and every species of crime are in this way most satisfactorily accounted for by this now generally received and thoroughly established science of mental philosophy; so that "the mystery of godliness," comprehended in the word *sin*, which for ages perplexed the student of theology, is now unraveled and understood by the scientific men of the age, and known to have a natural basis and natural origin.

This all-important discovery has driven the old orthodox Devil from the arena of human action. He no longer walks "to and fro in the earth, seeking whom he may devour." He is dead—dead—killed by the sledgehammer of science. And yet the fifty thousand clergymen who still "defend the faith once delivered to the saints" are (many of them) so far behind the march of human progress that the news of the mortal exit of his Satanic Majesty scorns not yet to have reached them; or, if it has, it is because they are unwilling to lose the services of a long-cherished and highly valued friend that they refuse to credit the report of his demise. Take away their Devil, and their whole theological scaffolding falls to the ground. Revivals could no more be carried on without his aid, than a watch could be kept running without a main-spring. And with the departure of the Devil must go "salvation by Christ," as there is then nothing, in a theological sense, to be saved from.

It is an important fact, of which the clergy seem to be ignorant, that the march of science has exploded all their old theological dogmas. Phrenology has banished the Devil; physiology explains the *modus operandi* of repentance; psychology, the process of "getting religion"; philosophy analyzes their Bible miracles; geology has expanded their six days of creation into six thousand years; astronomy has displaced Moses' theory of creation and demolished St. John's little eight-by-ten heaven. (See Rev. chap. 21.) And yet the orthodox clergy refuse to shorten their creed by leaving out these old, exploded dogmas. Like moles, they continue rooting and digging away among their musty creeds, dogmas, and catechisms, seemingly unconscious that the sun of science is now shining with dazzling brilliancy in the moral heavens.

Some of them manifest a tenacity in holding on to musty and antiquated dogmas equal to that of the butcher's dog in the army which seized a slaughtered ox by the caudal appendage, with the intention of monopolizing the meat, and held on with a "manly grip" until limb after limb had been torn off, and piece after piece had been cut away from the body by the hungry soldiers, and nothing was left but the tail and the backbone; and then his canine majesty growled at passersby, as much as to say, "I am master of the situation." The fossilized clergy are "masters of the situation," while the old orthodox carcass is now minus every part but the tail and naked backbone, to which they cling with a deathly grasp worthy of a better cause. They remind us of the hotel-keeper in Vermont who, in answer to the interrogatories of some travelers, stated that he did not keep any kind of food for either men or horses. "What in the name of God, then, do you keep?" inquired one of the hungry guests. He replied, "I keep Union Hotel." The standstill clergy still keep the old theological hotel minus any spiritual food, or supplied only with old salt junk handed down from the camp of Moses or Father Abraham.

A word more with respect to the origins of evil: Is it not strange that Christians should deny their God to be the author of evil, when it is expressly so declared in their Bible? "I make peace, and *I create evil.* I Jehovah do all these things."

Here is the positive declaration that God is the author of evil and, if it were not this unequivocally taught, we could prove that the Bible teaches this doctrine *indirectly* by various texts. If "God made every thing that was made," then he either made evil or the author of evil, whether that was a devil or a serpent or a fallen angel; and this is substantially the same thing as originating evil—to originate the author of evil. We challenge refutation of the proposition. But a philosophical analysis of the question will show there is no such thing as evil in either the *abstract* or *absolute* sense. Good and evil are but relative terms, like heat and cold, light and darkness, etc. There is no distinct line of demarcation between any of these correlative terms. It is impossible to tell where one ends, and the other begins. And then there is no act but that may become either right or wrong under different circumstances. The Bible says, "Thou shalt not kill." But the man who should see an assassin pointing a pistol to the head of his wife, or a dagger to her breast, and refrain from killing him as the only means of saving her life, would be virtually himself a murderer. "Thou shalt not steal" (Exod. xx.); and yet stealing would become a *moral right*, as well as a physical necessity, to avoid starvation. And so of all other acts called crime and sin: they may become *absolute virtues.* How foolish, therefore, to erect inflexible standards for human action or conduct!

And then it should be noted that what is regarded as sin in one age or country may be imposed as a moral or religious duty in another. It is a sin to *disbelieve* the Koran in Arabia, and a sin to *believe* it in America. It is a *sinful act* to disbelieve the Christian Bible in this country, and a *moral* and *religious duty* in Japan. It is blasphemy and atheism to disbelieve in Jehovah and Jesus Christ in this country, but a still greater blasphemy and sin to believe in them in Arabia. And thus all human actions are modified by the circumstances under which, and the locality in which, they are committed.

A RATIONAL VIEW OF SIN AND ITS CONSEQUENCES

W e will now attempt to show what reason, science, and God's eternal Bible teach as the nature of sin and its consequences. The orthodox world represents sin to be a personal affront against a personal God. But we take a broader, and, we think, a more rational view of the matter. We believe that no act of ours, whether good or bad, can possibly affect an infinite, omnipresent, and impersonal Deity in any way whatever. Nothing we can do can either offend or gratify such a being. He is infinitely too far removed from our little narrow sphere of action. But everything we do can and *does affect ourselves*, and generally our friends and all connected with us.

Every wrong act we perform inflicts an injury upon our moral consciousness, and a wound upon our sense of right, and inflicts a lasting injury upon our moral dignity, if it does not create a painful sense of wrong. And when once committed, no repentance, no forgiveness, no prayer, no atonement, no pardon, can do anything toward arresting the baneful effects, or toward healing the wound it has inflicted upon our moral consciousness, or the injury it has inflicted upon others. Hence, we never ask for forgiveness, nor rely upon any atonement by men, animals, or Gods to cancel the effects, or mitigate the wrong, or alleviate the injury in the case. When you put your finger into fire and burn it, you violate one of God's laws written upon your own constitution—the law of self-preservation; and it inflicts a wound which the longest and loudest prayer ever uttered can do nothing towards healing. The effect will remain until healed by the working of nature's inherent laws. A similar effect is produced by every wrong act you inflict upon yourself or your fellow beings. It inflicts a wound that is beyond the reach of prayer, pardon, repentance, or forgiveness. It must work its natural cure, as in the case of physical injury.

All bodily suffering comes through the mind, and hence affects the mind as well as the body; and every moral wrong we commit inflicts punishment or suffering upon the moral feelings. Hence, it will be seen that sin does not have to wait for God to point out the penalty or punishment, but contains its own punishment, which no power in heaven or earth can arrest, avert, or set aside. This is evidently the only true doctrine respecting the punishment for sin; and it is the only doctrine that can stop the commission of crime, and the only doctrine that can ever reform the world; for, while the people are taught that sin can be atoned for by any power in heaven or earth, they will the more easily yield to the temptations to commit sin. They will feel that this doctrine is a kind of license for sin: at least it weakens the motive for abstaining from sin. For if a man may lead a life of crime, sin, wickedness, and debauchery, destitute of all moral principle, for ninety-nine years, as orthodoxy teaches, and then have the effect entirely canceled, and the sin entirely erased from his soul, by one short hour of prayer and repentance and forgiveness, and by acknowledging his faith in the atoning blood of Christ, and then stand before God without a moral blot upon his soul, all purified and ready to join the pure in heart—the white-robed angels who lived a life of self-denial and purity—in shouting glory to God, where is the motive for leading a virtuous life? It is entirely too weak to restrain from the commission of crime while the temptation is as strong as we usually find it in all countries, especially as there is apparently a large premium offered to sinners. Christ says, "There is more joy in heaven over one sinner that repenteth than over ninety and nine just persons who need no repentance" (Luke xv. 7). No wonder that sin abounds in all Christian countries; and it always will abound while people are taught such pernicious doctrines. Therefore, we hold the doctrines of repentance, atonement, forgiveness, etc., to be all wrong. They are subversive of the first principles of moral justice, and pernicious in their effects upon society.

Let the wrong-doer, instead of being taught these pernicious doctrines, be instructed in the true system of salvation, which will teach him there is no possibility of evading or escaping the punitive effects of wrong-doing; that every wrong act he commits will inevitably drive the iron into his soul—the two-edged sword of moral conviction; and that the blood of no goats or no Gods can do anything toward washing away the sin, or mitigating the punishment. And let him be rescued also from the pernicious error of the churches, that "sin is a sweet morsel to be rolled under the tongue," or that "there is a pleasure in the commission of sin." We hold no such views; we believe in no such doctrines. We do not believe there is any real pleasure in the commission of a moral wrong of any kind. We believe that only a life of virtue is productive of real happiness. Let the wrong-doer be taught this moral lesson; and let him be also taught that every humane and virtuous act of this life will expand his soul, and elevate him to a higher plane of happiness, and bring him one step nearer the door of the heavenly kingdom. Let the world of mankind all be taught these beautiful and soul-elevating doctrines, which many now know by experience to be golden truths; and we will soon witness a great moral revolution and renovation in society by the propagation of these doctrines. We shall soon see the proof that our system of faith, embracing these beautiful, philosophical, and elevating doctrines, is much better calculated to moralize and reform the world than the morally weak and unjust doctrines of repentance, atonement, and pardon now daily preached from the Christian pulpits.

Many cases could be cited to show that they do have a pernicious influence. I will adduce one example: When that *Christian* emperor,

A Rational View of Sin

Constantine, had murdered his wife, son, nephew, and several other relatives, he raised his hands toward heaven, and exclaimed, "The blood of Christ cleanseth from all sin." Here is an example of the pernicious and demoralizing effect of the Christian doctrines of atonement and forgiveness. We repeat, then, that such doctrines are demoralizing, as they must operate to retard the progress of truth and religion, and the moral reformation of the world. People should be taught that it is as impossible to escape the penalty for sin or wrong-doing as it is to escape the darts of death; and that any act of forgiveness or atonement by some other being is only calculated to aggravate the wrong, and augment the sin, and open the door for a future commission of the act.

All should understand that there is no one to pardon sins, and no savior but themselves. "The new religion," as it is sometimes called—though it is the oldest religion in the world, being founded in the moral and religions nature of man, and an outgrowth of his moral, religious, and spiritual elements—this religion, which is the religion of all the truly enlightened and scientific minds of the age, teaches that every person must be his own savior; that every man and woman must work out their own salvation, not with fear and trembling, however, but with joy and rejoicing. Hence, we ask no bleeding saviors, no atonements, no acquittals by pardon or forgiveness. We offer no such bribery for crime or sin—no such allurements and inducements for leading a life of vice; for many can testify, from their own experience, that they were more easily tempted from the path of virtue when they believed in these old heathenish, morally deformed, and morally dwarfing doctrines.

On the other hand, they have felt much more strongly wedded to a life of virtue, and more powerfully restrained from wrong-doing since they abandoned these pernicious doctrines, and embraced the healthful, beautiful, and elevating doctrines of the "Harmonial Philosophy." This system teaches we have to suffer the penalty in full for every wrong act we commit; that we *cannot escape in any case* by either *repentance, atonement, or pardon*; that we cannot swim off to heaven through the blood of a murdered or crucified God, and leave our sins behind unpunished, or pack them on the back of a savior as the Jews did theirs on the back of a goat. It teaches us that the penalty is as certain as the commission of the crime; because one is the cause, and the other the effect. Hence, we could as easily replace a lost arm, torn off in the field of battle, by prayer, or stop the descending lightning from splintering yonder tree into a thousand fragments, as to avert or set aside the penalty for crime by "supplicating the throne of grace." We hold that every wrong act we commit, if it does not destroy our happiness at the time, and operate as a barbed arrow sticking in

225

the soul, will at least weaken our capacity for happiness in the future, weaken our moral strength and resolution to abstain from crime, weaken our natural detestation of crime, and weaken our moral ability to resist the temptation to commit the same and other crimes in the future, and finally destroy our moral manhood and true dignity. Now, here is a series of powerful motives for eschewing evil, and leading a life of virtue, which will operate to arrest that river of crime and iniquity now flowing through all Christian countries as soon as the people are taught these rational and beautiful doctrines in lieu of those weak and foolish incentives to virtue which are taught them from the Christian pulpit. They possess a much greater moral force than the fear of angry Gods and horned Devils. *Reader, ponder these maxims.*

The True Theory of Reform. It requires but a few words to show what kind of moral teaching is required to reform the world. As happiness is the predominant desire and inalienable right of every human being, all aim to pursue that course best calculated to attain it; but, as men are now organized and circumstanced, they often pursue a course of life which infringes upon and destroys the happiness of others. Some of them commit acts known as crimes, which are simply trespasses upon the rights, peace, and happiness of their neighbors. If, in thus pursuing happiness they must destroy the happiness of others, then it follows that the happiness of others is incompatible with their own. If so, then God has made a serious blunder in making one man's happiness depend upon destroying the happiness of others; and, as their happiness would depend equally upon destroying his, the happiness of all would thus be destroyed. Hence, the theory will not work. It follows, then, that men lead a life of crime calculated to destroy the happiness of others, because they are ignorant of the fact that they can pursue a course of life that will secure their own happiness without destroying that of others. All that is necessary to reform them, therefore, is to convince them of this fact. This is the *true* theory, and the *whole* theory, of reform. And when people become acquainted with the modern discovery in moral philosophy, which teaches us that we cannot attain to complete happiness without consulting the happiness of others in every act which affects them, there will be a *double motive* for leading a virtuous and honorable life. Even Christian professors will profit by it when they find that the grasping avarice which prompts them to try to monopolize wealth, and thus withhold the means of comfort and happiness from their neighbors, is not the way to attain real happiness for themselves. When the glorious era arrives that men will daily look after the happiness of others as well as their own, then we shall have a true religion, and a true state of society, and a happy world.

CHAPTER 47

THE BIBLE SANCTIONS EVERY SPECIES OF CRIME

"Be ye perfect, as your Father in heaven is perfect" (Matt. v. 48). All Christian professors admit that this perfection is to be attained by following his practical example, and that the way to become acquainted with this practical example is to read the Bible. Let us see, then, where a practical compliance with this precept, as thus understood, will lead us. If the God of the Bible is to be accepted as our "heavenly Father," then a compliance with this precept will leave no crime uncommitted, and no sin not perpetrated; for he is represented as either committing or sanctioning every species of crime, wickedness, and immorality known to society in the age in which the Bible was written. That the truth of this statement may not be called in question, we will proceed to bring forward evidence to prove it.

MURDER

We finds scriptural warrant for the highest crime known to the law—that of murder. God is represented as saying to his holy people, "Go ye out and slay every man his brother, every man his companion, and every man his neighbor" (Exod. xxxii. 27). And, relative to the dissenter from the faith, he is represented as saying, "Ye shall stone him with stones that he die." Now, if such texts are not calculated to foster the spirit of murder, and to extinguish the natural repugnance to cruelty and bloodshed in the human mind, we can conceive of no language that would have such an effect, especially when it is taken in connection with Christ's injunction, "He that hath not a sword, let him sell his coat, and buy one."

And the practical lives of Christian professors, from the earliest establishment of the Church, furnishes proof of the demoralizing influence of such texts as these upon the readers of the Bible. These injunctions to murder and slaughter have been faithfully obeyed; and the effect has been to submerge Christendom in a sea of blood. Look, for proof, at the war among the churches for many years about the doctrine of the Eucharist, which resulted in the destruction of three hundred thousand lives; the fight about images, in which fifty thousand men, women, and children were murdered; the war of a dozen churches against the sect of the Manicheans in the ninth century (A.D. 845) about some trivial doctrine of the Christian creed, and which left on the battlefield no less than a hundred thousand murdered human beings; the Church schism, in the time of John Huss and Jerome of Prague, followed by the war of the Hussites, which resulted in a bloody slaughter of a hundred and fifty thousand fellow Christians; the war known as "The Holy Inquisition," established in the year 1208, made a record in its history of human butchery of two hundred thousand Christian professors, who had to atone in blood for assuming the liberty to differ from the popular creed; and, finally, the Thirty Years' war which strewed the earth with bloody corpses to the frightful number of five millions of human beings. The whole makes a sum total of eighteen millions, a large portion of which were Christian professors—all the work of Christian hands and Christian churches, professed followers of the "Prince of peace." But if the text quoted above means anything (requiring his followers to buy swords), he appears also to have been the Prince of war. All the bloody tragedies cited above, which form but a small number of the cases which indelibly stain the records of the Christian Church, show how faithfully Christian professors have lived out the demoralizing injunctions of their Bible, and prove that the Book has been a powerful lever for evil as well as for good.

Even the *shocking cruelties* displayed in the execution of these bloody tragedies finds a warrant in the Bible. In their efforts to carry out the Bible injunction to exterminate heretics, no species of cruelty was left untried as a punishment for the honest dissenter from the faith. The sword of the Church was unsheathed, and plunged with a fierce and relentless ferocity into the bosoms and bowels of their neighbors and fellow Christian professors, whose only offense was that of believing and worshipping God according to the dictates of their consciences. With a burning hatred for heretics, stimulated by reading the Bible injunction to put them to death in a cruel manner, they leaped upon them with the ferocity of tigers, and tortured them to death with every species of cruelty their ingenuity could invent. They tied them to the whipping-post, or chained them to the fiery fagot; lacerated their bodies; cut their tongues from their mouths; tore their flesh from their bones with iron hooks, tongs, and pincers; cut off their lips, and tore out their tongues, so that their piercing cries and heart-rending agonies could convey no intelligible sound; tore their nails from their fingers, and thrust needles into the bleeding wounds; melted red-hot metal, and poured it down their throats; plucked out their eyes, and threw them to beasts; and, in some cases, their bodies were stretched upon the rack, and flayed alive, or torn limb from limb. But I forbear: the picture is too shocking. Oh that the waves of oblivion could roll over and cover such deeds of cruelty forever! I rejoice that the age for such atrocities is passed, and, I trust, can never return. I hope the churches will never again hold the reins of government, and shape all the laws of the country. The reason we do not witness such horrible scenes now is that many church members have outgrown their Bible; and, if there are any who have not, they are restrained by laws enacted by liberal minds of too much good feeling and good sense to permit the churches to thus cruelly persecute each other, or those who conscientiously differ from them.

I have stated that the shocking cruelties and barbarities practiced by Christians upon each other in past ages, find a warrant in the Bible. The act of David, "the man after God's own heart," in placing the children of Ammon under saws and harrows of iron, is scarcely equaled in atrocity by any act recorded in the history of the Fiji cannibals. It is revolting to every impulse of benevolence, every feeling of humanity, and all ideas of mercy or justice. And his wicked prayer, contained in the one hundred and ninth Psalm, breathes forth the same spirit. It is a series of fiendish imprecations poured out upon the heads of those who differed from his creed, and worshipped a different God. We will quote some of his language: "Set thou a wicked man over him. Let there be none to extend mercy unto him; let his children be fatherless, and his wife a widow; let his children be continually vagabonds, and beg; let his posterity be cut off, and their name blotted out; let the extortioner get all that he hath; let his prayer become sin; let the stranger spoil his land; let not the sin of his mother be blotted out."

Here is a series of most malignant imprecations issuing from a mind rankling and burning with a feeling of implacable revenge, which is shocking to contemplate. It is murderous in its intent, and demoralizing in its effect upon those who accept it as being in accordance with the will of God. No person can contemplate the cruelties practiced by this "man of God" upon his unoffending neighbors, or read his vengeful prayer, and accept it as emanating from "the man after God's own heart," without having his moral strength and resolution weakened, his moral standard lowered, and his ideas of the moral perfection of Deity degraded. And it was by deriving their conceptions of God from such a source that the Christian world has come to entertain such low, belittling, and dishonorable views of "the Supreme Ruler of the universe," as is shown in their preaching and their writings; and it furnishes their children with a low and imperfect standard of morality. And this must always be the condition of things while the Bible, with its numerous bad examples and bad morality, is accepted as a guide by those teachers and preachers who mold the moral sentiments of the people. It will be observed that "the man after God's own heart" invokes the divine vengeance upon innocent children, and prays that they may beg and starve, merely because their father was not a worshiper of the savage Jewish Jehovah, which exhibits a mind devoid of all idea of justice or humanity. And this is a part of the religion of the Christian's "Holy Bible," claimed as the product of divine inspiration. Now, who cannot see that such a religion as this is calculated to engender bad feelings, bad ideas, and bad morals, and to repress the lofty moral emotions of the human mind?

THEFT OR ROBBERY

Robbery, practiced under the false pretense of borrowing, is another crime claiming the sanction of God's "Holy Word" and that "Holy Being" whose morality we are taught to imitate by the injunction, "Be ye perfect, as your Father in heaven is perfect." We are told (in Exod. xii.) that the Jews, or Hebrews, when leaving Egypt, robbed or stole from the inhabitants to such an extent that "they spoiled the Egyptians," which leads to the conclusion that the robbery must have been very extensive: and for this merciless, wholesale robbery, they claimed the sanction of a just and righteous God; for we are told he sanctioned or commanded the act. And this is a part of the code of morals "the Evangelical Christian Union" would have us incorporate into the Constitution of the United States; but it is evident, from the facts already presented, that such an act would be a step towards barbarism.

WAR

Another immoral feature of the Christian Bible, and one which proves it to be a relic or record of barbarism, and a very unsuitable book to "constitute the fountain of our laws, and the supreme rule of our conduct" (as recommended and urged by the Evangelical *Christian Union*), is found in its frequent sanction of human butchery; and a just and righteous God is represented as leaving his throne "in the heavens" to come down to take a part in their savage and bloody battles with different nations about their religious creeds. He is represented as standing in the front ranks during every battle fought by his "holy people." And, by long experience on the field of human butchery, he came to receive the military title of "God of War," "A Man of War," "The Lord of Hosts," etc.; and his success in destroying human beings won for him the reputation of a great and skillful general, and placed him above other Gods in valor in his own estimation.

He is represented as becoming so excited with anger, so blood-thirsty and revengeful in spirit, that he commanded his holy people to strike down every living creature with the sword, whether men or animals. The word of command was "to spare nothing"; "save nothing alive that breathes." He is even represented as commanding the slaughter of innocent babes. The order was, so says Samuel (1 Sam. xv. 3), "Spare them not, but slay both men and women, infants and sucklings." Now, of all the blood-dyed mandates that ever issued from human lips, or was heard on the plains of human butchery, none ever excelled it in cruelty and malignant barbarity, claimed as coming from the mouth of a God of infinite justice and infinite benevolence. Think of the murder, in cold blood, of thousands of little innocent, prattling babies, who never lisped an evil word, or conceived an evil thought, in their lives! And this by command of the loving Father of the human family! Who believes it? Who can believe it? Ay, who dare believe it, if he would escape the charge of blasphemy? Neither Nero nor Caligula was ever guilty of anything so ruthless, so fiendish, so cruel, and so vindictive.

And this is the God the Evangelical Union tells us the Constitution of the United States should recognize as the Supreme Ruler of nations. This is the Bible that they tell us should become "the fountain of our laws, and the supreme rule of our conduct." This is the religion that they are trying to revive and fasten upon us in this enlightened nineteenth century. This is the religion we are required to believe came from a God of infinite justice, infinite mercy, and loving kindness, or be denounced as infidels, and be eternally damned. But could a person be more damned than to believe in such a religion? Now, those who have studied the philosophy and impressibility of the human mind know that no extortion or contortion of the language of the text, no symbolical or spiritual construction that can be forced upon it, can prevent the reading and believing a book from producing pernicious effects, which represents such barbarous deeds as having the divine sanction. Nothing can prevent it from exercising a demoralizing influence upon a Christian community. The sooner, therefore, it can cease to be placed in the hands of the heathen and the young people of Christian lands, and cease to constitute the basis of our religion, the better for the progress of true morality, and a virtuous system of religion.

THE EVIL OF INTEMPERANCE

There are a number of texts in the Bible which, if human language can mean anything, most unquestionably furnish a warrant for drunkenness, whatever might have been the intention of the writer; and that they have had the effect to sustain and promote this evil, the practical history of Christian countries furnish proof that cannot be gainsaid. That teacher of Bible morality—that wise man who is said to have received his wisdom directly from God, and must consequently be considered good authority—is represented as saying, "Give to him that is athirst, and wine to those of heavy heart. Let him drink, and forget his poverty, and remember his misery no more." Here we are virtually recommended to drown our sorrows, and benumb the pangs of poverty, by becoming dead drunk; for it is only after the inebriate has quaffed the contents of the intoxicating bowl, or swung the bottle to his lips until he becomes stupefied and insensible (i.e., "dead drunk"), that he can "forget his poverty, and remember his misery no more." We dare not deny, then, that Solomon recommended a state of beastly intoxication as a menus of drowning our troubles; for no other meaning can be forced upon the text than that which we have assigned it, without assuming an unwarrantable use of language. Away, then, with such a book as "the source of moral and religious instruction for the heathen," or as a reading book for youth and children! The question is not what the Bible can be made to teach; but what is it naturally understood to teach, and what are the moral consequences of so understanding it?

And we find in Exodus a still more explicit license, not only for drinking, but for buying and selling intoxicating drinks. It is proclaimed, upon the authority of Jehovah, "Thou shalt spend thy money for oxen, or for sheep, or for wine, or for strong drink, or for whatsoever thy soul lusteth after" (Deut. xiv. 26). We are sometimes told, but without reliable authority, that the wine here referred to did not possess very intoxicating properties. But it will be observed that the text did not stop at wine, but "strong drink"; thus leaving no doubt upon the mind of the reader but that they used strong liquors, even if we were warranted in assuming the wine was not of this character, which, however, we are not, and which we know is not true: for, although like the wine of the grape in other countries, it would not intoxicate *while new*, yet in that warm climate, as travelers affirm, it will ferment in a few hours. It is evident, then, that wine was one of their intoxicating beverages in addition to "strong drinks." And here we find a license for buying and selling and using both in a book which the orthodox churches would have us adopt as "the fountain of our laws, and the supreme rule of our conduct," ostensibly for the improvement of the morals of the people; when it is known to unbiased investigators of the subject that these and similar texts have been a stumbling-block in the progress of the temperance reform among that class of people who take the Bible as it reads without studying the art of extracting the old meaning with the clerical force-pump, and coining a new meaning of their own especially adapted to the occasion—an art studied and practiced by the spiritually blinded devotees of all "the Holy Bibles" which God is assumed to have inspired for the salvation of the human race.

I will cite one case in proof of the statement that a Bible containing such texts as I have cited is calculated to do much mischief in the way of retarding the temperance reform by furnishing the plainest authority for drinking and trafficking in intoxicating liquors. A friend, upon whom I can rely, related to me the following case: A man addicted to intemperate habits was converted to religion, and induced to sign the temperance pledge, partly by the influence of a speaker who quoted from "the word of God" such texts as these: "Woe unto him who holds the bottle to his neighbor's mouth" (Hab. ii. 15); "Wine is a mocker, and strong drink is raging" (Prov. xx. 1). But a few days after his conversion, as he was turning the leaves of the Bible, his eye accidentally caught sight of one of the texts I have quoted, "Thou shalt spend thy money for strong drink," etc. Here he discovered that his Bible and his God both declared that buying and drinking intoxicating beverages was all right. It was enough. His resolution gave way; his firmness was unmanned, his moral manhood prostrated, his pledge overruled; and in less than two hours, he was again lying in the ditch "dead drunk." Here is a proof of the mischief that can be wrought by one single text upon those who have accepted the Bible as "the supreme rule of their conduct."

You may proclaim the evil of intemperance with the tongue of a Cicero, or paint it with the pencil of a Raphael, and muster all the texts you can find in the book condemning the practice, yet one such text as I have quoted will poison the moral force of it all while the Bible is read and adored as "the rule of their conduct." As one drop of belladonna or prussic acid will poison a whole pint of water, in like manner will one immoral text, when found in a book accepted by the people as their highest authority in practical morals, have the effect to neutralize the moral force of every sound precept that may be found in the book. It is useless, and labor comparatively lost, for a book or a moral teacher to inculcate good precepts, while it is known they are morally capable of teaching or preaching bad ones. One spark of fire is sufficient to explode a powder-magazine. Bad precepts and bad examples are both very contagious in a morally undeveloped and unenlightened age; and their pernicious effects cannot be wholly counteracted or prevented by any number of precepts of an opposite character.

But we are told the precepts above quoted are in the Old Testament, and not the New, which is now accepted as higher authority. But then it should be borne in mind, that the Old Testament is still being printed and bound with the New as a part of "the Holy Bible," and "God's perfect revelation to man" for "the guidance of his moral conduct." It is still circulated both in Christian and heathen countries by the million with the New, and as of equal authority with the New Testament. It takes both to make "the Holy Bible." It will be in vain, then, to plead any extenuation or apology for the immoralities of the Old Testament on this ground. They will both stand or fall together. The "new dispensation" could not stand a day without the Old Testament as a basis. And then, when we push our investigations a step further, we find the New Testament lending its sanction to most of the evils and crimes which are supported by the Old

The Bible of Bibles

Testament; and among this number is that under review—the vice or sin of intemperance. Paul, one of the principal founders and expounders of the religion of the New Testament, and one of the leading examples and teachers of its morals, in his letter of exhortation to Timothy, advises him to "drink no longer water, but take a little wine for the stomach's sake" (1 Tim. v. 23). As for the plea or purpose for which the intoxicating beverage was to be used on this occasion "for the stomach's sake," it is the same that dram-drinkers and drunkards have always had recourse to justify the use of strong drink. It is always drunk for "the stomach's sake." And, when we find Christ himself converting a large quantity of water into wine (see John ii.), we must conclude that the New Testament does not teach a system of morals calculated to arrest the sin of intemperance. Those, then, who wish still to continue floundering in the cesspool of drunkenness, can find in the New Testament, as well as the Old, a justification for this sin.

SLAVE-HOLDING

The Bible contains a warrant for the perpetual enslavement of men, women, and children. It is well known to the pioneer-laborers in the antislavery reform, that this book constituted a strong bulwark in support of the system; that it was one of the principal obstacles in the way of effecting its extermination. Its defenders quoted such texts as the following: "Of the heathen round about you, shall ye buy bondmen and bondmaids, and they shall be your possession for ever" (Lev. xxv. 44). Among Christian professors, such positive and explicit license for the practice of slave-holding was hard to be set aside; and it undoubtedly had an influence to perpetuate the accursed system of slavery.

POLYGAMY

The practice of polygamy is endorsed by the Christian Bible. It is frequently sanctioned in the Old Testament, both by precept and example, while it is nowhere condemned by the Book, either in the Old or New Testament. This fact makes Mormonism an impregnable institution; and this is the reason it bids defiance to the efforts of a Christian nation to put it down. It is a Bible institution. Hence, a Bible-believing nation dare not attack it. The hand of the government is powerless to put it down, because it is justified by the "Holy Book." Hence, it continues to exist, a stigma upon the nation. Were it as explicitly and strongly condemned by the Bible as idolatry is, it would have been banished from the country long ago.

The Bible Sanctions Every Species of Crime

It can hardly be wondered at that so many Christian professors fall victims to licentious habits, as is evident from reports almost daily published in the periodicals, from which one traveler has collected more than two thousand cases of priests, the professed teachers of morality, who have fallen victims to the vice of illegal sexual intercourse within a few years; and probably the number whose deeds are never brought to light is much greater. As we have already remarked, this licentiousness among Bible believers and Bible teachers is no cause of wonder when we reflect that it is taught in their Bible, both by example and precept, and even, we are told, commanded by Jehovah himself. In the thirty-first chapter of Numbers it is written that the Lord commanded Moses to slay all the Midianites, except the women and girls who "had never known man," amounting to about thirty thousand. They were even ordered to kill every male among the little ones; and it is declared they left "nothing alive that breathes," except the thirty thousand maids saved to gratify the lust of those murderous libertines. Who that has any mercy, justice, or refinement in their nature, can believe that such cruelty and licentiousness was the work of a righteous God?

Christian professors contemplate these revolting pictures with an anxious desire to save the credit of the Book, until, by dint of determination to believe (for they are afraid even to doubt), they finally persuade themselves that, somehow or other, they must be right, notwithstanding their revolting nature. They conclude they do not understand them, or that it is our fine moral sensibilities, and our natural love of virtue, that is at fault. And thus our moral manhood is deadened and sacrificed to our barbarous religion. It is an evident fact, and a sorrowful truth, that the moral sensibilities of all Christendom are more or less blunted and seared in this way, and their standard of virtue lowered. Such is the demoralizing influence of the "Holy Book" when idolized and regarded as the source of our morals, and "the supreme rule of our conduct." It is evident we never can reach that elevated standard of morals and true refinement which is the natural outgrowth of civilization until the Bible is lowered to a more subordinate position, and is no longer allowed to shape our morals, and mold our religion, and retard our civilization.

The texts I have cited are but samples of many similar passages that evince a sickly, licentious state of morals amongst "the Lord's holy people." By the moral code of Moses and Jehovah, a Jew was authorized to seize a beautiful woman (if he should see one amongst the captives taken in war), and take her to his house for his wife; but if he finds upon trial that she does not suit him, then he can turn her out, and let her go whither she will. He was licensed to turn her adrift upon the cold charities of the world. "If it shall be that thou find no delight in her, then thou shalt let her go whither she will" (Deut. xxi. 14). It does not appear that her wishes were consulted in any case. She was a captive at first, and a slave to the end. And these hard-hearted, licentious men were "God's holy people."

Those pious and devout Christians who are so inveterately opposed to, and horrified at, "Free-Lovers" should not let it be known they believe in the Bible, lest they should get into the same difficulty the Rev. Mr. Hitchkiss did while in Arabia. Having stated to a Muhammadan that there was a class of people in America known as "Free-Lovers," and that they were infidels and Spiritualists, the disciple of the Koran remarked in reply, "I suppose you are a Free-Lover also." — "What makes you entertain that supposition?" asked the reverend. "Because," said the Mussulman, "you are a believer in the Christian Bible, and I have observed, by reading it, that its leading men were practical 'Free-Lovers.' The wise Solomon was so highly esteemed by God, that he opened to him the fountain of wisdom; and hence he must have been looked up to by the Jews as a leading authority in matters of religion and morals, and an example to be followed in practical life; and he practiced 'Free-Lovism,' or licentiousness, on a very large scale. His subjects and victims were numbered by the thousand; and with three hundred of them he maintained no legal relation. Hence, they were what are now called prostitutes. And his father David, 'the man after God's own heart,' was also a Free-Lover,' and indirectly committed murder in order to increase his number of victims; and Abraham, the father and founder of the Jewish nation, also belonged to that class. I suppose, therefore, you consider it all right." The reverend gentleman replied, "I believe it was right for them, but would not be right for us." "Then," said the Muhammadan, "you believe that moral principles change—that what is right today may be wrong tomorrow, and *vice versa.* Now, it is evident that, if they can change once, they can change again, and may thus be perpetually changing; so that it would be impossible to know what true morality is, for it would be one thing today and another tomorrow. I hold that the principles of morality are perfect, and hence cannot change without becoming immorality." Thus reasoned the "unconverted heathen," and thus closed his controversy with the Christian missionary. The reader can judge which had the better end of the argument.

WIFE-CATCHING

In the Book of Judges (Judges xxi. 20) we learn that the Israelites of the tribe of Benjamin were instructed in the art of wife-catching. "Go and lie In wait in the vineyards; and behold, if the daughters of Shiloh come out to dance in dances, then come ye out of the vineyards, and catch you every man a wife" (Judges xxi. 21). "And they did so." Now it was certainly rather shameful business for God's oracles to be engaged in—that of advising rude and lustful men to hide in ambush in the vineyards and, when they saw the young maidens approaching, to pounce upon them while dancing, and carry or drag them off without a moment's warning. It was called catching a wife; but in this age of a higher moral development, it would not be designated by such respectful language, but would be placed in the list of crimes and punished as a State-prison offense.

TREACHERY AND ASSASSINATION

In the fourth chapter of Judges we find a case of barbarity related, comprising the double crime of treachery and murder, for which a parallel can scarcely be found in the annals of any heathen nation, and which appears to have received the approval of the Jewish Jehovah. It is exhibited in the history of Jael, the wife of Heber the Kenite. We read that, as a poor fugitive by the name of Sisera was fleeing from "the Lord's holy people," who were pursuing him with uplifted swords with the determination to kill him, not for any crime whatever, but because he professed a different religion, and refused to worship their cruel God (for they seemed to consider themselves authorized by their God to exterminate all nations who dissented from their creed)—as this fugitive was flying from the swords of the worshipers of Jehovah, Jael went out to meet him (Sisera), and said unto him, "Turn in, my lord; turn in to me. Fear not." And, when he had turned in unto her in the tent, she covered him with a mantle, and feigned much pity for him; and, when he asked for a little water, she gave him milk: but, as soon as he had fallen asleep, "she took a nail of the tent and a hammer, and went softly unto him, and smote the nail into his temple, and fastened it into the ground." Who can read this deed of treachery and cruelty without emotions of horror, and thrilling chilly sensations at the heart? And yet Jehovah, the God of Israel, is represented as saying, "Blessed above women shall Jael, the wife of Heber the Kenite, be" (Judg. v. 24). Now, what is this but a premium offered for treachery and cold-blooded murder?

I believe, with Lord Bacon, that "it is better to believe in no God than to believe in one possessing dishonorable traits of character"; and I cannot see how it would be possible to ascribe more dishonorable traits of character to any being than are ascribed to the Jewish Jehovah. And this is the God the orthodox world wants put into the Constitution of the United States; but most unfortunate for our progress in morals and civilization would it be to adopt such a measure. And this is the book which the churches are constantly appealing to the people for aid to circulate among

237

the heathen as necessary to improve their morals, and save their souls; but no other book could be put into their hands so completely calculated to deaden and obliterate every feeling of humanity, every natural impulse of justice and mercy, and kindle feelings of murder and revenge. Such a book should not be admitted into their families to corrupt their natural sense of right and justice.

I will cite another case evincing the same spirit, and teaching the same kind of moral lesson. We are told in Judges (chap. iii.) that the Lord sent a man by the name of Ehud to murder Eglon, King of Moab, and sent him with a lie upon his lips. As he came near to the king, he said unto him, "I have a message from God unto thee" (Judg. iii. 20, 21). And, while conversing with him under the guise of a friend, he drew out a dagger, which he had concealed under his garments, and plunged it into his body, and killed him. And the Lord, "the God of Israel," is represented as raising up the bloody-minded Ehud for the special purpose of perpetrating this shocking deed of murder. To circulate a book among the heathen, detailing such revolting deeds of cruelty as consistent with sound morality, and approved by a just and righteous God, is an evil of no small magnitude.

I will cite one other case illustrative of Bible intolerance. It is found in the history of the godly Phinehas, related in the twenty-fifth chapter of Numbers. He was one of "the Lord's peculiar people," who were such violent sectarians that they showed no mercy towards any nation or any individual who dissented from their creed. Hence, when it was reported to Moses and his God that Zimri and his wife Cozbi had become converts to the Baal-peor religion, they sent Phinehas after them with deadly weapons to slay them for heresy; and he chased them into their tents, and slew them with a javelin upon their own hearthstone for no crime whatever against the moral law, but for simply exercising their God-given right to worship God according to the dictates of their consciences. It was a feeling of sectarianism, intolerance, and bitter animosity that prompted the act. We cannot wonder, therefore, that Christian Bible believers, who have chosen this book as "the supreme rule of their conduct," should have written their history in blood, and that the whole pathway of their pilgrimage is strewn with the bones of their murdered victims, who were slain for being true to their consciences, and for believing in and worshipping God according to their convictions of right and duty.

In addition to the long list of crimes already enumerated as being sanctioned by the Bible, we will name a few others:

Lying. We find that nearly all the leading characters who figure in Bible history, and who are held up as moral exemplars of the human race, were guilty of lying either directly or indirectly. We will cite a few cases.

The Bible Sanctions Every Species of Crime

It is shown that Abraham and his wife (Gen. xx.), and Isaac (Gen. xxvi.), and Jacob (Gen. xxxi.), were all guilty of falsehood; also Rachel, Jacob's wife (Gen. xxxi.), Jacob's sons (Gen. xxxvii.), and Samson (Judg. xvi.), and Elisha (2 Kings), and four hundred prophets (1 Kings xxii.). And Jeremiah makes out all the prophets were virtual liars (Jer. vi. 13). Peter lied three times in about seventy-five minutes (Luke xxii.). And Paul justifies lying (Rom. iii. 7). With so many examples of lying by "inspired and holy men of old," the custom became popular among the early Christians, and was upheld and justified by them, as stated by the popular Christian writer, Mosheim. And some of "the heathen nations," for this reason, were accustomed to calling the Jews "the sons of falsehood." Now, we appeal to the moral consciousness of every honest reader to decide in his own mind whether it is possible for a book containing such defective moral inculcations to be calculated to promote true virtue, or a love of truth, in either Christian or heathen nations, and whether it should not, on this account, be kept out of the hands of the heathen, as being calculated to weaken their natural appreciation of truth.

Swearing. Let the reader turn to his Bible concordance, and observe the hundreds of cases in which God and his people are represented as swearing. He can then understand why profanity is now more prevalent in Christian than in heathen countries. God himself is several times represented as swearing in his wrath (Ps. xcv. 11). It should therefore be expected to be prevalent amongst Christian Bible believers.

As a Christian missionary was recently returning from India on board a British vessel, observing a Christian professor frequently swearing, he stepped to him, and observed, "Here, sir, is my son, twenty-one years old, born and raised in a heathen land, and today is the first time he ever heard a profane oath." Rather a withering lesson for a Christian professor. There are obviously two causes for the great prevalency of profane swearing in all Christian countries. One is its frequent endorsement in the Bible, and the other is the common custom of the priesthood apparently indulging in the practice in the pulpit. In their godly zeal to convert sinners, they exclaim, "God will damn you." The boys in the congregation catch the refrain, run into the street, and repeat the oath (dropping one word), "God damn you." Before we can expect this foolish and demoralizing practice to be abandoned, we must have a different Bible and different religious teachers; and also before we can prevent the heathen who read our Bible from imitating our example in swearing, or using profane language.

Cursing. The numerous cases of cursing recorded in the Bible from Jehovah to Elisha, who cursed the sportive, saucy boys, and then destroyed them with bears, are calculated to engender and foster the worst and most

239

malignant passions of the human mind. The very name of the Jews' God, Jehovah (Elohim), is derived from a root that signifies "to curse and to swear." And the immoral practice of cursing is continued from the Old Testament through the New.

Murder. We have spoken of murders perpetrated by the Jews under the authority of a theocratic government. We will now cite some cases of a more private character: Cain, the first man born into the world, was a murderer; and, instead of being punished for it, he appears to have been honored. He went into the land of Nod, and built a great city. "The man after God's own heart" (David) indirectly killed Uriah; Judith cut off the head of Holofernes while in bed with him—a most shocking case; Jehoiada, the priest, murdered his queen at the high gate in cold blood; Jael, the wife of Heber, murdered the flying fugitive Sisera by driving a nail though his head; Ehud murdered the King of Eglon under the guise of friendship; Absalom murdered Ammon; Joab murdered Absalom; Solomon murdered his brother Adonijah; Baasha murdered Nadab; Zimri murdered Elah; Omri murdered Zimri; Ahab murdered Naboth; Jehu murdered Ahab and Joram; Shallum murdered Zachariah; Hoshea murdered Pekah. Numerous other cases might be cited. Some of these murderers were leading men among the Jews—men whose life and character exercised great influence; and consequently such examples were very pernicious, and the moral lesson they impart to Bible readers must be corrupting to their moral feelings, if not their moral conduct.

Flogging. The practice of flogging is regarded as a relic of barbarism by all modern writers on moral ethics. We find it was prescribed by law under the Hebrew monarchy. Forty lashes, in some cases, while the victim was tied or held down, was the penalty for certain crimes. (See Deut. xxv.) If they were schooled in the councils of infinite wisdom as they claimed to be, their God should have taught them a less severe and more enlightened method of treating offenders.

Witchcraft. "Thou shalt not suffer a witch to live" (Exod. xxii. 18) has been the watchword and the authority for the slaughter of great numbers of human beings. Figures cannot compute the tortures, the shocking cruelties, and the heart-crushing sufferings that have been endured as the legitimate fruit of this superstitious, barbarous law of "God's holy people." It was continued in force to a late period, and has been more extensively practiced by Christians than by Jews. The number of victims in Christian England alone amounts to hundreds of thousands. A large portion of them were tied hand and foot, and thrown into the water. If they sank, that terminated the case, guilty or not guilty; if they swam or floated, that was regarded as an evidence of guilt, and they were taken out, and burned or hanged. During its reign in England, thirty thousand harmless women were burned as witches, mostly poor women who had no means of self-defense.

Even the learned Sir Matthew Hale, one of England's most enlightened Christian jurists, sentenced a number of poor women to be hanged in 1664 as witches; and the reason he assigned for it was that "the Bible leaves no doubt as to the reality of witchcraft, and the duty of putting its subjects to death." Thus, we have an illustration of the enormous evils that have grown out of Bible superstitions, perpetuated by those who were so ignorant as to accept the book as authority. Witchcraft, which was believed by Bible writers and Bible Christians to be the work of the devil or of evil spirits, is now well understood in the light of modern science as to its causes, of which Bible revelation was ignorant.

As the want of space will permit no further exposition or enumeration of Bible crimes, we will sum up the whole thus: Murder, theft, robbery, war, slavery, intemperance, polygamy, concubinage, fornication, rape, piracy, lying, assassination, treachery, tyranny, revenge, persecution for religious opinions, vagabondism, degradation and enslavement of women, hypocrisy, breach of faith, suicide, vulgarity or obscenity, witchcraft, flogging, cursing, swearing, etc.

We have cited texts and examples in proof of the statement that all these crimes, and others not here enumerated, are sanctioned by God's "holy word," and were perpetrated by God's "holy people," as they are called. And yet a Christian writer declares, "The Lord kept his people pure, holy, and upright through every period of their history." A statement could hardly be made that would be farther from the truth. It is another evidence or the blinding effect of a false religion.

Again we ask, should a book, lending its sanction to the long catalogue of crimes herein enumerated, and which represents them as being in accordance with the will of a holy and a righteous God, be placed in the hands of the illiterate and credulous heathen as a guide for their moral conduct? Most certainly, it must have a deleterious effect upon their morals; and yet hundreds of thousands are distributed amongst them every year by the Christian churches and missionary societies. And then think of making such a book "the fountain of our laws, and the supreme rule of our conduct," as urged by the Evangelical Alliance and the orthodox churches. We almost tremble at the thought of such a step toward barbarism and demoralization.

CHAPTER 48

THE IMMORAL INFLUENCE OF THE BIBLE

With the characteristic moral teaching of the Christian Bible, presented in the preceding chapter and throughout this work, we see not how to escape the conviction that the Bible has inflicted, and must necessarily inflict, a demoralizing influence on society wherever it is read and *believed*. It is morally impossible for *any person* to read and believe a book sanctioning, or appearing to sanction, so many species of crime and immorality without sustaining more or less moral and mental injury by it. For whatever views he may entertain with respect to the numerous crimes therein reported as having been committed with the approval, and often at the command, of a just God, it must naturally and inevitably have the tendency to weaken his detestation of those crimes, and also weaken his zeal and effort to extinguish them and other similar crimes now existing in society. It must also lower his conception of the moral attributes of Deity. However honest, and however naturally opposed to such immoralities at the outset, it is impossible for him to entertain the belief that they were once approved, or even connived at, by a morally perfect being, without becoming unconsciously weakened in his feelings of opposition to, and his hatred of, such deeds.

It may be alleged that these practices are at war with those precepts that enjoin us to do unto others as we would have them do unto us; and that of loving our neighbors as ourselves, etc. This is true; but reason and experience both teach us, as an important lesson in moral and mental philosophy, that when a book which is accepted as a guide for the conduct and moral actions of men contains contradictory precepts, the people will seize on and reduce to practice those most consonant with their natures, and most congenial to their natural feelings and inclinations. Hence, it can easily be seen that, as the animal feelings and propensities which lead to the commission of crime, when unduly exercised, have always been stronger with the masses or the populace than the moral feelings, they have consequently always been more disposed to yield a compliance with those precepts which sanction, or appear to sanction, the commission of crime than those which are condemnatory of crime. All persons in whose minds the animal propensities are the strongest will seize with eagerness the least authority, or appearance of authority, for committing those crimes which they are naturally inclined to commit, and for which they are glad to find a license or encouragement to commit. Under such circumstances they will ignore the virtuous precepts, and yield a compliance with those of an opposite character. Therefore, Christian professors who expect the Bible to exert a moral influence in reforming the world and freeing it from crime, because it contains some beautiful and sound moral precepts, will be

Immoral Influence of the Bible

disappointed; for those precepts will be neutralized, and their effects destroyed, by those of an opposite character. A majority of the people in all countries have always possessed a strong inclination for committing those crimes which, we have shown, the Christian Bible appears to sanction. Hence, the Bible, with all its counteracting precepts, will only add fuel to the fire, for the reason already pointed out. Those who do not know this must be ignorant of the most important principles of moral science, and the elements of human nature.

Right here is where Christians commit a serious mistake. They scatter their Bibles among the heathen by the thousand, assuming that it will have the effect to moralize and civilize them, while they can find a warrant in it (as shown in the preceding chapter) for every species of crime they have been in the habit of committing. This is a solemn error they have been committing for ages. Hence, their missionary labors, instead of reforming the heathen, have only tended to demoralize them, where they have not been counteracted by the more rational religion of science and nature, as they have been in many cases. Many facts could be adduced to prove this statement, some of which may be found in chapter 50 ("Bible a Moral Necessity"). Wherever the Bible has been introduced, without the arts and sciences to counteract its influence (as in Abyssinia and the Samoan Islands), crime has increased. History proves that wherever the Bible has been circulated without any counteracting influences, both in Christian and heathen nations, it has had the effect to weaken the moral strength of the people, lower their natural appreciation of virtue and a true moral life, and has had a tendency to popularize crime by making it more respectable. It is therefore an *unsuitable book* to circulate as a guide for the moral conduct of man *in any country.*

CHAPTER 49

THE BIBLE AT WAR WITH EIGHTEEN SCIENCES

The word "science" is from the Latin *scire* ("to know"). Hence, every statement incompatible with the teachings and principles of science is simply *ignorance* arrayed against *knowledge*. It may surprise some who have been taught that the Bible contains "a perfect embodiment of truth," or who believe, with the redoubtable Dr. Cheever, that "the Bible does not contain the shadow of a shade of error from Genesis to Revelations"—it will doubtless surprise all such persons to be told that, so far from Dr. Cheever's statement being correct, "the Holy Book," by a fair estimate, is found to contain more than nine thousand scientific errors alone; i.e., more than nine thousand statements and assumptions which conflict with the established principles of modern science, besides errors in morals, history, etc. It is believed there is not one chapter in the book that does not contain several errors of this character. This, perhaps, should not be a matter of surprise to any person after viewing the character and condition of philosophy and the widespread scientific ignorance which reigned over the world at that period. Let it be borne in mind that science was but just budding into life, and philosophy had attained but a feeble growth amongst that portion of the earth's inhabitants who constituted the representatives of the Jewish and Christian religion. Not only does their history and their writings show that they were, for the most part, ignorant of what little science there was in the world—which was small compared with the present period—but they opposed it whenever they came in contact with it. Everything was ascribed to supernatural power.

The word "science" only occurs twice in the Bible—once in the Old Testament, and once in the New; and, in the latter case, it was used for the purpose of condemning it. Paul advises Timothy to "beware of the babblings of science" (1 Tim. vi. 20). The word "philosophy" is used but once in the Bible, and then not to recommend it; but Paul uses it to condemn it, as he does science, or at least to discourage it: "Beware lest any man spoil you through philosophy and vain conceit" (Col. ii. 8). It will be observed, then, that there is apparently a veto placed upon the study of science and philosophy in the only two instances in which reference is made to them in the Bible. We cannot wonder, therefore, that its devout disciples have in all ages, until a very recent period, set themselves squarely against the propagation of science and philosophy. It was but carrying out the spirit of their Bible.

The early Christians, almost to a man, discouraged the study of science, and condemned and persecuted those who attempted to propagate its principles, and even put some of them to death. Copernicus was persecuted for setting forth principles of astronomy which conflicted with the teachings of the Bible; Galileo was sentenced to death because he taught the rotundity and revolution of the earth in opposition to the Bible, which declares, "The earth has foundations, and can not be removed" (Ps. civ. 5); and Bruno suffered the penalty of death for teaching substantially the same doctrine. And every discoverer in science was condemned and persecuted.

Much was written by the early fathers in acknowledgment of the incompatibility of science with religion and the teachings of the Bible, and to warn the pious disciple of the danger of occupying his mind in the investigation and study of science. Even Eusebius, the popular ecclesiastical writer of the third century, and one of the most intelligent Christians of that age, acknowledged he had a contempt for "the useless baubles of the philosophers": "We think little of these matters, turning our souls to the exercise of better things." And Lactantius, a Christian of the same century, pronounced the study of physical causes of natural things "empty and false." And St. Augustine, "a shining light of the Church," treated with contempt the notion that the earth is round, as "trees on the other side would hang with their tops down and the men there would have their feet higher than their heads." He condemns it as false, "because *no such race is recorded in Scripture* among the descendants of Adam." What profound reasoning! Martin Luther utters his malediction against astronomy in the following language: "This false Copernicus will turn the whole art of astronomy upside down; but the Scripture teacheth another lesson, when Joshua commanded the sun to stand still, and not the earth." Of course, Joshua's order for the sun to stop knocks the science of astronomy on the head, and extinguishes it forever with all true Bible believers; and men have had to outgrow their Bibles before they could accept the teachings of astronomy. When we take into consideration the almost boundless acquisitions that have been made in the field of science since the invention of the printing art, and the many discoveries evolved in every department of science and art, now classified into a long list of new sciences, and which throw a flood of light on almost everything taught by the ancients in morals, religion, or science, we should not be surprised to find more or less error in everything they taught.

Let us look for a moment at the long list of sciences now taught in our schools, most of which were unknown two hundred years ago: Astronomy, geology, chemistry, mineralogy, meteorology, pneumatics, hydrostatics, mechanics, psychology, paleontology, anthropology, ethnology, archaeology, biology, history, chronology, botany, zoology, philosophy, physiology, ornithology, geography, mathematics, optics, acoustics, phrenology, animal magnetism, etc. The facts and principles now comprised in these several branches of science have mostly been developed within a comparatively recent period of time; and almost every department of science here enumerated embraces facts and discoveries which reveal important errors in the religious creeds of the ancient representatives of the Christian faith. To illustrate this statement, we will cite some examples:

1. *Astronomy.* More than forty errors in astronomy will be found exposed in chapter 15, treating on the Mosaic account of creation, and here may be added a few more to the number. Several texts in the Bible speak of the stars falling to the earth, or traveling in some lawless direction. Even Christ committed this error. (See Mark xiii. 25.) How ridiculous is this conception when viewed in connection with the fact that these stars are many of them larger than the earth! Saturn is about a thousand times larger, and Jupiter twelve hundred times larger, than our planet. John speaks of one-third of the stars falling at once (Rev. xii. 4). If these two large planets (Jupiter and Saturn) should be of the number, our little earth would fare rather badly, though it is evident they could not all have room to strike it. If they should strike it from opposite sides, they would effectually grind it to powder. The inspired writers of the Bible seem to have had their minds so filled with heavenly things that there was but little room left for scientific knowledge appertaining to the earth. The idea of the sun being made "to rule by day, and the moon and stars to rule by night," as taught in Gen. i. 16, discloses still further the ignorance of Bible writers on astronomy.

2. *Geological Errors.* The story of the creation in Genesis (as exposed in chapter 15 of this work) contains many geological errors. Almost every statement, in fact, conflicts with the teachings of geology, and especially the assumption that the earth, with the retinue of worlds which roll through infinite space, was brought into existence by a fiat of Omnipotence, and only about six thousand years ago; while many facts in geological science disprove its creation, and prove that it existed hundreds of thousands, if not millions, of years ago. For the numerous Bible errors under this head, see chapter 15.

3. *Errors in Geography.* The language applied to the earth by various writers of the Bible show quite plainly that they entertained very erroneous conceptions of its form and size, and the laws that govern it. Such language as "the foundations of the earth" (Ps. civ. 5; Job xxxviii. 4), "the ends of earth," "the corners of the earth," "the pillars of the earth" (1 Sam. ii. 8), clearly indicate that Bible writers entertained the common erroneous conceptions of that age, that the earth is a flat, square, angular figure, only inhabited on one side. Matthew, who represents Christ as seeing all the kingdoms of the earth from the top of a mountain, plainly discloses the same error.

The Bible at War with Eighteen Sciences

4. *Errors in Ethnology.* The Bible assumption of the origin of man within a period of six thousand years, and the descent of the whole race from a single pair, is directly at variance with the teachings of ethnological science, which discloses the true history of man, and proves, according to Agassiz and other modern naturalists, that the human race has descended from at least five pairs of original progenitors. See a work entitled "Types of Mankind," compiled from the writings of the ablest naturalists of the age.

5. *Archaeology,* which treats of antiquity, presents us with nearly the same series of scientific facts to disprove the Bible history of man. It presents us with many facts in the history of the ancient empires of India, Egypt, Greece, China, and Persia, which directly contradict many statements found in the Christian Bible, which the want of space compels us to omit any notice of here. (See chapters on Bibles.)

6. *Biology.* The Bible statements which make a son two years older than his father (2 Chron. xxi. and xxii.), a girl only three years old when she married, and two millions of people spring from seventy persons in two hundred and fifteen years, are all at variance with the teachings of biology.

7. *Botany.* The origin of thorns and thistles, and the preservation of the whole vegetable kingdom during Noah's flood, as inferentially taught by the Christian Bible, conflict with the present established principles of botany.

8. *Zoology.* This science, which discloses the true history of animal life, completely disproves some statements of the Bible relative to the animal kingdom. The hare is pronounced unclean in Leviticus, "because he cheweth the cud, but divideth not the hoof" (Lev. xi. 6). Here are three incorrect statements. The hare does not chew the cud, and does divide the hoof, and is not unclean (i.e., not unsuitable for food).

9. *Ornithology.* The writer who represents God as showering down nine hundred square miles of quails, three feet thick, around the Jewish camp to serve as food (see Numb. xi. 32), must have been ignorant of the size of this bird, if not of the whole featured tribe.

10. *Physiology.* The apostle James must have been ignorant of the science of physiology when he declares the prayers of the elders of the Church would heal the sick (Jas. v. 15). It is not denied but that the presence of the elders could exercise a healing influence on the sick, but it should be ascribed to their magnetism, and not to their prayers. The numerous cases in which disease is represented by Christ and his disciples as being produced by devils or evil spirits, and a cure effected by ejecting the diabolical intruder, shows them to have been ignorant of physiology; as does also the story of the sons of God cohabiting with the daughters of men (Gen. vi. 4), and producing a race of giants which, according to the Book of

247

Enoch, were three hundred cubits high. Rather tall specimens of humanity. Their heads would be above the clouds, so that they could not see which way they were traveling. This story finds a parallel in the traditions of India, which once produced a race of giants so tall that they could neither sit down in the house, nor stand up out of doors. Their eyes were so far from the ground that they could not see their feet. All these stories originated in an age which was destitute of a knowledge of physiology; and, as this amalgamation of Gods with human beings did nothing to improve the race, the story is destitute of a moral, and proves (if it proves anything) that the Gods were no better than men.

11. *Mental Science.* The two hundred texts, which represent the heart as being the seat of the mind or soul, furnish conclusive evidence that the writers were ignorant of the first principles of mental science. "My heart uttereth understanding" and "a pure heart" are examples. "An upright liver" or "a pure liver" would be just as sensible language. There is not one text in the book that implies a knowledge of the brain as being the organ of the mind, which is a scientific fact now well established.

12. *Animal Magnetism.* The exposition of this science by Mesmer, Deluse, Townsend, and other writers, renders it clearly evident that the phenomena of witchcraft, trance and many cases of spiritual vision, were nothing more nor less than the products of animal magnetism superinduced by the action of mind on mind, or the control of the mind by magnetic substances—the science of magnetism being entirely unknown in that era of the world. Every case reported of restoring life to a dead person by Christ, Elijah, Elisha, and other God-men, if they had any foundation in truth, are explained by the principles of this science. Similar cases have been witnessed in these modern times.

13. *Philosophy.* The science of philosophy, in its matured aspect, is of modern origin, and furnishes the true explanation for many of the "mysteries of godliness" and other mysteries of the Christian Bible which, by the illiterate writers of that age, were ascribed to the direct manifestation of deific powers. They are now known to be natural occurrences, instead of supernatural, as assumed by the writers. The Bible story of the rainbow furnishes one example. Moses must have been ignorant of philosophy when he selected the rainbow as an evidence there should be no rain in the future in sufficient quantities to inundate the earth again, when it is known that the rainbow is a certain evidence of rain, as it is produced by the rain in the act of falling. This is but one of many errors which the ignorant, illiterate Bible writers have made for want of knowledge on scientific subjects, such as the history of creation, the story of the flood, etc. The several cases in which thunder is spoken of as being the voice of God

disclose great ignorance of philosophy; and several instances in which God promises to take away the sickness of the people evince an entire ignorance of the natural laws which control health and disease. (See Exod. xxiii. 25; Deut. vii. 15.)

14. *Mathematics.* The Bible is deficient in many cases with respect to the correct observance of the rules and principles of mathematics. Its assumption that there can be but one God, and at the same time acknowledging three, furnishes a striking proof of this. Its enumeration of the families and tribes furnishes another evidence of this. Its calculation of numbers rarely coincides with the names. For example, Matthew, in his gospel, states there are forty-two generations from David to Joseph; but his list of names only makes forty-one. And Matthew says, "From Adam to David are fourteen generations," but by counting his list of names, we find but thirteen. The date of Methuselah's birth and his age, when compared together, extend his age ten months beyond the inauguration of the flood. How he sustained life, and avoided drowning during that time, must be one of the "mysteries of godliness." These are a few specimens of Bible mathematics.

15. *Chemistry.* A specimen of Bible chemistry is found in the story of "fire and brimstone descending from heaven together" without a coalescence, or the chemical combination and product which usually result from a contact of these two elements. Another specimen is presented in the process of manufacturing a golden calf by merely casting gold earrings, finger rings, etc., into the fire; and also Moses' invention for grinding the same gold into powder, and sprinkling it on the water, and compelling the people to drink it. No process is known in modern times by which gold can be ground to powder, nor for holding it in solution if ground and thrown into water. The specific gravity of all gold now in use causes it to sink to the bottom as soon as it is thrown into water. Bible chemistry seems to differ from natural chemistry.

16. *Pneumatics.* Had Jehovah been acquainted with this science, he could not have become alarmed about having his kingdom invaded by the builders of Babel; for we learn, by an acquaintance with the principles of this science, that the air becomes so rarefied as we ascend, that we soon reach a point where human life must cease. Hence, it was unnecessary to confound the language of the people in order to arrest the completion of the tower. They would have been compelled to desist before they had got many miles from the earth.

17. *Acoustics.* Moses must have been ignorant of this science, or presumed his readers would be, when he related the numerous cases of himself and Joshua and others reading and talking to two millions of people,

some of whom must have been several miles distant. No human voice in modern times could reach one-half of such an audience.

18. *Hydrostatics.* This science teaches us that several cases reported in the Bible of the waters of rivers and seas being separated and erected in perpendicular columns so as to form embankments, are contradicted by all the laws governing fluids, and hence are wholly incredible. The sciences of optics, meteorology, philology, and psychology might also be included in the above list as being ignored and practically set aside by Bible writers. And yet, in the face of all these facts, Dr. Cheever says, "There is a beautiful harmony between the principles of science and the teachings of the Bible throughout the whole book." And this seems to have been the universal conviction of the disciples of the Christian faith before the progress of scientific discovery in modern times laid bare the errors of the Holy Book. Since that juncture in biblical theology culminated, a new theory has been set on foot to dispose of the scientific errors of the Bible. We are told, as an apology for these errors, that "the Bible was designed to teach religion and morality, and not science." This is too true, but a true system of religion must be based on the principles of science. The plea also discloses a scientific ignorance on the part of the objector in not knowing "there is science in everything." Hence, it is impossible to write on any subject without coming in contact with the principles of science, which you must either conform to or violate. Persons destitute of scientific knowledge, as were Bible writers, are liable, in their ignorance, to stumble into scientific errors in writing on any subject.

CHAPTER 50

THE BIBLE AS A MORAL NECESSITY

The question is frequently asked by Bible adherents, What would be the moral condition of society without the Bible? Would it not again relapse into barbarism? Such questions manifest an ignorance of history and the moral instincts of the human mind, and are easily met and answered by other questions indicating broader views. We ask, then, what was the moral condition of the world, or that portion of it included in the Jewish nation, during the two thousand years that elapsed before any part of our Bible was written? Was it any worse than the next two thousand years after it was written? And what is the moral condition of five-sixths of the human family now, who never had our Bible? Facts in history prove that the morals of some of the nations included in this class are superior to that of any Bible nation, either now existing, or figuring in past history.

Take, for example, the Japanese. We will present the testimony of an English officer, Col. Hall. Reporting his own observations and experience, he says, "During more than a year's residence in Japan, I never saw a quarrel among young or old. I have never seen an angry blow struck, and have scarcely heard an angry word. I have seen the children at their sports, flying their kites on the hill; and no amount of entangled strings, or kites lodged in the trees, provoked angry words or impatience. In their games of jackstones and marbles, I have never seen an approach to a quarrel among them. They are taught implicit obedience to their parents; but I have never seen one of them chastised. Respect and reverence for the aged is universal. A crying child is seldom seen. We have nothing to teach them out of the abundance of our civilization." And a description of this nation by Dr. Oliphant fully confirms the above. He says, "Universal testimony assures us that, in their domestic relations, the men are gentle and forbearing; the women, obedient and virtuous. Every department of crime is less in proportion to the population than in Christian countries. The native tribunals prove their competency to deal with criminals by giving general satisfaction. Unlike any Christian country, locks and keys are never used, yet theft and robbery are almost unknown. Although we had the most tempting curiosities with us, and left them laying about our lodgings for months, not one of them was carried off, though our room was sometimes crowded with people. During the whole of our stay in Yeddo, we never heard a scolding woman, nor saw a disturbance in the streets, nor a child struck or otherwise maltreated. In cases of disputes between neighbors, their children are often selected as arbiters, and always give satisfaction. And parents in their old age often give their property and the entire management of their affairs into the hands of their children, who never betray their trust."

Now, it must be evident to every reader that no such a moral picture of society can be presented of any Christian country. And yet the Christian Bible is not only scarcely known among them, but they have resisted the most determined efforts of the Christian missionaries, for more than two hundred years, to introduce it and circulate it amongst them, and have kept it out by positive prohibition most of the time. Do such facts tend to confirm the statement often made by devout Christians that "the Bible must be introduced and read by the people before they can have good morals in any country"?

As a still further proof of the erroneousness of this statement, we will now contrast the state of morals in the most religious Christian countries with that of the heathen nation just referred to. And this moral picture of our country is from the pen of a Christian writer, the celebrated Parson Brownlow. He tells us, "The gospel is preached to the people regularly all over the country.... And yet, notwithstanding all this, rascality abounds in all classes of society.... Cheating and misrepresentation are the order of the day. In politics there is very little patriotism or love of country. In religion there is more hypocrisy than grace; and the biggest scoundrels living crowd the church with a view to hide their rascally designs, and more effectually serve the Devil. Pious villains, as sanctified as the moral law, are keeping false accounts, and resort to them for the sake of gain.... In a word, rascality abounds among all classes." Now look on this picture, and then on that.

We will now present another contrast. We will look at another specimen of morality among the heathen. The portraiture is furnished us by the celebrated Christian missionary, Dr. Livingstone. Speaking of some of the African tribes he encountered in his travels, he says, "The inhabitants have many wise laws and politic institutions, which would not discredit any nation in Europe. They are not a warlike people, but appear to hold martial achievements in great contempt or abhorrence. They have such a nice sense of justice and equity, that they will by no means make any encroachments on the territory of their neighbors. Their dealings with each other are characterized by mutual confidence, which *Christians would do well to imitate.*" No man is afraid of being cheated. No precautions are used to prevent theft and robbery; and yet no theft and robbery are committed. Their goods to be sold are stored in an open bazaar, left without any attendants, and the purchaser fixes his own price, and leaves what he considers a fair equivalent in its stead; and all parties are satisfied. It would seem, then, that while in Christian countries "it requires two to make a bargain," in heathen countries it requires but one. Here, then, we have the morals of a heathen nation, who not only knew nothing of Christianity, but would not condescend to talk with the missionary on the subject, but put him off with the plea, "It makes no difference what a man's religion is, if his morals and practical life are right." *Sensible reasoning.*

We will now turn another leaf in Christian history with the inquiry, Is every country honored with the name of Christian distinguished for morality, and every nation stigmatized as heathen practically immoral? We will present another specimen of Christian morality from the pen of that popular Christian writer, Mr. Goodrich. Speaking of the moral condition of one of the oldest Christian nations now existing (the Abyssinians), he says, "They are restless, savage, and brutal, almost beyond any known tribes of men. The Scotch traveler, Mr. Bruce, was at Gondar, the capital; and he tells us that he seldom went out without seeing dead human bodies lying in the streets, left to be devoured by the dogs and hyenas. Alnary, who lived there some years since, says he was invited to a feast, where, amongst the dishes he was offered, was flesh with warm blood. We are told the people eat the flesh from the cattle while alive; and sometimes, after a large piece has been cut out, the skin is drawn over it, and the bleeding beast driven on its way. Sometimes, when a party is assembled for a feast, and are seated, the oxen are brought to the door, the flesh is cut off the living animal, and the meat devoured while the agonized brutes are filling the air with their bellowings.... And the manners of the people in other respects are horrible in the extreme. Yet, strange to say, *they profess Christianity*, and *have numerous churches.* Their saints are almost innumerable, and surpass in miraculous power those of the Romish Church. The clergy do not attempt to prevent divorces, nor even polygamy."

In confirmation of the above graphic picture, we will quote also from an English geography by Guthrie and Ferguson, F.R.S. (p. 923): "The inhabitants of Abyssinia *consist of Christians.* Some ecclesiastical writers would persuade us that the conversion of Abyssinia to Christianity happened in the time of the apostles; but others state that this was after—in the year 333. There is no such thing as marriage in Abyssinia, and no distinction made between legitimate and illegitimate children, from the king to the beggar." *Here, then,* is *"Christian" morality*, and here is a specimen of *Christian "free-lovism"* too, in a country where the *Christian Bible has been circulated by the thousand, and read and adored for at least fifteen hundred years.*

Such facts furnish a complete refutation of the popular Christian assumption that "true and pure morality is inseparable from Christianity and the Bible." The truth is, the Bible alone has *never done anything* to advance

The Bible of Bibles

the cause of *either morality or civilization in any country*, because it is interdicted from improvement. It may be asked here, Why is it, then, that both religion and morality prosper in most countries where the Bible has been introduced? The answer to this question is found in the *important fact, overlooked by the Christian world,* that the *arts and sciences* generally accompany, or soon follow, the introduction of the Bible; but where this has not been the case, and the Bible has been circulated alone, as in the case of Abyssinia, *no progress whatever* has been made towards the establishment of true morality or a rational religion, or any of the adjuncts of civilization, thus proving that the causes for the moral growth and improvement of society are outside of, and independent of, the Bible and, we will add (in view of the many immoral lessons taught in the book), in spite of the Bible. A little rational reflection must convince any unbiased person that Bibles, in the very nature of things, must retard the moral and intellectual advancement and prosperity of society in every respect, notwithstanding they contain many good and beautiful precepts, for representing, as they do, the imperfect state of morals in the age and country in which they were written; while their teachings are assumed to be a finality in moral and religious progress, and hence are not allowed to be transcended in precept or practice. The consequence is, society would be pinned down immovably and perpetually to the same barbarous religion and morals of that age, if it were not pushed forward by the irresistible influences of the arts and sciences. Hence, we owe our advancement and prosperity *not to Bibles, but to causes adequate to counteract and overcome their adverse influences.*

THE MORAL BENEFITS OF INFIDELITY

An additional argument to prove the Bible is not a moral necessity to teach the practical duties of life is the fact that that class of persons known as "infidels," who entirely reject the book as a guide or as a moral instructor on account of its very defective and contradictory system of morals, are admitted by leading orthodox journals and representative men in the nation to possess better moral characters and habits, and to lead better moral lives, than Bible believers. As a proof of this statement, we will here present the most wonderful and humiliating concessions of that leading religious journal of the nation, "The New York Evangelist." On this subject it speaks thus: "To the shame of the Church it must be confessed that the foremost men in all our philanthropic movements, in the interpretation of the spirit of the age in the practical application of genuine Christianity, in the reformation of abuses in high and in low places, in the vindication of the rights of man and in practically redressing his wrongs, in the moral and intellectual regeneration of the race, *are the so-called infidels in our land.*
254

The Bible as a Moral Necessity

The Church has pusillanimously left not only the working oar, but the very reins of salutary reform, in the hands of men she denounces as inimical to Christianity, and who are doing with all their might, for *humanity's* sake, that which the Church ought to be doing for *Christ's* sake; and if they succeed, *as succeed they will*, in abolishing slavery, banishing rum, restraining licentiousness, reforming abuses, and elevating the masses, then must the recoil upon Christianity be disastrous in the extreme. Woe! woe! woe to Christianity when infidels, by force of nature or the tendencies of the age, *get ahead of the Church in morals*, and in the practical work of Christianity. In some instance they are already far in advance. In the vindication of truth, righteousness, and liberty, they are the pioneers beckoning to a sluggish Church to follow in the rear."

To this we will add the testimony of another orthodox writer (the eminent Catherine Beecher) as to the superior practical morality of infidels as compared with that of Christians. She says, in her "Appeal to the People" (p. 319), "It has come to pass that the world has been improving in practical virtue, while the Church has been deteriorating. The writer, in her very extensive travels and intercourse with the religious world, has had unusual opportunity to notice how surely and how extensively this fact has been observed and acknowledged by the best class of clergymen and laymen." She says one of the most laborious Episcopal bishops of the Western States declares that "the world is growing better, and the Church is growing worse." She next cites the testimony of an eminent lawyer and church member who is carrying on an extensive financial business throughout the country, and who makes the remarkable statement that, "the better class of *worldly men are more honorable and reliable in business than the majority of church-members.*" (Let the reader mark this statement.)

And this declaration was concurred in by another eminent lawyer, banker, and church member, who is doing a more extensive business in the Northwestern States than any other man. And he states that the most extensive businessman in Central New York has arrived at the same conclusion as the result of his observation. And the greatest businessman in Boston is also referred to, whose experience led him to this conclusion. And other businessmen in different parts of the country testify to the same effect. We may, then, set it down as the universal testimony of businessmen that infidels and "outsiders" are more honest, more reliable, more truthful, and more honorable than church members. What a fatal argument these facts furnish against the religion and morality of the Christian Bible! They indicate that the religion and morality of nature and science are superior.

255

The Bible of Bibles

It will be perceived, from the preceding orthodox testimonies, that the class of people usually stigmatized as infidels are the true exemplars in practical morality, and the true benefactors of society. And Christian countries owe them a debt of gratitude for all the reforms and improvements which have proved such signal blessings to society within the last few hundred years, and for their own elevation out of the groveling ignorance of barbarism into the glorious sunlight of civilization. What withering self-reproach, what shameful mortification and self-condemnation, they ought therefore to feel in view of having committed so many of them to the flames, or otherwise maltreated and killed them! For, according to the above Christian testimonies, they were the world's real benefactors and the following list will show that those victims *perished at the hands of Christians as infidel martyrs*:

In 1511 Herman of Ryswick was burned for heresy; in 1546 Aonius Polearius was hung and then burned for skepticism; in 1574 Geofroi Vallie was burned for publishing a heretical book; in 1546 Stephen Dolet, a printer and bookseller, was burned at Paris for atheism; in 1579 Matthew Hamont had his ears cut off and was then burned alive, in England, for denying that Christ is God; in 1583 John Lewes was burned at Norwich, England, for "denying the Godhead of Christ"; in 1589 Francis Kett, a member of a college in Cambridge, England, was burned for holding "divers detestable opinions against Christ, our Savior"; in 1611 Bartholomew Legate was burned to ashes at Smithfield for denying that Christ was God; in 1644 Edward Wightman was burned at Litchfield for denying the divinity of Christ; in 1619 Lucilio Vanini, an Italian, was burned for atheistical opinions; in 1574 John Gonganelle was poisoned for his *infidelity by the Holy Sacrament*; in 1629 Alexander Leighton had his nose slit and his ears cut off, and was imprisoned for eleven years for publishing a work against miracles. To make the matter short, without extending the list, it has been estimated that *forty thousand* perished at the hands of Christians in *forty years* for *infidelity, heresy*, or other opinions deemed unsound by orthodox. And thus it will be perceived that infidelity has had its martyrs as well as Christianity; and that Christians, in putting these men to death, were robbing the world (according to "The New York Evangelist") of its real benefactors. Oh shame! Christianity, where is thy blush?

CHAPTER 51

SEND NO MORE BIBLES TO THE HEATHEN

A recent work by a Christian writer states that there are now employed in the work of converting the heathen to Christianity fifteen thousand missionaries, and that they succeed in converting about ten thousand a year. From this statement, it appears that ten thousand missionaries make annually one convert apiece, while five thousand make none. And the cost the writer estimates to be about twenty thousand dollars for each convert. C. Wiseman estimated it, about thirty years ago, to be ten thousand dollars apiece. And, while these ten thousand converts were made, the heathen population increased in numbers five millions. Thus, it appears they increase two hundred times faster than they are converted. How long will it take, at such rates, to effect the entire conversion of the world? And what will be the cost? All the gold ever dug from the mines of Golconda and California would be but a drop in the bucket compared with the requisite amount. The question naturally arises here, Do the results justify such an enormous expenditure of time and treasure, say nothing of the loss of health on the part of the missionaries? A learned Hindu stated, in a speech made in London in 1876, that the conversions made in India are confined principally to the low, ignorant, superstitious class, who do not possess sufficient sense and intelligence to know the difference between the religion they are converted to and the religion they are converted from. Are such converts worth ten thousand or twenty thousand dollars apiece? The case suggests the story of the Hibernian who stated his horse had but two faults: "First, he is hard to catch; second, he is no account when caught." The heathen must be hard to convert if it requires an expense of ten thousand dollars apiece, and of but little account when converted if they know nothing about the nature of the religion they are converted to. There are various considerations which go to prove that the hundreds of millions of dollars expended annually in this enterprise are worse than wasted:

1. One missionary, becoming discouraged at the prospect, once made the statement that nine-tenths of the converts have not sense enough to understand the Christian religion, nor moral principle enough to live up to its precepts, and that a considerable portion of them relapsed into heathenism. It should be borne in mind that it is not the most intelligent nor the most moral portion of the heathen who profess to embrace Christianity, but generally the credulous, ignorant, and fickle-minded class, who are ready for any change that may be offered.

2. No real good seems to be accomplished by the introduction of the Christian Bible among the heathen, but much evil. Its thousands of bad moral precepts and bad moral examples, and its sanction of every species of

crime, must inevitably have the effect to weaken their moral resolutions, and deepen them in the commission of crime. And hence, as missionaries themselves indirectly confess, crime has increased in almost every nation where missions have been established. It is true that, in those nations where the arts and science have been cultivated, they have operated to some extent in counteracting the bad moral lessons they learn by reading the Bible; and in some cases, in this way, some improvement has been made. But no instance can be found in the history of the missionary enterprise where any improvement has been made in the morals of the people, where their instruction has been confined to the Bible, without the arts and sciences. On the contrary, their morals have grown worse, or remained unimproved, as in Abyssinia and the Samoan Islands, where after more than a thousand years' instruction in Bible religion, without the arts and sciences, they are still in the lowest stages of barbarism. (See chapter 50.)

3. It is a policy that must be deplored by every true philanthropist, that the Christian world expends millions of dollars every year to convert the heathen to a religion that can neither improve their morals or their intellect, but inculcates bad lessons in morals and science and, in many cases, is a worse religion than that already established in those countries. (For evidence, see chapter 50.)

4. And this policy becomes still more reprehensible when coupled with the fact that there are sixty thousand Christians living in a state of want, beggary, destitution, and suffering in Christian cellars in New York City; and two hundred thousand, including Boston and Philadelphia, who are in a state of degradation and suffering almost beyond description, who might be relieved and placed in a situation to improve their morals and their physical condition comfortably if the millions of money, time, and labor were spent on them which are uselessly expended on foreign missions. Think of two hundred thousand church members living in dark, damp, dreary, sickly cellars with grim starvation daily staring them in the face, while their purse proud Christian landlords are living in luxury over their heads. No such cruel, inhuman religion can be found in any heathen nation.

5. And then the missionary enterprise inflicts physical evils, as well as moral, upon the foreign heathen. It introduces habits and customs amongst them which, in some cases, destroy their health, as well as corrupt their morals. Look, for example, at the Sandwich Islands. Since the establishment of Christian missions amongst them, the population has decreased thirty percent. Twenty thousand children in schools in 1848 are dwindled down to eleven thousand. Marriages have decreased, and divorces have increased. Nine hundred divorces took place in four years, while previous to the introduction of Christianity, we are told, divorces

were almost unknown. Missionaries, ignorant of physiology and the laws of mental science, and in total disregard of natural law, establish habits among the heathen that destroy both their health and their happiness.

6. The people in several heathen countries have proved to be sharp-sighted and intelligent enough to detect the errors in the Bible and religious system presented to them by the missionaries. Bishop Colenso states that, while serving as missionary among the Zulu tribe, some of the natives started objections to statements found in the Bible which had not occurred to his own mind. And this fact made him resign his mission and return home, and read his Bible with more care, which resulted in detecting hundreds of errors in the Holy Book, which he has published to the world in a large volume. We are informed that the Hindus told some of the missionaries while among them that such a God as the Christian Bible describes would not be allowed to run at large in their country. He would be taken up as a criminal.

7. The natives in several countries where the missionaries have been operating, on becoming acquainted with the character of the teachings of the Christian Bible, have raised objections to its being circulated amongst them, and, in some cases, have besought the missionaries to leave. The Rev. Mr. Hall, a missionary in India, states that a public meeting was called at Madras by the natives to draw up a petition to Lord Stanley of England to send no more missionaries, and also entreat him to withdraw those then operating there; and such was the interest manifested that the meeting called out ten thousand people. The Chinese also have manifested strong opposition to the movements of the missionaries among them, while the Japanese have kept out from amongst them both Bible and missionaries by positive law until a recent period.

8. The inhabitants of the Friendly Isles of Honolulu, of India, and also of Japan, have all discussed the subject of sending missionaries to this country to improve the morals of the Christians; and it is certain that some of them are practically acquainted with a better system of morals than that which prevails in this country.

Here we will note the remarkable circumstance that a learned Hindu has recently held a two days' debate with a Christian missionary, which excited such an interest that it drew together from five to seven thousand of the natives, who desired to see the missionary beat in the debate. A writer states that the Hindu handled the missionary's arguments as a cat would a mouse, thus intimating that the missionary was completely vanquished in the logical contest; and yet this Hindu is called a "heathen." Pshaw! It would be a blessing to Christian countries to be supplied with a few

The Bible of Bibles

millions of such heathen. It would improve both their morals and their intelligence.

Note: Many anecdotes are afloat tending to prove the superior moral honesty of the Hindus and other "heathen." As a traveler was walking the streets of an Asiatic city with one of the natives, he proposed to step into a store and purchase some article. "No," said the native, "see that chair in the door to let us know the merchant is absent." — "What!" exclaimed the traveler. "Do merchants go away and leave their goods exposed in that way?" — "Yes," responded the honest native, *"when there are no Christians about."*

CHAPTER 52

WHAT SHALL WE DO TO BE SAVED?

"What shall we believe and do in order to be saved?" is an all-important query, and one which daily occupies the minds of millions of earth's inhabitants of all countries and all climes. There are ten thousand answers to this question, and they are as conflicting as the confusion of tongues at the Tower of Babel. No two religious orders, and scarcely any two religious believers, agree with respect to the all-important answer to be rendered to this all-important question. To prove this, we will interrogate the disciples of all the leading religious orders who have found a place in the world's history, and compare their answers, and observe the result. Commencing in the order of time, the disciples of the Vedas will be the first we will interrogate, as they represent the oldest religious faith that has ever been promulgated in the world.

THE HINDU ANSWER

Well, brother Hindu, will you be so good as to answer this question, "What shall we do and believe in order to be saved?" "Oh, yes!" responds the devout worshiper of Brahma, pointing to a stone arched pagoda. "Go and prostrate yourself in that holy building, made venerable by a thousand years' devotion, and offer up prayer and praise to Brahma, and, if you have committed any sins, implore his forgiveness. You must also believe in his Holy Book, the Vedas, and obey its precepts, which enjoin virtue and holiness, and forbid theft, robbery, murder, lying, dishonesty, adultery, and other crimes; and you must not only believe in the Holy Book as God's revealed will to mankind, but you must believe *it is all true—every word of it*. You must believe, also, that it existed in the mind of the great God Brahma *from all eternity*; and some nine thousand years ago was revealed by him to certain holy men, known as rishis, or prophets, who recorded it in a book for the instruction and salvation of the world; and that this divinely revealed and perfect book contains all knowledge, past, present, and future, and *all the religion necessary to save the whole human race*. And, if you would become a true-born saint [i.e., in Christian language, "regenerated and born again"], you must read the Holy Book through upon your bended knees. [And thousands of its most pious and devout disciples have performed this humble and laborious task.] And if you would advance still farther in soul-purification and true sanctity, so as to become a thrice-born saint [for they hold that the oftener you are born the better], then you must commit the divine volume all to memory. [And many of them, we are assured, have accomplished this herculean task.] But you cannot attain to complete and perfect holiness as a Hindu saint unless you forsake the busy scenes of life, retire to lonely places, and devote yourselves to a life of religious contemplation." By leading this austere, self-denying life, they hold that men and women can attain to complete holiness, and draw near to the spirit of God, and become so exalted in his favor as to receive important revelations from him, and be enabled by him to perform great miracles, such as casting out devils, raising the dead, handling fire without being burned, and swallowing poison without being killed or injured, and finally become Gods, and ascend to heaven in mortal bodies after the manner of Enoch and Elijah.

In one respect, some of the sects are much more consistent than Christian professors. Believing, as Christians have always professed to do, that sickness is often sent by God as a punishment for sin, they never send for a physician, nor allow one to treat the case, because, as they argue, trying to cure it would be trying to counteract the judgment of God, and thus bring down his vengeance upon the heads of those guilty of this sin. Here Christians might learn an important moral lesson of the heathen—that of living up to the doctrines they preach.

We have, then, the Hindu answer to the question, "What must we do and believe in order to be saved?"

THE EGYPTIAN ANSWER

Well, brother disciple of the old Egyptian religion, let us hear your answer to the question, "What must we do and believe in order to be saved?" "Well," replies the believer in this ancient order of faith, "if you would make a sure thing of escaping the pangs of hell, and being saved in the heavenly mansion, you must not neglect to pray daily to the great God Tulis, crucified some twenty-eight hundred years ago for the sins of mankind; and if you have committed any sin, you must pray to him to have them canceled from 'The Book of Life.' [For the ancient Egyptians believed and taught that our evil deeds, as well as our good deeds, are recorded in "The Book of Life," in which St. John represents (see Rev. xxii. 19) our good deeds alone as being registered.] And if you would make a sure thing of being saved in 'the day of judgment,' you must intercede with Divine Mercy to erase your evil deeds from this Book of Life, so that they will not stand against you in that solemn hour." Here we find a few of the duties enumerated which the disciples of that ancient system of religion believed and taught were necessary to be comprised in your religious creed in order to be saved in the great day of accounts.

THE CHINESE ANSWER

We will now interrogate the representative of the religion of "The Five Volumes," and hear his answer to this most important question that ever occupied the thoughts of the human mind. Well, then, brother Chinaman, please tell us what we shall do and believe in order to reach the heavenly kingdom when compelled to quit the things of time. "Why, the most important thing of all is to perform your daily vows to God, and worship him through images prepared to represent him, whether those images are made of wood or stone or metal, though you are not to consider these images as the veritable living and true God."

For no nation was ever so brainless or stupid as to believe that idols or images made of mere inanimate matter were living beings, much less a living God. No! The images which have been represented by Christian writers as being objects of worship in numerous heathen countries have been nothing more than mere imaginary likenesses of the Divine Being, and were gotten up for the same purpose that Christian men obtain photograph likenesses of their absent friends, and hang them on the walls of their dwellings. The object is simply to keep the images of our friends impressed on our minds in their absence; and the same motive actuates the idolater in making supposed images of an absent God. The object is simply to have something before them that will keep them in remembrance of him, and his laws and commandments—a very laudable motive, most certainly. They are idolaters, it is true; and so are all nations who believe in a personal God, whether called Jew, pagan, or Christian: for idolatry is defined to be "image-making and image-worship"; and both of these acts all religious nations have been addicted to (Christians not excepted). This can be seen in a moment, when we look at the essential nature of idolatry—that is, the making and worship of images. All images are first formed in the mind. The Christian forms his conception of a personal God in his mind; and the pagan does the same. Both thus make their mental images of God. The only difference in the two cases is the pagan goes one step farther, and represents his image in wood, stone, or metal; but it is no more an image than while it existed only in the mind. Then it is evident there is no essential difference between them. Both are idolaters. For further elucidation of this subject, see the chapter on idolatry.

And, if you would be saved by the Chinese religion, there are some practical duties you must perform. You must live up to the golden rule incorporated in their Bible nearly twenty-five hundred years ago. You must also observe the rite of water-baptism, for it has been a religious ordinance amongst them for several thousand years. And if you would attain to complete holiness, you must be kind to all human beings, and even all animals. Kill no living thing, and eat nothing after sundown. Then you can be saved by their religion.

The Bible of Bibles

THE PERSIAN AND CHALDEAN ANSWER

Brothers of the religion of Iran, can you tell us what to do and believe in order to be saved? "Yes, indeed. First of all, you must believe 'God's Living Word,' the Zend Avesta, for that is the meaning of the term. *Zenda* means 'the life' or 'the living,' and *Avesta,* 'the word of God.' And you must live up to its holy precepts, which will keep you from committing sin, and prompt you to lead a virtuous life. You must also say grace, both before and after eating, as that was their ancient custom. But you are forbidden to speculate in any of the necessaries of life so as to cause suffering among the poor. And their Bible declares that he who hoards up grain, and holds it for a high price, is responsible for all the famine and all the misery that may take place among the people. [I would recommend modern Christian speculators to borrow this heathen code, and learn from it some important moral lessons.] To insure salvation under this religion, you must also believe in 'Mithra the Mediator,' crucified for the sins of the world some three thousand three hundred years ago by wicked hands, but in no case make any idols or images of God; for their religion practically condemns idolatry."

THE JAPANESE ANSWER

We will now hear from a "heathen" nation distinguished for good sense, good morals, and practical honesty.

Tell us, then, brother Japanese, what we must do and believe in order to be saved. "Well, first of all, you must keep the Christian Bible out of your houses. Don't suffer it to enter your doors. Let all Bibles alone, and obey the inward monitions of your own souls. Your own conscience and experience and moral sense will teach you that it is wrong to lie, wrong to swear, wrong to steal, wrong to cheat, wrong to get drunk, wrong to fight, and wrong to kill." Now let us learn something about the moral character and practical lives of this "heathen nation," who, for more than two hundred years, have kept Christian Bibles and Christian missionaries out from among them, most of the time by positive law. Dr. Oliphant and Col. Hall, who both spent some considerable time amongst them, states that they are an honest, upright, moral, and sober people. With respect to honesty of dealing, sobriety, and abstinence from swearing, quarreling, fighting, or any of the common vices of society, the best authorities assure us that no Christian nation on earth will compare with them; and yet they conscientiously refrain from reading the Christian Bible. (See chapter 50 of this work.) What a startling disproof is here furnished to the declaration of Christian writers that the introduction of the Christian Bible, and the establishment of the Christian religion amongst the heathen, are essential to the existence of good morals amongst them! In many cases more good would be effected by reversing the practice, and sending heathen missionaries into Christian nations, as the pious pagans of China, India, and the Friendly Isles have all been talking of doing; some of the godly people of India have already entered upon the work.

THE MUHAMMADAN ANSWER

Brother disciple of the Koran, will you please to tell us what the one hundred and fifty million of followers of the great prophet believe is necessary to do and believe in order to be saved? "Yes, certainly. The devout believers in this soul-saving religion have understood this question for more than a thousand years, and know exactly how to answer it. You must believe that the Holy Book (the Koran) is God's last revelation, and his last will and testament to mankind; and you must shape your practical lives by its precepts, which will make you 'true saints,' and honest, upright, and righteous men and women. You must also believe that the great prophet is the true, holy, and appointed messenger of God, and that Allah is the only true God. To believe, as Christians do, that God is divided into three persons or beings, or three attributes, or three branches, known as Father, Son, and Holy Ghost, is not only a monstrous absurdity, but a monstrous sin and an unpardonable blasphemy; and no man or woman who holds such doctrine can be saved. God is but one, and Allah is his name, and you must worship him seven times a day; and on the sabbath day (Friday) you must present yourselves at the mosque with the Holy Book in your hand, which, having kissed, you are then to place it upon the holy altar, and listen while the priest explains its great truths and its profound and godly mysteries." And "on such occasions," says Major Denham, "tears flow in abundance, as under Christian preaching."

Here, then, you have the terms of salvation and the road marked out to heaven by the believers in the Koran.

THE JEWISH ANSWER

Brother Jew, can you show us the road to salvation, or tell us what to do and believe in order to be saved? "Oh, yes! It is a plain question, and easily answered. You must believe that the Old Testament Scriptures are the inspired word of God, and believe in its miracles and prophecies, though you are not to interpret or construe any of its prophecies as foretelling the coming and mission of Christ; for, as we wrote them, we of course know exactly what they teach, and how to understand them. And we know most *positively* that they do not foretell the coming and mission of any such a being as Jesus Christ as the promised Messiah."

The Bible of Bibles

"Now, look here, you wicked Jews," exclaim a hundred Christian sects, "you are denying 'the Lord who bought you,' and therefore cannot be saved." So six millions of Jews are consigned by their Protestant brethren to endless torment—given over to the buffetings of Satan to all eternity.

THE CHRISTIAN CHURCHES' ANSWER

And now, brethren of the Christian faith, we will listen with attention to your answer to the important question, "What shall we do and believe in order to be saved?" But Christian sects are so numerous, and their views so conflicting, we can only find room for the answers of a few of the leading churches.

The Catholic's Answer

Well, brother Roman Catholic, as you represent the oldest Christian denomination in existence, we will first hear from your Church in answer to this great question, "What shall we do and believe in order to be saved?" "Well, the question is easily answered. You must believe that the Bible is the inspired word of God; that Jesus Christ is the son of God; and that St. Peter, succeeded by the Pope, is his vicegerent on the earth. You must also worship, or at least believe in the divinity of, the Father, Son, and Holy Ghost, and the Virgin Mary; and adhere to the various rites and ceremonies of the Church."

The Greek Christian's Answer

Well, brother disciple of the Greek Church, "what shall we do and believe in order to be saved?" What do you think of the Roman Catholic's answer? Is it correct? "No, indeed; far from it. It is an insult to God the Father and God the Son both to put either St. Peter or the Pope at the head of the Church. That is the office and mission of Jesus Christ the Savior; and he will *never save you* while you believe such blasphemous doctrine." Away then goes the old mother-church, with her hundred and fifty millions of souls, down into the bottomless pit, being ruled out of heaven by the Greek Church; that is, doomed to eternal perdition, according to the testimony of the Greek Church.

The Presbyterian's Answer

Well, brother of the Presbyterian order, we will now listen to your answer to the great question, "What shall we do and believe in order to be saved?" How about the Greek Christian's answer to the question? Is it right? Does he hold the true doctrine, or not? "No. Very far from it, indeed. Like the Roman Christian, he believes in the divinity of the Virgin

What Shall We Do to Be Saved?

Mary, and consequently he is an idolater; and no idolater can be admitted into the kingdom of heaven." So away goes the old Greek Church, with her seventy million disciples, down into the world of endless woe, if the testimony of our Presbyterian brother is to be relied upon. And thus two-thirds of all Christendom, comprising the disciples of the Romish Church and the Greek Church, are doomed to an endless hell, according to their own witnesses.

The Unitarian Christian's Answer

Our Unitarian brother will now please come forward, and tell us "what we must do and believe in order to be saved." Do you endorse any of the answers already obtained, or agree with any of the churches which have been interrogated upon this subject, or not? "No. Very far from it." What! You don't dissent from the views of the Presbyterian Church upon this question, do you? "Yes, I do, for they worship 'the man Christ Jesus' (as Paul truly calls him) and, being but a man they are idolaters (like the Roman and Greek Christians) for worshipping him as a God, and therefore cannot be *saved*, according to the Bible. He was born as a man; he lived as a man; he ate as a man; he walked as a man; he talked as a man; he slept as a man; and finally died as a man. And he calls himself 'the son of man' more than forty times, which would *make* him a man. For these and various other reasons we believe he could not have been a God, but only a man, and therefore those who worship him *as a God* are guilty of idolatry—the most *heinous sin* a man can commit, according to the Bible. And hence they cannot *possibly* be saved, if the Bible teaches truly." Away then goes four hundred Protestant sects to the regions of eternal torment, if the testimony of Christian witnesses is to be believed and accepted in the case.

The Methodist's Answer

Brother Methodist, perhaps you can do something towards settling this vexed and puzzling question, "What must we do and believe in order to be saved?" "Certainly," exclaims the pious disciple of Wesley. "It is perfectly plain, and easily answered. You must believe in the Bible as the revealed will and word of God, and in Jesus Christ 'the Son and sent of God'; and pour out your souls in prayer and praises to God, and shout '*Glory*' to his holy name." "Stop, stop!" cries out the good, pious, quiet, broad-brimmed Quaker. "You cannot be saved in that way. You drown the inward monitor of the Holy Spirit, which must be listened to and obeyed in order to insure salvation. You, by your noisy way of worshipping God, drown the voice of this inward monitor, and consequently *hear* and *heed* not its admonitions; thus proving that you know nothing about the true way of worshipping God, or what true religion is. And therefore there is no chance for you to be saved." And thus two millions of Methodists are doomed to eternal woe by their Quaker brethren.

The Baptist's Answer

Brother Baptist, will you give us your opinion, or answer the question, "What shall we do and believe in order to be saved?" "Oh, yes! The Bible is so plain upon that subject that no honest reader can misunderstand it. You are to believe in the Bible; believe in Jesus Christ, and live up to his precepts; and believe in, and practically observe, the sacred ordinance of water-baptism—without which, according to the Bible, it is impossible to reach the kingdom, or inherit life everlasting." "Stop, stop!" exclaims the drab-cloth Quaker again. "I perceive that the Baptists, as well as the Methodists, are not on the road to salvation. No man or woman can be saved who believes in, and relies upon, the external and carnal rite of water-baptism. It is a reliance on such outward performances that causes millions of ignorant and unconverted heathen to sink to endless ruin every year. They and you are dwelling in the outer court, and practically know *nothing* about the true religion essential to salvation and hence cannot be saved." "Now, look here," exclaims the Campbellite Baptist, "water baptism is one of the *positive ordinances*; and the Bible declares that *no man or woman* can be saved without a compliance with *all* the ordinances, from the least to the greatest. Therefore, there is no chance for you infidel Quakers to get to heaven; but you will, sooner or later, be consigned to the pit 'where the worm dieth not, and the fire is not quenched.'"

And thus we might pursue the conflicting jargon of answers through all the churches. But we stop confused and confounded amid chaos, confusion, and contradiction. All seems to be wild conjecture and blind guesswork with regard to what we must do and believe in order to be saved. There appears to be no way of learning anything about the road to salvation by the churches. What is to be done?

The Quaker's Answer

Brother Quaker, as you profess to get light from above, perhaps you can throw some light on this dark question. We have not yet heard your answer to this puzzling question. Can your tell us "what to do and believe in order to be saved"? "Most certainly I can," replies the inspired disciple of Fox and Penn. "There can be no mistake about what the Bible teaches on the subject. It is perfectly plain, and easily understood. You are to retire into the quiet, and turn your minds inward with a prayerful desire to know the will of God. In this state of mind, open your Bible, and you will learn that you are to do justly, love mercy, and walk humbly with God, and become established in the true faith: for the Bible declares that 'without faith, it is impossible to please God'; that is, faith in his beloved Son, whom he sent into the world to die a propitiatory offering for the sins of man." "What!" exclaims the Hicksite Quaker, "do you mean to teach the dark and bloody doctrine of the atonement? Do you mean to say that we have to swim through blood to get to 'the house of many mansions'? If you do, you are egregiously mistaken. You are teaching and preaching an old, worn-out, bloody, heathen doctrine that never did and never can save a single soul." "Now, look here," cries the orthodox Quaker, "the Bible declares, 'There is no other name given under heaven whereby men can be saved than that of Jesus Christ,' and you are blaspheming his name by denying the efficacy of his death and sufferings. Therefore, your chance for salvation is a *hopeless one.* You will be *lost,* and consigned to the pit where there is eternal weeping and wailing, and gnashing of teeth." So away go both the Quaker orders, each booked by the other for eternal perdition.

But we must stop, or we will swell this chapter on the war of conflicting creeds to a volume. We have now interrogated all the leading churches relative to what it is necessary to do and believe in order to make a sure thing of salvation, and escape the awful and dreadful fate of endless damnation. And what is the result? No two churches—and it could easily be shown that scarcely any two Christians—agree upon this all-important question, upon which they tell us is hung the salvation of the world. As we have shown, the churches all virtually shut the door of heaven against each other. They are *all off the track, all on the road* to eternal damnation, according to the testimony of *their own* witnesses. In the name of God, what is the use or sense, then, of professing to believe in the Bible, or claiming to be Christians, when it is thus demonstrably proved that nobody knows anything about what the Bible teaches, or what it takes to make a Christian? The picture we have presented is no mere fancy sketch. It is not the work of mere imagination. Hundreds, if not thousands, of quotations could be furnished from the writings of eminent Christian writers of the different churches to show that it is a solemn reality, and that they differ in the way, and as widely, as we have represented. And what is the solemn lesson taught by it? Why, the absolute impossibility of our finding the road to heaven through the churches and it is an entire waste of time, besides being demoralizing to the mind, to attempt it. We are often told by the orthodox Christians, by way of defending their creeds, that the churches are agreed upon all the leading doctrines of the Christian faith.

Well, let us see how this is, and whether they in reality agree upon *anything.* We will institute another court of inquiry, and briefly examine and compare the views of the various churches relative to the cardinal doctrines of the Christian religion.

1. *Moral Depravity.* The first in order will be the fall and depravity of man.

Well, brother Calvinist, as you hail from the oldest Protestant Church, we will first solicit your views upon this all-important question. We wish to know whether you believe that man fell from a state of purity, and became morally depraved by the fall. "Oh, yes! We believe he fell so low that he became *totally depraved* by the fall; so that *all seen* are now the children of wrath, born in sin, and conceived in iniquity, and covered with corruption from the crowns of the head to the sole of the foot."

Brother Arminian, what do you think of this view of the matter? Is it Bible doctrine, or not? "No, it is neither according to the Bible, nor according to common sense, but a damnable doctrine, that will send any man's soul to hell who believes in such outrageous doctrine. It is not only untrue, but it is demoralizing to rob man so completely of his moral attribute as to make him feel like a brute and, consequently, act like one."

2. *Man's Restoration.* How is this to be effected, brother Calvinist? "Why, by the outpouring of the blood of Christ, the propitiatory offering." Brother Arminian, is this true Christian doctrine? "No, it is not. Man's salvation is effected in no such a way. Every man is to work out his own salvation. I can prove it by the Bible."

3. *Endless Punishment.* Most Protestant sects hold and preach that the wicked, when they die, are consigned to a place or state called "the bottomless pit." (How they are kept in it with the bottom out, the Lord only knows, or perhaps we should say the devil.) But the Universalists affirm that the Bible teaches no such doctrine, but tells us that, "as in Adam all die, so in Christ sinners shall all be made alive," which proves, as they affirm, the ultimate salvation of all the human race. But the Restorationists prove that there is "a mediate place for souls, which is neither heaven nor hell, but a preliminary and a temporary abode for all souls, good and bad."

And there is another class of Christians who find in the same book a still different doctrine, that of the *absolute and total destruction* of the wicked. They quote Phil. iii. 19. Which of these four Christian sects teach the true Bible doctrine? Who can tell?

4. *Divinity of Christ.* Most of the Protestant sects tell us that the Bible makes a belief in the supreme divinity of Jesus Christ essential to salvation; but the Parkerite Christian, the Hicksite Christian, and the Unitarian Christian affirm that it does not, that it only makes him a perfect or superior specimen of manhood. Which is right? Who can tell?

What Shall We Do to Be Saved?

5. *Polygamy*. Most of the churches once believed that polygamy is a Bible doctrine, and practiced it for eight hundred years. But now they tell us it is not. The Mormons, however, declare that it is sanctioned in the Old Testament, and not condemned in the New, and hence *is* a Bible doctrine. Which is right? How can we tell?

6. *Marriage*. Nearly all the sects hold that marriage is a Bible institution. But the Shakers declare that it is not, and quote Christ's own words to prove it as found in Luke xx. 35. "The children of this world marry and are given in marriage; but they who shall be counted worthy of that world, and the resurrection, neither marry nor are given in marriage." They reasonably conclude that those who shall not be considered *worthy* of being saved (which includes *all* married people) *will not be saved*, being cut off by Christ's positive prohibition of marriage. Which is right? Who can tell? The text, however, furnishes a consoling hope for old bachelors and old maids, to say the least.

7. *The Sabbath*. Most of the churches keep the first day of the week as the Bible sabbath. But the Seventh-day Baptists affirm that it is not, that the seventh day of the week is the true sabbath of the Lord; while other sects tell us that Christ, both by precept and example, labored to do away with *all Sabbath observances* and all *holy days*. Which is right? Who can tell?

8. *The Godhead*. All Trinitarians teach that there are three persons in the Godhead. The Paulite Christians say there are but two, while the Unitarians affirm there is but one. Which is right? Who can tell?

9. *Baptism*. The churches are not agreed with regard to baptism as to what it is, how, and when it should be applied and on whom it should be administered. Some hold to dipping, some to douching, and some to sprinkling, as the scripture mode of administering it. Which is right? Who can tell?

I should prefer the dipping process. It would do something toward saving the body of the sinner from disease, if not the soul from hell *if frequently applied*. He should be baptized once a week, if not once a day, with water and soap. We have now enumerated nearly all the leading doctrines of the Christian faith, and shown that the views of the churches, with respect to them, are about as different as day from night. The important query then arises, What progress have we made towards determining, by the Bible or by the churches, what we must *do and believe in order to be saved?* Why, about the same progress the boy had made toward reaching the schoolhouse, who, on being interrogated by the teacher as to the cause of his late appearance, replied, "Why, master, you see the road was so slippery, that when I attempted to take one step forward, I slipped two steps backward." "How did you manage to get here, then?" asked the teacher. "Why," replied Tom, "I turned round and went the other way." I would suggest that the churches try this policy of turning round and going the other way. My conviction is they would find the true road to salvation much sooner, and be better prepared to settle the question as to what they should do and believe in order to be saved. It is a question, however, they never can settle. The Bible is a very old book, and the farther we get away from the age in which it was written, the more difficult it will become to understand it: for human language, and even human thought and the meaning of words, are constantly changing. These circumstances will constantly augment the difficulty of even understanding any old Bible, or of determining what it teaches or designed to teach with respect to an important doctrine.

10. *The Number of Hells.* When the disciple of the Christian faith talks of a hell in the presence of a Hindu, he tells him he does not know anything about the matter; that there are no less than *three* institutions of this kind. But here the Muhammadan rises up and says, "You, too, are totally ignorant on the subject, for there are no less than *seven* institutions of this character. One of them is set apart for Christians who believe in the divinity and atonement of Christ." Lieut. Lynch, of the United States Navy, says that a Muhammadan told him, "No man or woman can be saved who believes that God was born of a woman, and then became a malefactor to a human tribunal; for the doctrine is blasphemous." Which of all these opinions is right? Who can tell?

11. *Bible Doctrines Constantly Changing.* The increase of intelligence and the growth and expansion of the human mind have the effect to change the views of the people generally and constantly upon almost every subject that occupies the mind; so that the creeds of the churches are constantly changing. Hence, the Bible is made to teach widely different doctrines in different ages; and what is Christianity today is infidelity tomorrow, and *vice versa.* (See chapter 58.) And so thorough is the change wrought upon the meaning or interpretation of nearly all the important text in "God's perfect revelation," that it virtually makes a new Bible for each generation. I will present some proofs and illustrations of this statement by comparing the doctrine of the churches of the last century with those of the present. In the days of Jonathan Edwards, a hell, constituted of a lake of fire and brimstone, was preached in nearly all the Christian churches; also the doctrine of infant damnation, when the Methodists sang that beautiful and charming hymn—

What Shall We Do to Be Saved?

"For hell is crammed
With infants damned,
Without a day of grace";

also the doctrine of predestination, the doctrine of election and reprobation, the doctrine of purgatory, the doctrine of Christ's descent into hell, etc. All these and other similar doctrines were preached in nearly every pulpit nearly every sabbath; and the preacher who would have neglected to preach these doctrines would have been denounced as on the road to hell. But now the clergyman who should attempt to preach these old Calvinistic tenets would be denounced as "an old fogy." Hence, the important query arises, When were the churches preaching Bible doctrine, *then or now*? Who can tell? Such changes are increasingly going on. Important changes are sometimes made in the popular creed in a few years' time, as we will cite a case to prove.

Just before the last war the peace doctrine was becoming quite popular in nearly all the churches, and sermons were even preached from such texts as the following: "Nation shall not lift up sword against nation; neither shall they learn war any more." But when the war broke out, new texts were hunted up, and the preaching all ran in the opposite direction. "Cursed be he who holdeth back his sword from blood" (Jer. xlviii. 10); "He who hath not a sword, let him sell his coat, and buy one" then constituted the texts for a sound sermon. Now it is evident that a book which thus teaches opposite doctrines virtually teaches nothing. Its moral force is destroyed. If a man wants to perform a certain act today, and an act of an opposite character tomorrow, and can find a warrant for both in the Bible, then it is evident the Bible can have no effect whatever towards changing his course of life. When every moral duty is both commanded and countermanded, and every crime both sanctioned and condoned, as appears to be the case with the Christian Bible, then it is evident that a man with the Bible would act exactly as the man without the Bible; for whatever he may naturally feel inclined to do, or whatever he wants to do, he finds Bible authority for. Hence, it is evident the Bible cannot change his conduct in the least; for it merely tells him to do what he wishes to do, and had made up his mind to do. I will prove this position by citing several cases for illustration.

We will suppose a man has become convinced by observations, or his own experience, that it is wrong to drink intoxicating liquors, and wants Bible authority for preaching temperance. He can find it by turning to Isa. v. 22: "Woe unto them that are mighty to drink wine." But a friend of his, a member of the same church, living in the city, where there is great demand for intoxicating beverages, wants to make some money by selling it. He finds the authority for that act also in Deut. xiv. 26: "Thou shalt spend thy money for oxen, or for sheep, or for wine, or for strong drink, or for whatever thy soul lusteth after." Another Christian becomes very angry, and filled with the spirit of a murderer towards a neighbor, and concludes to kill him. He finds Bible authority for it in the text, "Go ye out and slay every man his companion, every man his brother, and every man his neighbor" (Exod. xxxii. 27). Another pious Christian has become convinced, by "the logic of history," that all war and fighting is wrong, and hence concludes to preach the doctrine of peace. He finds Bible authority for that in the Decalogue: "Thou shalt not kill." Another devout Christian, whose common sense has taught him that it is wrong for one human being to enslave another, wants Bible authority against the practice. He finds it in the text, "Thou shalt proclaim liberty through all the land," etc. Another godly saint, living in a slave-holding country, and being both a tyrant and a mammon worshiper, wants Bible authority for trafficking in the blood and bones of his fellow beings, finds it in Lev. xxv. 45: "Of the heathen round about you shall ye buy bondmen and bondmaids, and they shall be your possession for ever"; so he knows it is all right.

And thus this exposition might be continued so as to show that there is no crime, no sin, no vice, and no wicked deed but that is both sanctioned and condemned by "God's Holy Word," and no moral duty that is not both commanded and countermanded; thus proving it to be absolutely impossible to follow it as a guide without being led into the commission of every species of sin, crime, and abomination, as well as prompted to the practice of virtue. Every person who has not made shipwreck of common sense must see at once that it is utterly impossible to learn anything about what is right and what is wrong, what is sin and wickedness and what is virtue, what is morality and what is immorality, or what he should approve, and what condemn, what he should do and what leave undone, or, finally, anything about the duties of life or the rules and principles of morality, by such a book. What *can* such a book, then, be worth, either in the cause of religion or morality? Where, oh! where is the common sense of Christendom? It is wonderful to what extent rationality and good sense have been banished from the human mind in all Bible countries by a false and perverted education. It cannot be wondered at that we have so many antagonistic churches with innumerable conflicting creeds, when we examine and learn something about the endless contradictions and confusion of the teachings of the book on which they are founded.

What Shall We Do to Be Saved?

SIX HUNDRED ROADS TO HEAVEN

We are swamped with endless difficulties in determining what to do and believe in order to be saved either by the Bible or the churches, when we look at the fact that there are, as some writers have computed, more than six hundred conflicting churches, each one claiming to preach and to teach the only true and saving faith of the gospel, and yet differing heaven-wide with respect to what constitutes that true and saving faith. They point out six hundred roads to heaven, when Christ says there is but one—"One Lord, one faith, and one baptism." The churches are simply guessing institutions, and their creeds so many stereotyped systems of guesswork. How much has been learned, or what important questions have been settled, either in religion or morals, by the nearly two thousand years' reading and study of the Christian Bible? The six hundred jarring churches, and their constantly increasing number, furnish a sufficient answer to this question. What a ludicrous aspect would the cause of science now be in, and what torrents of ridicule and contempt would be poured upon our institutions of learning, if they differed in their principles, or with respect to the principles of any branch of science, as the churches differ with respect to the doctrine of the Bible!

We will illustrate by an imaginary examination of the statements of one of our institutions of learning with respect to their attainments in mathematics. A class having recited, we will interrogate each one separately. "Well, John, as you have been studying figures several years, can you now tell us how many are twice two?" — "Yes, sir. Twice two are six." — "Very well. Take your seat. The next student will rise. James, can you tell us how many are twice two?" — "Yes, I can. Twice two are eleven." — "Very well. Be seated, and let Tommy rise. Tommy, as you are a diligent student, and have been through the arithmetic and the principal textbooks, please tell us how many are twice two." — "I will. It is a plain case: twice two are fourteen." — "Very well. Stand aside. That intelligent-looking boy yonder we will hear from now. Well, Moses, can you tell us, as the result of your five years' close study of mathematics, how many are twice two?" — "Certainly, I can. To be nice and exact about the matter, twice two are nine and a half." — "Very well. I am done with you. There is one more student to be interrogated. Well, Solomon, can you do anything towards settling the disputed question, how many are twice two?" — "Yes. I am astonished there should be any difference of opinion about the matter, when it is plain that no person who is really in earnest to understand it can fail to see that twice two are seventeen."

Such an institution of learning as this would be broken up as a nuisance in less than two hours after it was known to exist; and yet it furnishes a

275

striking illustration of the character and condition of our theological institutions in which are professedly taught the science of Christianity and the Bible. The difference among the professors and students of theology is as great and important as in the former supposed case; and were not the eyes of the soul put out, and the Christian sectarians rendered blind by their false or mistaken teachers, they would see that this is a true picture of their condition. We will institute another illustration.

The Christian churches are virtually six hundred guide-boards professedly pointing the way to heaven. Let us suppose a traveler, hunting his way to "the Queen City of the West," finds on a hill a tree or post, to which are nailed six hundred guide-boards pointing in six hundred different directions, and all labeled "To Cincinnati." How much would he learn from them about the proper road to travel to reach the city? The chance of striking the right course would lay within six hundred guesses, and those guesses could be made as well without the guide-boards as with them. And it is equally certain, and most self-evidently certain, that the road to heaven could be found as well if there were no churches and no Bible pointing six hundred different directions. Indeed, the chances of finding it would be much better without them, because the minds of the people are confused and confounded, and their time wasted, their mental and spiritual vision darkened, and their judgments weakened, by attempting to grope their way through such a labyrinth of chaos, confusion, and uncertainty, which really incapacitates them for searching and finding the right way and the sure road "to the kingdom."

ONE HUNDRED AND FIFTY BIBLE TRANSLATIONS AND COMMENTARIES

When we learn that there have been no less than one hundred and fifty different translations and commentaries upon the Bible put in circulation, we can see at once that this is calculated to greatly augment the difficulty of ever arriving at anything like a unity of belief among the churches, or of settling the question as to what it is necessary to do and believe in order to be saved, or of finding the road to heaven through the churches. Translation after translation of the Bible has been made by different churches, each one alleging that all preceding translations were full of errors. The learned Dr. Robinson of England has estimated that some of the modern translations of the Bible, made for the special purpose of getting the errors out of "the Holy Book," contain the frightful number of one hundred and fifty thousand errors; and the American Christian Union, now engaged in translating the Bible, declares that our present popular version, translated by fifty-four of the most learned Christian scholars, and which has long been an established standard authority in a large portion of Christendom and regarded as nearly perfect, yet contains twenty-four thousand errors. How many more translations we are to have, God only knows. The thought occurs here that, by the time all the errors are gotten out of the Bible in this way, there will not be much of it left—that it will not be much larger than "Poor Richard's Maxims" or a common-sized almanac. Now, to show the utter impossibility of establishing any doctrine or settling any question in theology by the Bible, or of learning anything about what constitutes Christianity, or what we are to do and believe in order to be saved, we have only to compare some of these translations together, and observe the wide difference in their teachings, and the fatal contradictions in their doctrines and precepts. We will cite a few examples by way of proof and illustration.

In our translation, known as "King James Bible," a text makes Christ say, "A spirit hath not flesh and bones, as you see I have" (Luke xxiv. 39), but in the most popular translation in Europe (the Royal), this text is made to read, "A spirit hath not flesh and blood, as you see I have not." Here is a direct contradiction. One of these Bibles makes Christ say he is a spirit, and the other that he is not, which is a flat, and almost a fatal, contradiction. Now, where on earth is the tribunal to which we can appeal to find out which of these translations is right? Or how can the matter be settled? Again, the text which in our own version is made to read, "There are three that bare record in heaven—the Father, Son, and Holy Ghost," reads in another translation, "There are three witnesses—the *water,* the *blood,* and the *spirit,*" which knocks the trinity and divinity of Jesus Christ both out of the Bible, so far as they are founded upon this text. We will cite one more example: "The wonderful Messianic prophecy," as it is called (found in Isa. ix. 6)—which reads in our translation, "Unto us a child is born, unto us a son is given, he shall be called Wonderful Counselor, the Mighty God, the Everlasting Father," etc.—is made in another translation to say instead of "the Mighty God," "the Mighty Hero," and instead of "the Everlasting Father," "the Father of the everlasting age," etc., which shows that the text is not a prophecy at all, and has no more reference to Jesus Christ than to Muhammad. "The Mighty Hero" is not a term that is ever applied to God, but to bloody warriors.

Now, who is to settle the question as to which of these translations is the right one? It will be observed, then, that we have, in the fifty contradictory translations of the Bible, no less than fifty contradictory moral codes and fifty contradictory systems of doctrines, which are virtually fifty assumed-to-be-perfect revelations from God (of course, all *infallible*). Now, let us multiply the number of Christian sects (six hundred) by the number of Bible translations and commentaries (one hundred and fifty), and we will have indicated the number of roads marked out to heaven by the churches. The result is ninety thousand (600x150=90,000). Here, then, we have ninety thousand roads leading to "the house of many mansions," which suggests the conclusion that nobody can possibly miss getting there; for we must presume that it would be impossible to travel in any direction without striking one of these numerous roads: so that the world of sinners may be comforted with the assurance they will all be saved. "The broad road" they are traveling must be intersected at many points by some of these many pathways to paradise; and they have only to turn off at the last crossing to be landed safe in "kingdom come." They have therefore ninety thousand chances of being saved by traveling "the broad road," if they prefer that to one of "the straight and narrow roads." This soul-saving system may be regarded as a lottery scheme in which there are eighty-nine thousand nine hundred and ninety nine blanks, and but one prize. Who would risk a farthing in such an investment, with eighty-nine thousand nine hundred and ninety-nine chances against drawing anything? Certainly no person with common sense or any intelligence. We will use an illustration.

We will suppose the proprietor of a brick building comprising ninety thousand bricks, one of which contains a gold medal worth one thousand dollars, says to one of his neighbors, "Sir, the walls of this building comprise ninety thousand bricks, and one of them contains a gold medal worth one thousand dollars. If you will step to it, and put your finger on it, you can have it." Can we suppose he would be very sanguine about winning the gold medal? Certainly not. We will make another illustration. We will suppose the Queen of England sends a company of a thousand men to Australia to dig for a treasure known to have been buried there during a war, the locality of which she describes in writing so accurately that she presumes there can be no difficulty in finding it. In a few weeks, she dispatches a messenger to the island to ascertain what progress the miners are making. But imagine his surprise on reaching the place, to learn that the laborers are divided up into six hundred companies, and each company stoutly insisting that the spot where they are digging answers exactly to the locality described by the written instrument. Now, on the messenger reporting the case to the queen, what would she conclude—ay, *what could she conclude*—but that she had made some serious blunder or omission in her attempted description of the place? It is not possible that an explicit revelation of the matter could have led to such endless confusion and disputes.

In like manner, we are morally compelled to conclude—yes, every principle of reasoning and common sense impels us to the conclusion—that God has made a serious blunder in attempting to give forth a perfect revelation to the world, if (as it seems) he has left it so ambiguous, so unintelligible, and so contradictory in its doctrines and teachings, that six hundred churches have risen up, and are now disputing about what its doctrines and teachings are. These six hundred churches comprise a hundred and fifty millions of guessing Christians, all guessing their way to heaven, with ninety thousand chances against their ever reaching the heavenly kingdom. To "the angel host" looking down, observing this infinite diversity, demoralization, and conflict among the disciples of the Christian faith, it must be regarded as a species of religious monomania; for we may assume that no intelligent mind, which is not blinded by religious superstition, could be drawn into such a delusion as to conclude that such a book or such a religions or revelation is from an all-wise and all-powerful God, or that it is necessary to believe it, or that it is possible to believe it in any rational sense, or that it can have the remotest connection with our salvation. It makes God a fool, man a lunatic, religion a farce, and the Bible superlative nonsense.

Revelation is defined to be "the act of making known." But what is made known by a book whose language is so contradictory and so ambiguous that no two persons in a million agree with respect to all it teaches? Every preacher and teacher simply makes known his ignorance whenever he assumes to *know* what the Bible teaches; and yet it is called "a perfect revelation of God's will." It is an assumption that makes God an ignoramus and a tyrant to suppose he would give forth a perfect revelation to the world, and require us to accept it as such on pain of endless damnation, and yet leave it in such a jumbled, bungling, and unintelligent condition that it is impossible to understand it. Such an assumption certainly borders on blasphemy. We would charge him with no such driveling nonsense. It is the legitimate prerogative of reason to assume that a perfect being could make a perfect revelation or Bible, the language of which should be so absolutely perfect and plain that no person of ordinary understanding could possibly fail to understand every text, every word, and every syllable of it, and no two persons could possibly differ about the meaning of one text in the whole book. Such a revelation or Bible, and only such, could be ascribed to an all-wise God. Even men and women can now be found who are so far masters of human language that they can write books so plainly that there can be no dispute about the meaning of one sentence in them. To assume, then, that an infinitely wise God could not produce such a book is to place him lower in the scale of intelligence than a common schoolboy. When, therefore, I find the Christian Bible so far from possessing such characteristics, I set it down as *prima facie* evidence that an intelligent and all-wise God had nothing to do in originating it. And if he were not superior to, or incapable of, such human weakness, he would reject with contempt and disdain the honor, or rather dishonor, ascribed to him in the authorship of such a book—such a medley of contradiction, ignorance, superstition, and barbarism as is ascribed to him.

It is sometimes alleged (as we have already observed) in defence or mitigation of the endless disputes among Christian professors about the teachings of the Bible, that this disagreement does not appertain to any of the essential doctrines of Christianity, but only to minor points, or doctrines of minor importance. But such an admission is fatal either to their honesty or to their good sense. It concedes that the quarrels among the churches for ages have been about mere trifles, not worth spending breath about. It concedes that it is "non-essentials," or mere trifles, that keep them apart, and that have led them to build five or six churches, and hire five or six priests, in every little village throughout the country, at an expense of many thousand dollars. It is certainly a criminal waste of time and money to spend it by the million for churches and priests to propagate doctrines which they themselves admit possess no real intrinsic importance. It shows they have been actuated by selfish, dishonorable, and ignoble motives in fighting each other for a thousand years, and in some cases murdering each other by the thousand, for a difference of opinion they admit to be of no importance. Those murdered Christians and devout Bible believers were charged with preaching damnable doctrines and devilish heresies; but now we are told it was minor and unimportant doctrines that they were quarreling about, and for which they were tortured and killed for preaching. Yes, non-essential doctrine! *O tempora! O mores!* But they make a serious blunder when they talk about non-essential doctrine; for their Bible teaches that all doctrines are essential—that there is no such thing as a non-essential doctrine; for it first proclaims "one Lord, one faith, and one baptism," and then declares that "he who offends in the least, offends in the whole."

These two declarations taken together prove (if they prove anything) that there is no "non-essential doctrine," and that the slightest departure from the right faith, or the least disregard of the *most trivial doctrine* of the Christian creed, will land the soul of the man or woman in endless perdition who is guilty of it. The solemn question arises here, then, Who can escape eternal damnation? For, if there is only one true faith, then the hundred and forty thousand different and conflicting faiths cherished and propagated among Christians must all be wrong but one—a fact which impels us to the awful and inevitable conclusion that not one Christian in a thousand—no, not in ten thousand—can be saved by these terms of the gospel. The thought sometimes occurs to the writer that no truly enlightened person, possessing a true moral dignity of character, could consent to hang his salvation upon a book which, after eighteen hundred years of the most critical investigation and explanation by the most learned minds in Christendom, still remains a mystery with regard to all its most important doctrines, so that more than six hundred churches are now disputing about what it teaches; and the difficulty is still increasing by the uprising of new churches with new creeds and new interpretations of the Bible.

Let the reader observe the striking difference in the harmony of views which prevail in the various scientific societies throughout the country and those of the churches, and he will discover at once that there is no science in our religion. Take, for example, the astronomical societies. They are all perfectly agreed with respect to what the great Bible of nature teaches concerning that science. There is no contention and no dispute with respect to the doctrines and principles of that grand revelation of nature, because they are all susceptible of proof and demonstration. Were it otherwise— were the amateurs and students of that science divided into six hundred conflicting factions, like the churches, each with a different theory with respect to what it teaches—one contending that the sun rises in the east, another that it rises in the west; one arguing that the sun is the revolving center of our solar system, another contending that the earth is; one teaching that the starry orbs which roll their massive forms through infinite space are mere wax tapers stuck in the azure vault to light this pigmy planet, or mere peep-holes for Gods to look out upon our world; and one arguing that they were all knocked up in a single day out of that singular substance called *nothing*, and another that they are the outgrowth of other worlds, or have existed from all eternity.

Had the author, who was once a member of one of those societies, observed such a chaos of confusion and conflict of opinion, he would have discovered at once that nothing is really known about the science of astronomy—that what is called such is nothing but a jargon of conflicting dogmas and wild speculations. Hence, he would not have remained with them a single day after making such a discovery. Having learned that the churches are in such a condition, he withdrew, and has not been a member of one of those discordant institutions for many years. He considers it a waste of time to be a member of a religious body that only increases this difficulty and confusion. He has but one life to live, and does not wish to waste that in a mere wild-goose chase after religious speculations that can never be settled. Why fool away our lives in chasing theological butterflies that can never be caught, when there is a hundred times as much to be learned within the domain of positive science as can be acquired in a lifetime, that is practically useful and calculated to enlarge the boundaries of our knowledge and elevate us to a higher plane of happiness, while the occupancy of the mind with theological dogmas is only calculated to "lead to bewilder, and dazzle to blind"?

Yes, we shall make more progress in learning our duties, in learning "what we must do in order to be saved," if we would look about us and forward, and endeavor to read the great Bible or book of nature illuminated by the rays of science, in which there are no contradictions, no confusion, and where we may learn of, and, in our finite measure, grow into and partake of the attributes of the Infinite Father, instead of looking backward and searching amongst the jarring contradictions, the creeds, dogmas, myths, and traditions of the past, covered as they are with the mold and dust of ages.

CHAPTER 53

THE THREE CHRISTIAN PLANS OF SALVATION

" "Without the shedding of blood there can be no remission for sin." The doctrine of this text constitutes the basis of all the plans of salvation which various ages and nations have founded on dead Gods and living devils. Nearly every religious nation known to history cherished the belief that God is an irritable, irascible, and vindictive being, subject to fits or paroxysms of anger; and when in this furious and unbalanced and ungovernable state of mind, he frequently poured out his vengeance upon his disobedient children, often subjecting them to the most terrible penalties in this life, and then threatened them with a still worse doom in the next. To avert this direful calamity—at least so far as it appertained to the life beyond the grave—most religious nations invented schemes which came to be known as systems or plans of salvation. The original model seems to have been furnished by the Hindus, and borrowed from them by the Egyptians, and thence transmitted to the Persians and Grecians, and was finally incorporated into the Christian system, and now constitutes what is known as "the Christian plan of salvation." Each system was composed of three cardinal principles: 1. the primeval innocency and moral perfection of man; 2. his temptation and downfall into a state of moral depravity; and 3. his restoration to the divine favor by the voluntary sacrifice and atoning offering of a God (one of the three members of the trinity). These three cardinal doctrines constitute what Christians denominate "the great and glorious plan of salvation," and on which a thousand volumes have been written, and ten thousand sermons are preached every year. As it professes to point out the road, and the only road, to heaven, it merits a somewhat critical examination. We will therefore analyze and examine its several principles to see whether it has a true moral basis, or is in strict accordance with the principles of natural justice.

The first proposition assumes that man primordially occupied the highest moral plane of moral perfection, and that all his animal propensities were held in strict abeyance to his moral convictions, and that he consequently led a morally pure, perfect, and holy life. The first and most important query to which this proposition or assumption gives rise is, Can it be shown to be true? Can it be sustained by either the principles of natural or moral science, or by the facts of history comprised in man's practical life? Now, it so happens that facts have been accumulating for thousands of years, gathered from almost every department of science and history, to prove and demonstrate that the proposition is entirely untenable—that it is not true. Geology alone demonstrates its falsity. It has written its negative verdict upon a thousand rocks beneath our feet.

These rocks contain the fossiliferous and organic remains of the early and primitive inhabitants of the earth, and indicate the order of man's moral and intellectual development; for as each successive layer or stratum of fossiliferous rocks, in which the organic remains of man are found, marks a distinct period in his history, and the growth of his moral and intellectual brain is found in all cases to correspond to the age and growth of these strata, the question is thus settled and demonstrated by the facts of geological science. As the older the rocks, the more remote period they mark in man's history; and the more remote the period to which it is thus traced, the lower the position in the scale of moral and intellectual development his organic remains prove him to have occupied. The question is thus reduced to a scientific problem, which admits of no disproof or refutation. It is, then, a settled scientific truth that the further we trace the past history of man by the footprints of geological science, the nearer he approaches to the condition of an animal—when he was almost totally devoid of intellectual perceptions and moral feelings, and was consequently a victim to his lusts and animal propensities. When, then, was his moral purity and perfection, or his angelic holiness? The doctrine is thus shown to be false and fabulous. All the skulls of the primitive races that have been found by geological research show that man, in his first rude type, had scarcely any moral brain; and the history of the race at that period shows that he possessed a corresponding low, weak, defective moral character, so much so that he could scarcely be considered a moral, accountable being. To talk, then, of his occupying a high moral plane at that early period, is to contradict every principle of science and every page of history. His animal propensities and selfish feelings must have held complete sway over the whole empire of mind for thousands, if not for millions, of years, so that his moral status was but little above that of the brute. The facts of science and history to prove this proposition are abundant; but as we are compelled to constantly observe the most rigid rules of brevity, we can only find space for one or two proof-illustrations.

Human skulls have been found embedded in the rocks of Gibraltar with retreating foreheads, prognathous jaws, and frontal bones an inch thick, and the receptacles for both the moral and intellectual brain very small—all of which denote very weak moral and intellectual minds, and a preponderance of the animal feelings; and geologists have decided that sixty-five thousand years must have elapsed since those bones and skulls were deposited in those rocks. Hundreds of similar facts have been gathered by geologists, and might be cited, but this one case is amply sufficient, and furnishes as conclusive proof as a thousand could do that the primitive inhabitants of the earth were on a low mental status, and that they were greatly inferior in morals and intellect to the least-developed minds of the present age; and consequently man's course has been upward, and not downward. There has been no falling, but a gradual rising, in both the moral and intellectual scale. It shows that man was at the very foot of the ladder at the commencement of his moral and intellectual career—that he was flat on his back in the ditch; and, consequently, there was no lower place to fall to. The first proposition, then, is shown to be false—that man originally occupied a high moral position, and that he was in a state of moral purity and perfection.

The second proposition—that of man's fall and moral degeneracy—is likewise shown to be false by the same facts; for, if he was never in a state of moral purity and perfection, then it is evident he never could have fallen from such a state. It would be superfluous, then, to attempt to show that man never fell, after having shown that he never occupied a high moral position to fall from. He could only fall in the sense the Scotchman did, who stated he fell up a well sixty feet in a bucket. It is settled, then, geologically, scientifically, and demonstrably, that man never fell in a moral sense.

We will now proceed to present what is presumed and assumed to be the scriptural exposition of man's original condition and fall.

We are told in the first chapter of Genesis that, when God had completed the work of creation, he pronounced it all not only good, but "very good," which indicates a state of perfection; but it appears the words were hardly out of his mouth until a very bad being, called a serpent, came crawling into the garden on his back, to furnish practical evidence that Moses' God was mistaken in having pronounced everything so "very good." We have to assume that he came into the garden of paradise on his back, because the reverse mode of traveling was not adopted until after the fall; that is, until after he was doomed to that mode of travel as a punishment for having tempted and beguiled Mother Eve to try her new molars and incisors on some fruit (supposed to be pippins) hanging on a tree, which, it appears, underwent the rapid process of blossoming, and bearing fruit that ripened in a few hours after it was planted. And thus the serpent, although a senseless reptile, committed the first sin—the first violation of moral law.

The first question that naturally arises here is, Why was not the fence around the garden of paradise made snake-proof, so as to keep his snakeship out? Or shall we presume the gate was left open, and that he entered in that way? This, however, would indicate a blundering carelessness on the part of Jehovah, which we dare not assume. Another question arising here is, Why was not the angel with the flaming sword, which, we are told, was placed over the door or gateway to guard it from intruders—why was he not placed there sooner? Why was he not placed there before the fall, instead of after, so as to bruise the serpent's bead, or behead him, on his attempting to enter? To place a guard over the gate after the Devil had entered, and caused the effectual downfall and ruin of the human race, and thus perpetrated all the mischief he could, looks very much like "locking the stable-door after the horse is stolen."

And the query also arises here, Are we not compelled to conclude that Moses' God was a little shortsighted, and rather hasty in his conclusion that everything was so *very good*," when the serpent proved to be so *very bad*? The only way to escape this dilemma is to assume that God did not make him, and that consequently he was not included in the original invoice of goods and chattels which were pronounced "very good"; but in adopting this expedient, we only leap "from the frying pan into the fire": the assumption does not do away with the difficulty, because it is declared that God made everything that was made. Hence, it is evident that, if he were made at all, the God of Moses made him; and, if he were not made, then it follows that he is a self-created or self-existent being, and invested with all the attributes, powers, and prerogatives of God Almighty himself. And thus we would place two omniscient, omnipotent and omnipresent beings on the throne of the universe, which is not only a moral contradiction, but a moral impossibility. We will assume, then, for the sake of the argument, that God did create the Devil—an assumption, however, which brings us into still greater difficulty.

Christ says, by way of illustrating human character, that "a tree is known by its fruit. A good tree can not bring forth evil fruit; neither can a corrupt tree bring forth good fruit." In this case, God the Creator is the tree and the Devil the fruit; and one is good, and the other evil. Here, then, is a good tree bearing evil fruit, which seems to furnish the most positive proof that Christ's moral axiom, "A good tree can not bear evil fruit," is false. There is evidently something wrong somewhere in this moral picture. Either Christ was mistaken, or the Christian world is wrong in assuming the existence of this omnipotent and independent being of an opposite character. It presents us with a moral paradox that no theologian in Christendom has yet been able to solve. We are compelled to assume that both beings are good, or both evil, and that they cooperate and act in harmony; or that a good God made a wicked Devil—i.e., "a good tree brought forth evil fruit"; or else we must reject the Christian system of salvation, and assume the existence of but one invisible and Almighty Being, who orders everything for the best. The absurdity we have just noticed is but one of many, both of a moral and of a scientific nature, equally senseless and foolish, which we find involved in the Christian plan of salvation. We will notice a few others.

According to Christian theology and Christian logic, all evil or sin that is committed is prompted by an evil tempter. Scientists and Harmonialists account for such actions by tracing them to the abnormal or perverted action of natural faculties, powers, and propensities, which, in their healthy state, are productive of good alone, and not evil; and thus making them the product of the mind itself in its unhealthy condition. But Christian theologians tell us it is a separate, evil genius operating in the "inner man" which does all the mischief and prompts the possessor to the commission of sin. But this assumption gives rise to endless difficulties, some of which we will state in the form of questions. We would ask, then, in the first place, if all sin or evil is prompted by an evil tempter, how came the original tempter himself to fall victim to sin? Who put him up to it, seeing there was no tempter in existence but himself? In such a dilemma, we must either assume that Divine Goodness was his tempter, or that he tempted himself. To make him his own tempter would involve us in an egregious absurdity, equal to that of Guy Faux lifting himself by the straps of his boots; and to make God the tempter would relieve his Satanic Majesty of all responsibility in the case, and make God alone accountable for the sin, and also the author of sin. This, however, they do by other assumptions. Books enough have been written to form a library by orthodox writers in the attempt to rescue their God from the odium and responsibility of being the author of sin; but under their system of theology, he cannot escape the stigma.

No sensible construction of any orthodox system can save God from the authorship and responsibility of sin. They all teach that God created man, and man committed sin. This makes God the author of sin, either directly or indirectly, in spite of all the logic and lore that ever has been, or ever can be, made use of to escape the conclusion; for even if it could be successfully shown that God did not implant in man the desire or inclination to commit sin, and he derived this inclination from the devil, it cannot be denied that God is responsible for allowing the Devil to exist, or, if this could be denied, would still be responsible for leaving man so morally weak as to be overcome by the Devil. If he is infinite in goodness and infinite in power, as they teach, then, if he did not fortify man with sufficient moral strength to resist all temptation to sin, the act of sinning becomes his own. No logic and no sophistry can resist this conclusion. It is now a settled principle in moral ethics, that what any being does through an agent he does himself, and is as responsible for it as if he performed the act with his own hands *de facto*. If, then, God created the Devil, and he turned out to be the agent of evil or sin, it was only a roundabout and indirect mode of performing the act himself. This is a logical syllogism that defies the ingenuity of the orthodox world to overturn. The most plausible plea in the case is that the Devil was originally a good being, but fell from grace. According to several Bibles, he is a fallen angel; but it is evident that he could not fall unless he possessed some inherent moral weakness that caused him to fall. A perfect being could not fall. It is, then, self-evident that inherent moral weakness was implanted in him by his Creator. This would make his Creator responsible for his moral weakness, which caused him to fall. And thus the question is settled logically, philosophically, and morally.

We will now proceed to examine the nature of the diabolical act that caused the downfall of the human race—"the original sin," as it is called. We are told it consisted in eating some fruit which grew on a tree God himself had planted in the Garden of Eden, and forbidden to be used. Why it was interdicted from use is not explained in the Christian Bible; but it is rendered plain by the relation of the same story in other Bibles.

In the Persian version it is stated that the tree bore the twelve apples of immortality, and that the Devil, in the shape of a monkey, guarded the tree to prevent the *genus homo* from partaking of the fruit; as tradition had taught them that, by so doing, man would become immortal like the Gods, and live forever. This the Gods deprecated, as they allowed no other beings to become equal to them, and hence had the tree guarded to save the immortal fruit. But the Christian Bible is entirely silent as to the purpose of planting the tree, or forbidding its fruit to be eaten. It cuts short many stories which we find more amplified and in fuller detail in older Bibles.

No reflecting or unbiased mind can see any wisdom or any sense in permitting or causing a tree to bear fruit, and then decreeing that it shall all go to waste by interdicting it from being used, as Jehovah is represented as having done. Certainly, no sensible God would act thus. And if Adam and Eve were "very good," as he himself declared them to be, must we not consider it an ungodly and a tantalizing act to place fruit within their reach, and then forbid them to touch or taste it? It looks more like the act of a fiend than that of a kind and loving father who, we would naturally suppose, would be so pleased with his newly made children that he would do everything possible to please them and make them happy. If the fruit was an improper article of diet, it should have been placed out of sight, or rendered unpalatable, so that they should not desire to eat it. If Adam and Eve were very good beings, and God both *infinitely* good and *infinitely* wise, he could and should have placed them in a condition from which they could not fall, and in which they would have possessed no inclination to do anything wrong. I can see no possible benefit to arise from surrounding them with temptations to commit an act that would ruin them eternally, and their posterity after them. The plea is sometimes urged that it was morally necessary for the original progenitors of the race to possess the power and liability to sin, in order to make them free agents. Free agents, indeed! That is certainly a novel kind of free agency, which not only makes a man free to commit an act which it is known will lead to his own destruction and the ruin of the entire human race, but implants in him the inclination to do it. This is free agency run mad.

We will illustrate the principle. A mother sees her little child approaching an open well, and turns heedlessly away, and lets the child rush into the jaws of death; and, when reproved for the act, she raises the plea, "Oh, I did not want to interfere with its free agency!" Here is the Christian logic of free agency put in practice. God is represented as setting traps around the human family, knowing they will be caught; and this is called moral freedom or free agency. The rat enjoys the same kind of moral freedom when he creeps beneath the deadfall in quest of food, and takes the chance of misplacing the triggers. There is no free agency in any rational sense in furnishing a man with a rope to hang himself, knowing that it would be used for that purpose; and this the orthodox God has done for the whole human family, so that we are all now suspended on the gallows of total depravity and moral death.

THE FALL AND CURSE

We will now notice some of the "awful consequences" said to have resulted from eating the forbidden fruit—"the *world-wide curse*" pronounced upon the human race as the penalty for that act. Several distinct effects are enumerated as consequences of the deed. But a critical investigation of the matter in the light of present age will show that, instead of being curses, they are blessings, and have added greatly to the enjoyment and happiness of the human family; and, consequently, we should now be in a more deplorable condition than we are if "our primitive parents" had heeded the divine interdiction, and let the fruit alone. We will look briefly at some of the consequences, and observe whether they have really turned out to be curses or not.

The first effect produced by the act of Father Adam and Mother Eve eating the forbidden fruit appears to have been that of opening their eyes so that they could see and distinguish objects around them. It certainly was a very singular way of cursing human beings to grant them the glorious boon of vision, and thus relieve them from the necessity of groping their way through life. As to the gift of sight being a curse, there are thousands of human beings now in the world who would like to be cursed in that way—those who were born blind, or have lost their sight. "The rest of mankind" would consider it to be a great misfortune or curse to be placed in the original condition of Adam and Eve in this respect. We must admit, then, that this *curse* turned out to be a blessing, and that we are indebted to the serpent-devil for it; and, consequently, he should not have been doomed to dine on dust as a penalty for conferring this blessing upon the human race.

The second commandment growing out of the act of eating the interdicted fruit appears to have been the acquisition of a knowledge of good and evil; that is, the power of distinguishing between good and evil. But this, so far from being a curse, was an inestimable and indispensable blessing; for, without the attainment of this knowledge, they could not have known that any act was evil, and hence would have been liable to plunge into all manner of crime, pillage, debauchery, murder, etc., until they effected the entire extinction of the human race. The acquisition, then, of the knowledge of the moral difference between good and evil was an invaluable blessing, and no curse at all; and, having been brought about through the agency of the serpent-devil, he should have the credit of it.

The third effect produced by plucking and eating the prescribed fruit was the discovery that they were naked. Why they had not made the discovery before is a mystery of godliness. The people of the present age, although presumed to be in a state of degeneracy, if not total depravity, do not require the use of their eyes to know when they are naked; but it seems that, before the fall in a state of moral perfection, such knowledge could only be acquired through the optic nerves. Hence, "the perfection of our first parents," so often spoken of and lauded by the orthodox world, must simply have been the perfection of ignorance; and it is true, if their history is true, that they were most consummately ignorant until they were enlightened by the serpent. They were too ignorant to clothe themselves. God Almighty had to forsake the throne of heaven and come down to earth, to make garments of goatskins for them, before they could be sufficiently habilitated to go abroad, or admit company. Their two sons, however, were the only company they were permitted to enjoy at that time.

One of these turned out to be a murderer; and, having killed his only brother, he fled to the land of Nod, and married a wife, although, according to the "inspired account," his mother was the only woman then living. It seems strange, under such circumstances, that he should marry a wife when there were no women to make wives of. After he had killed his brother, and repented of it, a mark was set upon him, that "whosoever found him should not slay him." But how could this "whosoever" know what the mark meant? And who was this "whosoever," when he himself had killed off the whole human race, excepting his father and mother? And we presume they would not be likely to slay their own and only son if there were no mark set upon him to prevent it.

Up to this period, the conduct of the serpent-devil had been very respectful, and every act performed had resulted in a direct benefit to the human family. Even his conduct towards Mother Eve seems to have been marked by politeness, for he served her with fruit before partaking of it himself. For these good acts he deserved the use of his legs, which, we must presume, he lost by the fall, when he transgressed, fell, and was cursed; and a part of this curse consisted in taking his legs from him, and compelling him to crawl. But it appears his legs were afterwards restored to him; for, when he came with the sons of God to attend a picnic at the house of Job, and was asked where he came from, replied, "From walking to and fro in the earth." This feat of walking he could not very well have performed without legs. Hence, we naturally conclude they had grown out again, or had been restored to him in some way, notwithstanding it had been decreed he should "crawl on his belly all the days of his life." The whole story of the serpent, as presented in Genesis, is a borrowed and laughable fiction; and the reader will excuse us for presenting it in that light.

We have shown that the violation of the command of Jehovah to Adam and Eve not to partake of the fruit of the tree of knowledge, so far from being attended with any evil result, gave rise to several important benefits, and was therefore a praiseworthy act. And if they had carried the act of disobedience a little further, and plucked and eaten of the fruit from the "tree of life" also, it would, according to the context, have produced results still more important, as it would have immortalized their physical bodies, and prevented the ingress of death into the world; and we should have been spared that dreadful calamity. But a worse calamity would have overtaken us; for it is easily seen that, in the course of a few centuries, our planet would be overstocked with inhabitants. And, as a part of Adam's curse consisted in being doomed to eat the ground (see Gen. iii. 17), it follows that, if none of his posterity had died, they would have become so numerous in the course of time as to have eaten up all the ground (there being nothing else for them to eat), and leave not a mole-hill of *terra firma* for a living being to stand upon. The conception is really ludicrous, and yet a legitimate inference from the story which presents us with a series of laughable ideas from beginning to end.

We will now notice the sentence pronounced upon the several participants in this fabled rebellion against the divine government, and observe how, or to what extent, they were realized. Adam, Eve, and the snake were culprits arraigned at the bar under charge of being rebels; and, al! being found guilty, a sentence was pronounced upon each separately. We will examine them in their order.

The first part of Adam's curse consisted in being doomed to die: "The day thou eatest thereof, thou shalt surely die" (Gen. ii. 17). The serpent, however, took the liberty to contradict and counteract the sentence, and told him he should not die, but that partaking of the fruit would make him "wise as the Gods, knowing good and evil." Now, the first question that arises here is, Who told the truth in the case—Jehovah or "the father of lies"? In the eighth chapter of Genesis we read, "All the days of Adam were nine hundred and thirty years, and he begat sons and daughters." It will be seen, then, that he did not die in "the day thereof," nor the year thereof, nor the century thereof; so it appears the serpent told the truth, and Moses' God told the falsehood, or was mistaken. Hundreds of Christian writers and commentators have racked their brains to find some plausible mode of disposing of these difficulties. The most specious one they have resorted to is that of assigning the text a spiritual signification, and alleging that it was a spiritual death that was intended in this case. But the text does not say so and the context shows it was not so: for it is declared, "Dust thou art, and unto dust shalt thou return" (Gen. iii. 19), which shows it was not spiritual but physical death that was meant; and this did not take place for more than nine hundred years after the sentence was pronounced.

The second part of Adam's curse consisted in being driven out of the garden, and compelled to engage in agricultural pursuits; that is, he was sentenced to earn his bread by the sweat of his face. (See Gen. iii. 23). But the experience of nearly the whole human race, from that period to the present time, proves that the sweating part of the operation is no curse at all, but a real blessing, for no person in warm climates can enjoy good health without perspiring occasionally; and as for labor being a curse, because said to have been pronounced upon Adam as a penalty for transgression, the experience of all who have tried it, and the present condition of the civilized world, proclaim it to be untrue. Indeed, we must consider it a very fortunate circumstance that he was driven out of the garden and compelled to embark in agricultural pursuits, not only on account of such employments being conducive to health, but because the very existence of human life depends upon it in all civilized countries. It is the source whence we derive all our food, all our clothing, and nearly all the comforts of life. No, it is laziness, not labor, that curses the race; and the most accursed set of beings are the drones, the soft-handed gentry, who are almost as afraid of a hoe, axe, or spade as they are of the measles or smallpox, having been erroneously taught that labor is a curse.

The Three Plans of Salvation

The third item in Adam's curse consisted in being doomed to eat the ground: "Cursed is the ground for thy sake, and in sorrow shalt thou eat of it all the days of thy life" (Gen. iii. 17); but we have never seen any report of either Adam or any of his posterity eating the ground, or making it an article of diet. It will be observed, then, that no part of the sentence pronounced upon Adam turned out to be a curse, but, when realized at all, was realized as a blessing.

The sentence pronounced upon the woman was also of a threefold character. In the first place, she was doomed to "bring forth children in sorrow" (Gen. iii. 16). And her posterity, we are told, inherited the curse, and must suffer in the same way; but the history of the human family shows many individuals, and whole nations in some cases, have never suffered this affliction. It is well known that the mothers of some of the African tribes, also some of the tribes of Americans, never suffer in childbirth. Hence, it will be seen that the curse in the general sense implied by the text is a failure in this case also.

The second punishment to which woman was to be subjected was that of being ruled over by her husband. This portion of her curse, we must confess, has not been an entire failure. Many women, even in civilized countries, are not only ruled over, but tyrannized over, by their husbands. Yet this state of things has by no means been universal. On the contrary, in many cases, woman has been the ruling party; and, in some instances, they have not merely ruled their own husbands, but all the husbands in the nation. Queen Mary, Queen Anne, and Queen Victoria, and many others, are examples of this kind; and then there have been thousands of women in all ages and countries who never had any husbands. Consequently, the curse is a failure in their cases. The curse of husband-dominion, then, has not fallen upon woman as a sex.

There was to be enmity between the seed of the woman and the seed of the serpent (i.e., their offspring) as the third part of woman's curse, but we find no evidence that this part of the curse has ever been fulfilled. We observe no more enmity between men and serpents than between men and other noxious reptiles and ravenous beasts. How much enmity exists between the Hindu juggler and the serpent that twines around his arm and neck, and crawls through his bosom? We may be told in reply that it is not the common serpent that is referred to here, but the serpent-devil that beguiled Eve; but we do not learn that his Devilish Majesty ever had any offspring. So this part of the curse, in a general sense, is a failure also.

293

THE CURSE OF THE SERPENT

The curse pronounced upon the serpent was of a twofold character. He was doomed to crawl upon his belly. How he traveled previous to that period we have no means of knowing, as revelation is silent on this momentous subject. He must have crawled on his back, or hopped on his head or tail—either of which we should consider a much more difficult mode of travel than that inflicted on him by the curse. I can see no curse or punishment in an animal or reptile traveling in its natural way, and by the easiest mode known in the whole animal kingdom. To make a curse of his mode of travel, he should have been turned the other side up, so that, while wiggling or wriggling along on his back, his eyes and mouth would get full of dust and mud. This would have been much more like a punishment—a more real and sensible curse than his present mode of traveling.

The second mode of punishing the serpent was to compel him to eat dust as an article of diet, but some difficulty must have arisen in attempting to comply with the injunction. When the ground is saturated with water, he would have to take a meal occasionally of mud, which would not be more nutrition than dust, and would not be fulfilling the law. But it is needless to speculate. It is evident he does not subsist in that way, but, like the other culprits, escaped the penalties or punishments due to his crime.

I have now examined all the items of that curse—eight in number—said to have been visited upon Adam, Eve, and the serpent, and what do they all amount to? Not one of them has been realized as such; but most of those that were practically realized turned out to be real blessings. And yet they have been proclaimed to the world by the clergy as the missiles of wrath hurled upon a guilty world for the sin of rebellion against the divine government. Whether any of these so-called "visitations of divine displeasure" were designed as penalties for disobedience or not, it is evident they have not in a moral sense been realized, or had any beneficial effect whatever. And we must conclude that it was rather short-sighted in Moses' God to attempt to bring his children into obedience by pronouncing curses upon them. He himself virtually acknowledges it; for, after having tried these expedients and found they availed nothing, he became so discouraged that he said, "It grieved him to the heart" (see Gen. vi. 6) that he had made so rebellious a creature as man.

THE SECOND SCHEME OF REDEMPTION

The God of Moses, after having tried the expedient of cursing his children—the cunning workmanship of his hands—and grieved over the failure for more than a thousand years—he (the God of Moses) came to the conclusion to try another expedient. He concluded to select a few of the choicest specimens of the *genus homo* in order to preserve the race, and start anew with some of the best stock or material that could be found.

Accordingly, old drunken Noah—the most righteous man that could be found amongst the millions of the inhabitants of the globe—was chosen to build a schooner, yacht, canoe, or some kind of a vessel, called an *ark*, into which he stowed millions of birds, bipeds, and insects of all species and all sizes, from the ostrich and condor down to fleas, flies, mosquitoes, spiders, and bedbugs; and millions of animals and reptiles of all kinds and all sizes, from the mammoth and the mastodon down to skunks, lizards, snakes, gophers, and grasshoppers; together with himself and family of eight persons, and food sufficient to last them ten months while in the ark, and several years afterwards, as we must presume was done from the fact that it is declared that the waters destroyed every living thing upon the face of the earth. And it must have required several years to restock it with grass and animals to serve as food for the granivorous, herbivorous, and carnivorous species; this would make a bulk sufficient to fill forty such vessels, and a weight sufficient to sink the whole British navy. And all this living mass of respiring and perspiring animals were dependent upon one little window twelve inches by fifteen for light and air, which had to be kept shut most of the time to keep out the rain. If some giraffe or cameleopard had been disposed to monopolize the window by thrusting his head out, we can easily imagine what would have been the fatal consequence to this living, breathing cargo. And then we have to entertain the thought that lions and lambs, wolves and sheep, dogs and skunks, hawks and chickens, owls and doves, cats and mice, men and monkeys, all ate and slept together in immediate juxtaposition like a band of brothers. Perhaps more glorious times never were realized since "the sons of God shouted for joy."

But it appears the whole thing turned out to be a failure. The drowning process was no more effectual in producing the desired reformation than the first scheme that had been tried; for, only a few hundred years after the culmination of this world-drowning experiment, Moses' God is represented as crying out in despair, "The imagination of man's heart is evil, and only evil continually." This was certainly a deplorable and disheartening state of things witnessed so soon after it had been presumed that all the bad folks had been drowned; but it appears that, if all that class had been drowned, there would have been no human beings left. David, therefore, was probably right when he exclaims, "There is none that doeth good, no not one" (Ps. xiv. 3).

THE THIRD AND LAST PLAN OF SALVATION

The atonement was the third and last resort. The third experiment in any case generally ends the siege whether successful or unsuccessful. After a few thousand years more had elapsed of grief, anger, and disappointment in the practical history of Moses' God, he ventured to try one more experiment in the effort to get his people on the right track—not so much, however, to get them in the right way as to have his own wrath appeased. In this way he sanctions the greatest crime ever perpetrated by the hand of man—that of murder. God the "Father," in order to cancel the sins of his disobedient and rebellious children, and mitigate his own wrath, is represented as proposing to have his "only-begotten son" killed—at least, as consenting to the act. This looks like "doing evil that good may come of it," which is a very objectionable principle of moral ethics, according to Paul. How the commission of the greatest of all sins can do anything towards reforming other sins, or how the punishment of an innocent being can do anything towards atoning for the sins of the guilty, presents us with a moral problem, shocking both to our common sense and common reason. If the Father's anger could not be appeased or his vengeance satisfied without the perpetration of a horrible murder, and the knowledge that some victim had died a slow and agonizing death, we are forced to the conclusion that he is a cruel and revengeful God, and that his passions overrule his love of justice and his paternal regard for his son. But it appears that this last experiment, whether right or wrong, was attended with as complete a failure as the two preceding ones; and yet it assumes to be the best that "Infinite Wisdom" could devise. And the resources of divine knowledge and skill were apparently exhausted when this scheme culminated. And yet it also failed, according to the admission of its own friends and ardent supporters (the clergy); for they tell us that, notwithstanding all the schemes and systems that Omniscience and Infinite Prescience could devise to save man, he does not get saved: at least but few are saved, and they have to "work out their own salvation with fear and trembling."

Nineteen-twentieths of the human family, the clergy tell us, are still traveling on "the broad road," and are finally lost, notwithstanding all the labored experiments and expedients of omniscient or Jehovahistic wisdom to save them. With this view of the case, the thought is suggested that it was hardly worthwhile to have gone to the trouble and expense of fitting up a heaven for the few that are saved. It certainly "doesn't pay." And this conclusion is the more forcible in view of the fact that it must be rather a lonesome place, and consequently not a very desirable home or situation to live in; for we are told it is "a house of many mansions," "and yet few there be that find the strait and narrow road" leading to it. Hence, we may conclude that many of the rooms or mansions are empty. Such a lonesome heaven could not be congenial or adapted to any class of saints but monks and hermits.

We have now briefly examined the three plans of salvation that lie at the formulation of the Christian religion, and shown that they are all failures according to their own witnesses. In view of this fact, we cannot wonder that Moses' God is represented as saying that he repented for having made man, and that it grieved him to the heart (Gen. vi. 6). Such a series of signal failures is enough to discourage even a saint or a God.

CHAPTER 54

THE TRUE RELIGION DEFINED

True religion sees God in everything, reads his scriptures on every page of Nature's open Bible, and feels him in the inspiration of the soul. It calls God father, not king; Christ a brother, not a redeemer. It loves all men, but fears no God. Its God is not a tyrant, but a loving father. It looks upon Jesus Christ as a truly good man, but not a God; as a noble, loving, benevolent being, but endowed with human frailties. It considers him a martyr to truth and right, but not a just victim to his father's wrath, or the just object of a bloody sacrifice. It regards the laws of nature as sufficient, if diligently studied and strictly observed, to serve as a guide for man's earthly life without any special revelation. It holds that man's natural love of goodness, justice, mercy, and honesty is capable of endless expansion and augmentation. It walks by the light of science. The many grand truths of the age, developed by the onward march of mind, form its infallible laws, and constitute its living virtues. It uses reason for a lamp, and an enlightened intellect for a guide. It ties no martyr to the stake, piles the faggots around no heretics. It issues no dogmas, no bulls, no canons, and hangs man's salvation upon no infallible revelation. Christians say, Give us a better revelation; Christ said, "Cease to do evil, and [then] learn to do well." All wrong and hurtful institutions should be pulled down or abandoned, and trust to finding better ones. Remove the weeds from the soil, and a healthy and useful vegetation will spring up in their place. The true religion grants perfect freedom to all human beings; leaves human thought as free and unfettered as the wind, as free as the rays of sunlight which fall upon every hill and every valley, and rest upon the bosom of the deep.

True religion does not regard God as a personal monarch, governing the universe by the caprices of an angry and fickle mind, but as the living, moving, all-pervading, self-sustaining, energizing, vivifying power which moves and sustains the machinery of the whole universe, and controls, by a concatenation of laws, the myriads of worlds which move in majestic grandeur through infinite space, and causes them to act in concert and harmony without a discordant jar. It does not write its inspiration and revelation in a dead language or unintelligible Hebrew, but in living characters, which all can read and understand. It indulges in no spirit of bigotry, consigns no man or woman to endless torment, never talks of total depravity or original sin. It is a natural and godlike religion, calculated to satisfy the deep, unutterable longings of the *soul*, and bring blessings and happiness to all who live up to its requirements. It is a tree bearing the fruit of practical righteousness. It does not teach that all of God's truth is shut up in a printed book. It knows no sects, no creeds, and no thirty-nine articles.

The True Religion

It does not pilot the pilgrim through life with a dark lantern, nor search for living truths among the religious mummies of the dark ages, but regales itself upon the living truths of the age. Its devotees do not require temples made with hands in which to worship the Father. It does not require holy houses, holy days, or holy sacraments. It recommends all to search for truth as a pearl of great price. It teaches all to worship God by a life of practical goodness, and by cherishing kindly feelings toward every human being. This is a religion that will impart true pleasure in life, and afford sure comfort in a dying hour.

THE RELIGION FOR THIS AGE

It is a religion founded upon truth and goodness—a religion freed from the old, worn-out, superstitious, Oriental myths. The people are becoming too enlightened to tolerate them much longer; they are becoming tired of being fed on the stale food of past ages; they have been kept in a state of spiritual stagnation long enough. They are becoming too intelligent to wish to listen to old mythological doctrines that have been preached by Christians for centuries. We want a religion better adapted to the wants of the age. We want a religion that will furnish better nourishment for man's moral and spiritual nature—a religion calculated to develop true manhood, instead of repressing it; a religion whose doctrines do not conflict with established principles of science; a religion which our moral sense does not condemn, and against which our reason will not rebel. We want a religion that puts no walls between reason and revelation, and forms no creeds and no barriers to the spontaneous outgrowth of every faculty of the soul. We want a religion that does not require men and women to be born several times before they can be honest, truthful, and reliable, or "good enough to enter the kingdom of heaven." We want a religion that acknowledges no law but truth and justice—a religion that will tolerate no wrong, and forgive no sin. We want a religion whose bond is love, whose temple is truth, whose altar is a guiltless conscience, and whose creed is a life of practical righteousness. We want a religion which will teach us to cherish kindly feelings toward all mankind, and which will prompt us to labor to spread flowers instead of thorns in the pathway of everyone with whom we come in contact, and thus make them better and happier beings; for this is the true end of all true religion and all true preaching.

> "For modes of faith let zealous bigots fight:
> He can't be wrong whose life is in the right."

The Bible of Bibles

We want a religion that will estimate men and women for what they are, and not for what they believe—a religion that does not measure their moral worth by their creeds, but by their practical lives. We want a religion that will banish all creeds and mind-enslaving dogmas from the earth, and substitute in their place brotherly love and goodness. We want a religion that will do away with ignorance and poverty, that will labor to prevent anyone from suffering for the needful things of life, and that will bind all together in ties of universal brotherhood. In fine, we want a religion that will make truth and love and true practical righteousness the pole-star of every man and woman who embrace it. This is the religion we need; this is the religion for the age; this is the religion that would and will banish all unrighteousness from the earth, and elevate the race to a higher plane than they ever have or ever can attain under their soul-cramping, creed-bound religions; this is the religion the author is laboring for, and has earnestly desired for twenty-three years to see established among "all nations, tongues, kindred, and people." This religion is not derived from any Bible, but is an outgrowth of man's moral and religious nature, as all true religions in all countries have been. A religion derived from this source would prompt us to labor daily to promote the happiness of our neighbors and fellow beings generally, instead of studying every hour of our lives to practically rob them, as do most men in civilized countries, including nearly all Christian professors, who are *positively forbidden* by their Bible and lawgiver (Christ) to *lay up any treasure* on earth; yet it is their constant study how to draw all the money possible out of the pockets of their neighbors, with but little regard to their wants, necessities, or even sufferings, that they may die in the midst of wealth. It is a strange, yet almost universal, infatuation that the inauguration of the true religion will banish from the earth.

300

CHAPTER 55

"ALL SCRIPTURE IS GIVEN BY INSPIRATION OF GOD"

If this statement be true, then God must have "led a very busy life," for the world is literally loaded down with scriptures. There are not less than eleven hundred and fifty pious effusions that may come under this head, and at least that number claiming to have originated from the fountain of divine inspiration. But the religious sects and religious orders will tell us that but one of those eleven hundred and fifty scriptures is the product of the Divine Mind, and but one of them has received the seal and sanction of Almighty God. Then our salvation hangs by a very slender thread, for no rule has been furnished us by Infinite Wisdom by which we can distinguish which is the spurious and which the genuine, or which is the scripture given by inspiration of God. All pious nations have had their scriptures in profusion. Let us hold a court, and hear the testimony of some of the witnesses with respect to the validity of their respective claims.

Here is a Hindu, a pious soul of the Brahmin order. Well, brother, we wish you to tell us whether you know anything about "the scriptures given by inspiration of God." "Most certainly I do." Well, where and what are they? "Why, after existing in the mind of the great God Brahma from all eternity, they were revealed by him, about nine thousand years ago, to the holy rishis (prophets), who penned them into a Holy Book for the instruction and salvation of the world, now known as the Vedas. They are pure, holy and divine, and point out the only sure road to salvation."

Here comes a Chinese mandarin. Well, brother, what light can you throw upon this subject? Have you ever seen "the scriptures given by inspiration of God"? "That is a question easily answered. The Five Volumes are the purest, the holiest, and the most sublime production ever given to the world. There is nothing immoral, no obscene language, to be found in this 'Holy Book.' Its precepts are matchless, and it is the only book whose teachings are calculated to 'make wise unto salvation.' It will save all men who receive it and obey it."

Take a seat. We want now to hear from a disciple representing the land of Iran. Brother Persian, the question is, Where is "the scripture given by inspiration of God"? "Your question surprises me. The Holy Zend Avesta has been circulating for thousands of years; and have you not seen it? It points out the only sure road to the kingdom of eternal bliss, and contains the only true religion for the human race."

Very well; be seated. There is yet another class of devout worshipers we wish to interrogate on this all-important subject. Brother Muhammadan, will you please to step forward, and help us solve this difficult problem? Where are "the scriptures given by inspiration of God"? "Have you never read that holy and inspired book, the Koran? If so, you ought to be able to answer the question; and, if not, you are risking your eternal salvation by remaining ignorant of its beautiful truths; for it consigns to an endless fiery hell all who disbelieve and reject its sublime teachings, and refuse to travel the road it has marked out to paradise and eternal bliss."

Thus, we are making but little progress toward settling the question, Where is "the scripture given by inspiration of God"? We will now question the Christian Church. Here we are met at the very threshold with two hundred answers. "Join our church, and beware of counterfeits" meets us at every church door. We do not mean to say that every church has a separate Bible, though virtually it almost amounts to this, as each denies to all others that use of the Bible and construction of its doctrine and teachings which alone can insure salvation. But, in a broader sense, there are two hundred answers to the question, Where are we to find "the only scriptures given by inspiration of God"? The two hundred translators and four hundred commentators make out more than two hundred distinct systems of faith, and virtually more than two hundred Bibles. When we look at the numerous and widely different translations of the Bible, and the numerous collection of books by different churches which have been made to constitute the Bible at different periods, and the numerous alterations which Christian writers tell us have been made in all of the books of the Bible, and the great number of gospels and epistles floating over the world at one period and afterwards denounced as spurious, and the constant alteration of the Bible by adding some books and rejecting others, we can see at once that it is impossible ever to find any way of determining which are "the scriptures given by inspiration of God."

Here let it be noted that, for nearly three hundred years, the Christian world had no Bible but the Old Testament, and that during that period, hundreds of gospels and epistles were written, and thirty-six Acts of the Apostles, by all kinds of scribblers, or, as one Christian writer calls them, "ignorant asses." These were put in circulation as constituting "the only scriptures given by inspiration of God." Most of them were afterwards condemned by the Church fathers as being the product of the Devil, and as being calculated to lead every soul down to hell that should read and believe them. But there never was any agreement among church leaders as to which of the three hundred gospels and epistles in circulation were spurious, and which were genuine; nor has there ever been any rule for distinguishing them, or determining which was which. How, then, was it possible to know which were "the scriptures given by inspiration of God"?

Here arises a query of most striking import, which should sink deep into the mind of every honest investigator of this subject. Should it not be set down as a moral impossibility that an all-wise God would inspire men to write gospels and epistles for the instruction of mankind and the salvation of the world, and then let them get mixed up with hundreds of others "inspired by the Devil," and calculated to "lead to perdition"? It must have been the means of effecting the eternal ruin of thousands, if not millions, of immortal souls. And nearly all Christian writers admit there was no way of distinguishing the poisonous and pernicious productions from the "inspired." It is also admitted that the former were more read than the latter. Now, we must assume that a God would be essentially lacking in the ingredients of good sense (or rather would be a mere imaginary being) who would do business in such a bungling and reckless manner as to furnish man with a revelation of his will, hang his salvation upon it, and then abandon the field for three hundred years, and let everything run to ruin. Such a God *ought to "repent, and be grieved to the heart."* Look what kind of stuff the people swallowed for gospel during that period!

The Gospel of the Infancy, which was afterwards condemned as the work of devils and impostors, was, during this period, accepted as inspired by nearly the whole Christian world; and see what it contains. In the first chapter it is related that a woman had a son who was, by the intervention of some witches, turned into an ass, when she hastened off to the mother of the young Messiah (Jesus), and related her grievance to that amiable personage, which so excited her compassion that she forthwith seized the young child Jesus, and set him astride the ass's neck, when, "lo and behold!" it took all the ass properties out of the animal, and restored him back to manhood, or rather boyhood. And all the biped asses then in Christendom swallowed this asinine story as "scripture given by inspiration of God." The same book relates that various sick and impotent persons visited the child Jesus, and were cured of their diseases by having his swaddling-clothes wrapped about their heads, necks, or other portions of the body, and forthwith the devils departed (on one occasion in the shape of a dog). If there is a lower plane of senseless superstition than this, I pray God I may never know it. And all this was gospel and "inspired scripture" for whole centuries, with the *majority* of Christendom. Both preachers and laymen read and believed those "Holy Scriptures." This is about as senseless as the story of some devils coming out of a woman, and taking up their abode in a herd of swine. These stories are all "chips of the same block," and all equally incredible.

CHARACTER OF THE VOTERS WHO DECIDED
WHAT SCRIPTURES SHOULD BE CONSIDERED INSPIRED

It is now well known that the first authentic collection of Gospels and Epistles, called "the Bible," was made by the Council of Nice 325 A.D.—a body of drunken bishops and lawless bacchanalians. The Christian writer,

Mr. Tyndal, says they got drunk, came to blows, and kicked and cuffed each other; and that "the love of contention and ambition overcame their reason." They claimed to be under the influence of "the spirit." Undoubtedly they were; but it was a kind of spirit that men hold intercourse with by uncorking the bottle, and not the spirit of gentleness and peace. He says, "They fell afoul of each other," and such was the severity of their blows that one member was mortally wounded, and died a short time after. It was simply a disgusting and disgraceful row—a scene of rowdyism of at first seventeen hundred, and finally about three hundred, Christian bishops, without a character for either virtue, sobriety, or honesty. One writer says, "They were abandoned to every species of immorality, and addicted to the most abominable crimes"; and such was their extreme ignorance that but few of them could write their names. Their method of deciding which Gospels and Epistles were divinely inspired was quite unique. It is stated they were all placed under the communion table, and when the proper signal was given (so says Irenaeus), the inspired Gospels "hopped on to the table," which separated them from the spurious. Why the spurious Gospels did not possess the hopping power and propensity is not stated. Two of the bishops, Chrysante and Musanius, died during the council, before the vote was taken; but such was the importance of the occasion that they did not withhold their votes on that account. The proper documents being prepared and carried and placed near their defunct bodies, they mustered all the force their dead bodies could command, and signed them; and thus, between the living and the dead, we have got a Bible which, it is presumed, contains all "the scripture given by inspiration of God" under the new dispensation.

The Gospels and Epistles thus voted into favor were not arranged together in the form of an authentic Bible until nearly sixty years after. This was done by the Council of Laodicea in the year 363. After this, council after council was called to *vote in or vote out* some of the books adopted by previous councils, and to settle some important church dogmas. The first council voted the Acts of the Apostles and Revelation out of the Bible (i.e., voted them down); but the second council, which met in 363, voted them in again. Another council, which met in 406, voted them, with several other books, out of the Bible again. And thus were books and dogmas voted in and voted out of "the infallible and inspired word of God," and altered and corrected, time after time and century after century, by twenty-four different councils, composed of bigoted bishops and clergymen, so quarrelsome and belligerent that they resorted to fisticuff fighting in several of the councils; and thus was "God's Holy Word" and "perfect revelation" tossed to and fro like a battledore—this book voted in, and that one voted out, and sometimes half a dozen at a time. And where was the "all scripture given by inspiration of God" at the end of this revolutionary and demolishing clerical crusade? And where was its author, that he would suffer the whole thing to be taken out of his hands, altered and corrupted until he could not know his own book, and would not have been willing to father it if he had been able to recognize it? William Penn says that "some of the scriptures which were taken in by one council as inspired were rejected by another council as uninspired; and that which was left out by the former council as apocryphal was taken in by the latter as canonical. And certain it is that they contradict each other. And how do we know that the council which first collected and voted on the scriptures—voting some up, and some down—were able to discern the true from the false?" Here the whole thing is set in its proper light by a devout Quaker preacher. The extract contains a volume of instruction and shows the impossibility of our determining the "all scripture given by inspiration of God."

ADDITIONS, ALTERATIONS AND INTERPOLATIONS

We have a vast amount of testimony to prove that councils, churches, and clergymen arrogated to themselves a lawless license to change, insert, and leave out various texts, chapters, and even whole books, from "God's unchangeable word," until it may now be assumed to be thoroughly changed. From a large volume of testimonies we will cite a few: The version of the Old Testament made under Ptolemy Philadelphus, 287 B.C.—the most reliable version extant—Bishop Usher pronounces a spurious copy, full of interpolations, additions, and alterations. He says, "The translators of the Septuagint added to, and took from, and changed at pleasure"; and St. Jerome says that Origen did the same thing with the New Testament. Bishop Marsh testifies, in like manner, that Origen, who first collected the Bible books together, confessed that he made many alterations in them before they fell into the hands of the Council of Nice. Dr. Bentley admits that the best copy of the New Testament contains hundreds of irreparable omissions, errors, and mistakes. The Rev. Dr. Whitby says, "Many corruptions and interpolations were made almost in the apostolic age." Dupin says, "Several authors took the liberty to add, retrench, correct divers things." Some of the clergy and churches rejected books that did not suit them, while others altered them to suit their fancy. We are told that Lanfranc, Archbishop of Canterbury, made countless numbers of alterations in the Bible in the sixth century for the purpose of making them suit his Church. Eusebius says he found so much proof that the Gospel of Matthew had been altered and corrupted, that he rejected it as being unworthy of confidence. Victor Wilson informs us that a general alteration of the Gospels took place at Constantinople in the year 506 by order of the

Emperor Anastasius. St. Jerome complains that in his time many alterations had been made in the Bible, and that its different translations were so essentially changed that "no one copy or translation resembled another." Scaliger testifies that the clergy and the churches put into their scriptures whatever they thought would serve their purpose. Michaelis says, "They thrust in and thrust out as best suits fancy." In the name of God, we would ask how any person in his sober reason can think of finding "all scripture given by inspiration of God" in the midst of such a general wreck, ruin, and demotion of the original scriptures. It is as impossible as to raise the dead or to find Charlie Ross. The Rev. Dr. Gregory says that no profane author has suffered like the Bible by profane hands. Where, then, can we find "all scripture given by inspiration of God"?

FORGED GOSPELS AND EPISTLES

The Unitarian Bible says, in its preface, "It is notorious that forged writings, under the name of the apostles, were in circulation almost from the apostolic age." Mosheim testifies that "several histories of Christ's life and doctrines, full of pious frauds and fabulous wonders, were put in circulation before the meeting of the Council of Nice"; and he states, like William Penn, that he had no confidence in their ability to distinguish the true from the false. We will here quote another statement of William Penn: "There are many errors in the Bible. The learned know it; the unlearned had better not know it." Here is another sad proof of the blinding effect of reading and believing a book that abounds in errors. He would have the unlearned and honest reader swallow all the errors of the Bible, and be thereby morally poisoned by them, rather than have the book brought into discredit by having its errors exposed. This circumstance of itself is sufficient to seal its condemnation. Belsham says, "The genuine books of the Bible were but few compared with the spurious ones." This would be inferred from the circumstance of only four Gospels being adopted out of fifty, and only seventeen Epistles out of more than one hundred. Daille says, "The Christian fathers forged whole books"; but neither he nor anybody else can furnish any rule for determining which they are.

LOST BOOKS FOUND OR RE-WRITTEN

Dupin says a portion of the books of the Old Testament were burned in wars, and others lost by the Jews themselves; and in the Second Book of Chronicles (xxxiv. 14) we are told that Hilkiah found the Book of the Law after it had been lost eight hundred years. This law appears to have constituted the most important portion of the Jewish sacred writings. The circumstance gives rise to some very strange reflections and conclusions. It appears from this circumstance that the Lord's holy people had been without any law to guide or govern them for eight long centuries. Now, can we suppose for a moment that their God, Jehovah, was a being of infinite wisdom to write or dictate a law, and base the happiness and welfare of his people if not the world on that law, and then, through carelessness or otherwise, suffer it to get lost and remain unfound for eight hundred years, so that nobody could have the benefit of it during that long period? The very thought is a trespass upon our good sense, and does violence to our reason. And where was the law during all that time? And how was it preserved for so long a period of time? If written on papyrus or parchment, it would have perished in less than a century from being exposed to the weather: for we can't assume it was preserved in a drawer or box as, in that case, it would not have been lost; and, if engraven on stone, the weight would have been fifty times as much as Hilkiah could carry.

We are told that when Josiah the king heard the law read, he rent his clothes (2 Chron. xxxiv. 19). Well, that is strange indeed. It must have been a very curious law, or he must have been a very curious man. Why the reading of a few plain moral precepts should drive a man to insanity, and cause him to tear his clothes, is something hard to understand. And it is evidence that the whole Jewish tribe had never known or read much about the law: otherwise a knowledge of it would have been preserved by tradition, and the king would not have been so profoundly ignorant of it. If the law was the Pentateuch, as some writers assume, the king would have had to stand a week to hear it all read; and it seems strange that "Shaphan the scribe" could pick up a document covered with the mold, rust, and dust of eight centuries, and read it off with sufficient expertness for the king to listen to with patience.

But the wonder and difficulty do not stop there. It was only about a quarter of a century until this great "holy and divine law" was lost again, which left "the Lord's holy people" again without any moral code to guide them, or a governing law, for six centuries longer. No wonder they preferred worshipping a calf (see Exod. xxxii.) to paying homage to a God so reckless of their welfare and happiness. On this occasion it became so thoroughly lost that it never "turned up" again; and there seemed to be no way to remedy the deplorable loss but to have it written over again. At least that appears to have been the impression of Ezra the priest, who set himself to the onerous task of reproducing the long-lost document from memory or from a second installment of divine inspiration. (See Esdras.) Such a memory does not often fall to the lot of mortals to possess—a memory that could enable a man to reproduce a document which neither he nor any other person had read for six hundred years. If the world could be furnished with such a mental prodigy at the present day, we might again have the benefit of the numerous books and libraries that have been destroyed by fire in modern times. It would require no previous knowledge of any of those works to achieve the task of reproducing them. Perhaps we may be told that we are becoming "wise above what is written." It would require no mental effort to attain to this eminence, and become obnoxious to such a charge. In this case, a few brief sentences, and the whole thing is dismissed: no details are given.

The story of Hilkiah finding the Book of the Law sounds very much like Joe Smith finding the Mormon Bible; and the case of Ezra's re-writing it is matched by the story of "Vyas the Holy" finding the divine law of the Brahmins some three thousand years before Hilkiah was born. Mr. Higgins says that nearly all ancient religious nations had the tradition of losing and finding their holy books, holy laws, and holy languages. The query is here suggested that, if such an important document could be restored to the people in the manner adopted by Ezra, why was not this expedient resorted to a thousand year sooner, and thus save the demoralization of the Jews? The policy adopted is too much like "locking the stall after the horse is stolen."

IMPOSSIBILITY OF POSSESSING A RELIABLE TRANSLATION

It is quite evident, from the facts presented and from others which will hereafter be presented, that, if God ever gave forth a revelation of his will to the founders of the Jewish and Christian religions, the world is not in possession of it now, and cannot find it in a book as old as the Christian Bible, and written by simply stringing consonants together in a line without any vowels, and without any distinction of words, and which must necessarily be an enigma that would puzzle any scholar to decipher. Hence, the learned Le Clere says, "Even the learned guess at the sense in an infinity of places, which has produced a prodigious number of discordant interpretations." And Simonton, in his "Critical History," says, "It is unquestionable that the greater part of the Hebrew words of the Old Testament are equivocal in their signification, and utterly uncertain; and that even the most learned Jews doubt almost every thing in regard to their proper meaning." To talk of finding "all scripture given by inspiration of God" environed with such difficulties, is to talk nonsense. We will illustrate the nature of these difficulties by citing a case.

We will look at the random guessing at the meaning of a single word of a single text by the most learned students and scholars in biblical literature. The word indicating the material of which Noah's ark was composed, our translation says, was gophir-wood, but the Arabic translation says it was box-wood; the Persian translation says it was pine-wood; another translation makes it red ebony; and still another declares it was wicker-work. Davidson, assuming to be "wise above what is written" in the case, says it was bulrushes cemented with pitch; another writer translates it cedar-wood, etc. And thus God's Holy Book, designed for the guidance of man, has been the sport and the bauble of learned guessers in all ages of Christendom, who evidently know as much about it, in many cases, as a goose does about Greek.

MANY DIFFERENT CHRISTIAN BIBLES

Owing to the multiplicity of Bible translations, which differ widely in their doctrines, precepts, and the relation of general events, making a different collection of books to constitute "the word of God," various churches, and even individual professors, have assumed the liberty to compile and make a Bible for themselves. The Roman Catholic Bible differs essentially from that of the Protestants', having fourteen more books. The Bible of the Greek Church differs from both. The Campbellites have a translation of their own. The Samaritan Bible contains only the Five Books of Moses. The Unitarians, having found twenty-four thousand errors in the popular translation, made another translation containing still many thousand errors. The American Christian Union, having found many thousand errors in King James's translation, is now engaged in a new translation. How many more we are to have, God only knows. Martin Luther condemned eleven books of that Bible, as we have already stated, and thus made a Bible for himself. Paul's Epistle to the Hebrews he denounced in strong terms. Eusebius, the learned ecclesiastical writer, throws eight Bible books overboard, and had a Bible to his own fancy. Dr. Lardner and John Calvin each condemned five or six books, and had a Bible peculiar to themselves. Grotius places the heel of condemnation on several books of the Bible. Bishop Baxter voted down eight books as uninspired, and unworthy of confidence. Swedenborg accepted only the Four Gospels and Revelation as inspired. The German fathers rejected the Gospel of St. Matthew, and I know not how many other books. The Bible of the learned Christian writer Evanson did not contain either Matthew, Mark, or John. The Unitarian Bible does not contain Hebrews, James, Jude, or Revelation. The Catholics denounce the Protestant Bible, and the Protestants condemn the Catholic Bible, as being full of errors. A number of other churches and learned Christians might be named who had Bibles of their own selection and construction. And thus every book in the Bible is passed under the flaming sword of condemnation, and has been voted down by some ecclesiastical body or learned and devout Christian. Each church has either made out a

309

Bible for itself, or accepted that which came the nearest teaching the doctrine of their own peculiar creed. In the midst of this rejection, expulsion, and expurgation of Bibles and Bible books, where can we find "the scripture given by inspiration of God"? We have it upon the authority of Dr. Adam Clark, Eusebius, Bishop Marsh, and other writers, that many texts and passages contained in our Bible cannot be found in the earlier editions; thus showing that many gross interpolations and forgeries have been practiced by the Christian fathers. Christ's prayer on the cross, "Father, forgive them," etc., the story of the woman taken in adultery, the passage relative to the three that bare record in heaven, etc., they assure us, cannot be found in any early translation of the Bible. Where, then, are "the scriptures given by inspiration of God"? Who can tell?

CHAPTER 56

INFIDELITY IN ORIENTAL NATIONS

It is an interesting and instructive historical fact that in all religious countries—Christian, heathen, and Muhammadan—as the people become educated and enlightened, a portion of them improve the teachings of their Bible by new interpretations; while another portion, possessed of still more intelligence, abandon the book altogether and become infidels to the prevailing religion of the country. I have spoken of the former class in another chapter. In this chapter, I shall present a brief history of the latter class, who are known as infidels under different systems of religion. We find, by our historical researches, that in India, Egypt, Persia, Chaldea, China, Mexico, Arabia, etc., a portion of the people outgrow the religion of the country in which they have been educated. And it is an important fact, observable in all religious countries, that *that* portion of the population who become dissatisfied with the established religion of the country are the most intellectual, the most intelligent, and very generally the most moral also. We desire the reader to notice this, as it tends to prove that the cause of infidelity in all countries is intelligence and intellect, and to establish the converse proposition that the mass of people who adhere so rigidly to the religion in which they were educated are people of limited intellect, large veneration, and not very progressive by nature, and very generally have but little historical or scientific knowledge. They consequently have not observed the errors and defects of their religion, or its cramping and stultifying effect upon the mind, or its effect upon the morals of the country. They prefer having somebody else to do their thinking for them. This will be fully illustrated by the brief historical sketch we will now present of the practical operation of infidelity under several forms of religion.

RELIGIOUS SKEPTICS OF INDIA

It is generally assumed by the disciples of the Christian faith that the people of India are on a low scale of mind and intelligence, and that this accounts for the tardy success of the missionaries in the work of converting them to the Christian faith, and the obstacles which lie in their pathway, which makes the cost of conversion bear an enormous proportion to the few proselytes won over to the religion of Jesus. This matter is interestingly controverted by the Rev. David O. Allen, who spent twenty-five years in that country as a missionary. We will make an extract from his work, "India, Ancient and Modern." Speaking of the obstacles the two hundred missionaries encounter in the work of conversion, he says, "It is now some years since a spirit of infidelity and skepticism began to take strong hold of the *educated* native minds of India. This spirit was first manifested in

Calcutta, Madras, and Bombay, and it is making rapid progress in all the large cities" (p. 584). Let the reader mark the word "educated" in this extract. Most cogently does it sustain the assumption we have several times made in this work that it is intellect and intelligence that cause infidelity under every form and system of religion. It denotes an upward tendency from the brute creation, which is devoid of intellectual brain.

Mr. Allen says, "This class of persons [the infidels] has associations and societies for debates, discussions, and lectures; and, among the subjects which engage their attention at such times, religion, in some of its forms and claims, has a prominent place. Their libraries are well furnished with infidel and deistical works, which have been provided from Europe and America. The historical facts and doctrines of the Bible, the ordinances of the gospel, and certain facts and periods of the history of Christianity are made the subjects of inquiry, discussion, and lectures. At such times Christianity and all connected with it—the scriptures, doctrines, and characters, as well as parts of its history—are often treated with levity, scurrility, and blasphemy." Let the reader bear in mind that it is a Christian missionary speaking, who is in the habit of styling everything "blasphemy" in the shape of argument against his idolized and superstitious religion. We are assured from other sources that their language, although freighted with argument and wit, is always respectable. "On such occasions," continues Mr. Allen, "they make a free use of the works of infidel writings, and the sneers and cavils and arguments of deists in Europe and America.... This same class has also, to a great extent, the management and control of the national press in India. [This statement suggests that infidelity in India is becoming deep, widespread, and popular.] In their journals much appears of an infidel and scurrilous nature against Christianity in perverted and distorted statements of its doctrines and duties, of its principles and its precepts, of the conduct and character of its professors, and of the ways and means used for propagating it....

The following facts show the state of the native mind in India: The proprietor and editor of one of *the oldest and best-supported* newspapers in Bombay some time ago expressed his views of the state of religion among all classes, and suggested what course should be pursued. After inserting two or three articles in his paper, to prepare the minds of his readers, he said it was obvious to all that the state of religion was very sad, and becoming more so, and that all classes of people appeared to have lost all confidence in their sacred books; that Christians do not believe in their Bible, or they would practice its precepts; that the Jews, Muhammadans, Hindus, and the Zoroastrians do not believe in their sacred books, because, if they did, they would not do so many things which their Bibles forbid, and neglect so many things which they command. He then proceeds to say that the sacred books of all these different classes may have been of divine origin, and when first given they may have been adapted to the then state and circumstances of the people, and may have been very useful, but that they had become unsuitable to the present advanced state of knowledge and improved state of society; and that none of these sacred books could ever again have the confidence of the people, and become the rule of their faith and practice.... He then suggested that a religious convention be called in Bombay, and that each class of people send a delegation of their learned and devout men with copies of their sacred books, and that the men of this convention should prepare from all these sacred books a Shastra suited to the present state of the world, and adapted to all classes of people. And he expressed his belief that a Shastra thus prepared and recommended would soon be generally adopted. In his next paper he proceeded to mention some of the doctrines which such a Shastra should contain; and among them he said it should inculcate the existence of only one God, and the worship of him without any kind of idol or material symbol. And then he would have no distinction of caste, which he thought was one of the greatest evils and absurd things in the Hindu religion.

Now, these opinions and suggestions are chiefly remarkable as exhibiting the state of the native mind. [Do you mean to say, Mr. Allen, that the hundred and fifty millions of the native minds in India are all tinctured with these doctrines? If so, it is glorious news indeed.] It is unnecessary to say that these views are entirely subversive of Hinduism, involving the rejection of its sacred books as well as its preceptive rites and most cherished practices. The writer of these articles for the public *was a respectable and well-educated* Hindu.... He was proprietor as well as editor of his paper, so he had much interest in sustaining its popularity and increasing its circulation. Indeed, I was told he had but little property besides his paper, and that he relied chiefly upon it for his support. He knew the state of religious opinions among the Hindus; and he was well assured that such opinions and suggestions would not be to the prejudice of his character, or to the injury of his paper. [Glad to hear this, Mr. Allen, on his account, and as showing that a remarkable amount of good sense, intelligence, and infidelity predominate over the Christian religion in India.] Now, this man, the readers of his paper, and the circle of his acquaintance, *show the state of hundreds of thousands* in India, who are dissatisfied with the Hindu religion, and, having no confidence in it, would gladly embrace something better, more reasonable, and calculated to exert a better influence upon society and the character of their nation." All hail to such intelligence

313

as this! It shows that the heathen of India have more reason, sense, and intelligence than many professors of Christianity.

Now, mark the cause that Mr. Allen assigns for this intellectual skepticism of India. He says, "It is in part the effect of the knowledge they acquire which removes their stupidity and ignorance, and imparts power to think, compare, reason, and judge on religious subjects; and in part from the principles and facts of modern astronomy, history, geography, etc., being utterly at variance with the declarations and doctrines of the Hindu Shastras; so that no person who believes in the former can retain any confidence in the latter. [And, if he had included the Christian Bible with the Shastras, the statement would have been almost equally true.] The natural consequence of this course of education is to produce a spirit of skepticism in *respect to all religions*. [Another wonderful admission, and more proof that infidelity, brains, and intelligence are correlative terms.] The effect is now seen in the religious, or rather the irreligious, views of a proportion of the young men who have been educated in European science and literature in the institutions established by the government of India. They are strongly opposed to Christianity, and often ridicule its most sacred and solemn truths [errors more probably]. They openly avow their skepticism and deistical sentiments; but they have hitherto generally conformed to the popular superstitions so far as to avoid persecution, and retain their sacred positions, and to secure and enjoy their property rights.... Motives of worldly policy may lead most of the present generation of *educated young men* through life to show some respect to notions, rites, and ceremonies *which they regard as false, unmeaning*, and superstitious; but should these views pervade the masses of the native population (which they are now doing rapidly), they may be expected to develop their genuine spirit in very painful consequence, ... unless Christianity acquires sufficient power to restrain them" (pp. 574 and 321).

The painful consequence here apprehended is simply the triumph of religious skepticism based on, and growing out of, a broad and thorough literary and scientific education over the senseless dogmas and superstitions of Christianity. Such "painful consequences" will always follow in any country the enlightenment and expansion of the minds of the people by a thorough acquaintance with the principles of science and literature. It is just as natural as that light should dispel darkness, and that is exactly what is realized in such cases. Mr. Allen's statement that motives of worldly policy restrain many of the educated young men of India from avowing their real convictions on the subject of religion shows that the same spirit of mental *surveillance* and priestly despotism prevails in India that prevails in all Christian countries, and prevents thousands from letting their real sentiments be known. This mental slavery has filled the world with hypocrites; but it will soon burst its bonds in India, or would, if the two hundred Christian missionaries could be called home. And then I would suggest that the tide of missionary emigration be reversed, and that some of those highly enlightened, educated men of India be sent to throw some light upon this country.

Mr. Allen, in the continuation of his subject, states that the government councils of education in India are publishing various works on science and literature—the production of the minds of its own citizens—and that they have published a large number of works of this character within a few years past. And he states that, "if this course is continued, India will soon have a valuable indigenous literature" (p. 321). This statement tends to enlighten us still further as to the cause of the recent rapid spread of infidelity in that country; for science and literature are certain to precede infidelity. But he complains that the government system of education, which simply teaches science without superstition, while "it is destroying the confidence of the people in their own system of religion, is also introducing speculation, skepticism, and deism" (p. 321). If he were an enlightened philosopher, he would understand that this is the legitimate operation of cause and effect. Mr. Allen, in concluding this sketch of the rapid progress of skepticism in India, says there are many thousands in India who have passed from conviction of the falsehood of the Hindu religion into a state of skepticism and indifference to all religion, unless when the progress of Christianity now and then rouses them to oppose it. This must be cheering news to every enlightened philanthropist. This whole sketch of Mr. Allen's is very interesting, as it discloses the real causes of infidelity or skepticism in all religious countries, and shows that every form of superstition is giving way and sinking before the march of science, literature, and education in the most populous nation on the globe. It is indeed a soul-cheering thought. And where is there a Christian professor who is so bigoted as not to derive the hint from these historical facts that he can find the cause of his rigid adherence to his own religion, with all its errors, by simply placing his hands on his head? It is true. There are, however, many persons who still believe in an erroneous system of religion, simply because they have had no opportunity of obtaining light on the subject.

SECTS AND INFIDELS IN GREECE AND ROME

When we arrive at Greece, we find a nation possessing a mental caliber seldom equaled, and furnishing many philosophers with brains sufficient to enable them to see through the errors and the absurdities of any system of religion. Hence, infidels were more numerous than sectarians; and those infidels (better known as philosophers) nearly succeeded, by the force of superior logic and wisdom, in banishing all systems of religious superstition from the nation. But questions of controversy were more on philosophical subjects than on religious themes; because the dogmas of the popular religion of Greece, like that of all other countries, were so absurd that the Grecian philosophers could dispose of them without much mental effort. As a proof and illustration of this statement, we will cite the case of Stilpo, who, on being asked by Crates (B.C. 331) whether he believed that God took any pleasure in being worshipped by mortals, replied, "Thou fool, don't question me upon such absurdities in the public streets, but wait until we are alone." Greece, and also Rome, furnished intellectual minds of a high order, and all their numerous philosophers were skeptical on the prevailing forms of religion in those and other nations. It will be observed, then, that nearly all the religious orders of antiquity gave rise to numerous sects, and also numerous infidels and skeptics, *alias* philosophers.

Sects and Skeptics in Egypt

Ancient Egypt was characterized by a considerable amount of intellectual mind, and no inconsiderable proficiency in the arts and sciences. And hence, as would naturally be expected, a considerable portion of her people, in the course of time, broke from the trammels of the popular religious faith, and became infidel to all the systems and sects in the nation; while those of a secondary order of intellect abandoned some dogmas, modified others, and started new sects. This gave offense to the parental religious order, which resulted in one or two cases in a serious quarrel, though not with the bloody and deadly results which have marked the religious quarrels among the sects and followers of "the Prince of peace," which have been so sanguine, cruel, and bloody, as to leave eighteen million human beings on the battlefield, or consumed by fire, or consigned to a watery grave. Religious wars among the heathen have not been half so fiendish or fatal as those waged by the disciples of the cross. The number of sects in Egypt is not known, but they were numerous.

Sects and Skeptics in China

China, though characterized by less mental activity than most other religious nations, has had her sects and her skeptics, and not a very small number of the former, though less in proportion to her religious population than either Egypt, India, Persia, Chaldea, or Arabia. Some of her sects manifested a disposition to borrow dogmas from other religions, while others attempted an improvement on the ancient faith established by Confucius, although in its moral aspects it was the best system of religion extant. The oldest sect known was founded by Laotse, and was known as Taotse. His religion differed more from that of Confucius with respect to its ceremonies than its doctrines. On the whole, there has not been sufficient intellectual growth in China to produce any very marked changes in the long-established religion of the country. Innovation and religious improvement in China are checked and almost prevented by a sort of ecclesiastical tribunal, which has existed from time immemorial, known as "the Court of Rites," which is invested with authority to suppress religious innovation, and thus put an extinguisher on infidelity.

PERSIAN SECTS AND SKEPTICS

Persia has possessed sufficient intellectual mind to make very considerable changes in her religion. According to tradition, she was once overrun with idolatry. But now, and for at least three or four thousand years (and before the time of Moses), that nation has manifested the greatest abhorrence to images, excelling in this respect even Moses, who probably borrowed his antipathy to idolatry from that country. Sects have arisen which have condemned not only the doctrines of the primary system, but its mode of worship. There has been considerable controversy among the sects in Persia upon the question whether God should be worshipped in temples made with hands, or in the open air; also with respect to the origin of evil, and whether the Devil (Ahrimanes) was eternal, or co-eternal with God (Ormuzd). These questions of dispute, and various others, have given rise to more than seventy different sects, while the most intellectual and best-improved minds have outgrown and renounced them all, and assumed the character of infidels.

MUHAMMADAN SECTS AND SKEPTICS

Muhammadans have paid very particular attention to education, and the cultivation of the arts and sciences, and have produced and published a number of literary works. A number of scientific men have arisen among them from time to time, and schools and colleges have been established, in which many have obtained a literary and scientific education. Hence, there will be no difficulty in understanding why thousands of infidels or skeptics have arisen amongst them, and avowed their disbelief in the religion of the Koran. Some of them have spent much time in writing and speaking in their attempts to expose its errors and absurdities; and a large number of sects have sprung up amongst them from time to time, numbering, on the whole, not less than fifty. All these sects mark the progress of religious thought, and each sect made some improvement in the prevailing creeds and dogmas, or some of the religious customs and ceremonials.

The Bible of Bibles

One of the oldest and principal sects was the Sabeans, who claim to be the original founders of the Muhammadan religion. They are very devout, pray three times a day—morning, noon, and evening. They also observe three annual fasts, offer animal sacrifices, practice circumcision, and cherish other foolish customs, and preach other superstitious doctrines, which the cultivation of the sciences has had the effect to open the eyes of some of its devotees to see the absurdity of. Hence, they have left and founded new sects with new and improved creeds. In this way a great many new sects have sprung up from time to time, as in Christian countries, which marks the progress of religious improvement. A great amount of religious controversy has been carried on between these belligerent sects, which has had the effect, to some extent, to liberalize all.

One of the largest and most important of these sects has arisen in modern times—"the anti-Ramazan" sect—which now numbers not less than forty thousand adherents. They discard the feast of Ramazan, condemn polygamy, and contend that no man ought to be persecuted for his religious opinions or his infidelity. It will be perceived they are somewhat radical, and this is easily accounted for. Their origin dates since the dawn of literature in that country; and they number in their ranks the best educated, most enlightened and intelligent professors of the Muhammadan faith. Here is suggested again the cause of infidelity, or the act of outgrowing the popular faith, which has characterized a portion of the disciples of nearly every form of religion known to history.

Some of the Muhammadan sects rose up against one form of popular superstition, and some another. One sect opposed the prevailing belief in a physical resurrection, and argued that the soul rises only as a spiritual entity. Another sect opposed and exposed the absurdity and obscenity of the rite of circumcision. Another argued that punishment after death would be but for a limited period. Another sect opposed the savage superstition of animal sacrifice, etc. While the mother institution, which worshipped in the ancient, moss-covered mosque, condemned them all as infidels, none of them seem to have possessed the amount of intellectual acumen or scientific intelligence to enable them to perceive that the whole system was defective. Hence, they labored to improve it, instead of laboring to destroy it, and supply the place with something better; though hundreds and thousands of the educated classes had their mental vision sufficiently enlightened and expanded to enable them to see truth beyond the narrow confines of creeds and dogmas. Hence, they abandoned their long-cherished religious errors, and have since lent their influence to expose them, and put them down.

"Thus round and round we run;
And ever the truth comes uppermost,
And ever is justice done."

318

CHAPTER 57

SECTS, SCHISMS AND SKEPTICS IN CHRISTIAN COUNTRIES

The practical history of Christianity, ever since the dawn of civilization, has been that of schisms, sects, and divisions, all indicating the natural growth of the human mind, and its thirst for knowledge, its struggles for freedom, and its unalterable determination to be as free as the eagle that soars above the clouds. The number of church sects is estimated to be more than five hundred, and the number is still increasing. And the multiplication of infidels has kept pace with the increase of the churches; and skeptics are now increasing much more rapidly than converts to the churches. This fact accounts for the lamentations with which church organs and religious magazines are now filled with respect to the rapid falling off of church membership, and the decline of church attendance. The people are rapidly outgrowing their creeds and dogmas. This causes the decline of the churches. We will cite a few facts by way of illustration: A recent number of "The Christian Era" states that there has been twenty-two thousand more deserters from the Baptist Church than conversions to it within the brief period of five years. This does not look like converting the world, as they have avowed their determination to do. And the Methodist Church, according to "The Watchman and Reflector," is losing its members still faster: several thousand have left within the past year. "Zion's Watchman" presents us with a still sadder picture of the evangelical churches in general. It states that religion is on the decline in all those churches, and that in some of them it is rapidly dying out. It states that, where one new church is erected, two are shut up; and concludes by saying, "Zion indeed languisheth, and religion is at a low ebb." It means churchianity religion; "for pure religion and undefiled," the outgrowth of modern intelligence, is on the increase, and increases in the ratio of the decline of the churches.

The cause of Zion in old England appears to be in as lamentable a condition as in this country. A recent number of "The English Recorder" makes the solemn declaration that there are five millions of people living without the means of grace in that one province, and that, if arranged in a continuous line in single file, they would reach the distance of fourteen miles. This is rather a large number of immortal souls to be traveling the broad road in one nation. And we are informed that in Canada a large number of the people have no religion, and are on the road to infidelity.

To return to this country: A colporteur of the American Bible Society informs us that three-fourths of the citizens of Philadelphia, and four-fifths of those of New York and vicinity, have no religion and no faith in the religion of the Bible. They must therefore be set down as infidels. And the American Christian Commission, which assembled not long since in New

York, has made some startling developments with respect to the decline of church attendance throughout the country. This body, I believe, represents nearly all the evangelical churches, and is composed principally of clergymen. They have had census committees traveling the whole country over to ascertain the proportionate number of church members and churchgoers in every city, town, and village in the country. Their report is really astonishing; and, as figures will not lie, these reports prove that the orthodox churches are rapidly declining.

As indicative of the state of the whole country, look at the condition of some of our large cities. This vigilance committee tells us that three-fourths of the citizens of St. Louis never attend church, making about two hundred thousand out of the whole population. And in Boston, according to their figures, the proportion of church members and churchgoers is still smaller, being only about one-fifth, which leaves two hundred thousand persons "out in the cold"; but it is a kind of cold that is very comfortable compared with the cold, chilling dogmas of orthodoxy. Statistics similar to the above are furnished for many of the cities, towns, and villages throughout the country, by which it appears that many people are forsaking these old, obsolete institutions, and that the credal churches are really in a dying condition. The State of Vermont, taking it at large, furnishes a moral lesson worthy of imitation. It is one of the best educated, moral, enlightened, and intelligent States in the Union. Crime is but little known compared with the world at large; and yet only about one in twenty of her citizens is a sound church member. Thus, we see that Vermont is about the best educated and most moral State in the Union, and, at the same time, the most infidel State. Put this and that together.

It will be seen at once that education, intelligence, morality, and infidelity go hand in hand, and that morality grows out of infidelity, instead of Christianity; and that science and infidelity, and not the Bible or Christianity, are to be the great levers and instrumentalities for reforming the world. Where, then, is the moral force of Christianity, so much talked of by the clergy? And we have it, upon the authority of this national body of clergymen, that there are not a sufficient number of church edifices in the country to hold one-half of the people if they wished to attend "divine service"; and that, on an average, the churches are not half-filled on the sabbath. From this statement it is evident that only about one-fifth are churchgoers; and a large number of these are not church members, but attend, as the committees state, for mere pastime. This state of things forms a striking contrast with the condition of things only eighty or a hundred years ago, when nearly everybody attended church. To sum up the thing in a few words, the case stands about thus: A hundred years ago from three-fourths to nine-tenths of the people were church attendants, and the most of them church members; but now not more than one in eight or ten is a church adherent, and not the half of these are sound or full believers.

A gentleman, who has recently traveled in every State in the Union for the purpose of critically investigating the matter, concludes, as the result of his inquiries, that not one in fifteen of the entire population of the United States is a sound orthodox believer. This, contrasted with the state of the country and churches a hundred years ago, shows the difference is great, and that the decline of the orthodox faith is rapid, and their approach to their final destiny *swift* and sure. Calculating from the present rates of decrease in church interest and belief in church creeds, there will not be an orthodox church in existence sixty years from this time. Truly does the committee making this report say, "The state of the churches is alarming"; but it is only alarming to the unprogressive adherents to old, musty, mind-crushing creeds and dogmas. To us it is not alarming, but cause of rejoicing, in view of the fact that the disappearance of these old soul-crushing institutions will give place to the glorious and grand truths of the Harmonial philosophy—a religion adapted to the true wants of the soul, and calculated to save both soul and body from everything which now mars their health, beauty, and happiness. Then everyone can "sit under his own vine and fig-tree, where none can make him afraid" of orthodox devils or an angry God.

We bring these things to notice for the purpose of showing that a religious body which persists in preaching, from year to year and from age to age, the same creed, dogmas, and catechisms, without any improvement, or even conceding the possibility that they can be improved, will fall behind the times, and finally be abandoned by all growing and intelligent minds. They cease to answer the moral and spiritual wants of the people, and become as cramping to their souls as the Chinese wooden shoes would be to their feet. "Excelsior, onward and upward," is the motto for this age. And that institution, whether moral, religious, or political, which obstinately refuses to live out this motto, will die as certainly as that the stopping the circulation of the blood will produce death.

Having spoken of the decadence of the churches, we will now look at the counter-picture—the progress of infidelity. And here we observe that leading church members not only confess to the decline of the churches, but concede, on the other hand, that what they are pleased to stigmatize as infidelity is rapidly increasing. We will refer to some of their alarming reports. A recent number of "Scribner's Monthly" says that, "at this very moment a black cloud of skepticism covers the whole moral horizon"; and the Right Reverend Bishop of Winchester corroborates the statement by exclaiming, "Infidelity is everywhere: it colors all our philosophy and our commonplace religion." Professor Fisher, in a warning note to Christian professors, says but few religious teachers are aware of the strength of the infidel party, and the alarming prevalence of infidelity throughout the country—that "it pervades all classes of society, and is in the very atmosphere we breathe." If this be true, that infidelity pervades the atmosphere, then all must inhale it, and become contaminated by it, and thus become infidels naturally, and in spite of any godly resistance. Hence, they should not be blamed for what they cannot help.

The Rev. David K. Nelson, author of "The Cause and Cure of Infidelity," makes some wonderful concessions in regard to the alarming prevalence of infidelity among the higher classes. He tells us that three-fourths of the editors of our popular newspapers are infidels, that nearly all our law-makers are infidels, and that "even the Church itself is full of infidels." If these statements are to be credited, the reverend gentleman may as well abandon all efforts to arrest it; for it evidently has the reins of government, and cannot be stopped, and will ultimately rule the nation, and finally the world. Then will we have a rational religion; then will the millennium, so long predicted by seers and sung of by poets, be ushered in as an earthly paradise. This statement of Mr. Nelson's is corroborated by the religious magazines of the day. "The American Quarterly Review" asserts that seventeen-twentieths of the people are tinctured with infidelity. This leaves but a small handful of the faithful and zealous defenders of the "faith once delivered to the saints." The editor of "The Baptist Examiner" says that a member of the United States Senate remarked to him, "There are, I assure you, but very few members of this body who believe in your evangelical religion." This is confirmatory of the statement frequently made in this work, that our current religion is not adapted to the times; that it is practically outgrown by the better informed classes of society. Mr. Beecher says, "Four-fifths of the educated young men of the age are infidels." Take notice, "the *educated*." Here is further evidence that infidelity and intelligence are almost synonymous terms—further proof that education and intelligence alone are needed to banish Christian superstition from the world.

Let it be borne in mind that infidelity, in its true sense, simply means want of faith in the worn-out creeds and dogmas of past ages, but no lack of faith in anything good and true. If we were to accept the orthodox definition of infidelity—"Want of faith in the precepts and practice of Christ"—then it would apply to every Christian professor on earth. There is not one of them that is not tinctured more or less with this kind of infidelity. There is not a Christian professor who believes as Jesus Christ did, or who practices the life he did. For example: no civilized Christian in this enlightened age believes with Christ that disease is produced by devils, and that to cure the "obsessed," the diabolical intruder must be cast out "of the inner man." In this and other respects, all enlightened Christian professors of the present day differ from the precepts and examples of Christ; hence, strictly speaking, are not Christians, but infidels. And we are warranted in saying that Christ himself, if living in this more enlightened and scientific age, would reject some of the superstitious notions which he cherished in common with the religious professors of that dark and illiterate era. He was most devoutly honest, but very ignorant on scientific subjects.

Here, permit us to note the fact that a very great change has taken place within half a century in the practical lives, as well as the religious views, of those who still profess to believe in the Christian faith. The time has been when nearly all religious professors, including even officers under the government, kept a diary of their religious experience, about which they talked whenever they met together; daily engaged in vocal prayer, and daily read their Bibles and catechisms, and the latter many of them *committed to memory*. But now it is doubtful whether one-half of even the clergy themselves ever read it. And as for the Bible, which used to be read every day by Christian professors, probably not one-half of them ever see inside of it once in six months, unless it is when they wish to settle some controverted question in theology. Some modern works of fiction or of travel have taken the place of "the Holy Book" on the centre-table, while the newspaper has supplanted the catechism. These are some of the extraordinary changes which have recently taken place, and are still rapidly going on, in the practical lives of Christian professors, which tend to show that their faith is daily growing weaker in the soul-saving efficacy of their religion, or in the belief that it possesses any intrinsic importance. This rapid decline in practical Christianity will land nearly all its professors on the shores of infidelity in less than half a century.

CHAPTER 58

MODERN CHRISTIANITY ONE-HALF INFIDELITY

When Martin Luther left the Roman Catholic Church and adopted the motto, "Liberty to investigate," he sounded the death-knell of every orthodox church that should afterwards spring up outside the jurisdiction of the Pope. Luther was bigotedly orthodox, and something of a tyrant, but he had more intellectual brain and mind than most men of his time; and that intellectual ability, though warped by education and enchained by bigotry and superstition, struggled for freedom as minds of that character always do. Luther commenced reasoning (most unfortunate for his orthodoxy); but he had been living in the murky atmosphere of superstition all his life, and preaching a creed that had been stereotyped for a thousand years: so that his reasoning powers had been much weakened, and he had not sufficient intellectual light to see his way out of the dark prison-house of superstition in which the whole Christian Church was then enslaved. But he had intellect enough, when exercised, to convince him there was something wrong in the popular religion of the times; and he commenced reasoning, though in a very narrow circle. He did not attack orthodoxy, but only the tyranny of its misrule and the audacity of the Pope. It was only a reasoning mind beginning to feel the impulse of intellectual growth. The method that he adopted—"liberty to investigate"—was a dangerous experiment for orthodoxy, and will yet prove the death warrant of all Protestant churches.

The Pope has adopted the only true policy for keeping the light of the grand truths of science and infidelity from entering the darkened doors and windows of the Church, and producing schisms and disputes—that of binding the intellect in chains, and laying it at the feet of the Pope. But Luther, by adopting the motto, "Liberty to investigate," set some orthodox minds to thinking and reasoning; and a religious mind that is allowed to think for itself will eventually think and reason its way out of its soul-enslaving creed, or at least make some progress in that direction. Hence, ever since Luther adopted this grand motto, the Christian Church (except that part kept in fetters by the Pope) has been gradually moving every hour since Luther entered upon this hazardous experiment of allowing religionists to reason and think for themselves. Orthodoxy has been growing weaker. It is becoming gradually diluted with the grand truths of science and now entertains broader and more enlightened views. Thus, this bigoted spirit of orthodoxy is dying by inches. Its days are numbered; and the last orthodox Protestant church will die in less than a century. This is no mere visionary dream or random guesswork: it is a scientific problem, which can be proved and demonstrated by figures. The progress of the churches in the past, in permitting the truths of science and the infidelity of the age to displace its mind-crushing dogmas, and modify its creeds, furnishes a certain criterion for calculating their final destiny; and, by this rule, we are assured its years will be few.

Let us look and see what progress the Protestant churches have already made towards "abandoning the faith once delivered to the saints." Some of them are much farther advanced in the line of progress than others; and each new church that has sprung up since the days of Luther dates a new era in the religious progress and onward march of infidelity; and yet each one professed to be sound in the faith, and forbid anyone to advance beyond its landmarks. Every one proclaimed, Thus far shalt thou go, and no farther, in the line of religious progress. We will notice them in their order.

The old Romish Church held all Christians in its iron grasp for eleven hundred years, and hung its dark curtains in the moral heavens to exclude the light of science. Reason was held in chains, and the intellect crushed beneath the foot of popish infallibility. But after this night of intellectual darkness, Luther rebelled, broke the spell, and set what little intellect there was left in the Church to thinking. Its doctrines were heathenish. It taught the infallibility of the Pope, and the divinity of the Virgin Mary. In this respect, they were more consistent than the Protestant churches, for the divinity of Christ presupposes the divinity of both his parents; otherwise, he would be half human and half divine. It also teaches the doctrine of election and reprobation, endless punishment, and other silly superstitions. In this state of mental darkness, Greek literature made an attempt to invade its ranks and dispel its ignorance with the light of science, but failed—not, however, until it had let a few gleams of light into the intellectual brain of some of the best minds, and set them to thinking. This caused a few members to reject the infallibility of the Pope, and a division in the Church was the consequence. A new Church was instituted, which received the name of "the Greek Church." Here we find a slight improvement in the Christian creed. The Greek Christians rejected the doctrine of the infallibility of the Pope, but still held to the divinity of the Virgin Mary, and all the other senseless dogmas of the Church. But as it abandoned one of the most popular but unreasonable doctrines of the Church, it was an important step toward advancement. They did not, however, look upon it in that light, but declared it was the true doctrine of the Bible, and here planted their stakes, and forbade any further improvement.

After gathering a Church of seventy million souls, another night of intellectual darkness set in, and continued for four hundred years, which brings us down to the fifteenth century, when Luther rebelled against the Pope, and again broke the spell of mental lethargy and intellectual darkness, and set what little intellectual mind there was left in the Church to thinking.

The Bible of Bibles

Another slight improvement was made in the Christian creed. The Lutherans not only rejected the doctrine of the infallibility of the Pope, but also the divinity of the Virgin Mary, but here stopped, and planted their stakes, and issued a bull to interdict further progress; but the ball, once set in motion, cannot be stopped. As well attempt to bind the ocean with a rope of sand as to attempt to stop the march of thought when one link is broken which binds it to the Juggernaut of superstition. This is true, however, of but few minds. But few church members possess thought and independence enough to advance faster than their leaders.

Luther did not live long enough to outgrow all the superstitious dogmas in which he had been educated; but he made such rapid progress in infidelity that he condemned the doctrines of eleven books of the Bible, and consequently rejected them: viz., Chronicles, Job, Ecclesiastics, Proverbs, Esther, Joshua, Jonah, Hebrews, James, Jude, and Revelation. He was then an infidel with respect to eleven books of the Bible; and, had he lived in an age of progress like the present, he would have become an out-and-out infidel. But the mass of his followers did not possess minds so susceptible of intellectual growth; hence, they lived and died in faith with the creeds he made for them. There were, however, a few exceptions to this rule. In all ages and all religious countries, and under every form of religion, there have been a few minds gifted with thought and reason beyond that of the multitude. A few of this class figured under Lutherism, who eventually, by virtue of their tendency to mental growth, discovered some defects in his creed and system of faith.

Among this number was Arminius, who rejected the doctrine of total depravity, original sin, the eucharist, purgatory, etc., and, with this change of Lutherism, founded what became known as the Arminian Church. But as no mind and no set of minds in any age have possessed the mental capacity to discover all error, or to grasp all truth, so Arminius only outgrew a few of the erroneous dogmas of the Christian faith, and then stopped, and planted his stakes, and stereotyped his creed; and any opinion or doctrine that advanced beyond that was infidelity. He did not live quite long enough to discover the absurdity of the atonement and an endless hell, and hence those doctrines are found in his creed; but the change he made in the popular religion furnishes another indubitable proof of the progress of mind, and the progressive improvement of the religion of Christianity, and another proof of the steady progress Christianity has made towards infidelity. So distinct and marked have been these changes, that they furnish *data* for calculating proximately the period when the last dogma shall drop out of the creeds of the churches, and bring them into conformity to the teachings of reason and science—in other words, when Christianity shall merge into infidelity. And what is meant by infidelity is the want of faith in the false and morally injurious dogmas of the superstitious ages.

Another step in the road of religious progress brings us to the Unitarian Church. Here we find still longer strides in the direction of the Christian faith towards infidelity. The Unitarians rejected the doctrine of the divinity of Jesus Christ. And why? Simply because the founders of that church had expansive intellectual minds that enabled them to perceive the absurdity and logical impossibility of the truth of the doctrine. Their enlightened reasoning powers enabled them to discover these objections to the doctrine: viz. (1) the impossibility of incorporating an infinite being into a finite body or into the human body; (2) the absurdity of considering any being on earth a God while there was acknowledged to be one in heaven, making at least two Gods; (3) the difficulty of accepting the Bible history of Christ as furnishing proof of his divinity, while it invests him with all the qualities of a human being. These and numerous other absurdities, which are treated of in "The World's Sixteen Crucified Saviors," lead them to reject the doctrine of the divinity of Christ, while most other Protestant churches consider a belief in the doctrine essential to salvation. Thus, they make a long leap towards infidelity. Having intellectually outgrown the doctrine, they set themselves to work to get it out of the Bible. This was no difficult task: for as many texts as may be found in the New Testament in favor of the doctrine, a much larger number may be cited in opposition to it.

A similar history may be given of the Universalist Church. It, too, has run into infidelity. The doctrine of Universal salvation is a beautiful doctrine: it had its origin in the noblest and kindest feelings of the human mind. Messrs. Murray and Ballou, founders of the church, were men of broad philanthropy and human sympathy, and possessed the kindest feelings. Such men could not brook the idea of endless misery for a single soul in God's universe. They were also men of a liberal endowment of reason and logical perception, and hence rejected the doctrine from logical considerations. Being intellectual and intelligent men, they became convinced that the doctrine was wrong. They set themselves to work to get it out of the Bible. Their object in doing this was more to save the credit of the Bible than to make it an authority to sustain their own position. The Bible, being a many-stringed instrument on which you can play any music, they found about as little difficulty in disproving the doctrine by the Bible as others do in establishing the doctrine by that authority. It is wonderful with what ease and facility a dozen conflicting doctrines may be drawn from the same text. This is because all human language is ambiguous, and that of the Bible pre-eminently so; and this fact demonstrates the absolute impossibility of settling any controverted theological question by the Bible.

The Bible of Bibles

Controversialists who should argue a question before a jury on Bible ground, for a week or a mouth, should, in most cases, have a verdict given in favor of both parties; for, usually, both "beat" and also get beaten. Universalists, taking advantage of this ambiguity and uncertainty of Bible language, are now able to show that the doctrine of endless punishment is not taught in the Book. They succeeded in ruling the doctrine out of all the punitive terms to be found in "Holy Writ." The word "devil," on being traced to its origin, was found to be a contraction of "do evil." With this discovery, they cast the "devil" out of their Bible. The word "hell" was found to be derived from the Saxon word "hole," and hence, if it can have any application in the case, must mean "Symm's Hole." "Hell-fire" originally meant a fire kindled in the vicinity of Jerusalem to consume the offal of the city. And thus, according to Universalism, the doctrine of future endless torment is no longer a Christian doctrine. Whether their position is correct or not, it is rather comforting to believe that none of us are to be eternally roasted in the future life, and that even Satan himself has been released from the "painful duty" of ruling that kingdom.

The history of both the Unitarian and Universalist Churches furnishes evidence of the rapid advancement of Christianity toward infidelity; and also the conclusion that the natural desires and moral feelings, and also the reasoning faculties, have much to do in forming the opinions of Christian professors as to whether certain doctrines are taught in the Bible—whether they are scriptural or antiscriptural. The wish is often father to the belief. Just let a certain Bible doctrine become repugnant to the natural feelings of some pious professor, or at war with his enlightened reason, or instinctively repulsive to his moral sense, and he will find some way to convince himself that it is not a Bible doctrine. A new light springing up in the mind has, in many cases, led to new and improved interpretations of the Bible. It seems strange, indeed, that none of the two hundred millions of Christian professors have been able to discover that it is the improvement of the moral and intellectual faculties that has done so much to improve the doctrines and general teachings of the Bible in modern times. The old absurdities and heathenish ideas of the Bible are pumped out by the clerical force pump, and a new set of ideas substituted in their place. This keeps it from falling immeasurably behind the times. It is a work of moral necessity to keep it from being condemned and set aside, or trampled under foot. Christian professors can all find abundant scripture to prove anything they desire to prove; but let them change their belief and adopt the opposite doctrine, and they can find as much scripture to prove that also. There is no difficulty in making out any kind of a creed or code of faith that may be desired. Hence, a man may change his creed or his conduct as often as he pleases, and still be a Christian, or at least pass for one.

Who that is not blinded by priestcraft, or a false religious education, cannot see that it was the natural growth of the moral and intellectual faculties which gave rise to those new churches to which I have referred, with their new and improved interpretation of the Bible? Step by step along the pathway of human progress, the churches are forced against all resistance to make occasional improvements in their creeds; but so strong is their resistance to any change, and so determined to keep their creeds and dogmas unalterably stereotyped, that their improvements are too slow to suit the most progressive minds amongst them. Hence, they leave the churches to which they have been tied, and in some cases form new ones, with new creeds, better adapted to the improved taste and improved moral code of the times. There is not a Protestant church in existence that does not furnish incontestable proof that Christian doctrines are perpetually changing. There is not a Protestant church that is not on the high road to infidelity. They have all unconsciously broken loose from the old landmarks. There is not one of them that is not now preaching doctrines which they would fifty or sixty years ago have denounced as infidelity. This may be to some a startling statement, but I will prove it.

I have pointed out numerous changes in doctrines made by all the modern churches, and their rapid tendency to infidelity. I will now show that the churches from which they emanated, on account of their immobility and conservativeness, have also made radical changes in their creeds, and are moving on in the same direction, being pushed forward by the irresistible tide of modern innovation and improvement. They have made more or less change in nearly all the doctrines of their creeds. Then look at the numerous doctrines once regarded as the very essence of Christianity, which they have entirely abandoned. We will enumerate some of them: The doctrine of casting out devils; the doctrine of a lake of fire and brimstone; the doctrine of Christ's descent into hell; the doctrine of purgatory (these two last-named doctrines, Mr. Sears says, "were once the doctrines of the Church universal, which nobody called in dispute"); the doctrine of election and reprobation, foreordination; the doctrine of infant damnation; the doctrine of polygamy, etc. These were all once regarded as prime articles of the Christian faith; and most of them were preached by all the churches, and now they are all abandoned by most of the churches, thus showing that they improve their creeds as they advance in light and knowledge. Thus, the enlightenment of their own minds leads them to preach more enlightened doctrines, which they erroneously suppose are the teachings of the Book, when they are really the product of their own minds.

The Bible of Bibles

The Indian, when he halloos to the distant hills and receives back the echo of his own voice, erroneously supposes someone is responding to him. In like manner, Christians, when reading and interpreting their Bible, receive the echo of their own minds, which they mistake for the response of the Bible writers, and the true meaning of the text.

Each new church, springing up from time to time, is founded on some new interpretation of the Bible, and flatters itself that, for the first time since the establishment of Christianity, it has found the true key for unlocking all the mysteries and explaining all the doctrines of the Bible; and that all the churches which preceded it were in the dark, each of which interpreted the same texts differently, with the same conviction that they had found the true key for laying open the hidden mysteries of the "word of God." But the probability is that, if the Bible writers could be called up from their graves and interrogated about the matter, they would declare that not one of the churches had guessed at the real meaning of those texts which they are quarreling about the meaning of; that they are all far from the mark; and that they have all saddled a meaning on the texts which the writers never intended, and never thought of, and would make them smile to hear of—though, in many cases, they have made decided improvements on the original meaning, so as to make them more acceptable to the enlightened and thinking and intelligent minds of the age. This saves the Book from being rejected.

Did the clergy preach the same doctrine they did fifty or a hundred years ago, they would find themselves minus a congregation. It is the improvement they are constantly making in the Bible that keeps up its reputation, and saves it from the ruinous criticisms and condemnations of the scientific men of the age. And yet these changes are wrought unconsciously to the great mass of Christian professors; and many of them would have been startled had they been told in early life that the time would come when they would believe as they do now—perhaps horrified at the thought—and would have denounced it as the rankest infidelity. The question, then, naturally arises here, Where is the use of erecting standards of faith, when you believe one thing today and another tomorrow? You admit you were mistaken in the belief you entertained a few years ago; and in a few years more, if you have a progressive mind, you will admit that your present position is wrong and susceptible of improvement. Every Christian professor of much intelligence makes some improvement in his creed in the course of his life. Hence, it is impossible for him to know what he will believe tomorrow, or how much more of an infidel he will be than he is today. One change makes way for another. The wheels of progress move steadily onward: they never stop, and never run backward. It is impossible, after you have made the slightest change and improvement in your religious belief, which is a step in the direction of infidelity, to know how many steps you will take in the future. You may resolve and re-resolve, as most religious professors do, that there shall be no change in your present views; but that will not prevent it. One change proves not only the possibility, but also the probability, of another change.

Martin Luther once believed, like Rev. Dr. Cheever of New York that, "There is not the shadow of a shade of error in the Bible from Genesis to Revelation"; and yet he afterwards found eleven books of the Bible so full of errors that he decided they were not divinely inspired, and rejected them from his creed; and, had he lived fifty years later, he might have rejected all the other books of the Bible, and become as rank an infidel as Paine and Voltaire. They became infidels to the whole Bible in the same way he became infidel to nearly a fourth of it. The mind that loosens itself from the trammels of its early education, and begins to think for itself, has launched its bark on the sea of infidelity. One free thought is one step toward infidelity; that is, a disbelief in the dogmas, superstitions, and traditions of the dark ages. It is just as useless and just as foolish for a man to resolve he will never be an infidel, as to resolve it shall never rain, or that the hair on his head shall never turn gray; for he has just as much control over one as the other.

We have shown that the Protestant churches are sailing out on the ocean of infidelity, and are making steady progress in that direction; and it is only a question of time when they will be entirely infidel. It is true that, owing to the conservative character of the church creeds, and the inveterate hostility the priests have ever manifested to changing them, upon the assumption that they are too holy and too sacred to be criticised and too perfect to be improved, the churches have made slow progress in the way of improving their creeds compared with what would have been witnessed in this respect under a more liberal and tolerant spirit. Owing to this impediment, the improvement in Christian doctrine has not kept pace with improvements in other things. The progress in the arts, science, agriculture, political economy, the mechanic arts, the fine arts, etc., has far outstripped the improvement of our religious institutions, and their relinquishment of the errors and superstitions of the past, and nothing but the most absolute compulsion by the moral force of the progressive spirit of the age has induced the churches to make any improvement in their creeds and doctrines. The spirit of improvement is manifested in every department of business, and in all our numerous institutions but that of our religion. When it comes to that, it is "Hands off! There shall be no changes here." It must still continue to wear the same old garments it has worn for nearly two thousand years, though they have become musty, soiled, and worn, and directly opposed to the spirit of the age. In view of this strongly opposing conservative spirit, it is remarkable that so much improvement has been realized in our national religion as we now witness.

This improvement has been effected more by the process of changing the meaning of words and language than that of changing the text by a new translation, as I have already shown. This surgical operation has been inflicted upon thousands of texts; and so frequently and so generally has this expedient been adopted by churches to get rid of the errors of the "Holy Book," that the meaning of some texts has been changed hundreds of times. There is one text in Galatians (iii. 20) which, Christian writers inform us, has received no less than two hundred and forty interpretations at different times by different writers; that is, two hundred and forty guesses have been made at the meaning of this one text. "Revelation" is defined as "the act of making known." But what is made known by a book, one text of which you have to guess two hundred and forty times at the meaning of, and then don't know whether it is right or not? And this is but a sample of many texts scattered through the Book, which have been overburdened with meanings in a similar manner in order to get a sufficient amount of science and sense into them to make them acceptable to the enlightened minds of the age.

This renovating and revolutionizing process makes Christianity a mere system of guesswork, and salvation a mere lottery-scheme. Thousands, in view of this ambiguity and precariousness, have come to the conclusion that it is easier to find what is right in any question of morals, without recourse to the Bible, than it is to find out what the Bible writers desired to teach in the case. Why, then, waste such a vast amount of time in attempting to find the meaning of thousands of texts, as many Christian writers have done in all ages of the Church, when, if the meaning could be determined with certainty, there would be but little accomplished by it? For, after all, we have to test the truth of the doctrine or precept by our own experience, in the same manner they proved it—if they proved it at all. There has been time enough wasted in this kind of speculation to build the Pyramids, and the world is no wiser or better for it. As there is no certain rule for interpreting one text in the Bible (and every word originally written in Hebrew had from four to forty meanings), we may guess at the meanings until our heads are gray, and then die in doubt. To show how the meaning of Bible texts has been improved by successive constructions, I will cite one case.

For more than a thousand years, the various texts that refer to casting out devils were accepted as literally true. It was supposed they mean just what they say, and that "the old fellow" (King Beelzebub) is to be cast out of the inner man—body, head, horns, and hoofs. But when the age of reason dawned upon the world, it began to be discovered that the notion of casting out devils was an old heathen tradition, and too senseless for sensible people to believe in. Hence, to save the credit of the Book and the credit of the Church, casting out devils was interpreted to mean casting out our evil propensities, which, although a perversion of the meaning of the writer, was an improvement on the original. The further acquisition of scientific knowledge, accelerated by the invention of the printing press, revealed the fact that man never parts with his evil propensities, or any other propensities, however much they may be subdued. Hence, Bible-mongers set themselves to work to ferret out another meaning for the text. They finally decided that casting out devils means *restraining* our evil propensities. This, although far from the meaning of the writer, is another improvement on "God's perfect revelation." In this way, step by step, this and thousands of other texts have been improved from time to time by successive translations and interpretations, until "God's Book" has become partially purged of the errors it would seem he put into it. It may yet, in this way, become a sensible book.

The interpretation of the Bible has been (as already stated) an art in all Christian countries for ages. The original object was to obtain the meaning of the Bible writers, but in modern times, the object seems to be to obtain a meaning to suit the reader, without much regard to the meaning of the writer. This statement may be, to some readers, rather startling, but there can be no question of its truth. Some of our most popular Christian writers have avowed it, though in rather an indirect way. Hear what the Rev. John Pye Smith, the leading Christian clergyman of England, and one of the ablest and most popular in all Christendom, says with respect to Bible interpretations: "I would advise the clergy everywhere to interpret the Bible according to the spirit of the age." Most wonderful advice truly, and a dead shot at the Bible. Let it be understood, then, that according to this Christian divine, Bible readers hereafter are to pay no attention to the plain and obvious meaning of the Bible language, or to the writer's intended meaning (which is the only true meaning), but force a meaning into the text which you know will be acceptable "to the spirit of the age"; that is, to men of reason and of scientific attainments. The Bible, then, is to be venerated henceforth, not for what it teaches, but for what it ought to teach, or what the fanciful reader would have it teach.

Verily, verily, we have fallen upon strange times when "God's word," like a nose of wax, is to be molded into any shape to suit "the spirit of the times." But don't let it be supposed that the Rev. John Pye Smith is the only Christian professor who makes God's infallible revelation succumb to the good sense and intelligence of the age—"the spirit of the times." There is not an orthodox clergyman, not a Christian church, and scarcely a Christian professor, who does not make the Bible a mere tool in that way. None of them, in all cases, accepts the literal meaning of the Bible. None of them takes the dictionary for a guide in all cases to determine the meaning of the words of the text. As we have said, there is not an orthodox church or clergyman who does not frequently abandon the dictionary, and travel outside of it, coin a new meaning of his own for many of the words of the Bible, and ingraft into those words a meaning they never possessed before. They thus assume a license that would not be tolerated with respect to any other book; yet, notwithstanding those countless alterations and changes in "God's unchangeable word"—changes in the language, changes in the meaning of its words, changes by translation, changes in the import of its doctrine, and changes in the teaching of its precepts—millions cling to it as "God's perfect, unalterable revelation," his "pure and unadulterated word."

They seem to take the same view of it the old lady did of the carving-knife, which although it had been mended sixteen times, had had seven new blades and nine new handles, yet it was the same old keepsake which her father had given her forty years before. The Bible, in like manner, has been altered and amended by fifty translations and a hundred and fifty thousand alterations, according to the learned Dr. Robinson of England, and is still believed by millions to be the same old book—just as God gave it to man. What superstitious infatuation! It is an instructive fact, which we will note here, that all this labor of amending and enlightening the Bible is the work of the very best minds in the churches—the growing, thinking, intellectual minds in those institutions; minds that are in a state of unrest, that are hungering and thirsting for something better; minds which are unconsciously struggling to get free from the trammels of priestcraft and superstition, and the religious creeds in which they were educated, and are unconsciously aspiring for something better, something higher, holier, and purer, but cannot give up the idolized Book which has been so long enwrapped among their heart-strings that it has seemingly become a part and parcel of their souls. Hence, rather than abandon it and leave it behind them, they prefer to remodel and reconstruct it, and bring it up to their own moral standard, and thus make a better and more sensible thing of it than God himself did in the first place; that is, assuming that he had anything to do with it. And they generally put newer and better ideas into the Book, and better morals, than they ever got out of it; and finally, in many cases, outgrow the current theology, and become more enlightened, more intelligent, and more useful members of society, than they were in any period of their lives.

CHAPTER 59

CHARACTER OF THE CHRISTIAN GOD

The object in selecting and presenting the list of texts quoted in this chapter is to show that Bible writers entertained a very low and dishonorable conception of the "all-loving Father," and that, on this account, the reading of these caricatures of Infinite Wisdom must have a demoralizing effect upon those who habitually read them and accept them as truth. Even if they were all accepted as metaphors, or mere figures of speech, that would not prevent or destroy their injurious effect upon the mind; for descriptions by metaphor or pictures have the same effect upon the mind as literal descriptions or representations. And what must be the effect upon the mind of the ignorant heathen, who read the Book with no suspicion of its being aught but reality, as much of it was unquestionably designed to be?

1. "There went up a smoke out of his nostrils, fire out of his mouth devoured: coals were kindled by it" (2 Sam. xxii. 9). Suggestion of a volcano.

2. "He had horns coming out of his hand" (Hab. iii. 4.).

3. "Out of his mouth went a sharp two-edged sword" (Rev. i. 16). Rather a frightful monster to look at.

4. "He shall mightily roar from his habitation" (Jer. xxv. 30). Wonder if it frightened the saints in glory.

5. "He shall give a shout, as they that tread the grapes" (Jer. xxv. 30).

6. "He awakened as one out of sleep" (Ps. lxxviii. 65). The presumption would be he had been asleep.

7. "And like a mighty man that shouteth by reason of wine" (Ps. lxxviii. 65). Would not this lead to the conclusion he was drunk?

8. In his anger, he persecuted and slew without pity (Lam. iii. 43). Good authority for persecuting and killing enemies. No wonder all Christendom is noted for persecution and bloodshed.

9. "His fury is poured out like fire" (Nah. i. 6). Rather a frightful God.

10. "The rocks are thrown down by him" (Nah. i. 6). Throwing stones is rather a ludicrous business for a God to engage in.

11. He became angry, and sware (Ps. xcv. 11). It is easy to see why swearing is so common in Christian countries.

12. He burns with anger (Isa. xxx. 27). Who would wish to live in heaven with such a being?

13. "His lips are full of indignation" (Isa. xxx. 27). Who saw his lips? And what peculiar aspect did they present to lead to this conclusion?

14. "And his tongue as a devouring fire" (Isa. xxx. 27). How came the writer to see his tongue?

15. He "is a jealous God" (Exod. xxxiv. 14). Jealous of what? "Jealousy is a hateful fiend" (Cato).

16. "He shall stir up jealousy like a man of war" (Isa. xiii. 13). Of course, if he indulged in jealousy himself, his example would stir up this vile passion in others.

17. He rides upon horses (Hab. iii. 8). In what part of the universe are those horses kept? And how many does he ride at a time?

18. "He shall cry, yea, roar" (Isa. xiii. 13). Rather a frightful object.

19. "He that sitteth in the heavens shall laugh: the Lord shall have them in derision" (Ps. ii. 4). "But thou, O Lord, shalt laugh at them; thou shalt have all the heathen in derision" (Ps. lix. 8). Whoever heard him laugh?

20. "The Lord is a man of war" (Exod. xv. 3). What kind of arms does he use?

21. "I will make mine arrows drunk with blood" (Deut. xxxii. 42). A good archer.

22. "They have provoked me to anger." — "Anger shows great weakness of mind" (William Penn).

23. "I will heap mischief upon them." — "Mischief-makers are enemies to society" (Socrates).

24. "I will spend my arrows upon them" (Deut. xxxii. 23). "Arrows are the weapons of savages" (Goodrich).

25. "A fire is kindled in mine anger" (Deut. xxxii. 22). "Anger resteth in the bosom of fools" (Solomon).

26. "I will also send the teeth of beasts upon them, with the poison of serpents" (Deut. xxxii. 24). This exhibits a more fiendish spirit than that of Nero.

27. "I myself will fight against you in anger and fury and great wrath" (Jer. xxi. 5). "Anger and fury disclose a weak and unbalanced mind" (Publius Syrus).

28. "I will laugh at your calamity" (Prov. i. 26). "Only brutal savages can be happy while others are miserable" (Publius Syrus).

29. "I frame evil against you" (Jer. xviii. 11). Who, then, can deny that God is the author of evil?

30. The spirit said, "I will be a lying spirit in the mouth of all his prophets" (1 Kings xxii. 22). Of course, then, all the lies they told would be his, and not theirs.

31. "If I whet my glittering sword" (Deut. xxxii. 41). What a frightful picture for the all-loving Father!

32. "Spare them not, but destroy both men and beasts, infant and suckling" (1 Sam. xv. 3). We would neither worship such a God on earth, nor dwell with him in heaven.

33. "He was unto me as a bear lying in wait, and as a lion in secret places" (Lam. iii. 10). Think of the God of the universe descending from heaven, and crouching in ambush, like bears and lions, to spring upon the unsuspecting traveler! The tendency of such a thought is to weaken both moral and intellectual growth.

34. He will "cry like a travailing woman" (Isa. xiii. 14).

35. He is full of vengeance and wrath, and is furious (Nah. i. 2). A savage monster. Who would worship such a God?

36. "The sword without, and terror within, shall destroy both the young man and the virgin, the suckling also with the man of gray hairs" (Deut. xxxii. 25).

37. "The sword shall devour, and make drunk with their blood" (Jer. xlvi. 10).

The language of the above is blasphemous and shocking to refined feelings, whether accepted as literal or figurative.

Though but just begun, we will pursue this sickening theme no further at present. It is an unpleasant task to pen these shocking pictures of "Divine Goodness"; but the time has arrived when these evils should be fully exposed, that Christian professors may see the error of preaching the doctrines of the semi-barbarous ages, which have the effect to dwarf the intellect and repress the growth of every healthy moral emotion of the mind, and thus retard the moral and intellectual progress of society. Such considerations loudly call for a full exposition of the errors and evils of biblical theology, so long concealed under the sacred garb of "inspiration."

Note: This chapter might easily be extended to a hundred pages of similar examples.

CHAPTER 60

ONE HUNDRED AND FIFTY ERRORS OF JESUS CHRIST

In "The World's Sixteen Crucified Saviors," under the head of "The Two hundred Errors of Christ," the author has pointed out sixty errors in his teachings and practical life. It was the intention of the author to have completed the exposition in this chapter, but he has discovered that a full and thorough elucidation of all the errors would swell this volume beyond its proper size. He has therefore concluded to present a mere abstract of one hundred and fifty of those errors in this work, and reserve a fuller exposition to be comprised in a pamphlet to be published soon, and to contain also thirteen powerful and unanswerable arguments exposing the numerous absurdities and impossibilities of the orthodox theory that Christ possessed two natures, human and divine—that he was both God and man. This assumption is known as "the hypostatic union," or dual nature of Christ. The pamphlet comprising these two subjects can be had when published, of the usual booksellers or the author, for twenty-five cents.

The admirers and worshipers of Jesus Christ adore him as a being of absolute perfection—perfect in intelligence, perfect in wisdom, perfect in power, perfect in judgment, perfect in his practical life, and perfect in his moral inculcations. We are told, "He spake as never man spake"; and, finally, that he taught a system of religion and morals so absolutely faultless as to challenge the criticism of the world, and so perfect as to defy improvement: and to doubt or disbelieve this dogmatic assumption is to peril our eternal salvation. With this kind of teaching and preaching in the Christian pulpit for nearly two thousand years, it is not strange that the great mass of Christian professors have been blinded and kept in ignorance with respect to his numerous errors, which modern science has brought to light both in his teachings and his practical life, a portion of which will be found briefly noticed in this chapter under three heads: viz., (1) "Christ's Moral and Religions Errors," (2) "Christ's Scientific Errors," and (3) "Christ's Errors of Omission."

THE MORAL AND RELIGIOUS ERRORS OF CHRIST

In "The World's Sixteen Crucified Saviors," we have, under the above heading, shown (1) that Christ possessed a very ardent religious nature; (2) that he was unenlightened by scientific culture; (3) that consequently he often indulged in the most extravagant views of the duties of life; (4) that he inculcated a moral and religious system carried to such extremes as to render its obligations utterly impossible to be reduced to practice; (5) that his injunction, "Take no thought for tomorrow," is of impracticable application, and never has been lived up to by any of his disciples in that age or since; (6) that, if reduced to practice, it would starve the world to death in less than twelve months; (7) that his injunction, "Lay not up treasures on earth" (Matt. vi. 19), has been ignored and trampled under foot by the whole Christian world; (8) that his injunction to his disciples to part with all their property (Matt. xix. 21) would soon fill the world with paupers; (9) that his promise to supply all the necessaries of life to those who shall "seek first the kingdom of heaven" (Matt. vi. 33) has never been fulfilled; (10) that his injunctions, "Resist not evil," (11) when smitten on one check, turn the other also, are virtual invitations to personal abuse; (12) that his mandate, "Love not the world," (13) also, "to hate father and mother, brother and sister," etc. (Luke xiv. 26), (14) also, to give up voluntarily our garments when attacked by a robber (Matt. v. 40), (15) also, to make no defense of our lives when they are sought by murderers (Luke xvii. 33), are all extravagant, unnatural, and unreasonable moral obligations; (16) that his declaration to his disciples that they would be "hated by all men" (Matt. x. 22), (17) and his injunction to shake off the dust of their feet against their skeptical hearers, (18) and "go and teach all nations," (19) and "take nothing for your journey" (Mark. vi. 8), are all indications of a mind run wild with religious fanaticism; (20) as is also the declaration, "He that believeth not shall be damned"; (21) and "He that believeth and is baptized shall be saved" is equally unreasonable; (22) that all things asked for in prayer believing has never been realized by any person; (23) that it sets aside all natural laws. (24) It is calculated to encourage idleness and sloth, (25) and thus bring on misery and starvation. (26) The commands to "call no man 'father,'" (27) also, "Call no man 'a fool,'" (28) also, to "pray without ceasing," (29) also, to forgive our enemies four hundred and ninety times ("seventy times seven"), (30) also, to "love your enemies" (Matt. v. 46), (31) also, to pluck out our eyes and cut off our hands if they offend us, (32) and also to become eunuchs for the kingdom of heaven's sake, are utterances which bespeak a mind devoid of a knowledge of either natural or moral philosophy; (33) as does also the injunction to become perfect as (God) our Father in heaven (Matt. v. 48). (34) His belief in an angry God; (35) his injunction to fear God (Matt. x. 28); (36) his advice to his followers to live like the lilies of the field (Matt. vi. 26); (37) his statement that "the meek should inherit the earth," (38) that his disciples would be hated by all man; (39) his reasons for forbidding them to swear; (40) his blessing on the poor; (41) his denunciation of the rich; (42) his parable of Dives; (43) his encouragement to mourn; (44) his blessing on the pure in heart, (45) and on the hungry and thirsty; (46) his choosing the ignorant for companions; (47) his setting the mother against the daughter (Matt. x. 36); (48) his getting angry (Matt. xxi. 12); (49) his treatment of his mother, (50) also of the money-changers, (51) and of the Pharisees; (52) his usurpation of property (Matt. xxi. 2); (53) his calling men "fools and hypocrites," (54) also "vipers," (55) and "children of the Devil" (John viii. 44); (56) his enjoining his disciples to shake off the dust of their feet against them, (57) and to call no man "rabbi," (58) and no man "master"; (59) his falsehood about going to Jerusalem (John vii. 8); (60) his substituting water for wine; (61) his strong sectarianism (John x. 1); (62) his treatment of the Gentiles (Matt. x. 5); (63) his threat toward Jerusalem; (64) his calling honest men "robbers" (John x. 8); (65) his denunciation of Sodom and Gomorrah, (66) and Chorazin and Bethsaida (Matt. xi. 21), (67) and Capernaum; (68) his answer to the woman of Samaria, (69) and his calling Peter "Satan"; (70) his hatred of the world, (71) and contempt of life—all these precepts and practices, when critically examined, are found to be at variance with the laws of moral science as taught in this enlightened age, which establishes the fact that Christ was no moral philosopher.

THE SCIENTIFIC ERRORS OF CHRIST

The following scientific errors of Christ, a portion of which are exposed in "The World's Sixteen Crucified Saviors," show that he was neither a natural nor a moral philosopher: (1) He assumed that disease is produced by demons, or evil spirits. (2) He generally treated disease, not as the result of natural causes, but as produced by evil beings. (3) His rebuking a fever (Luke iv. 39) discloses an ignorance of the science of physiology. (4) His declaration about the stars falling (Matt. xxiv. 29) evinces his ignorance of astronomy; (5) as does also his belief in the conflagration of the world (Matt. xxiv. 34). (6) His belief in a personal devil (Matt. xvii. 18), (7) also his belief in a literal hell (Matt. xviii. 8), (8) also a belief in the unphilosophical doctrine of repentance (Mark ii. 17), (9) and also that of divine forgiveness (Matt. vi. 12); (10) his repeated assumption that belief is a voluntary act of the mind; (11) his frequent reference to the heart as being the seat of consciousness; (12) the great importance he attaches to a right faith; (13) his unpardonable sin against the Holy Ghost; (14) his superstitious idea of casting out devils; (15) his comparing faith to a grain of mustard-seed (Matt. xi. 23); (16) the promise of "well done" (Matt. xxv. 21) as a reward for well-doing; (17) his statement about man increasing his stature, (18) and about two men joining in prayer (Matt. xviii. 19); (19) his promise to come in the clouds of heaven (Matt. xxiv. 30); (20) the time that event was to take place (Matt. x. 23); (21) his penalty for wrong-doing, or sin; (22) his penalty for falsehood (John viii. 44); (23) his superstitious belief in an undying worm; (24) his penalty for idle words; (25) his statement about speaking in new tongues

One Hundred and Fifty Errors of Jesus Christ

(Mark xvi. 17), (26) about handling poisonous serpents, (27) also swallowing deadly poisons, (28) and that these acts should furnish a proof of divine power; (29) his frequent confabs with imaginary devils; (30) his views of the marriage relation (Luke xx. 34), (31) why a certain man was born blind (Matt. vii. 22); (32) his ignorance of the natural causes of physical defects; (33) his conduct toward the fig-tree (Matt. xxi. 20); (34) his statement relative to the Queen of Sheba, (35) and relative to Noah's flood (Luke xvii. 27); (36) his frequent denunciation of unbelievers; (37) his injunction to become perfect as God; (38) his erroneous views of love, (39) and of the peacemakers, (40) and of the tax-gatherers, (41) and of divorce; (42) his views of alms; (43) his statement about Moses (John v. 46), (44) about Nicodemus, (45) about bearing witness, (46) about letting our light shine, (47) about his disciples praying, (48) about praying for the kingdom of heaven, (49) about the law (Matt. v. 17), (50) about his being the Christ (Matt. x. 23), (51) about performing miracles, (52) about bringing a sword, (53) about his disciples sitting on the twelve thrones, (54) about judges in heaven, (55) about the fate of Judas; (56) his deception by Judas; (57) his mistake about Peter; (58) his promise to the sons of Zebedee (Matt. xx. 23); (59) his parable of the unjust judge; (60) his new commandment; (61) his promise of a hundred-fold reward; (62) his ideas about paying tribute, (63) also about marrying a divorced woman; (64) his promising Peter the keys of the kingdom of heaven; (65) his declaration relative to binding things in heaven; (66) his notion of merit in religious belief, (67) and that faith is the gift of God; (68) his ideas of lust, (69) and about earthly treasures, (70) also treasure in heaven, (71) about tombstones, (72) and about an arbitrary personal God; (73) his ignorance of science and natural law. (74) He never spoke of a natural law, (75) nor used the word "science," (76) nor "natural philosophy." (77) And, finally, his spending nine-tenths of his time in idleness or obscurity is historic, scientific, and practical proof against his divinity. From all the facts and precepts enumerated above, we are compelled to conclude he was no philosopher, and was ignorant of the principles of natural science. And this accounts for the numerous scientific errors which abound in all his teachings and preachings and his whole practical life, as set forth in the work of which this is a synopsis.

CHRIST'S ERRORS OF OMISSION

Had Christ been an all-wise omniscient God—the character his orthodox disciples claim for him—he would have noticed and understood, and consequently have condemned, various demoralizing practices, customs, and institutions then existing in society. He would also have discovered and taught the grand moral and scientific truths and principles which have since been brought to light, and have proved such signal blessings to society, so that the world could have enjoyed them two thousand years ago.

(1) He would, in the first place, have discovered and exposed the evils of the despotic form of government under which he lived, (2) and have suggested a better system. (3) He would have taught the people the beauties and benefits of a true democracy, (4) and would have exposed the evils of physical as well as mental slavery; (5) also the deleterious and demoralizing effects of intoxicating drink, instead of manufacturing it. (See John ii. 7-9.) (6) He would also have exposed the errors and evils of the many popular religious superstitions then and there prevalent, instead of endorsing them. (7) He would have taught the science of anthropology as essential to human happiness, (8) including the principles of mental science; (9) and likewise the true principles of moral science, (10) and the necessity of mental culture, (11) and the most important lesson of all—that of self-development. (12) He would have taught the people that everything is controlled by natural law, (13) instead of by the caprices of an angry God. (14) He would have taught the people that right and wrong are natural principles, (15) that virtue contains its own reward, (16) and sin or crime its own punishment. (17) He would have taught the science of life and the laws of health as essential to human happiness; (18) and that the violation of natural law must be attended with suffering; (19) and that every immoral act a man commits against another must injure himself, (20) and destroy his true happiness, (21) and tend to make him a victim to his own passions. (22) He would have taught the true principles of mental freedom, (23) and the rights of conscience in matters of belief; (24) and that man is responsible to himself alone for his belief. (25) And, finally, he would have taught the modern doctrine of evolution as furnishing the true and philosophical solution of all human actions, both good and bad.

Certainly a being possessing infinite wisdom could have discovered and brought to light these grand practical truths, and thus greatly augmented the sum of human happiness, instead of leaving the world to drag on in suffering ignorance. And his omitting to do it must be characterized as an error of omission. For a fuller exposition, see the pamphlet.

CHAPTER 61

CHARACTER AND ERRONEOUS DOCTRINES
OF THE APOSTLES

Christ's apostles, although reputedly inspired, were very far from being exemplary characters. Quarrels, jealousies, and emulations are frequently disclosed in their practical lives. We are told there were "envyings and jealousies and divisions" among them (1 Cor. iii. 3), and that "they disputed among themselves who should be the greatest" (Mark ix. 34). This implies that there was selfishness and worldly ambition at the bottom of their movements. Paul also represents them as "*defrauding*" and lawing each other (1 Cor. vi. 7, 8); and Paul himself had a serious quarrel with Barnabas, as we are told: "The contention was so *sharp* that they departed asunder one from the other" (Acts xv. 36). These incidents in the practical lives of the apostles show that they were frail and fallible mortals, and under the control of selfish feelings like the rest of us, and that their "inspiration," if they possessed any, was not of a very high order. Such men are very unsuitable examples for the heathen to imitate, as they are impliedly recommended to do when the Bible is placed in their hands.

With respect to the doctrines taught by the apostles or New Testament writers, we will here assume the liberty to say they contain more errors than we can allow space to enumerate. For those of Paul and Peter, we shall appropriate a separate chapter, but will only cite a few of the errors of the other New Testament writers as mere samples of others.

James's superstitious idea of curing the sick by prayer and oil we have already noticed (chapter 41). He also endorses the foolish and incredible story of Elijah controlling the elements so as to cause a three-year drought (chap. v. 17). He tells us we can *get wisdom by simply asking* it of God (chap. i. 5). Then why do millions of people devote years to hard mental labor to acquire it? He speaks approvingly of the practical life of Abraham, also of the miserable harlot Rahab (chap. ii. 23, 25), and avows his belief in a devil, etc. John also avows his belief in this superstition (1 John ii. 13), and likewise in the bloody atonement (1 John i. 7) and the doctrine of predestination (1 John v. 18); and, worse than all, he issues the bigoted mandate, "Receive no man into your house" who does not preach the doctrine I do (2 John i. 10). Jude endorses the foolish story of Sodom and Gomorrah, the contest between Michael and the Devil, the second advent, a day of general judgment, etc. These will do for specimens of apostolic errors.

CHAPTER 62

CHARACTER AND ERRONEOUS DOCTRINES OF
PAUL AND PETER

I. CHARACTER OF PAUL

Paul, standing at the head of the Church in the apostolic age, and being the principal New Testament writer and the principal teacher and doctrinal expounder of the New Covenant, or gospel dispensation, his practical life and his doctrines must therefore be regarded as constituting a part, if not the principal part, of the basis of the Christian religion. We shall therefore make no apology for presenting here a brief exposition of his character and his doctrines; and we shall show that both present numerous defects and inconsistent and contradictory features.

1. In his First epistle to Timothy (i. 13), he states that he had been "a blasphemer and persecutor, and injurious," and confesses that he was *particeps criminis* in the martyrdom of Stephen; yet, in the Acts of the Apostles, he declares "I have lived in all good conscience before God unto this day" (Acts xxiii. 1). Here is one specimen of his many incongruous statements.

2. He relates the account of his miraculous conversion three times, and in three different ways. In the first statement he says, "The men stood speechless, *hearing a voice*, but seeing no man" (Acts ix. 7). In the second account he says, "*They heard not the voice* that spake to me" (Acts xxii. 9). In the third statement, when relating the case to King Agrippa he says, "They were all fallen to the earth" (Acts xxvi. 14); while, in the first account, he had stated, "The men stood speechless." It is evident they could not stand speechless while they were all fallen to the earth.

3. In one account he states that Jesus told him to stand up and receive his mission; but in another place he says he was ordered to go to Damascus to receive the message.

4. He told the king that he showed himself first at Damascus, and then at Jerusalem (Acts xxvi. 20); but in his Epistle to the Galatians he declares that he did not go to Jerusalem.

5. Again, he says he went to Jerusalem, and Barnabas took him by the hand and brought him to the apostles (Acts ix. 27).

6. And then, again, to the Galatians he declares he saw none of the apostles, "save James, the Lord's brother" (Gal. i. 18).

7. In 1 Cor. x. 35 he says, "I please all men in all things"; but in Gal. i. 10 he says, "If I yet pleased men, I should not be the servant of God." Here, then, is another palpable contradiction.

8. In Rom. xi. 5 he speaks of the "election of grace," but in Tit. xi. 9 he says the grace of God has appeared to all.

9. In his letter to Timothy he says, "God will have all men to be saved (1 Tim. ii. 4), but in Rom. ix. 22 he speaks of "the vessels of wrath fitted to destruction"; and in Rom. ix. 27 he says, "A remnant shall be saved." All will not be saved if only a remnant is saved.

10. When about embarking for Rome he stated, "I perceive the voyage will be of much hurt and damage to life" (Acts xxvii. 10); yet on the voyage he declared, "There shall be no loss of any man's life among you" (Acts xxvii. 22). An "inspired apostle" and oracle of God should be punctiliously accurate in all cases, or all his statements will be brought under distrust, and it will be impossible to arrive at the truth in the case; or, in any case, all will be involved in doubt and conjecture.

11. Paul's errors in doctrinal inculcations are numerous. His confessions to the Corinthians that, "being crafty, I caught you with guile" (2 Cor. xii. 16), sets forth a bad example, and indicates a bad system of morals, which is calculated to have a demoralizing effect upon Bible readers and believers, especially the heathen and the youth of Christian countries.

12. And his statement that the truth of God "hath more abounded through my lie unto his glory" (Rom. iii. 7), is still more demoralizing in its tendencies. Many have looked upon it as a justification for lying. It seems to imply that lying is all right if done for the glory of God; and as he states in 1 Cor. x. 31, that whatsoever we do should be done to the glory of God, it logically follows that lying is justifiable in all cases. Mr. Higgins states that such doctrine had the effect to reduce lying to a system among the early Christians, and that they considered it a duty to lie when the interest of the Church could be promoted by it. A book inculcating such bad morality should not be circulated amongst the heathen.

13. Paul's reason for recommending a life of single blessedness is deserving of notice. He says the unmarried man careth for the things of the Lord; but the married man careth for the things of the world—"how he may please his wife" (1 Cor. vii. 33). The last act he named here does not trouble men much nowadays, at least after the honeymoon is passed; and a man who considers God worthy of more attention than wives, as Paul did, would not be likely to bestow a very high appreciation on the latter. But the greatest objection to the doctrine is that, if practically carried out in accordance with his recommendation, there would soon be no wives to please.

14. We must notice another objectionable doctrine of Paul with respect to marriage. Instead of acknowledging an honorable and virtuous motive for marriage, he would tolerate it as the least of two evils; that is, as a means of mitigating a burning lust (1 Cor. vii. 9). This makes marriage a mere animal attraction—the union of a man and woman drawn together

from lustful motives. Paul advises bachelors not to marry or touch a woman, but remain single like himself (1 Cor. vii. 1). But such advice, if practically complied with, would soon depopulate the globe. If not so strongly adverse to human nature, it would doubtless ere this have filled the world, first with Shakers, and then with the graves of an extinct race.

15. Paul says to the Romans (Rom. vii. 17), "It is no more I that do it, but sin that dwelleth in me. For I prove ... that in my flesh dwelleth no good thing." Here are taught two erroneous doctrines: (1) the essentially corrupt and sinful nature of the human body, taught anciently by the Hindu ascetics; (2) that sin or the Devil operates on the mind independent of the human will or volition, which savors of fatalism. And his statement that some vessels are made to honor, and some to dishonor (Rom. ix. 21), seems unequivocally to set forth the same doctrine. Many commentators have puzzled their brains over it to make it mean something else, but with ill success: the declaration is not that men *become* vessels of honor and dishonor, but that they *are made so*.

16. Paul's exhortation to servants to be obedient to their masters has furnished pious Christian slaveholders a good text to preach from throughout slaveholding Christendom, and has done much to rivet the chains tighter upon the limbs of the slave.

17. When Paul calls the Cretans "liars, evil beasts," etc., he descends to a low position, both in the scale of manners and morals: he is not only uncivil, but exhibits bad passions. They did not merit such personal abuse, as they had never done him an injury, at least we have no proof of it.

18. Paul tells us that God sends people a strong delusion, that they may believe a lie and be damned (2 Thess. ii. 12). More fatalism. To delude people with lies in order to damn them is worse than hardening Pharaoh's heart in order to find a pretext for drowning him. Let it be borne in mind that, if there is any spiritual signification justly assignable to this text, it can only benefit the few, as the common people always accept language with its common signification. But can we assume that Paul was such a blunderer that he frequently used language conveying exactly the opposite meaning from that intended, and that in this way he taught fatalism and immoral doctrines when he did not intend to do so? And then, as it is claimed he was inspired, is it not a slander upon Infinite Wisdom to assume that God was so ignorant of human language that he put these pernicious doctrines in Paul's mouth by mistake? One or the other of these conclusions we are driven to accept, in order to save Paul from condemnation; but this only saves his moral character at the expense of his good sense. The most rational assumption appears to be that Paul lived in an age and country which knew nothing of mental or moral science, and honestly believed and

taught these pernicious doctrines. We will now learn something about the moral code of bachelors.

19. "I suffer not a woman to speak in the church." "It is a shame for a woman to speak in the church" (1 Cor. xiv. 35). He says, if they want to know anything, let them ask their husbands at home. But this, in some cases, would be the blind leading the blind; and, in other cases, only the leaders would be blind. Paul should have learned the lesson of O'Connell, the Irish agitator, who said, "Since I have learned that my mother was a woman, I have great respect for women, and advocate their rights."

20. We will now notice the reason Paul assigns for having wives subject to their husbands: it is simply because man was created before woman (1 Tim. ii. 13). What profound logic! Worthy of a Locke or a Newton! But if there is any logical force in the argument, then monkeys should have the preference of men in the churches, as they came still earlier in the order of creation.

21. Paul's doctrine that all governments are ordained of God, and that those who resist them shall receive to themselves damnation (Rom. xiii. 1), is a virtual condemnation of those noble philanthropists who in various ages and countries resisted the authority of tyrants. It makes Washington, Jefferson, Franklin, and others sinners and criminals for opposing the tyranny of King George.

22. Paul evinced a very intolerant spirit when he said, "If any man preach any other doctrine than that which I declare unto you, let him be accursed" (1 Gal. i. 9). This is the spirit of intolerance, persecution, and bigotry—the spirit which has erected the scaffold, piled the fiery fagots around the stake, wielded the guillotine, adjusted the halter around the neck of the martyr, and crimsoned the earth with the blood of the righteous. This very text has had the effect to fire up such a spirit, and it has frequently been quoted as authority for such cruel deeds as those just cited.

23. Paul gives utterance to a very high singular doctrine when he says that even nature teaches that it is a shame for a man to wear long hair, but the glory for a woman, because nature gave it to her for a covering. (See 1 Cor. xi. 14.) He was certainly not much of a philosopher, or he would have made the discovery that nature promotes the growth of the hair upon the heads of men and women exactly alike. If nature did not permit any hair to grow upon the head of man, or did not allow it to grow more than an inch in length, there might be some plausibility in the assertion. But, as the case stands, it is the shears, and not nature, which teaches that it is a shame for a man to wear long hair; or rather, if there is any shame in the case, it consists in man cutting off his hair after nature has been so kind as to supply him with such a useful covering.

24. Paul's endorsement of the doctrine of the atonement, and his declaration that "without the shedding of blood there can be no remission for sin" (Heb. ix. 22), show that he had not advanced beyond the old Jewish and pagan superstition of "blood for blood." The doctrine is a relic of heathen barbarism, and is shocking to persons of fine moral sensibilities; but this subject is treated in another chapter.

25. Paul also endorses the old heathen tradition that God is an angry, revengeful being. He lent the influence of his powerful mind and pen to perpetuate this demoralizing and blasphemous doctrine, which has had an injurious effect upon the minds and morals of the people in all past ages.

26. We again call attention to Paul's declaration that God sent the people a strong delusion that they might believe a lie and be damned. Think of a just and righteous God deluding people in order to damn them! The doctrine is certainly blasphemous. It is enough to charge a demon with such acts as this. Some writers suppose that Paul did not mean what is here literally expressed, but it is probable he did, for it is the old Jewish idea that everything that takes place is the achievement of a God. We must assume that the Devil, who now attends to such business, had not been sworn into office at that time. Hence, he supposed that Jehovah still attended to such business.

27. One indelible stigma on Paul's character is found in his endorsement of the pagan and Jewish rite of circumcision—a cruel and bloody custom—which no truly enlightened and sensible man would lend his sanction to perpetuate, much less perform with his own hands, as Paul did on Timotheus (Acts xvi. 3). Paul also contradicts himself with respect to the matter. He says, "If ye be circumcised, Christ shall profit you nothing" (Gal. v. 2). Yet he afterward performed the act on Timotheus, as stated above. This is preaching one doctrine and practicing another.

28. Paul said that he was a Roman citizen; but no Jew could be a full Roman citizen until the reign of Philip or Decius, long after. He also passed for Paul of Tarsus, but Tarsus was not a Roman city at that time, not until about a hundred years afterward. This was being all things to all men in order to gain a few proselytes; and truly, he carries out the doctrine quite well. At one time he professes to be a Roman (Acts xxii. 26); at another time he professes to be a Pharisee, and says that his parents were Pharisees (see Acts xxiii. 6); and then, again, he was an apostle of Jesus Christ (Acts xv. 10).

29. Paul uses some rather doughy arguments on the subject of the resurrection. He says that on the last day, at the sound of the trumpet, we shall all be raised, the dead in Christ first (1 Cor. xv. 52). We are also told that "this mortal shall put on immortality." We are compelled to believe,

from the language here used, that Paul believed in the sleep of the soul in the grave; and the resurrection of the natural body is a ridiculous absurdity and a physical impossibility. The sleep of the soul is a still worse assumption. Why should the soul lay in the ground covered with filth and worms? What possible benefit could it derive from laying in a state of insensibility for centuries? And what would become of it if someone should remove the decomposed remains of the body, and all the earth contiguous, to some other locality, or toss it into a running stream? And this has been done. What becomes of the soul in such a case? Does it float down the stream with the physical debris? If so, where will it stop, and how will it be found in the day of resurrection?

30. And the doctrine of the resurrection is attended with still greater difficulties and logical obstructions. The physical body, according to Paul, is to become a spiritual body. But a portion of the body is consumed by worms during the process of decomposition in the grave; and those worms, when they die, are consumed by other worms. Will it not, then, require a search warrant in the day or resurrection to find all those worms, and to gather every minute particle of the old body together to form the spiritual body? Why not make the new body of a stone or a stump, or some other material, instead of the old, decayed, decomposed body? It would require a miracle in either case. Cases have been reported of Christian missionaries being eaten up by cannibals. The flesh of the Christian in such cases becomes a part of the physical body of the cannibal; and the cannibal will, according to Christian theology, come forth unto "the resurrection of damnation," and will take a portion of the body of the missionary with him to the bottomless pit. How will it be obtained? A serious difficulty, certainly! How is it to be met and surmounted? Many other logical difficulties lie in the way of making a practical application of the doctrine.

31. When Paul calls our physical tenements "vile bodies" (see Phil. iii. 21), he reveals the old pagan idea of the body being sinful. They looked upon it as a kind of prison for the soul, and a thing to be hated and contemned as you would a tyrant with a rope around your neck. This error discloses great ignorance of the functions of the human body and its relation to the soul or mind. It would be impossible to have a pure soul in a vile body. Here Paul discloses still further ignorance of science.

There are other acts and other erroneous doctrines, which mark the practical life of Paul, that are quite obnoxious to criticism: as, for example, the curse he pronounced upon Elymas, whom he stigmatized a sorcerer, though he does not prove he was one, but says that was his name by interpretation (Acts xiii. 8). This act, which it is stated produced total blindness, must be regarded as an act of bigotry and intolerance. Elymas is not charged with any crime or immoral conduct, and, so far as we can learn his history, he was an honest, upright man: but he sought "to turn away the deputy from the faith" (Acts xiii. 8); that is, like the Greek philosophers, he attempted to point out the absurdity of some of Paul's doctrines. There is something very significant in the statement of Paul that some of his doctrines were "to the Greeks foolishness" (1 Cor. i. 23), for they were a learned, intelligent, and sensible nation of people. And no such nation ever has, or ever will, accept as true and sound doctrine some of the theological nonsense and absurd doctrines that Paul preached. Future generations will wonder that such doctrines were ever taught by people claiming to be sensible and intelligent.

The circumstance that Paul relates of a viper coming out of a bundle of sticks, and fastening on his hand without inflicting a deadly wound, evinces a degree of superstition which no philosopher could entertain. The assumption is that God, after bestowing upon the reptile the disposition and means of defending itself, interposed by a divine act to prevent their action.

Christ and his apostles (including Paul), instead of studying and understanding the laws of nature, were constantly looking for something to contravene them, and set them aside. Of course, they were honest in this; but it shows their want of scientific knowledge, which was characteristic of the age.

The circumstance of Paul's handkerchief and apron healing the sick, as related in Acts xix. 12, is evidently regarded as another interposition of divine power. But cases are frequently performed in this manner in various parts of this country by Dr. Newton and other healers, who impart their magnetic aura to a handkerchief, or some other article of clothing, or a piece of paper, and send it to the sick, who are cured as effectually as those were by Paul's magnetized handkerchief; for it was undoubtedly his magnetism imparted to the handkerchief that effected the cures. Modern science is solving the mysteries and miracles of the past.

We will only observe further that Paul lays down three systems of salvation, which, when arranged side by side, certainly make the road broad enough to enable nearly every son and daughter of Adam to reach the heavenly kingdom:

Salvation by Faith. "By faith ye are saved, and not of yourselves: it is the gift of God" (Eph. ii. 8). It being the gift of God, we, of course, can have no agency in the matter. "A man is justified by faith without the deeds of the law" (Rom. iii. 28). This is a direct contradiction of James, who declares, "Faith, if it hath not works, is dead" (Jas. ii. 17).

Salvation by Works. "God will render to every man according to his deeds" (Rom. ii. 6). "The doers of the law shall be justified" (Rom. ii. 13).

Thus, it will be observed, Paul, in the above-cited texts, not only contradicts James, but also contradicts himself.

Salvation by Divine Predestination. "As many as were ordained to eternal life believed" (Acts xiii. 48). This is not given as Paul's language, but it is spoken with respect to his preaching. And Paul sets forth the same doctrine in Rom. xi. 5, when he speaks of a remnant being "saved by the election of grace." Here, then, are three roads to heaven, which so multiply the chances of being saved that but few can be lost.

Such conflicting statements show that confusion and ambiguity characterize the Bible, and render it impossible to learn anything definite from its statements.

Note: How can Christians believe in the immortality of the soul after reading Paul's declaration that "God alone hath life and immortality dwelling in the light"? If so, then man is not an immortal being (see 1 Tim. vi. 16).

II. CHARACTER OF PETER

In his practical life, St. Peter was a singular and angular being. He presents us with the oppose extremes of virtue and vice. He appears to have been about as distinguished for wickedness as for piety. He told the same falsehood repeatedly, and backed it up with an oath (Matt. xxvi.): hence, lying, cursing, and swearing are laid to his charge. And then, we are told, he was put in possession of the keys of the kingdom of heaven (Matt. xvi. 19). How a man, guilty of such moral derelictions, could have had a higher honor bestowed upon him than was ever bestowed upon any other human being, or how he could have been considered a safe custodian for such an important charge, it is difficult to see; and then it looks too much like a bribe for immoral conduct. It weakens the incentives to a virtuous life to reward the criminal, and shows imperfection in the moral system which he was allowed to represent. As for his doctrines, they are characterized by the same moral and scientific errors and defects as those of St. Paul and embrace some of the same doctrines of heathen mythology.

1. He speaks of the earth as "standing out of the water and in the water" (2 Pet. iii. 5). Here is the old Hindu tradition which taught that the earth floated on a sea of water, traces of which are also found in Genesis.

2. He tells us, also, that the earth has been once destroyed by water, and in the day of judgment will be destroyed by fire (2 Pet. iii. 6, 7). It has been from time immemorial a very prevalent tradition amongst the Oriental nations that the world had been, and would be again, alternately destroyed by water and fire. Peter and Josephus also seem to endorse this tradition.

3.　Peter also endorses and teaches the absurd and unphilosophical doctrine of fore-ordination (1 Pet. i. 20).

4.　He also enjoins "servants to be in subjection to their masters," not only the good, but also the froward (1 Pet. ii. 18). This is absolute tyranny. There is to be no resistance to the bloody lash. The motto of Patrick Henry is much better—"Resistance to tyrants is obedience to God."

5.　Wives are to be in subjection to their husbands (1 Pet. iii. 1), even as Sarah obeyed Abraham (verse 6). There is nothing said about husbands obeying wives, probably because, as he says, woman is the weaker vessel (1 Pet. iii. 7). Wonderful logic! A sage conclusion for a Christian moralist! He thus places Christian morality below that of the ancient Druids, who placed women on a level with men in both Church and State.

6.　Peter tells us, "Christ bore our sins in his own body on the tree" (1 Pet. ii. 24). This is the old Jewish idea of carrying away sins by scapegoats, and the Oriental heathen doctrine of putting innocent Gods to death as a punishment for the sins of the people—a doctrine which posterity will condemn as barbarous. (See "The Sixteen Crucified Saviors," chapter xxi.)

7.　Peter says a "dumb ass spoke with man's voice" (2 Pet. ii. 16). He thus endorses the story of Balaam's ass becoming endowed with human speech.

8.　Peter, like Paul and Christ, endorses the absurd story of Noah and the flood (1 Pet. iii. 20).

9.　But space will not permit us to notice all the erroneous doctrines set forth by Peter. He teaches the doctrine of a general judgment (2 Pet. ii. 9), the doctrine of election and reprobation (2 Pet. i. 10), and the doctrine of a general conflagration of all things terrestrial (2 Pet. iii. 12).

10. But the most remarkable incident in the life of Peter is his connection with the fact of Ananias and Sapphira. We find many logical absurdities and moral errors in this story recorded in Acts v.: 1. It is very strange that Peter, who denied his Lord and master three times, and hence was repeatedly guilty of telling positive falsehoods, should be the chosen instrument under Christ's religion to pronounce sentence of death upon Ananias and Sapphira for the same sin. 2. Why should Ananias and Sapphira be punished with death for a crime that Peter, Abraham, and Isaac were all guilty of several times? 3. Is it not strange that Jehovah should be considered as being strongly opposed to lying, if he himself, as stated in 1 Kings xxii., converted four hundred of his prophets into liars, and then endorsed the lying Peter? 4. Is not the crime of Ananias and Sapphira—that of attempting to withhold a little money from the priests by lying–of less magnitude than that of ruining a whole nation by robbery, as we are told God's holy people did? They robbed and "spoiled the Egyptians" (Exod.

xii. 36). 5. Is it not probable they needed it more than the priests did? The moral law teaches that it is necessity, and not might, that makes right. 6. Does it not look rather unreasonable that Sapphira should repeat the same falsehood for which her husband had just been struck dead, as it must have been known to her? Who can believe it? 7. And can we suppose that God would be so partial as to kill a man and woman for the first offense of lying, and let Abraham, Isaac, and Peter and others escape after committing the sin several times? These considerations seriously damage the credibility of the story.

CHAPTER 63

IDOLATROUS VENERATION FOR BIBLES

Should reason, science, and philosophic lore
Against my faith combine,
I'd clasp the Bible to my breast,
Believing still that it's divine.

Here I am told how Christ hath died
To save my soul from hell:
Not all the books on earth beside
Such heavenly wonders tell.

This simple book I'd rather own
Than all the gold and gems
That e'er in monarch's coffers shone,
Than all their diadems.

Nay, were the seas one chrysolite,
The earth a golden ball,
And diadems the stars of night,
This book were worth them all.

Christian writer, in attempting to portray the Protestant view of the Bible, says, "It is a miraculous collection of miraculous books. Every word it contains was written by miraculous inspiration from God, which was so full, complete, and infallible that the authors delivered the truth, and nothing but the truth. The Bible contains no false statements of doctrine or faith, but sets forth all religious and moral truth which man needs to know, or which it is possible for him to receive, and not a particle of error; and therefore the Bible is the only authoritative rule of faith and practice."

These two pious effusions—one in prose, the other in poetry—exhibit the views and feelings very prevalent among the disciples of the Christian faith only a few centuries ago; and they are cherished yet, to a considerable extent, by a large portion of Christian professors. This blind, idolatrous veneration is gradually giving way to the light of science and general intelligence, and the thick mental gloom and darkness of superstition out of which they grow is being dispelled. When the intellectual mind becomes fully developed and enlightened, the Bible will find its true level, and will command no more homage than other books. It will be read and estimated, like other human productions, according to its real merits. In this enlightened and scientific age, Bible devotees never go to such extreme lengths in pouring fulsome adulations upon the idolized book. They would be laughed at for their ignorance and superstition if they should attempt it. But the time has been when every religious nation which possessed a "Holy Book" attached extreme sacredness and exalted holiness to the book and all its contents, and often indulged in the most extravagant language and the wildest rhapsodies in their attempts to eulogize and idolize its virtues. In this respect, there was but little difference between Jews, pagans, and Christians: all idolized their Holy Books. A sacred regard was shown not only for the book, but often for every manuscript, scrap of paper, or text which it contained, or which was supposed to contain a message or revelation from God. But few religious nations have existed, even in the remote past, who have not possessed some kind of Bible or sacred record which they treated with an enthusiastic veneration bordering on idolatry.

The Hindus, the Egyptians, the Persians, the Chinese, the Muhammadans, and the early Christians were all Bible idolaters. The Hindus, like the Christians, were religiously enjoined to read and study "the Holy Scriptures"; and the priests, as those in Christian countries do now, made them a study, and reduced the interpretation of them to an art. And, like Christians in another respect, they were interdicted from transcending in knowledge what was taught in their assumed-to-be divinely illuminated pages. The disciple of the Hindu faith was not allowed to become "wise above what was written" in the Vedas (see chapter 6); and the same solemn prohibition, "Add not to, or take not from, the word of God," was reverently obeyed by the devout disciple of the Vedas.

The Muhammadans believe the Koran has been received and transmitted from generation to generation by the direct agency of God. They claim that it is not only an infallible rule of faith and practice, but "God's last will and testament to man," and that it is designed by God for the whole human family; and they pray and hope for its universal extension and adoption. One pious Mussulman (Sadak), on being asked why the Koran appeared to be newer every time it was read, replied, "Because God did not reveal it for any particular age or nation, but for all mankind down to the Judgment Day." Muhammadans tell us that, "such is the innate efficacy of the Koran, it removes all pains of body and all sorrows of mind. It annihilates what is wrong in carnal desires, delivers us from the temptations of Satan and from fears. It removes all doubts raised by satanic influences, sanctifies the heart, imparts health to the soul, and produces union with the Lord of holiness."

With the ancient Persians, the great test and touchstone of all faith and all moral action was their "Holy Word of God." To know whether a thing was right or wrong, they had only to inquire, "Is it taught, or is it forbidden, by the Zend Avesta?" The Persians, like the Jews, had four days set apart in each month for religious festivals, on which occasions, Mr. Hyde informs us, "they met in their temples, and read portions of their Holy Books, and preached and inculcated morality and virtue" (chap. xxxviii. p. 352).

But Bible exaltation and adoration ran much higher than is here indicated in some countries. They were not only believed to be "words" or "the word of God," but to have a portion of the spirit of God impressed into every chapter, every verse and every word; and hence they received a portion of that veneration and adoration usually ascribed to Deity. And here we find both Jews and Christians have been strict imitators of the heathen in the practical exhibition of this species of book idolatry.

We are told that the ancient Buddhists ascribed inherent sacredness and supernatural power to the identical Sanscrit word of their scriptures. Hence, it was considered sacrilegious to make any alteration in the arrangement of those words; and for fear some alteration of this kind might be made, they objected to the missionaries translating "the Holy Book" into the English language. Mr. Hyde informs us, they not only read their Bible in their temples, but at their festivals and in their families; and, like the Jews and primitive Christians and the Muhammadans, they carried them in their travels, and slept with the Holy Book under their pillows.

Nearly all Bibles in that age were treated with this kind of veneration. Brahmins, Persians, Jews, Muhammadans, and Christians, in their earlier history, were in the habit of attaching texts or detached portions of scripture to their clothes, or inserting them into their hats or shoes—an act prompted by the belief that they would impart some supernatural charm. The Persians, Hindus, and Muhammadans have been seen covered from head to foot with scripture texts. In the days of St. Justin and St. Jerome, such scenes were often witnessed among Christians also. Even the handling of the Bible was believed to impart a supernatural or miraculous power, manifested in the cure of diseases, driving away devils, etc. Several Bibles were thus deified. In some nations they were kept under lock and key, or cloistered in a golden box, to prevent unsanctified hands from opening them. The notion was prevalent with the devotees of several Bibles that they should be read differently, if not held differently, from other books. Kissing the "Holy Book" was also prevalent among the Hindus, Muhammadans, and early Christians—indeed, in nearly all religious countries. Bible worship knew no bounds in the days of ignorance and superstition, when people had more piety than philosophy. Believing that the spirit of God permeated their Bibles, nearly all the blessings of life were ascribed to their influence.

Such a belief, fostered from age to age, and transmitted from parent to child, could but operate to blind the judgment of all Bible believers so as to

Idolatrous Veneration for Bibles

disqualify them for detecting defects or perceiving their errors, though they may abound on every page. And these Bibles have been read by millions of their disciples with a kind of solemn awe or holy fervor, which not only wholly incapacitates the mind for perceiving its errors, but shuts out the possibility of a doubt of its truth. Indeed, they glory in assuming it to be "a perfect embodiment of divine truth," "without the shadow of a shade of error from Genesis to Revelation," to use the language of Dr. Cheviot with respect to the Christian Bible. The reasoning faculties are put to sleep, and the intellect bound fast in chains, before "God's Holy Book" is opened; and if the reasoning faculties should by chance arouse, and rebel against such tyranny, and try to assert their rights by permitting a doubt to spring up in the mind that some statement or text is not true, the Bible devotee becomes alarmed, and exclaims, with trembling fear, "Lord, I believe: help thou mine unbelief." In this state of fearful and prayerful mental strife against reason, doubt, and disbelief, he again sinks into the "darkness of devotion," determined still longer to hug his canonized and idolized book to his bosom with all its errors and immoralities.

This has been virtually the experience of thousands of Bible believers, to a greater or less extent, in all ages and all countries in possession of "Holy Books." In this way, Bibles have been an obstacle to the progress of mind and the progress of society. An unchangeable and infallible book must inevitably cramp the mind, and hold it in chains. Hence, a Bible-believing community can make no progress in morals, science, or civilization, only so far as they violate their own principles by transcending its teachings. Society would remain forever in an ignorant, uncultured state, were there not some minds in it possessing a sufficient amount of intellect to outgrow their Bibles; and, but for the publication and perusal of other books, society would make but little progress. A mind which is religiously and conscientiously bound to believe in a Bible is bound to all its errors and all its ignorance, and hence can make no progress while it adheres rigidly to its own principles or its own scruples; but thanks to the progressive genius of the age, the "Holy Books" which embody the moral and religious errors of the past are nearly outgrown, so that they are seldom read now even by their professed admirers. People are assuming the liberty of becoming "wise above what is written" in "God's Holy Book." Even Christians themselves often assume this liberty: otherwise we should have a community characterized by ignorance and superstition; and our writers would be as liable to stumble into errors and contradictions as the Bible writers when they penned "God's perfect revelation." It requires the acquisition of but little knowledge and intelligence to become "wise above that which was written" in that illiterate and ignorant age.

CHAPTER 64

SPIRITUAL OR IMPLIED SENSE OF BIBLES

The practice seems to have been very early conceived and adopted in various countries by the disciples of different Bibles which have been long extant in the world of attaching to all the offensive texts of their sacred books (which, when taken literally, convey either a vulgar, immoral, or foolish sense) a new and more acceptable meaning than earlier custom had sanctioned, or more devout minds had ever thought of. As the growing intelligence of the people was constantly disclosing long-unnoticed and important errors in the Holy Book, this expedient was adopted to cover them up, or put them out of sight. As Jesus, if not Paul, by virtue of the growth of the moral and intellectual perceptions, was able to distinguish some errors and moral defects in the first installment of Bible revelation as found in the Jewish Old Testament, so the people in every age since, in those countries where any cultivation has been bestowed upon the mind, have been capable of bringing to light numerous errors incorporated into the sacred books of past ages; and as some of those books called Bibles were claimed by their disciples to be perfect, divinely inspired, and infallible, and consequently free from error, some expedient had to be devised to sustain this claim, and show that the man of science was guilty of falsehood when he charged "God's Holy Book" with containing errors. The expedient finally adopted was to take the long-established signification of the words of the text out, and put in a new meaning, coined by the prolific brain of the devout defender of the Book for the occasion; and this new sense was called "the spiritual sense." It was presumed it would be more acceptable to the intelligent minds of the age. In this way, whenever a new scientific discovery has been announced, demonstrating some of the statements of the venerated volume to be erroneous, the clergy have set themselves to work with their clerical force-pumps to extract the meaning which our standard dictionaries assign to the words of every text that seemed to conflict with the newly discovered scientific truth, and ingraft into it a new meaning of their own invention. This practice finally became and has long been, an established practice and art in nearly every country where a Bible has been known, whether Jewish, Pagan, or Christian. In fact, no nation having a Bible has omitted to practice it.

No matter how vulgar, how disgusting, or how shocking to the better feelings or how immoral the literal reading of the text, a hundred ways could be found to get rid of its offensive signification; a hundred spiritual interpretations could be thrust under its verbal coverings. The most senseless, the most indecorous, and the most demoralizing verbiage could thus be made to pass for great "spiritual truths." The pagans and the Jews practiced this art laboriously and extensively; and the disciples of the Christian faith, in all ages of the Church, have been their strict imitators. That it is a very ancient heathen custom is evident from the declaration of "The Nineteenth Century," which quotes Plutarch as saying, "The spiritual or allegorical mode of interpreting words and language was applied to the poems of Orpheus, the Egyptian writers, and the Phrygian traditions" (p. 337).

Grote tells us that the plain and literal meaning would not have been listened to, as it did not suit the mental demands of the people. (See Grote's "History of Greece.") He assigns this mode of interpreting sacred books to ancient Egypt; and Mr. Wilson says the Christians caught the passion for spiritualizing and allegorizing their Bible at an early date, and of converting them on all occasions into spiritual mysteries, from the later Platonists, the example of Philo, and the Jewish rabbis. "The Muhammadans," Mr. Kant informs us, "gave a spiritual sense to the sensual descriptions of their paradise," and thus the Hindus also interpreted their Vedas. "The Muhammadans," says another writer, "indulge in glowing allegories concerning love and intoxication, which, like some of the Hindu devotional writings, seem sensual to those who perceive only the external sense, while the initiated find in them an interior meaning." The Greeks and Romans, according to the testimony of Mr. Kant, explained away some of the silliest legends of their polytheism by spiritualizing them, or giving them a mystical sense. Speaking in general terms, Mr. Taylor says, "An allegorical sense was the apology offered for the manifest absurdities of paganism." The Roman Julian once remarked that the poetic stories concerning the Gods, though regarded as fables, he supposed contained a spiritual treasury. Kant declares, in like manner, that the ancient pagans "gave a mystical sense to the many vicious actions of their Gods, and to the wildest dreams of their poets, in order to bring the popular faith into agreement with their doctrines of morality"; that is, they resorted to a spiritual interpretation in order to save them from being condemned as popular intelligence advanced. "All the learned ancients," says Mr. Higgins, "gave their sacred writings two meanings—one literal, and the other spiritual." Philo confessed that the literal sense of the Old Testament is "shocking": hence, "a divine science, believed by intuition, is necessary to penetrate the hidden meaning." The Essenses declared, the literal sense of their scriptures was devoid of all power.

Origen, finding Moses' writings replete with error and immorality, got rid of the difficulty by declaring, "It is all allegory." He makes the remarkable confession that "there were some things inserted in the Bible as history which were never transacted"; hence, he concludes they must be interpreted spiritually, or set down as false. And St. Hillary declares, "There are many historical passages in the New Testament, which, if taken literally, are contrary to sense and reason; and therefore there is a necessity for a mystical interpretation." Not that we have any evidence that such an interpretation was ever thought of by the writer; but this new and forced interpretation is the only alternative to save the credit of the Book. Any senseless expedient or subterfuge that could be invented was dragged in, rather than admit the Holy Book contained errors; for this would prove it to be the work of man, and not of God. This has been the policy from time immemorial of the votaries of all sacred books.

Origen—after declaring, "There is no literal truth in the story of Christ driving out the money-changers"—asserts that it is an allegory, indicating that we are to cast out our evil propensities. He says the early Christians seldom used the literal sense of the scriptures, because it taught something objectionable; and ever since the inauguration of this mode for concealing the errors and defective moral teachings of the Bible, all kinds of ridiculous interpretations of scripture have been resorted to by orthodox writers to make it teach what each one desired. Since they arrogated to themselves the liberty to depart from the literal meaning of the text, hundreds of meanings have been ingrafted upon the same text by as many writers and readers; thus launching all scripture import upon the quicksands of uncertainty. The Rev. Mr. McNaught of England points to one text in Galatians—on which, he says, two hundred and forty meanings have been saddled by different Bible interpreters—as a specimen of this kind of license, that is, two hundred and forty guesses at the meaning: thus making Bible interpretation, and the system of salvation founded on it, an entire system of *guesswork*; and I would suggest that, if we have thus to guess our way to heaven, we can do so as well *without* the Bible as *with* it. A God who is so ignorant of human language as to give forth a revelation to the world couched in such unintelligible and ambiguous terms that no two people can understand it alike, it seems to us, should not have attempted it.

All will be chaos and confusion and wild guesswork with respect to the meaning of a large portion of the Bible, while its readers are allowed to depart from the established meaning of words as defined by our dictionaries, and fabricate new meanings of their own. As for example: St. Andrew tells us that, when Christ spoke of removing mountains, he meant the Devil; and when he spoke of selling two sparrows for a farthing, Bishop Hillary says he meant "sinners selling themselves to the Devil." The red heifer offered by Moses on the day of Pentecost was "spiritually Jesus Christ"; thus identifying Gods with beasts. The wool and hyssop used for sprinkling the people, we are told, means spiritually, "the cross of

Christ." Christ's injunction to hate father, mother, brother, and sister, etc., we are told, means that we must love them; and many similar examples of manufacturing new meanings for obnoxious texts might be cited.

Now, we ask, of what practical value can the Bible be, when there is no certain clew to its meaning, or when any of its readers, on finding a word or text whose literal signification does not suit their religious fancy, can assume the liberty to renounce the dictionary, ignore the common and established acceptation of words, and fabricate a new meaning contrary to, and in direct conflict with, the common signification? To get rid of some obvious error in the text, they bestow upon it any kind of fanciful, and sometimes ridiculous, signification their imagination can invent, and then insist with a godly zeal that it is the intended meaning of the writer. If such lawless license in the use of words is to be tolerated, as Bible believes are in the habit of assuming, in order to make it teach something which they devoutly desire it should teach, then all rules with respect to the employment of language and the use of words are at an end: our dictionaries may be banished from the schoolroom. We will no longer have use for them if words are no longer the symbols of ideas, which must be the case if people are allowed to attach any signification to them they please, or assign them a meaning at variance with common custom; and a person can learn as much by casting his eyes over the blank pages of the book as by tracing its printed lines. And the art and labor of printing, so far as he is concerned, is superseded; for, as he fabricates his own meaning, this can be done as well without type as with it. Mr. Ernstein, in his "Principles of Biblical Interpretation" (p. 37), affirms that "a proposition may be strictly true which is not contained in the words of the text"; which is tantamount to saying, "The meaning exists independent of the text, and is to be found outside of it." So the text is not needed, and is of no practical use; for the sentiment of the text can be traced as well on the blank page. The unwarrantable license which Bible adherents assume of ingrafting new meanings into the words of a text when its literal reading shocks their moral sense by its immodesty, its falsity, or its puerility, would not be tolerated with respect to any other book; and, if it is just and warrantable in this case, why not adopt it for interpreting the pagan Bibles, and thus spiritualize *them* into truth and harmony? It would take every objectionable statement out of them, and make them pure, unmixed truth. With this kind of license a book can be made to teach anything desired. Grant me the liberty that Christians assume in deviating from the established use of language, and coining a new meaning for words, and I will take all the infidelity out of "Tom Paine's writings," and make them chime with the smoothest and soundest orthodoxy.

361

The Bible of Bibles

It should be borne in mind that the custom of spiritualizing the apparently immoral and obscene portions of the Bible is something the common people know nothing about, but suppose that Bible writers, in all cases, mean just what they say. Hence, it is evidence the practice has been attended with no practical benefit to society; and Infinite Wisdom should have foreseen (and would if it had been his production) that the use of such language would have a demoralizing effect upon the world, and consequently would have made use of *better* language. Bishop Holbrook says that the notion of inner sense to the Bible is a mere creation of fancy, and will take the errors out of any book. And, as different writers differ in their mode of spiritualizing the Bible, it proves it is a mere invention and forced expedient to save the credit of the Book. The resort to a spiritual sense for the Bible was simply an attempt to conceal *its bad sense—its nonsense*, its vulgarity, its immoral teachings, and its numerous contradictions, which scientific and progressive minds are constantly bringing to light. But it is as illusory and ineffectual as the ostrich hiding its head in the sand to evade its pursuers. In both cases the danger is blinked out of sight, but not removed.

Any sense of a text not clearly expressed or unequivocally indicated by the language, we claim, is a slander and a derogation upon Infinite Wisdom, as it assumes he was too ignorant of language to be able to say what he meant, thus placing him lower in the scale of intelligence than a common schoolboy; and assumes his priesthood are infinitely wiser, as they are able to reveal his "Holy Book" all over again, and thus make the numerous blunders of Infinite Wisdom plain and intelligible to common sense and the poorest understanding.

I cannot conclude this chapter without bestowing my thanks upon Emanuel Swedenborg for the service he has rendered the cause of truth and theological reform by an improved system of theology he has made out of the Bible, or rather out of his own brain. Being a man of unusual intellect and moral aspirations, and a man of considerable literary attainments, he could not brook the absurd system of theology taught in the pulpits, professedly drawn from the Bible. And whether his system is more conformable to the teachings of "the Holy Book" is a matter of no importance. It is in many respects a rational and beautiful system, and is thus far very acceptable, and must be very beneficial as a substitute for the irrational, and in some respects immoral, system taught by the orthodox churches; and, were it universally adopted by Christian professors, it would be a great improvement on the popular system, and a step toward the attainment of a true and perfect system.

CHAPTER 65

WHAT SHALL WE SUBSTITUTE FOR THE BIBLE?

The disbelievers in Christianity in all past time, when objecting to it as being fraught with too many moral defects to constitute a basis or guide for the religious opinions and moral actions of men in an age more free from superstition, and much farther advanced in a knowledge of the true science of morals and the general principles of philosophy, have been met with the reply, "Show us a better system before you pull down Christianity and throw aside the Bible. Let us know what you are going to substitute in their place." Very well, good friend, we will meet your objection, and hope we can remove the difficulty. We think that either of the following answers should prove satisfactory, and, all taken together, *more* than satisfactory:

1. We do not propose or desire to destroy or supersede any valuable truth, precept, principle, or doctrine taught in the Bible, or to set aside anything that can in any way prove to be practically useful. We only propose to sift out the errors from the truth, rejecting the former and retaining the latter, and to employ as many of the old timbers in constructing the new superstructure as are not rotten or otherwise defective.

2. Truth cannot be "pulled down" or destroyed, as it possesses an omnipotency of principle that is indestructible. Like gold in the refiner's crucible, it shines the brighter for every effort to destroy it.

3. It must be presumed, therefore, that whatever portion of your religion is susceptible of destruction is false, and *should be* destroyed.

4. It is the nature of truth to spring up voluntarily the moment error is removed, as naturally as air or water rushes in to fill a vacuum. The instant the clouds are rifted, the sun darts down its vivifying rays upon the earth. You want no substitute for weeds when exterminated from your garden. When eradicated, those plants which are more useful and beautiful, and which they have been choking and repressing the growth of, will then assume a more healthy appearance. You ask no substitute for sickness or disease, but desire it removed that you may again enjoy the blessings of health. Moral health will likewise ensue by the removal of noxious weeds from the mind.

And, finally, you can find a complete answer to this objection in your own Bible: "Cease to do evil, and (*then*) learn to do well"; that is, the moment you discover an error in your faith or practice, *abandon* it, and you will soon "learn" what its proper substitute is. *Truth* is always at hand as a substitute for *error*. We may assume, then, that if any of the erroneous doctrines now propagated were abandoned, they would find their own substitute immediately, as sickness finds its substitute in health. But we will not leave the pious Christian in this negative condition, but will furnish him with a "substitute" which holds out much better hopes and promises than he has anchored in his idolized system, whether those hopes appertain to a virtuous and happy life here, or to an ever-blessed eternity beyond the confines of time. That substitute will be found fully explained in chapter 14, under the head of "The Infidels' Bible." Or, if he desires a system in fuller detail, and one possessing great beauty, let him examine the principles of "The Harmonial Philosophy."

CHAPTER 66

RELIGIOUS RECONSTRUCTON, OR THE MORAL
NECESSITY FOR A RELIGIOUS REFORM

A philosophical analysis of the human mind, viewed in connection with the practical history of man from the early morning of his existence, fully demonstrates it as an important truth that individual happiness and the moral welfare of society depend essentially upon the uniform action and harmonious cooperation of all the mental faculties; and that, on the other hand, their individually excessive and inharmonious action constitutes the primary source of nearly all the crime, misery, and discord of society. And it may be well to note here, as another important preliminary truth, that the progressive development of the science of mental philosophy has settled the division of the mental faculties into the following classification:

1.   The animal, which imparts energy and impulsive strength to the whole character, mental and physical.

2.   The social, which is the source of family ties and the social and cooperative institutions of society.

3.   The moral, which makes us regardful of the happiness and welfare of other beings than ourselves.

4.   The intellectual, which is the great pilot-chamber or lighthouse of the whole mind; though it is but recently that discoveries in mental philosophy have fully disclosed this as being its natural and legitimate office. It has thus demonstrated it to be the most important department of the mind. Its position in the cerebrum—occupying, as it does, the superior frontal lobe of the brain—might, however, have suggested this.

Now, this is no fanciful delineation, no mere ideal mapping of the mind, but has been demonstrated thousands of times, since the discoveries of Gall, to be the true condition and classified analysis of the mental faculties.

The religious faculties constituting that department of the mind which often controls our actions and conduct toward others, and being situated at the apex of the brain—the point where the most intensified feelings and impulses are supposed to concentrate their misdirection or abnormal exercise, is consequently attended with more direful consequences to society than that of any other portion of the mind. All history demonstrates this as a tragical fact, for religion, more especially, *is always born blind.* This being a tenable fact, and the religious faculties being awakened to action at an early period of human society—before the intellectual chambers of the mind were lighted up by the illuminating rays of science, or supplied by a philosophical education and a thorough and untrammeled study of nature's laws—their natural intensity of feeling, thus uncurbed and unenlightened, drove their honest but dark-minded possessors into the most senseless and childish superstitions, the most absurd doctrines, the most relentless intolerance of belief, and the most bloody and murderous persecutions; thus proving that conscience unenlightened is a very unsafe and a very dangerous moral and religious guide. The popular Christian proverb, that "man cannot be too religious," comprehends a very fatal error in moral ethics: for the man who possesses more religion than intellect, or more devotional piety than intellectual cultivation and philosophical enlightenment, is sometimes a more dangerous man to society than the highway robber or the midnight assassin; because, always finding many accomplices to aid him in his direful deeds of bloody persecutions, and frequently being able also to invoke the strong arm of the law, his work of defamation and spoliation, if not of open persecution and bloodshed, is wider spread than that of the burglar or the stealthy assassin.

A review of history shows us: 1. That, up to the installation of the era of science, which dates back less than three centuries ago, the world—that is, the Christian world—was literally a vast prison-house of chains, and a theater of butchery and blood, the result of a practical effort of men, devoutly pious, to "promote the glory of God," and the establishment of a supposed-to-be true religion. 2. The perpetrators of those tragical deeds upon men and women were, many of them, as religiously honest and conscientious "as ever breathed the breath of life"; and they verily believed they were doing God service in thus punishing and exterminating dissenters and heretics. The very fact that some of these pious persecutors perished themselves at the fiery stake in the conscientious and unflinching maintenance of their principles, shouting "Hallelujah" while the burning fagots consumed their bodies, leaves no possible ground for doubt that a deep religious conviction had actuated them in the work of persecuting and punishing the enemies of their religion, and in attempting to convert the world to its "saving truth" by the sword.

Much is said about "conscience," "the internal monitors," "the still, small voice," etc., as a guide for man's moral actions; but if experience and history ever proved or can prove anything, they demonstrate most conclusively that conscience unenlightened by the intellectual department of the mind, or a conscience grown up amid the weeds of scientific ignorance, is as dangerous a pilot upon the moral ocean as the helmsman of a ship, in midnight darkness, surrounded by dangerous shoals and resistless whirlpools. Conscience without science or philosophy is a lamp without oil, which consequently, being without light, is more likely to lead us astray than to guide us to the temple of truth. Science is the pilot lamp by which we discern our way on the pilgrim-voyage of life; while religion is the feeling, the motive-power, which impels us onward. Hence, the latter should at all times be subservient to the former, and should be checked and restrained from spontaneous development and exercise until the former is duly installed upon the mental throne as ruler of the moral empire. It is as dangerous to cultivate and stimulate the religious feelings, until the fires of science or practical philosophy have been kindled up in the intellectual chambers to furnish the light necessary to guide them in their impulsive course, as it would be to steam up the boilers of a boat when approaching a precipice in the night, with the pilot asleep upon his hammock, and all the lights extinguished in his chamber. Neither religion nor conscience possesses primordially any light of its own. Both are born blind, and all the light they ever possess is by reflection from the intellectual lighthouse. Prolific, indeed, of the proof of this statement, are human nature, human experience, and universal history. Let the policy, then, be in all cases to cultivate science before religion. The intellectual mind, we repeat, should be thoroughly cultivated and enlightened before the religious feelings are called into action.

Query. Reader, what do you *now* think of Dr. Cheviot's statement, "The Bible does not contain the *shadow of a shade of error from Genesis to Revelation*"?

CONCLUSION

1.   As this work was announced several years ago, it seems proper to explain the causes of the long delay in its publication. Want of health for completing it, and want of means for publishing it, furnish the true explanation. But by the practical application of a remedy constituting a new and extraordinary discovery in the healing art, the author's health has so far improved as to enable him to resume the work, and re-write nearly the whole of it in a few weeks time. The work advertised embraced but forty pages. The present volume comprises nearly eleven times that number of pages, and includes only two chapters of the original, except the small portion that has been re-written.

2.   While "The World's Sixteen Crucified Saviors" was designed principally to trace the doctrines, traditions, and miraculous events of the Christian Bible to their primary pagan or Oriental origin, the main object of "The Bible of Bibles" is to expose their logical absurdity, and the evils resulting from their propagation and practical application.

3.   The objection is frequently raised in this work against placing the Bible in the hands of children, and in possession of the heathen.   This would, of course, keep it out of our common schools; and the author rejoices in knowing that, although the Bible was used as a regular schoolbook in his youthful days, it has been banished as a textbook from nearly every schoolroom throughout the country. This denotes progress.

4.   Christian professors regard it as a sufficient refutation of all the arguments and facts designed to prove and demonstrate the immoral influence of the Bible upon society, to assert that Christian countries are superior in morals to those not in possession of their Bible. But many facts cited in this work tend to prove that, if the assumption were correct, it could not with any show of reason or sense be attributed to the influence of the Bible.   It is clearly, if not self-evidently, impossible that such moral or immoral lessons as are derived from the history of such characters as the father and founder of the Jewish nation (Abraham), who is represented as living up to all the commands, all the statutes, and all the laws of God (see Gen. xxvi. 5), while practicing the abominable crimes of treachery, deceit, falsehood, incest or adultery, and polygamy, etc.—I say it is morally impossible for such examples and such lessons to exert other than a demoralizing influence upon society; or that of David, pronounced "the man after God's own heart," while practicing a long catalogue of the most shocking crimes (see chapter 30). Such cases blasphemously represent God as sanctioning the most atrocious crimes and the most revolting deeds, which is a virtual license to the whole human race to practice them. If a book containing such lessons does not exert an immoral influence upon society, then human language, when employed in writing Bibles, fails to make its ordinary impression upon the mind. But we will here cite three

Conclusion

cogent and incontrovertible historical facts, which will settle the matter at once and forever, by proving the truth of our oft-repeated proposition that the Christian Bible, notwithstanding the apparent improvement in morals of most Christian countries in modern times, has, on the whole, tended to demoralize every nation where it has been generally read, believed, and practiced.

First, look at the moral condition of the whole Christian world during the period known as "the Dark Ages," and you will see the proof in overwhelming torrents. During that long night of moral darkness and human depravity, which lasted nearly a thousand years, all Christendom was reeking with moral corruption, and practicing the most abominable crimes. Lying, deceit, hypocrisy, moral treason, licentiousness, adultery, fornication, fighting, and drunkenness were the order of the day among all classes, including the clergy and the deacons, simply because the light of science had not reached them, and the Bible was their sole guide in morals and religion. This state of things continued until the introduction of Greek literature dispelled the thick clouds of mental darkness, and arrested the swift tide of moral corruption. Second, the Greeks without our Bible were both morally and intellectually superior to any Christian nation. Third, "the Dark Ages" were brought to a close by the introduction of Greek learning and Greek morals into Christian nations. This dates their first tendency to rise out of the sloughs of heathen barbarism, and their first appearance of moral improvement. And thus the proposition is proved and demonstrated by the facts of history that the Bible continued to demoralize society until its influence was arrested by the dawn of moral and physical science. In no nation has there been any marked improvement in morals with the use of the Bible alone.

5. It will doubtless be regarded as an extraordinary circumstance that so many thousand biblical errors as are disclosed in this work should have passed from age to age unnoticed by the millions of disciples of the Christian faith, and more especially the startling fact that all the cardinal doctrines of the Christian religion are founded in error. But it should be borne in mind that it was regarded and taught as a religious duty to suppress and conceal all such errors, and absolutely wicked, sinful, and dangerous to admit the possibility that the Holy Book *can contain errors.* And this negative policy alone was sufficient to keep them concealed and out of sight.

6. It is stated in chapter 30 that none of the Old Testament writers teach the doctrine of immortality or the doctrine of future rewards and punishments. The proof and a full elucidation of this subject will be found in "The Biography of Satan."

7.   It is stated in chapter 55 that all human language is more or less ambiguous and uncertain, and in chapter 52 that skillful linguists of this age can construct language whose meaning cannot be misunderstood; and hence God should have been able to do so when the Bible was written. The first statement refers to language as ordinarily used when the Bible was written, and especially the imperfect Hebrew of the Bible. The last statement implies that with the modern improvements language can be so employed as to leave no doubt of its meaning in any case. Both statements, then, are correct.

8.   The author, in abridging citations from history and the Bible, has in some cases deviated from custom in using quotation marks. This is especially true of chapter 22 (on Bible contradictions).

9.   It is believed that no errors of any importance can be found in this work, unless some mistakes have been committed in making scriptural references.

10.   ☞Each reader of this work is desired to examine carefully and critically the author's exposition of "The Twelve Cardinal Doctrines of the Christian Faith," and report to him his views of that exposition. Those twelve leading doctrines are embraced in the twelve chapters commencing at chapter 33 (on revelation) and ending at chapter 44 (on a personal God).